Additional Praise for 37 WORDS

"*37 Words* is a stellar and moving tribute to Title IX's fifty years of gender equity progress in schools. The book centers the champions behind this landmark law—the authors and advocates, survivors and athletes, and every student breaking gender stereotypes to reach their dreams. Well-researched and brimming with hope, the book is an inspiration in our continued fight for gender justice for all."

—*Noreen Farrell, executive director, Equal Rights Advocates*

"Sherry Boschert captures the fight waged by feminists over decades against sex discrimination in education and to secure equal access and opportunity for women and girls. Setbacks and victories, protests and demonstrations, the fights in Congress and in the courts, are all chronicled by Boschert. *37 Words* is an important book at an important time, reminding us of the need to keep fighting for Title IX."

—*Katherine Spillar, executive editor,* Ms.

"The struggle to win, implement, and preserve Title IX, the bedrock 1972 law banning sex discrimination in education, comes alive in these pages. Boschert's vivid biographical portraits of key leaders of these efforts, from the 1960s to the present, make this a page-turner that illuminates the historical roots and antecedents of the #MeToo movement."

—*Ruth Milkman, professor of sociology and history, CUNY Graduate Center, and author of* On Gender, Labor, and Inequality

"Boschert's exquisite achievement in *37 Words* rests on deeply researched history, eloquent prose, and, perhaps most surprising of all, the page-turning story of how one unassuming yet brave woman—Bernice Sandler—turned sexist oppression into educational liberation for millions of women. There is sobering and uplifting brilliance dancing off the pages of this book, page after page. Do not miss it."

—*Jennifer Freyd, founder and president, Center for Institutional Courage*

37 WORDS

37 WORDS

Title IX and Fifty Years of
Fighting Sex Discrimination

SHERRY BOSCHERT

THE
NEW
PRESS

NEW YORK
LONDON

Requests for permission to reproduce selections from this book should be made through our website:
https://thenewpress.com/contact.

Published in the United States by The New Press, New York, 2022
Distributed by Two Rivers Distribution

ISBN 978-1-62097-583-1 (hc)
ISBN 978-1-62097-729-3 (ebook)
CIP data is available

The New Press publishes books that promote and enrich public discussion and understanding of
the issues vital to our democracy and to a more equitable world. These books are made possible
by the enthusiasm of our readers; the support of a committed group of donors, large and small;
the collaboration of our many partners in the independent media and the not-for-profit sector;
booksellers, who often hand-sell New Press books; librarians; and above all by our authors.

www.thenewpress.com

Book design and composition by Bookbright Media
This book was set in Bembo and Euclid

Printed in the United States of America

2 4 6 8 10 9 7 5 3 1

No person in the United States shall, on the basis of sex,
be excluded from participation in,
be denied the benefits of,
or be subjected to discrimination under
any education program or activity
receiving Federal financial assistance.

—Title IX's first 37 words

Contents

37 WORDS

1

Strong

1969

Alone at home, her husband at work and the kids at school, Bernice Resnick Sandler screamed. She exulted in her "Eureka!" moment. She'd found it—the missing card from a deck stacked against her. Her heart quickened with her scream of discovery.

She'd found it buried in a footnote in a dry government document, part of the voluminous reading she'd pursued to find a solution to her problem. Sandler's mother, Ivy Resnick, called this "bibliotherapy." "If you don't understand something, ask," she'd say. "And if you still don't understand, read." Read everything you can find about it. Ivy had been the first in her family of ten to graduate from high school. An avid reader herself, she instilled in Bernice a love of bibliotherapy.

Over the next four decades Sandler would use her discovery to change the lives of hundreds of millions of Americans, but on this day in 1969 she simply wanted a job. She knew she was qualified—at least as qualified as the peers she'd seen get hired over the last several months. The obscure note gave her the first evidence that the obstacle in her way might be illegal—might be discrimination.

At age forty-one, Sandler was about to earn a doctoral degree in education from the University of Maryland. She loved teaching college students while finishing her EdD work. Her students seemed to enjoy her classes. The department was growing, with seven tenure-track openings for new faculty. But when Sandler applied, she couldn't get an interview—not at Maryland or any other university. The men students in her program not only got interviews but received job offers from colleges around the country even without interviews. How could a college in rural Pennsylvania find these men and yet her own institution couldn't seem to see her? She didn't know that the faculty were promoting men students for jobs. She didn't know the words for "old boys' network" in 1969.

"If you don't understand something, ask," she could hear Ivy's voice saying. "The worst they can say is no." Bernice had grown up in a large, loud, and energetic Jewish family in the Flatbush section of Brooklyn, New York. Until early adulthood she thought of herself as shy and quiet, until she realized that this was true only in relation to her family. Walking into a room at the Resnick household, you'd likely hear six conversations going on at once among four people laughing and yelling and talking on top of each other. So, Sandler knew how to be social. She also understood that women were expected to be sweet and accommodating in public.

She was gifted, too, with great intelligence and high energy. Family and friends called her Bunny, a name morphed from a Yiddish version of Bernice—"Bunya." She learned from her family to take a stand for social justice. While shoe shopping one day, Ivy and six-year-old Bernice stopped at a picket line blocking the store. "We're not buying you shoes in *that* store," Ivy said. Bernice grew up wanting to do something to improve the world. She thought that being a college professor, teaching and doing research, might be that something.

Older than most of the students in her cohort and working part-time as a lecturer, Sandler had become friendly with some faculty when they invited her to parties. On campus one day, she worked up the courage to ask one of them about her situation.

Sandler sat down in his office. Why, she asked, couldn't she get a job interview at the University of Maryland?

Without skipping a beat, he replied, "Let's face it, Bunny. You come on too strong for a woman."

Speechless, she believed him. Why had she discussed professional issues with faculty members? Why had she spoken up in graduate seminars, and a few times at staff meetings? Why had she ruined everything after coming so far?

Bernice had known from a very young age that she wanted an education and wanted to work, both things that were not taken for granted among young U.S. women in the 1940s and 1950s. Both her father, Abraham, who owned a women's clothing store, and her mother, a bookkeeper and homemaker, emphasized learning. Bernice graduated from tuition-free Brooklyn College and worked part-time as a secretary while earning a master's degree in clinical and school psychology from the City University of New York. After graduation she found work again as a secretary, the most common job available to women at the time and, along with teacher, nurse, or homemaker, one of few that welcomed women if they were white.[1]

Then she met Jerrold Sandler. They married in 1952 and moved almost immediately to Bloomington, Indiana, for his new job at the university. Intent on pursuing a doctorate degree so she could become a professor, Bernice applied to the graduate program in psychology at Indiana University but wasn't accepted. The university favored men as students and faculty.[2]

With the Korean War escalating, Jerrold enlisted and became a naval officer. They moved eleven times in six years. Bernice was lonely, smart, and too restless to limit herself to housekeeping and raising daughters Deborah and Emily. She tried going back to school, but it was hard with a three-year-old and a four-year-old when the university wouldn't allow part-time attendance. She dropped out.

Instead, she learned guitar and taught it, playing Pete Seeger and other folk music—African American spirituals, songs of miners and union workers, songs of hardships, songs of fighting for freedom. She worked part-time stints as a preschool teacher and a research assistant. Occasionally, she met other women with college degrees among the gaggle of mothers at the children's playground, a few of whom even had part-time jobs. But all they ever really talked about, including Sandler, was their children. Never about politics, or their areas of expertise, or personal dreams and hopes. Work and public affairs didn't fit the confining definitions of femininity by which white women were judged, while Black women had to work to survive even if they'd prefer to be solely homemakers.

Then Betty Friedan challenged the concept in her 1963 book *The Feminine Mystique*. Friedan summarized the mystique as the artifice of defining women solely in relation to the needs of men—as sex objects, breeders, or caretakers.[3] The book sold millions of copies to smart, bored, restless upper- and middle-class women, giving them license to complain about their lives and to admit desiring something more. With both of her kids now in school and more time on her hands, Sandler decided to try again for a doctoral degree.

By then they were living in Silver Spring, Maryland, so she approached the psychology department at the University of Maryland in College Park. She couldn't get any faculty member in the small department to talk to her. How could she get in if they wouldn't even talk to her?

As luck would have it, Sandler met the head of the department's admissions committee at a mutual friend's party. Thinking quickly, she asked him, "Who are your best students?" Those would be the military veterans, he replied. "I'm like the veterans!" Sandler said. "I've been home taking care of my kids, and now I'm going back to school." He liked the analogy but cautioned that the department doesn't accept many women, especially older ones. Sandler was thirty-six. She got in anyway.[4]

She lasted one semester in the psychology department. Sandler and the half-dozen other women graduate students would gather outside the ladies' restroom before class and joke that "one day we're going to come here and the ladies' room is going to be locked." They laughed, but only because they didn't know how else to describe the ways they were made to feel unwelcome, much less why. They knew the all-men faculty didn't want them there, but they had no words for it.

Sandler transferred to the more welcoming education department, where she thrived. She found that she not only enjoyed teaching college students but was good at it. Eventually the university hired her as a temporary lecturer to teach a night class while she completed her doctorate in counseling and education services.

During all this, the social and political upheavals of the 1960s reached her only indirectly. Sandler followed news of the civil rights movement, had learned that what white people used to call racial "prejudice" (as if it were just an individual's feelings) now was understood to be "discrimination" (a larger societal pattern of prejudicial actions). The Civil Rights Act of 1964 created an Equal Employment Opportunity Commission (EEOC) to enforce its prohibitions against discrimination in employment. More than four thousand complaints alleged sex discrimination in the EEOC's first two years.[5]

But Sandler was still a student, not thinking much about workplace issues. What little she saw in the media about women demanding equal treatment didn't really apply to her, she thought.

She did learn of the new National Organization for Women (NOW), founded in 1966 by women's rights leaders including Friedan and attorney Pauli Murray, an African American legal genius active in the civil rights and feminist movements. In 1967 NOW endorsed an eight-part bill of rights for women demanding equal and unsegregated education, job training, and enforcement of laws banning sex discrimination in employment.[6] Women across the country swelled NOW's ranks, but not Sandler. Not yet.

In her proper, middle-class life, Sandler also didn't connect with the grassroots feminist revolution that emerged in the mid-1960s mainly among younger women who had honed their political chops as organizers in the civil rights movement and anti–Vietnam War organizations. By 1966–68, women who developed a sense of self-worth and capabilities in these movements began gathering in small groups to share their stories and discuss the sexism they experienced, both in their organizations and in society.

These "consciousness-raising groups" spread beyond activist circles, soon reaching hundreds of thousands of women. Many of them turned their newfound consciousness into a variety of actions, from staging confrontational street theater to organizing childcare programs, founding rape crisis centers, and much more. Occasionally, they'd get a bit of snide media coverage, such as TV reports of a hundred activists protesting the objectification of women at the 1968 Miss America pageant in Atlantic City, New Jersey. They symbolically tossed bras into trash cans and unfurled a banner inside the event proclaiming "Women's Liberation." A few blocks away, the first "Miss Black America" pageant convened to highlight racism in the Miss America contest.[7]

The momentum of this so-called second-wave women's movement (the first being the suffragist movement) already was altering U.S. society in fundamental ways, but Sandler consciously absorbed only some of this, unaware of most of it. Still, at some point in the 1960s while driving in her car she realized for the first time, "I am a *person!*" Not just a mother, a wife, a daughter, a sister. A person in her own right, as valuable and deserving as any other person. As she drove she starting singing, "I am a person. I am a person. I am a person!" again and again and again. She hardly could remember ever being so happy.[8]

She even suggested to her doctoral advisor that she was interested in doing her dissertation on how young women make vocational decisions. He looked horrified. "Research on women!? That's not *real* research," he told her. She quickly found a different topic.[9]

Sandler also absorbed news reports of massive unrest on college campuses in the late 1960s sparked primarily by the anti-war and civil rights movements. Police shot and killed three people at South Carolina State University after a civil rights protest at a segregated bowling alley in February 1968. Activists at Columbia University took over five buildings in the largest protest of its kind in May 1968; police arrested seven hundred people. Elite universities began to consider admitting women.

In rare instances, the mainstream media treated the women's movement seriously. In early 1969, as Sandler started to wonder why she couldn't get a faculty job interview, reporter Vera Glaser asked President Richard Nixon a pivotal question in a nationally televised news conference.

"Mr. President, since you've been inaugurated, you have made approximately 200 presidential appointments, and only three of them have gone to women. Can we expect some more equitable recognition of women's abilities, or are we going to remain the lost sex?" asked Glaser, the Washington bureau chief for the North American Newspaper Alliance syndicate.[10]

Nixon and the men journalists in the room chuckled at first, until Nixon realized this might not look good. He shifted tone. He would look into it. The question prompted calls from other media outlets and follow-up stories on women's limited roles in government. In response, Nixon created a Presidential Task Force on Women's Rights and Responsibilities, with Glaser as a member.

Not long after the press conference, Glaser received a surprise letter from Catherine East, a Labor Department researcher. "I gather from the tone of your question [to the president], you might be interested in a few statistics," she wrote. East had been gathering facts on employment practices for years in her behind-the-scenes bureaucratic career. She served as an unofficial networking node in pre-internet times, strategically connecting scores of professional women in and out of government who were concerned about sexism.

Glaser turned East's data into a five-part syndicated series on sex discrimination—a term starting to come into wider use. Launched in mid-March 1969, "The Female Revolt" series ran in nearly five hundred U.S. newspapers including the *Washington Post*, and got inserted into the *Congressional Record*.

In Sandler's mind, though, the articles didn't really apply to her. The women's libbers who complained of discrimination probably hadn't worked as hard as she had. She was a college lecturer. She soon would have a doctorate! Yet here she was, with her kids grown to teenagers and their mother about to fulfill her dream of becoming "Dr." Sandler, and she had screwed up any chance of a faculty job by coming on too strong.

That night, sitting with Jerry and away from the girls in a room converted from a porch, she sobbed her way through a box of tissues and told him what her friend had said. Jerry let her cry, then asked, "Are any of the men in your program strong?" Of course, Bernice said. They're all strong characters. They're men.

"Then it's not you" causing the problem, he said. "It's sex discrimination." The concept was relatively new at the time, but Jerry may have been more attuned because his work touched on other issues of discrimination. He led a Ford Foundation–financed project under the auspices of the Smithsonian to get books into the hands of poor urban children to boost their reading skills.[11]

Bernice wasn't convinced. She felt it must be her fault if she couldn't go any further. Sexism so deeply permeated the culture that she, like many men and women, didn't recognize it when it stared them in the face. As an elementary school student, Bernice had wanted to be one of the volunteer crossing guards so she could wear the guard's dashing sash and help students cross the street safely. But only boys were chosen as crossing guards. Only boys were allowed to help run the film projector. And only boys got picked to go to the school's basement—the mysterious, off-limits basement—to refill the classroom's inkwells. Bernice had wanted to be part of those adventures too, but she quickly resigned herself to her fate. This is how the world runs, she figured. It was as accepted as wearing clothes—most people just didn't question it. She had no words to question it. No one pointed to these standards and said "sex discrimination." So now, if she couldn't get a job, she figured it must be her fault. She didn't know yet that none of the other women in her cohort were getting jobs, either; only the men were.

Within three months she changed her mind. At an interview for a research position for which Sandler was highly qualified, the interviewer hogged the time by telling her why he doesn't hire women. They go running home when the kids get sick, mainly. During her only other job interview, at a temporary work agency, the interviewer said Sandler wasn't really a professional. She's just a housewife who went back to school.

Sandler finally saw a pattern. Her gut told her this was discrimination. Her heart told her it was immoral. But could it possibly be legal? As the days went by, she drove the kids to medical and dental appointments and solicited quotes on carpeting and painters for the house. She shuttled Deborah to piano lessons and Emily to dance recital, but she also took time for "bibliotherapy."

She found the Equal Pay Act of 1963, the first U.S. law prohibiting wage disparity on the basis of sex, which had finally passed after multiple attempts since 1945. The act made it illegal to pay men and women who work in the same place different wages for equal work. When President Kennedy signed it, women on average made 59 cents for every dollar paid to men. But the Equal Pay Act amended the Fair Labor Standards Act of 1938, which exempted professional, executive, and administrative positions. That meant women teachers, faculty, and administrators were not covered. Not because the bill's main sponsor, Rep. Edith Green (D-OR), wanted it that way. She'd had to accept this flaw in order to get the bill passed, a case of the typical sausage grind that is congressional lawmaking.

The Civil Rights Act of 1964 contained two sections that came close to helping Sandler, but not quite. Title VI of the act prohibited discrimination based on race, color, and national origin in programs or activities receiving federal financial assistance, but it omitted discrimination based on sex.[12] Title VII of the act did include sex under its employment protections for administrative and professional workers, but it specifically excluded employees of educational institutions "in their educational activities."[13] Again, women teachers, faculty, and administrators in any schools were not protected.

Baffled and frustrated, Sandler kept reading. She even read footnotes. She was, after all, an academic. And there it was, the lifeline she'd been looking for—a footnote in a U.S. Civil Rights Commission report on enforcing civil rights for African Americans that mentioned Executive Order 11246 as amended by Executive Order 11375.

Every U.S. president writes executive orders to manage the operations of the federal government. No one wrote more of them than Franklin D. Roosevelt. In 1941 he issued Executive Order 8802 in response to pressure from African American civil rights leaders and their allies including union leader Esther Peterson and First Lady Eleanor Roosevelt. Executive Order 8802 outlawed discrimination in the federal government and defense industries based on race, creed, color, or national origin—but not sex, to Peterson's great disappointment. Two years later, he amended that to also cover government contractors (Executive Order 9346).[14]

Peterson stayed active in politics, though, and kept pressing for fair treatment of women. President John F. Kennedy appointed her assistant secretary of labor and director of the Women's Bureau. She convinced him to create the first Presidential Commission on the Status of Women, which issued a groundbreaking report in 1963 (co-authored by Catherine East). The report launched forty-five state commissions by 1966 to study the status of women in their states. Sandler read the commission's report and a pile of others. She read bill after bill and articles and footnotes until finally there it was—a reference to President Lyndon B. Johnson's Executive Order 11375.

When Johnson appointed Peterson as a special assistant for consumer affairs in the early 1960s, she got him to promise that if he ever amended or expanded on Executive Order 8802 he would include a prohibition against sex discrimination.[15] Johnson did strengthen Executive Order 8802 by signing Executive Order 11246 in 1965, which put the secretary of labor in charge of enforcing the nondiscrimination provisions, but they still didn't include sex. Peterson was furious, and so were other advocates for women. When asked to explain itself, the Johnson administration said the order's drafters simply "forgot" to include sex discrimination. NOW turned up the heat on Johnson, demanding an executive order to "fix" 11246. Finally, in 1967, Johnson's Executive Order 11375 amended 11246 to prohibit sex discrimination by federal contractors as of October 13, 1968.[16]

When Sandler read that, an idea flashed in her head. Most colleges and universities get federal contracts. Under the executive orders, then, sex discrimination must be illegal there.

She screamed. "Colleges have contracts! They're covered!" she shouted to the empty chairs at the kitchen table.

But almost instantly, she doubted herself. The sum of her political experience consisted of voting and, one year, being a poll watcher. What did she know about executive orders? If she was reading these orders right, they had huge implications not only for her situation but for women all over the country. Now what should she do?

2

Complaints

1970

VINCENT MACALUSO WAS WAITING FOR HER CALL. NOT SANDLER IN PARticular, but he expected someone to discover Executive Order 11375—someone who had hit what we now call the glass ceiling and wanted to bust through it.

Macaluso believed that good things could be done in government service. A career bureaucrat, he worked as a deputy director of the Office of Federal Contract Compliance (OFCC) at the U.S. Department of Labor.[1] Once laws or executive orders get passed, bureaucrats must write regulations to implement them. Most of Macaluso's work focused on implementing laws prohibiting racial discrimination. Only in the past year had he and his team begun thinking about what they might do about sex discrimination under Executive Order 11375. He'd attended Labor Department hearings in the summer of 1969 on what the regulations should say. Macaluso felt grateful that his staff included one woman who could tell him—and even tell him off—when he got something wrong because of unconscious sexism. But he was growing concerned that others in the OFCC were ignoring the new executive order.

When Sandler looked around for someone to consult about executive orders that apply to federal contractors, she guessed that the Labor Department's OFCC was a good place to start. The front desk connected her to Macaluso; it was the first time she'd spoken to a federal official. He took her under his wing, going above and beyond his job description.

Macaluso liked fairness. He grew up in the 1930s with President Franklin D. Roosevelt as his idol, listening raptly to Roosevelt's fireside chats on the radio. He enthusiastically asked Sandler to meet with him.

Her insecurities grabbed her again. "Oh, god," she thought. "He must be coming on to me. How am I going to handle this? Do I really want to do this?"

She gathered her courage and went to meet him on December 10, 1969, at his OFCC office. Macaluso reassured her that she was interpreting the executive orders correctly. Sandler wanted to publicize the fact that colleges were discriminating against women in violation of the executive orders, she told him. Macaluso broke into a broad smile. "Why, it'll scare the hell out of them!" he said.[2]

Macaluso understood that he was taking a risk. He had no authority to promote issues or to coach advocates, so he avoided mentioning his meetings with Sandler in his work reports.

He knew that the OFCC could be Sandler's "big stick" when the carrots of persuasion failed to move stubborn institutions away from discrimination. Then, as now, a tremendous amount of the country's business flowed through government contracts. Usually just the threat of losing government funds persuaded contractors to say they would comply with antidiscrimination regulations. On rare occasions, the government had to follow through on the threat; in the 1960s, for example, it withheld funds to convince the construction industry in Cleveland to hire more minorities.

Macaluso advised Sandler to get faculty lists for departments at a university and compare them with government data on the proportion of doctoral degrees awarded to women in those fields. The government didn't gather much data on women in 1969, but it did have the number of doctoral degrees sorted by sex. If U.S. women earned 25 percent of advanced degrees in psychology but filled only 2 percent of faculty in a college's psychology department, for instance, Sandler could file a federal complaint charging a pattern of discrimination and violation of the executive orders. She could file on behalf of any women who might want to remain anonymous for fear of retaliation—a very realistic fear. He helped Sandler draft her first letter of complaint to serve as a template, and coached her to send copies to representatives, senators, and the secretary of labor, urging them to enforce the executive orders.

Even before she found Macaluso, Sandler sought allies and started gathering data. The broader women's movement included many activists in academia who challenged restrictions on their social and political opportunities. Food and Drug Administration approval of the first birth-control pill in 1960 gave women greater agency in their sexual lives and opened up more roles for them by reducing the risk of pregnancy. Young women active in the civil rights and anti-war movements spoke out against sexism in the Student Nonviolent Coordinating Committee and in Students for a Democratic Society. Women at the University of Chicago formed its first women's liberation group in 1967—the Women's Radical Action Project.[3] Rutgers, the State University of New Jersey, was one of the first in the country to offer women's studies courses in the late 1960s. Yale and Princeton in 1969 became the first of the elite all-male colleges to admit women—though the colleges were motivated mainly by a desire to keep applications coming from men, whose interest in single-sex education waned.[4]

Dozens of national and regional feminist groups sprouted up in the late 1960s and early 1970s with varying philosophies and strategies. Though relatively tame compared with some of the women's liberation groups in larger cities, the National Organization for Women (NOW) seemed too radical to Sandler and, well, not very ladylike. She was drawn more to the Women's Equity Action League (WEAL), a more conservative group that spun off from NOW in 1968 to avoid the polarizing issue of abortion.[5] Founded by Elizabeth (Betty) Boyer and others in Cleveland, Ohio, in 1968, the "respectable" women of WEAL focused more narrowly on employment, education, and economic issues. Publicity from Glaser's syndicated articles in 1969 nearly doubled the group's membership that year.

Sandler felt this was a group she could work with. They weren't the activists being mocked in the mainstream media as bra-burners and radicals. They were more like her! Because of WEAL's campaign against "Help Wanted" ads soliciting only men job seekers, Sandler noticed problems in the July 1969 Placement Bulletin for one of her professional groups, the American Personnel and Guidance Association (APGA). At least nine job ads specified sex, such as "Director of Counseling and Psychological Services . . . Male preferred," or "Clinical Psychologist . . . Man."

Sandler challenged the APGA in November 1969 to stop the discriminatory wording as a violation of Title VII of the Civil Rights Act. She sent WEAL's Boyer copies of her letters. After connecting with Macaluso, Sandler wrote to the APGA again, this time warning its lawyer to take a look at Executive Order 11246 as amended by Executive Order 11375. The APGA received federal contracts, making its discriminatory behavior illegal. Before the month's end, the APGA's lawyer conceded that she was right and referred the matter to a committee to change the association's ad policy.

It appeared Sandler had her first big win.[6]

In the fall of 1969, feminist academics in various fields—psychology, sociology, anthropology, and political science—collaborated with colleagues before their disciplines' annual meetings, where they took over sessions and staged protests about sex discrimination. At the American Sociological Association meeting, they pointed out that in 188 graduate schools, women were 30 percent of PhD candidates but only 4 percent of full professors.[7]

Inspired, Sandler contacted the instigators and started asking the University of Maryland for employment statistics that it normally didn't compile—numbers for graduate student applicants, cohorts, and faculty by sex. When requesting the data, she followed WEAL's advice to not mention discrimination or WEAL. "I merely mumbled on about 'some research I was doing,' 'problems in higher education,' 'perceptions about women's education,' etc. No one understood what I was talking about and so it naturally sounded very academically respectable," she wrote to a WEAL leader.[8]

Sandler sent a twenty-one-page report about the University of Maryland to WEAL in the fall of 1969 that didn't yet reference the executive orders but highlighted sex inequities.[9]

Encouraging letters from Boyer and support from Sandler's husband, Jerry, convinced Bernice to fly to WEAL's annual conference on December 6, 1969, despite her extreme fear of flying. She hadn't flown in years. Jerry even arranged a business meeting in Cleveland for the same time so that he could hold Bernice's hand during the flight.[10] The conference strengthened her feelings of connection and showed WEAL leaders who she was.

After Sandler's December 10 meeting with Macaluso, she knew she was onto something big. Maybe even too big for WEAL alone. "Hold your hat and sit down," she wrote to WEAL's new president, Nancy Dowding, the same day. "The Executive Order does indeed apply to sex discrimination in universities and Macaluso was very interested in our following through on this." She asked for permission to bring NOW in on their efforts because WEAL by itself won't get as much publicity. "Our first responsibility should be women, and WEAL second," even if the much bigger NOW runs away with the campaign, Sandler said.[11] Dowding gave her the go-ahead on December 18.[12]

Macaluso advised that Sandler's complaints would be more impressive if she had a title rather than simply signing her own name, so WEAL anointed Sandler the chair—and only member—of its new Action Committee on Contract Compliance. He also set up a lunch meeting for Sandler with Catherine East, the Labor Department employee who had long served as a hub for the informal women's network in federal government.

Seeking data from other schools, Sandler wrote to WEAL members and her few academic contacts on a tired old typewriter that couldn't be bothered to get all the letters in a straight line. She added sheets of carbon paper to get three or four copies as she typed. She typed letters more than once if needed, since there was no such thing as a personal computer and relatively few people had access to a Xerox photocopier. Some universities had them, though, and women on campuses photocopied Sandler's letters, shared them with colleagues, and spread the word by phone.

WEAL members in twenty-two states gathered information for Sandler from the start. Better than anecdotal reports would be academic studies, but there were few to guide her despite women's increasing activism on campuses. Reports from Chicago, California, New York, and elsewhere gave her something to go on.

Students and faculty at the University of Chicago had staged weeks of protests about the treatment of women there in early 1969. The university tenured only four women in its department of sociology since the school's founding in 1892, they noted, yet 30 percent of doctoral candidates in sociology were women—a pattern repeated in most departments of every institution of higher education.[13] In the previous seventy-seven years, Chicago's anthropology department had hired only two female professors and the political science department only one.[14]

A reporter for the *Washington Post* chose to start his otherwise substantive story on the Chicago controversies with this demeaning introduction: "Marlene Dixon is a round, 32-year-old blond who reminds you of the gal in the trailer park who's always bouncing around her kitchen in slacks pouring coffee and friendliness for the other women in the neighborhood. In fact, Marlene Dixon is a PhD in sociology at the University of Chicago, which dearly wishes it had never heard of her. It was the school's decision not to renew her contract that set off weeks of sit-ins, demonstrations and acrimony."[15]

On the West Coast, feminists at Stanford University released equally scathing reports at the undergraduate and medical schools in March and December 1969. Stanford's dean of admissions argued that admitting more than 40 percent women in an undergraduate class would limit spots for men and "in effect penalize them" by decreasing the favoritism toward them.[16]

On the East Coast, five women on the faculty at Columbia University, New York—all members of the group Columbia Women's Liberation—issued a ten-page report in December 1969 charging the university with tokenism and discrimination.[17] Columbia's graduate schools granted nearly a quarter of their doctoral degrees to women but hired women for only 2 percent of their tenured faculty. "We are puzzled by the Graduate Faculties' commitment to train women, but not to hire them," the report stated.

"All we want is for women to get jobs and be promoted consonant with their abilities," Rachel DuPlessis, a preceptor in the English department, told the *New York Times* in January 1970. "That doesn't sound like much, but it's a lot considering the current situation."

Sandler saw the *Times* article about Columbia and wrote to Ann Sutherland Harris, an assistant professor of art history and co-author of the Columbia Women's Liberation report. "The Women's Equity Action League is currently exploring some new legal avenues in this area," Sandler wrote, asking for a copy of the report. She also dug up a few older studies on discrimination by sex in hiring, salary (even for the same rank), and promotions.[18]

At Sandler's University of Maryland, nine of fifteen departments in the College of Arts and Sciences had no women as full professors.[19] Only one woman in the psychology department held tenure (3 percent), even though women earned 23 percent of all PhDs in psychology in the United States. That was better than at the University of California, Berkeley, which had no women faculty in its psychology department at all.

Sandler put together an eighty-page complaint drawing on all these reports. Four pages of quotes cited materials demonstrating Sandler's broad "bibliotherapy." Macaluso tried to get her to punch up the cover letter to Labor Secretary George P. Shultz. He wanted a very "direct attack" on the government for not doing anything about the "shocking" and "outrageous" problem of sex discrimination in education. "Lady-like" language will be interpreted as a sign of weakness, he insisted. Sandler put some of that in the letter, "but probably not as much as he would have liked," she wrote to Dowding.[20]

With help from a friend of her husband at the Ford Foundation who had access to a photocopier, Sandler made close to two hundred copies of the complaint. Jerry also suggested that WEAL send out a press release. On Saturday, January 31, 1970, roughly a year after Sandler cried because she thought she was "too strong for a woman," she and WEAL filed a historic class-action complaint of sex discrimination against all U.S. colleges and universities with specific charges against the University of Maryland, signed by WEAL president Nancy Dowding. The complaint asked Secretary of Labor Shultz for an immediate review of all higher education institutions holding federal contracts to assess compliance with Executive Order 11246 as amended by 11375.

Sandler carbon copied all eleven women in Congress and the secretary of Health, Education, and Welfare (HEW), Robert H. Finch. She also copied members of key House and Senate committees, multiple women's professional organizations, people who had sent her data, the press, and others.[21]

WEAL's complaint cited an "industry-wide" pattern of discrimination against women.[22] Part of the problem was that women couldn't even get into some colleges as students. The University of Virginia—the state's premier public institution of higher education—rejected 21,000 women applicants in the early 1960s alone and didn't turn away a single man in the same period.[23]

Sandler pointed to disturbing trends. A smaller proportion of graduate degrees in law, engineering, and medicine went to women in 1969 than in 1930. Subtly invoking Cold War competition with Russia, Sandler wrote, "Why are 85% of Finland's dentists and 75% of Russia's physicians women? In our country only 7% of our physicians are women." This could only be because of suppressive quotas, she charged.

Nationally, the few women who managed to get into college, earn advanced degrees, and get hired by colleges and universities found advancement difficult or impossible. The pattern was clear: the higher the rank, the fewer the women. Colleges and universities paid women faculty less than men with the same length of service and qualifications, multiple studies showed. The loophole in the Equal Pay Act—exempting professional, executive, and administrative positions—made this legal even if unethical.

The copies sent to members of Congress asked them to contact Labor Secretary Shultz for a response. Within a few weeks more than twenty members of Congress did so. WEAL's complaints landed on Macaluso's desk in the Labor Department for "comment."[24] The Labor Department forwarded the complaint to HEW, the agency that should be enforcing the executive orders in colleges and universities. Sandler busily wrote to many organizations after filing the complaint, asking them to write their congressional representatives and to consider filing their own complaints.

"I feel like I've opened Pandora's box," she wrote to Macaluso. "Thanks, very very much."[25]

The copies sent to local newspapers and a few other media outlets generated a story on the "women's page" of the *Washington Post*, which was more of a local paper at the time, not the national media powerhouse it became after the Watergate scandal.[26] The complaint drew little national attention at first but it did generate a small notice—less than an inch of copy—in the *Saturday Review of Literature* that included Sandler's contact information. That was enough to reach women across the country who began writing and calling Sandler and feeding her the stories and numbers she needed to file more complaints against individual colleges and universities.

Jo Ann Gardner, a leader in the Association for Women in Psychology, sent Sandler a breakdown by sex of University of Pittsburgh faculty on letterhead proclaiming, "Uppity Women Unite." Sandler fell in love with those words. A pejorative word most commonly applied to Black Americans since the 1800s who dared to challenge racist and classist hierarchies, "uppity" also was used against women or anyone who aspired to being treated better than the people in power thought they "deserved." Some feminists in the 1960s and 1970s, inspired by the civil rights movement, reclaimed or co-opted the word. They took pride in being uppity women, a phrase implicitly linking the women's movement to wider struggles for civil rights.

Sandler would hand out close to thirteen thousand buttons with the slogan over the next forty years. She wrote a thank-you to Gardner for sending her data: "I think we are probably beginning to see a snowball effect in the women's movement—each of us is encouraged by the activities of others."[27]

Snowball it did, part of the avalanche of the wider women's movement that tumbled into the 1970s. Women's revolts in many sectors of society drew increasing media attention. Female students at Yale University seized the microphone at an alumni dinner in February 1970 to complain and make demands about the treatment of women a year and a half after Yale first admitted women.[28] At the University of Chicago, women realized they'd earned advanced degrees without learning anything about women's history, literature, or art. Though proud of their academic accomplishments, they called a press conference and burned their degrees in public.[29]

Women's liberationists wrote position papers and sent them to groups in other cities; pamphlets streamed across the country. *Newsweek* magazine planned its first cover story on the burgeoning women's movement but assigned it to the wife of one of the editors because the magazine refused to hire women as staff writers. Women among *Newsweek*'s researchers and assistants waved the March 16 issue's bright yellow cover announcing "Women in Revolt" on publication day at a press conference in ACLU offices announcing their class-action lawsuit against *Newsweek* for sex discrimination. Within days, female staff at the *Ladies' Home Journal* staged a sit-in of their own. Similar uprisings broke out in law firms, businesses, and nonprofit organizations.[30]

Women got uppity outside major metropolitan areas, too, if somewhat less confrontational. When a male managing editor denied a reporter's request that women be allowed to wear pants to work at the *News Sentinel* in Knoxville, Tennessee, all the women in the editorial department showed up in pants or pantsuits on August 26, 1970. "I can't believe it," the managing editor muttered every time a woman walked in the door. After several hours of muttering and chain-smoking, he told a colleague, "I know what I'll do. I'll just ignore them." Women in pants were there to stay.[31]

Activists started opening women's centers in cities around the country. The Lutheran Church ordained its first female pastor. New York, Alaska, and Hawaii became the first states to liberalize abortion laws. When the head of the Democratic Party's Committee on National Priorities said women couldn't hold decision-making posts because of their "raging hormonal imbalance," public outrage forced him to resign.[32]

Sandler's life zoomed into the fast lane. She finally found temporary work in February as a psychologist helping HEW to revise merit system exams, part of its new Women's Action Program. She also taught two evening classes at the University of Maryland. Her volunteer work with WEAL thrilled her the most. For the first time in her life she conferred with lots of smart, professional women, some of whom she even met. "If you need a place to stay in this area, our house is yours, provided you don't mind sharing it with two teen age girls, our dog, guinea pig, hamster, and our one lone male, my husband," she wrote to a distant collaborator in February 1970.[33]

One key new ally noticed the *Washington Post* article about Sandler's complaint—Arvonne Fraser. The wife of a congressman, she managed his campaigns and had held state party offices herself. Fraser's insider knowledge of Congress and exceptional organizing skills took Sandler and WEAL to a new level of impact.

Raised on a Minnesota farm during the Depression, Arvonne declared in seventh grade that when she grew up and had five children, she wanted them all to be boys because boys have more fun. She worked her way through college. Arvonne met her second husband, Donald Fraser, through Minnesota Democratic politics and became his de facto campaign manager, helping him get elected to office and eventually to Congress. Don hurt her feelings when he hired a man with little experience as campaign manager just so he could have a man's name on the campaign literature.

She almost felt sorry for the guy, though, when he realized that she and Don called the shots.

Arvonne's own ego hit bottom when they moved to DC. No longer the victorious campaign manager, state vice-chairwoman of the Democratic-Farmer-Labor Party, leader of the Democratic Women's Forum, and member of the Minneapolis Board of Public Welfare, she felt like a non-entity—a housewife living in the suburbs, driving carpools for their six kids (not all of them boys).

She pulled out of her funk by returning to Don's office as a part-time volunteer, which was possible only because they could afford to hire household help, a Black woman named Rosetta McDonald. Things improved further when the Fraser family moved into DC. Arvonne attended a meeting of NOW's DC chapter but decided the women there were politically naïve. She tried the Woman's National Democratic Club but felt disappointed that they only featured white men as speakers. Her son Tom bought her a subscription to the tiny feminist newspaper *off our backs*, through which Fraser read about women's consciousness-raising groups, but she didn't feel drawn to them.

She and a friend organized their own path to feminism, an informal brown-bag lunch group in 1969 mainly for wives of political officials, diplomats, and journalists. It was a radical move for women in Washington at the time. They couldn't admit even to themselves that they were creating a support group just like the "women's libbers" were doing. One cardinal rule for their monthly meetings: Don't introduce yourself in relation to a man but rather in terms of what you're doing or thinking or want to talk about. A participant at the first meeting told Fraser, "This is the first time in my 20 years in Washington that anybody has ever asked me *who I am*."[34]

Reporters who caught wind of the meetings pestered attendees for the names of their husbands. Instead, the group dubbed itself The Nameless Sisterhood.

Fraser invited the Sisterhood's first outside speaker: Bernice Sandler. Her talk inspired Sisterhood members to join WEAL. Within a year Fraser organized a DC chapter. Soon after, she created a legislative office for WEAL and became the group's national president. Everyone shared their own Rolodexes full of names and phone numbers of friends and colleagues who might be interested. They were on a roll, building a network.

Meanwhile, Sandler filed complaint after complaint from WEAL—all but the first signed by her—against more than 250 colleges and universities over the next two years, approximately 10 percent of the 2,525 U.S. institutions of higher learning.[35] Boyer, WEAL's politically savvy founder, coached Sandler not to notify the presidents of universities when she filed complaints but to send a copy to the university's local newspaper. The president wouldn't know it was coming until he got a call from a reporter, and by then it was a public matter.

Sandler made sure that each complaint relied on statistical data or, in twenty complaints, on the basis of discriminatory advertising for faculty positions. None depended solely on anecdotal material, though stories of discrimination arrived in her mailbox often.

Emmy Booy sent Sandler her brief rejection letter for a job teaching geology at Bates College in Maine, which declared "we are interested only in a male applicant here." The University of Iowa's Department of Zoology in 1969 wrote to job applicant Dr. Eunice Kahan in New York demanding to know whether she and her husband would split up if they offered her a job.

Loraine Grant, a nurse in Euclid, Ohio, with a master's degree in education and health, sent Sandler a copy of a letter she'd mailed to Sec. Shultz about the difficulty of finding work because of the reluctance to hire women. Grant's daughter, a student at Carleton College in Minnesota, and other students there were starting to organize against sex discrimination, decrying the university's wording in its search for a new college president: "preferably male." Grant's son, a student at Cornell University in New York, also was harmed by sexism, she added. "I am concerned for him because I do not believe any man can develop into the kind of human being he ought to be when it is done at the price of holding others down," she wrote.[36]

Women who fed information to Sandler risked retaliation. The City University of New York formally censured two women who contributed to Sandler's charges, a move that could have gotten them fired despite having tenure.[37] Some other colleges terminated the teaching contracts of women who complained. Unable to find work, at least one applied for welfare.

Since the U.S. Office of Education didn't gather statistics disaggregated by sex, Sandler's files on sex discrimination in academia quickly became the most extensive in the country.

Her sources and WEAL's members wrote their elected representatives, as Macaluso had advised, generating a heavy stream of congressional letters that cascaded down and got sent back up the bureaucratic channels of HEW and the Labor Department. Eventually congresspeople and their constituents generated so many letters that the departments had to assign several employees to handle them all.[38]

Sandler's strategy of complaining under the executive orders quickly caught on with other women's organizations. She spoke at meetings and conferences whenever she could, almost always taking the train because she was afraid to fly. One ally, a Black woman, called to invite her to speak at a conference in Houston. "How about you come down and talk about women's issues?"

Excited by the prospect, Sandler asked, "So, is there a train that goes to Houston?"

"What do you mean is there a train? You fly down here!"

"Well, I don't fly," Sandler said, explaining her deep fear. Usually that prompted a sympathetic "Oh, isn't that a shame?" and brainstorming on other transportation options. Not this time.

"Listen. You learn to fly or get out of the women's movement," the woman said. Stunned, Sandler did as she was told. She was still afraid, but she flew.

At one of her speaking events she met Ann Scott, a professor of English at the State University of New York, Buffalo, who chaired NOW's new National Campus Coordinating Committee in early 1970.[39]

"Since WEAL's goals and ours are the same I have decided to mount through NOW a national campaign to back up WEAL's blanket complaint to the OFCC with individual complaints from universities," Scott wrote to Sandler in March. Over time, NOW filed nearly a hundred complaints in all—often in close communication with Sandler. Scott invited Sandler to stay with her in New York City in April while attending the

Professional Women's Caucus, where Sandler bonded with the likes of feminist author Kate Millett.[40]

Jerry met Bernice at the train station on her way back from New York and surprised her with a copy of *Playboy* magazine. "This is not like him," she thought. Inside was an article on "The Fiery Feminists," so he'd bought it for her. In her thank-you to Scott for her hospitality, Sandler mused, "How do you tell anyone that your husband buys you a copy of *Playboy* because you're a Feminist?"[41]

Scott joined WEAL; Sandler finally joined NOW.[42] Scott also compiled Sandler's tips on how anyone could file complaints; they distributed them across the country through NOW and WEAL.

On February 6, less than a week after WEAL filed Sandler's class-action complaint in January 1970, a coalition of local women's groups in the Boston area sent Harvard's president a "Statement and Proposals Concerning the Status of Women at Harvard University."[43] Though it didn't mention the executive orders, the report presented statistics and demands to remedy sex discrimination there. The local NOW chapter turned it into a formal complaint to Sec. Shultz on March 25.

The Labor Department already was investigating Harvard for race discrimination. Shultz tacked on a review for sex discrimination—the first of its kind in education.

Harvard boasted no women among 473 tenured professors in its Law School and the Graduate School of Arts and Letters, according to the women's groups' report.[44] The university intentionally kept the percentage of women low among its graduate students (8–22 percent, depending on the school), and its hiring didn't keep pace even with these low percentages. Yet Harvard received tens of millions of dollars from federal contracts, the equivalent of hundreds of millions in 2020 dollars.

Harvard initially refused to hand over individual personnel records on hiring, salaries, and promotions, calling the federal investigation a "fishing expedition." HEW in April gave Harvard a fifteen-day deadline to open its records. In a rare move, the government lowered the boom, withholding approximately $4 million in contracts (the equivalent of $26.7 million in 2020). Harvard begrudgingly opened its records.[45]

Women at the University of Michigan filed a complaint under the executive orders about wage inequities in May 1970, prompting HEW to open its first investigation of a public university for sex discrimination. As at Harvard, Michigan officials initially refused to cooperate, risking $66 million per year in federal contracts. But over time HEW froze federal funding under the executive orders at multiple colleges and universities. Michigan eventually backed down.[46]

By mid-April Sandler had filed charges against thirty-two institutions of higher learning. Two weeks later, the total reached forty-three.

HEW's Office for Civil Rights (OCR) finally opened an investigation of sex discrimination at Sandler's University of Maryland in April and said it would collaborate with the Labor Department to review the employment of women by colleges and universities.[47] "We are asking for the same kind of vigorous enforcement that the OFCC has shown in combatting racial discrimination in the construction industry," Sandler wrote in yet another letter to Shultz.

Though Sandler and WEAL didn't mention it in their complaints, women of color faced double discrimination in education. Black and Chicano and Puerto Rican liberation movements pressed colleges and universities to admit more minority students and fund ethnic studies programs. In 1969, a five-month student strike—the longest on any U.S. campus in history—forced San Francisco State University to create the Departments of Black Studies and Ethnic Studies. The Black Action Movement led a ten-day strike at the University of Michigan, Ann Arbor, that ended in early April 1970 with the university agreeing to increase the enrollment of Black students on campus to at least 10 percent in the fall of 1973, close to the Black proportion of the state's population. Black students had the same intelligence and ambition for higher education as any other subgroup but suffered from centuries of systemic racism blocking access and support.[48]

Like the protests at the 1968 Miss America pageant, though, women's and racial justice groups mostly moved in parallel worlds, occasionally overlapping.

Meanwhile, Catherine East in the Labor Department's Women's Bureau produced a five-page fact sheet reporting significant differences by sex in rank and salary at colleges and universities, backing up Sandler's complaints. Eight months earlier, the Women's Bureau published a nine-page data-driven pamphlet dispelling the myths that female workers "go running home" when their kids get sick (one of the excuses given Sandler for not being hired) or didn't stay in jobs because they quit when they married.[49] By the end of April, HEW confirmed it was investigating several universities for sex discrimination.[50]

Ann Scott homed in on the fact that the government did not enforce the requirement for affirmative action in hiring women in education the way it did for racial minorities. She crafted a model plan for affirmative action, the "NOW plan." At Sandler's urging she ran it by Macaluso. "He's really great about telling us how to get even tougher," Sandler said.[51]

Sandler, as WEAL, submitted the NOW plan to the Department of Labor in May, with little response. "Women (and men) from all over the country . . . are sending data about their institutions and asking WEAL to file formal charges for them. . . . All of this is a result of mouth-to-mouth communication, for there has been very little publicity on our activities," she said.[52]

Scott ended the affirmative action plan with a plea to free not just the oppressed but the oppressor: "The hidden cost to men is equally high; being favored puts men in the position of profiting at the expense of women. No profit could ever justify such a cost; no one is equal until everyone is equal," she wrote. "Men, too, are the prisoners of their cultural status, forced to maintain a socially determined superiority which is defined by women's inferiority. I cannot seriously believe that any man worth his salt wants to be defined as a man by how much better he is than a woman. I think too much of men to believe that, and I believe and hope men think too much of themselves to allow it."[53]

When Scott and Sandler got a chance to meet with Macaluso and other Labor Department officials, Sandler watched and learned from the more experienced Scott's political maneuvering toward their goal.

Slowly the mainstream media started recognizing the growing impact of the women's movement and being more respectful in its coverage, a notable instance of which was the first documentary on the subject, produced and reported by Marlene Sanders of ABC News and broadcast on May 26, 1970.[54] Getting broader respect from the public, though, proved more elusive.

When Sandler described her federal complaints to students in one of the classes she taught, a young man raised his hand. "Did your husband write that for you?" he asked. No one batted an eyelash. It seemed a reasonable question in that era.

"No," Sandler explained. "I wrote it myself."

Despite the vocal disapproval of some, Sandler remained pleasant and polite with her students and colleagues, except once.

A professor approached her in a hallway between classes. "I know what you're doing," he said. "Why can't you be more like a lady?"

His words stung Sandler deeply. Like many women of her generation, she tried exceedingly hard to remain "ladylike" in all that she did. She had been careful to dress professionally for work and press appearances, to control her emotions in public, and to use polite language even when discussing discrimination. She'd been filing federal charges, doing serious work to right injustice, and all he could see was the way it inconvenienced his notion of femininity. Sandler had had it.

"I've been a *lady* for more than forty years," she cried, "and where the hell has it gotten me?!"

She lost her lecturer position at the University of Maryland at the end of the semester.

Bigger things awaited her. Feminists inside and outside Congress were blowing up business as usual, igniting years of legislative battles to create stronger tools against sex discrimination. Among them—a law called Title IX.

3

Congress
1970–1972

SITTING IN THE SEATS FOR SPECTATORS IN ROOM 2261 OF THE RAYBURN House Office Building, Sandler bounced her right foot nonstop to release her pent-up energy. The first congressional hearings on sex discrimination in higher education! Hearings that she helped organize! The cranked-up air conditioning countered the humid June heat outside.[1]

Before her sat the polished wooden tables for witnesses and press, facing a long, raised semicircular table for subcommittee members, framed by the room's dark wood-paneled walls and plush blue carpeting. Rep. Edith Green (D-OR) presided in the center of the dais, one of eleven women among the 535 members of Congress and the rare woman with enough seniority to have any clout there.

These seven days of hearings in June and July 1970 focused on Green's Section 805 of H.R. 16098—a small but potentially mighty part of a large omnibus education bill. Section 805 would prohibit sex discrimination in any program or activity receiving federal financial assistance. Green knew it would be a tough sell to the other fifteen members (all men) of the House Special Subcommittee on Education that she chaired and then to the thirty-five members of its parent Committee on Education and Labor—all men save for Green and Rep. Patsy Takemoto Mink (D-HI), the first Asian American woman and woman of color elected to Congress, in 1964.[2]

Most of Green's colleagues and the Nixon administration gave Section 805 a chilly reception. Seven members of her subcommittee didn't bother to attend the hearings at all. Only one other member joined her on most days. The Labor Department refused to send anyone who had power to enforce the executive orders. Administration witnesses tried to get her to water down Section 805.

Sandler moved from the audience to the witness table on June 19, day two of the hearings and her first time testifying before Congress. She'd lost her university teaching gig but here she was, sitting alongside pioneering civil rights attorney and professor of American studies Pauli Murray of Brandeis University and assistant professor of art history Ann Sutherland Harris of Columbia University.

Astounding stories and statistics crossed her desk almost daily, Sandler told Green and Rep. William D. Hathaway (D–ME), the two subcommittee members present that day.[3] In one academic department, a female full professor earned less than a male assistant professor who was fresh out of graduate school. Elsewhere, an associate professor who'd been on a university's faculty for ten years discovered that her salary fell more than $1,000 below the bottom of the university's pay scale ($6,711 below in 2020 dollars).

"Women have been loath to complain about discrimination in their institutions because they risk academic suicide if they do so," Sandler added. She knew of several women whose faculty contracts were not renewed after they protested sex discrimination on their campuses.

"And all of this is legal!" Other laws did not protect against sex discrimination in education. The executive orders did, but only regarding employment, not other aspects of education. Plus, the executive orders did not have the status of law—they could be changed by any presidential administration. And federal contracts mostly went to larger universities, so the executive orders didn't apply to most small colleges and K–12 schools. The executive orders weren't enough; women needed a law like Green's proposed Section 805.

"As more and more information has been collected, there is no question whatsoever that there is a massive, consistent and vicious pattern of sex discrimination in our universities and colleges," Sandler said.[4]

Rep. Green ran the hearings with her usual no-nonsense style. A former schoolteacher, she'd been in office fifteen years, long enough to chair a House subcommittee, and authored or influenced nearly every bill on education during her time, earning the nickname "Mrs. Education."

Not many of her colleagues liked Green but they begrudgingly respect-
ed her. News accounts from late 1969 described the five-foot-four, sixty-
year-old Green as a "tigress," a diminutive gray-haired grandmother who
"certainly seems gentle" but makes "strong men quake with fear and fury"
in legislative battles because she was "a bareknuckle fighter who's capable
of really whiplashing her opponents." A *Washington Post* article about her
in 1969 used the sexist sub-headline, "LADY OR SHREW."[5]

Green grew up in a time when the Ku Klux Klan dominated Oregon
politics, yet she learned to think for herself.[6] She supported every civil rights bill that came before her, though not always in their entirety,
and led an eight-year battle to finally pass the Equal Pay Act of 1963. By
1970, though, Green opposed mandated busing to integrate schools on the
grounds that those decisions should be left to local control (a favorite argument of anti-integrationists, though she didn't see herself that way). Critics
referred to her as "the liberal racist," "the sweetheart of the southerners,"
and "the Nixon Democrat."[7]

Sandler wrote apologetically to NOW's Ann Scott: "I close my eyes to
her position on everything other than women. That may be a copout but
if I didn't do that I couldn't accomplish very much for women."[8]

Sandler spoke her mind at Green's hearings in part thanks to Phineas
Indritz, a NOW board member who influenced Congress from behind
the scenes as a lawyer for various House subcommittees.[9] Indritz had
helped connect Sandler earlier that year to Green, who asked Sandler
to suggest witnesses for a possible one-day hearing on discrimination
against women.[10] By mid-February her legislative counsel for the subcommittee, Harry Hogan, suggested that the hearings extend to two
days. Sandler connected Hogan with the "uppity" women faculty at
Columbia University. Plans quickly grew to five and then seven days of
hearings. Indritz also invited Sandler to draft a speech that Rep. Martha Griffiths (D-MI) might give to Congress about discrimination in
education.

In that first week of February 1970, as Sandler prepared for her new
temporary job at HEW and started teaching her last semester of two evening classes at the University of Maryland, she drafted a fiery first version
of a speech that served as a template for dozens of her own speeches and

congressional testimonies in the years ahead. Griffiths used most of what Sandler wrote in her March 9 speech, generating news stories.[11]

Sandler was getting a crash course on how Washington worked. Macaluso suggested that she might want to push to amend Title VI of the Civil Rights Act to prohibit discrimination not just based on race, color, or national origin but also based on sex. She mentioned that idea to Indritz, who nudged Green, and into Green's bill it went.[12]

On February 19, Green introduced the giant Omnibus Post-Secondary Education Act of 1970 (H.R. 16098), a large bill that had been in the works for some time to reauthorize higher education programs. Her Section 805 would fix the three laws that Sandler identified as deficient: Titles VI and VII of the Civil Rights Act, and the Equal Pay Act within the Fair Labor Standards Act.

The Equal Pay Act fix was deviously brilliant. A Labor Department employee who had helped Green draft and pass the Equal Pay Act, Morag Simchak, purposefully used obscure wording in that part of Section 805, knowing that legislators wouldn't think to object because they wouldn't make the extra effort to discern what it actually said.[13] Simchak's personal experience convinced her that sometimes things need to be disguised to survive. She had escaped Nazi-occupied Poland hidden in the back of a hay cart, she told Sandler, and arrived in the United States in 1941 as a refugee. Her first husband, a fighter for the Polish resistance, died in the 1944 Warsaw uprising.[14] Hogan and Green adopted Simchak's wording and relied on her counsel as Section 805 evolved.

Meanwhile, word spread about the WEAL complaints. Professor Pauli Murray and other academics reached out to Sandler that spring. She suggested them as witnesses for Green's hearings.

Some Republican congresswomen contacted Sandler too. Four of them had been raising the issue with Nixon's staff periodically since January 1969. His new Presidential Task Force on Women's Rights and Responsibilities issued a report in December 1969, though the administration did not publicly release it initially. *A Matter of Simple Justice* recommended specific steps to counter rampant sex discrimination.[15] "I believe the President" will do the right thing, task force member Rep. Florence Dwyer (R-NJ) wrote to Sandler, "but I also believe that there can be no further delay in attending to the very serious matter of eliminating discrimination and expanding opportunity" for women.[16] Someone leaked the task force report to the press.

WEAL and NOW continued to stoke public attention. Sandler filed complaints of sex discrimination in March against the University of North Carolina and all the colleges in the City University of New York.[17] She targeted Florida's entire state university system and its two-year colleges in May. In June WEAL filed a discrimination complaint against all California State Colleges and Universities, and NOW filed charges against the State University of New York, the largest university system in the world.

"You know, I think in the not so long run we are going to shake up a hell of a lot of universities," Sandler wrote to an ally.[18]

Neither Nixon's Task Force nor Section 805 in Green's bill attracted much attention. The public focused heavily instead on the proposed Equal Rights Amendment (ERA) to the Constitution, a separate bill being debated in Congress that women had been seeking for forty-seven years, and which could have prohibited sex discrimination in much more than education.[19]

The lobbyist for the powerful American Council on Education declined to participate in Green's Section 805 hearings, saying, "There is no sex discrimination in higher education and, besides, it's not a problem."[20] The hearings focused mainly on employment discrimination in multiple fields plus some attention given to student admissions, counseling, and textbooks. Most of the witnesses held advanced degrees. At a time when U.S. society had only recently begun to address still-persisting racist and financial obstacles to joining the professions, most of the witnesses were white.

Throughout the hearings, Green kept returning to the idea that sex discrimination was a bigger problem than race discrimination, a common type of thinking that put the two in competition.

Professor Pauli Murray tried to interrupt this train of thought. Testifying after Sandler, she spoke first on behalf of the ACLU and then for herself.[21] One of the few women—and even fewer Black women—to earn a law degree before 1960, Murray contributed her scholarship on segregation to Thurgood Marshall's case against racist education systems in *Brown v. Board of Education*. She'd served on President Kennedy's Commission on the Status of Women, became the first Black person to earn a doctorate in law from Yale, and co-founded NOW. At the time of Green's hearings she was a university professor and member of the ACLU's national board, and in 1976 would become the first woman ordained as an Episcopal Church priest.

The struggles against racism and sexism are "equally urgent," Murray said.[22] She related the racism of Jim Crow to the sexism of "Jane Crow," a term she popularized. Murray articulated the overlap of racial, gender, age, and class oppressions. (A 2017 biography drawing on Murray's voluminous personal records argued convincingly that she also was a transgender man, though Murray never talked about this publicly.)[23]

"I am led to the hypothesis that we will be unable to eradicate racism in the United States unless and until we simultaneously remove all sex barriers which inhibit the development of individual talents," she stated. "I am further convinced that the price of our survival as a nation is the sharing of our power and wealth—or rather the redistribution of this power and wealth—among black and white, rich and poor, men and women, old and young, red and brown and all the in-betweens." The different discriminations were entwined, she argued; solutions must address this simultaneously lest people facing more than one type of discrimination be left behind.

Rep. Shirley Chisholm (D-NY), the first Black woman in Congress and the only congressperson to testify at the hearings, agreed with many of Murray's comments in her own remarks on July 1. Her only reservation with Section 805 was a desire for even stronger enforcement mechanisms. Like Green, though, she experienced sexism as worse than racism: "During my entire political life, my sex has been a far greater handicap than my skin pigmentation."[24]

Chisholm attended grade school in Barbados and graduated from Brooklyn College as one of sixty or so Black students in a student body of ten thousand. She eventually landed a teaching job. With the full support of her husband, Conrad, Chisholm ran for and won election to the New York State Assembly and then Congress.[25] She eschewed public protests and demonstrations, staying within the electoral process to support civil rights, social justice, feminism, Black Nationalism (though she opposed the "masculinism" of many Black Nationalists), students, prisoners, and an end to the Vietnam War. She joined NOW as soon as it started. She constantly tried to build coalitions between white feminists and women of color, one of just a few politicians at the time who connected race, gender, and class issues. The inability of many white feminists of the time to address issues important to women of color frustrated her. "There's some aspects of women's liberation that relate to Black women," like advocating for day care, she said, "but the rest of it is baloney."

Frankie M. Freeman, the only woman and only Black person on the U.S. Commission on Civil Rights at the time, testified the same day as Chisholm. Racism was a bigger problem than sexism, she countered.[26] Her experience as a Black Southern woman differed from Chisholm's life as a Barbadian American living in the North. Freeman worried that Green's bill would dilute attention to discrimination based on race, color, or national origin.

She and Nixon's men frustrated Green by opposing nearly every part of Section 805. A Department of Education spokesman who testified echoed statistics on sex discrimination to acknowledge the problem, then reversed direction to oppose Green's remedies. Even Elizabeth Koontz, director of the Women's Bureau, toed Nixon's party line.

"I just have to say it is the biggest bunch of gobbledygook I have heard for a long, long time," Green said in response to Koontz's testimony.[27]

The Nixon administration especially argued against adding "sex" to the kinds of discriminations prohibited by Title VI, which banned discrimination based on race, color, or national origin. Amending Title VI would make it the strongest law against sex discrimination besides the ERA, if the latter passed, because it would cover many areas of society—not just education but also federally assisted housing, health care, and public accommodations such as hotels and transportation. Multiple administration officials testified that they worried it might eliminate single-sex dorms and threaten religious autonomy. They feared it would force institutions to provide shared restrooms, job training, physical education, and gyms—the only discussions of sports that the House would hear over the course of the bill's evolution.[28]

Sandler and the other women's advocates argued strongly for amending Title VI. Said Murray, "As a rule of thumb all antidiscrimination measures should include sex along with race, color, religion, national origin, age, and other prohibited bases of discrimination."[29]

Instead of amending Title VI, administration officials argued, Congress should make Section 805 separate legislation using the same wording as Title VI but limiting its purview to education. Over the next two years a provision to amend Title VI bounced in and out of the bills that evolved into Title IX as Green and her staff vacillated on the provision's inclusion.[30]

Sandler and Murray maintained a steady correspondence for a few years after the hearings, sharing news and testing ideas. "It's a great time to be alive and to be associated with women like you and so many others who are in the Movement today!" Murray wrote soon after Green's hearings, along with sharing some thoughts about strategy. A prolific correspondent in general, Murray sent a handwritten note a couple weeks later: "Dear Bunny! When you're written up in the history of this era, they should refer to you as the little woman who started the Academic Sex Revolution."[31]

Sandler replied with good news: Rep. Green hired her to work part-time on sex discrimination until January 7, mainly to put together the written record of the hearings.[32] "Life is busy, busy, busy. At least now with my new job I can spend virtually all of my working time on matters relating to the women's movement. I came back from vacation to find maybe 50–75 letters to answer, etc."[33]

A young law professor at Rutgers University, Ruth Bader Ginsburg, wrote to Sandler. (Ginsburg went on to be the second woman on the Supreme Court.) She asked for more information about the WEAL complaints for a seminar on women's rights she was planning for spring 1971.[34] Their correspondence had begun in 1969 and spanned the 1970s.[35] Sandler's feedback on Ginsburg's draft article for a law journal "saved me from the kind of error that can be particularly embarrassing for a lawyer," Ginsburg wrote in thanks.[36]

Sandler was feeling a bit more like an insider while still active as an outsider. On August 26, 1970, approximately fifty thousand people marched in New York City at NOW's hastily organized Women's Strike for Equality under the slogan "Don't Iron While the Strike Is Hot!" Sandler and twenty others addressed between a thousand and two thousand people at a rally that day in Lafayette Park, Washington, DC, across from the

White House, urging passage of the ERA. With her large glasses and gray-ing bangs framing her face, Sandler told the crowd, "There is something wrong in a nation where more than one-half the population—women—are second-class citizens. . . . It's time for the hand that rocks the cradle to rock the boat," a popular feminist slogan.[37]

She compiled 1,261 pages of records from Green's hearings into two volumes; Green printed three thousand sets—totaling six thousand books, six times the norm.[38] The records "are monumental and truly, Pauli, the discrimination is far worse than any of us could have imagined," Sandler wrote to Murray.[39]

She and NOW's Ann Scott consulted often about enforcing the execu-tive orders. "Dear Bunny," Scott wrote on September 30, 1970. "The most important thing that has happened to the movement in two years—you got a new typewriter!" The words that Sandler typed now lined up neatly in a row instead of individual letters forming hills and gullies across the page.[40]

Sandler filed a complaint on October 5, 1970, against all U.S. medical schools based on testimony at Green's hearings.[41] Media articles boosted her profile and her message. *Women's Wear Daily* called her "a diminutive waif-like education specialist" on Green's staff who "is a fire cracker when it comes to women's rights."[42]

By the end of 1970 women had filed at least eighty-four complaints against 262 colleges and universities for sex discrimination under the exec-utive orders.[43] But Green's higher education bill never made it out of her subcommittee, and Section 805 died with it.

Sandler, WEAL, and NOW filed sex discrimination charges against Yale University and all U.S. law schools to kick off 1971.[44] On Capi-tol Hill, the momentum of the women's movement flowed into a rela-tive grace period in the early 1970s before opposition to women's rights got better organized. "We put sex discrimination provisions into every-thing," Rep. Bella Abzug (D-NY) recalled. Much of it passed because most congressmen didn't really understand the implications, Sandler later said.[45]

Green relied on Hogan to draft iterations of her previous sex-discrimination bill to submit to the Ninety-Second Congress; he consult-ed frequently with Sandler and Simchak.[46] Green had her hands full with lots of other tasks, including deciding what to do about wild mustangs roaming her state and annoying ranchers.

In early April she introduced H.R. 7248, the giant Higher Education Act of 1971 that replaced the 1970 omnibus bill. In it, Title X replaced Section 805. Hogan sent Sandler a copy the next day, almost apologizing because Title X exempted single-sex colleges. Sandler, Ginsburg, NOW, and others tried to persuade Green to ban sex discrimination at *all* publicly funded schools, but women's and men's colleges successfully pressured legislators to exempt existing single-sex colleges.[47]

All spring and summer, Hogan shuttled between women's advocates and aides for other subcommittee members to find compromises on this issue and others on which they disagreed. Along the way, the bill shifted from amending Title VI to being a more constricted stand-alone law that used Title VI's wording but applied only to education. Perhaps Green felt that amending Title VI, which affected not just education but many corners of American life, would attract too much attention and opposition, dooming it. Maybe she deferred to the wishes of the Nixon administration and Civil Rights Commissioner Frankie Freeman, who testified at Green's hearings against amending Title VI. It may have been a reasonable strategy at that time, but it missed an opportunity to emphasize the cohesiveness of civil rights. From this point on, separate civil rights laws would try to stop discrimination based on sex, or age, or disability, or race, color, and national origin. As more people in ensuing decades came to better understand the multiple discriminations faced by women of color, for instance, these separate laws lacked the legal scaffolding to protect against the additive effects of these converging discriminations. They could address race or sex complaints separately but not the unique hardships of mistreatment based on race *and* sex.

Within a week of Green releasing her bill, Sen. Birch Bayh's office called asking for information. The young Democrat from a Republican state, Indiana, had found feminism through his brilliant wife, Marvella, and became a prime women's ally in the Senate. She'd been a star student who tried to go to the University of Virginia but was told, "Women need not apply." When they met in college and married in 1952, Marvella wanted a career, but at Birch's request she reluctantly agreed to wait until after their

child was grown. She urged Birch, a farmer, to run for the Indiana Legis-
lature and to go to law school. Marvella helped coordinate his successful
1962 campaign for Senate from their garage.[48]

As Birch throttled up his reelection campaign, President Lyndon Johnson said he wanted Marvella to be vice-chair of the Democratic National
Committee. Marvella was over the moon with happiness about the idea.
But Birch turned to his staff for advice. As the men met in the Bayhs'
home, Marvella paced the floor in the next room, looked out the window,
and cried. It would cost Birch votes, his aides said. Marvella never completely forgave Birch for telling Johnson he needed her to help with his
campaign instead of taking the job. Later in life Birch said it was the worst
mistake he ever made. He won reelection by a slim margin.

For years Marvella urged Birch to do something about sex discrimination in education and to get the ERA passed. He became a chief Senate
sponsor of the ERA. In December 1970 he announced a national childcare
proposal, deeply researched by Marvella. In 1971 he joined WEAL's advisory board.

When the full Senate debated its version of Green's higher education bill
(S. 659) in the summer of 1971, Bayh offered a sex discrimination amendment to complement Green's Title X. Sen. Peter H. Dominick (R–CO)
asked a series of questions about the intent of Bayh's bill.[49] It was one of
only five times that the topic of sports came up—three mentions in Green's
hearings and two in Senate debates.

"I do not read this as requiring integration of dormitories between the
sexes, nor do I feel it mandates the desegregation of the football fields," said
Bayh, a sports fan who was known to toss around a football on the roof
of his Senate office building. "What we are trying to do here is provide
equal access for women and men students to the educational process and
the extracurricular activities in a school, where there is not a unique facet
such as football involved. We are not requiring that intercollegiate football
be desegregated, nor that the men's locker room be desegregated."

Dominick commented, "If I may say so, I would have had much more
fun playing college football if it had been integrated." Bayh responded,
"The Senator from Indiana will resist the temptation to remark further on
that point." The men in the Senate laughed.

Then Sen. Strom Thurmond (R-SC) asked if the statute would force The Citadel, a public military academy, to admit women. Bayh said yes, which was not what Thurmond wanted to hear. He raised a point of order arguing that the sex discrimination proposal wasn't relevant to the education bill being discussed. The other senators agreed, pushing Bayh's amendment aside.[50] They passed the rest of the education bill that summer.

Bayh tried repeatedly and unsuccessfully throughout the remainder of 1971 to reintroduce the amendment. He also explored a possible run for president until a breast biopsy found cancer in Marvella in October 1971. Birch stayed in the Senate to be closer to Marvella. After treatment, she pursued the career she'd wanted, as a TV commentator and spokesperson for the American Cancer Society, until the disease killed her in 1979.[51]

Other legislators proposed bills overlapping what Green and Bayh were trying to do. Shortly after Green introduced Section 805 in early 1970, Rep. Abner Mikva (D-IL), with Rep. Mink and four others, introduced a bill, the Women's Equity Act, that incorporated the Presidential Task Force recommendations and more.[52] Various representatives introduced versions of that bill in 1971, 1972, and 1973. Bayh introduced a Senate version in June 1971. None passed.

A separate but related bill did pass—the first to prohibit sex discrimination in school admissions. It addressed the elite world of medicine.

Medical schools limited women on average to 7 percent to 10 percent of admissions in the 1960s.[53] To change this, Green and Bayh passed identical sex-discrimination amendments to the Comprehensive Health Manpower Training Act of 1971 and the Nurse Training Amendments Act of 1971, motivated by testimony at Green's 1970 hearings.[54] Schools and hospitals no longer could deny women entry into medical or health training programs without risking losing some of the $616 million in federal funding for 1972 ($4.1 trillion in 2020 dollars).[55] But the legislation, which became known as Titles VII and VIII of the Public Health Service Act, did nothing to stop sex discrimination against students once they enrolled; they still needed Green's Title X, which was threatened by disagreements over other parts of the larger education bill.

"Her bill is in trouble—she and [Reps.] Brademas and Quie will have to work out some sort of compromise, and I'm not sure what will happen to the sex discrimination provision once they start to trade off," Sandler wrote in late August.[56]

Sandler finally landed a permanent job in September as director of the new Project on the Status and Education of Women (PSEW), started by the Association of American Colleges (AAC), a trade association for "the best liberal arts colleges you never heard of," as she liked to call it. Tucked away on the second floor of one of the AAC's two adjoining townhouses near Dupont Circle, Sandler had a lovely view of the trees on R Street and enough physical distance from the rest of the AAC to follow her instincts.

She ignored PSEW's purported but somewhat vague focus on women's studies and liberal education to spotlight discrimination and fairness instead. It meant she could no longer be the one filing complaints through WEAL; other members picked up that role.[57]

Sandler anguished over her first hire for PSEW staff—Francelia Gleaves, a magna cum laude graduate of Howard University already working at the AAC.[58] "Was much distressed while looking for a secretary. So many bright college graduates with so dim a future," Sandler wrote to Murray. The head of personnel warned Sandler that Gleaves was a troublemaker, a trait that Sandler thought might be an asset.[59] She managed to get Gleaves a better title—research assistant—and a bit more pay than originally budgeted, "but oh, I feel like I have indeed joined the establishment, and am exploiting women like the rest of them."[60]

An African American woman, Gleaves believed that progress for Black women depended as much on stopping sex discrimination as on stopping racial discrimination. The many calls and letters to PSEW that Gleaves handled—quite a few from women of color—showed her that the Project mattered. Gleaves helped produce PSEW's newsletter and wrote several resource papers on minority women in education, women in nontraditional jobs, and other topics. She represented PSEW at conferences of some fledgling Black feminist organizations, most of them short-lived. It felt good to get together with other Black women. So many of them felt like they walked a tightrope—they couldn't speak out for women's rights without alienating many Black men. But how do you elevate the race to some level of equity, she wondered, if you leave half the people dangling in the abyss? Gleaves couldn't choose between being a Black person or a woman.

When she met with officials or gave public talks she often was the only African American in the room. That didn't faze her—not since age twelve when, at the height of the civil rights movement, the segregated Methodist Church invited her to speak to a summer conference of thousands of white youths in North Carolina, many of whom had never spent time with a Black peer. She went by herself, scared but committed. Talking with adults in academia was easier than that.

After a marathon session, Green's subcommittee sent the massive higher education bill to the full Committee on Education and Labor on September 23, but by an 8–7 vote the subcommittee replaced Green's Title X with a version that exempted all undergraduate admissions at coed institutions, private or public. That would exclude 95 percent of college women from protection against discrimination in admissions, Green complained.[61] "There's going to be a battle in the full Committee next Tuesday," she wrote to a friend.[62] With five women now on the thirty-seven-member committee, including Chisholm and Mink, and Democrats outnumbering the sixteen Republican men, her chances were good.[63]

Green offered an amendment to the full committee on September 29 to restore her original Title X. Rep. Al Quie (R-MN) complained during debate that telling schools they couldn't discriminate in admissions would be harmful. Asked to cite specific examples, he replied weakly, "Stewardess schools?" If Green's bill passed, "you are going to have male stewards" serving drinks and food on airlines—clearly women's work, he implied. The committee members laughed.[64] They voted along party lines to go with Green's wording.

During four days and one night of debate on the education bill starting October 27, the House rejected what had been Title IX (a measure related to political interns), so Green's sex-discrimination amendment changed from Title X to Title IX. Both the *Washington Post* and *New York Times* editorialized against it. "Though motivated by the best of intentions, such legislation is unsound" because the sexes have different needs and aspirations, the *Times* argued.[65] Elite private colleges like Harvard and Yale that didn't want the government telling them what to do generated a slew of letters to Congress opposing Title IX.

Opposition to Rep. Green's 1971 bill came "primarily" from "a very limited number of the so-called 'prestigious' or 'elitist' colleges and universities on the Eastern Seaboard," Green wrote. "These twenty or thirty colleges and universities do not and never have represented higher education in the United States."[66]

Rep. John N. Erlenborn (R–IL) parroted the Ivy universities' talking points when he moved on November 4 again to exempt all undergraduate admissions. The university leaders wanted "diversity," which they defined as more choices than either single-sex colleges or schools that treat the sexes equally—namely, schools that admit more men than women based on sex, not merit.[67]

Democrats rose to oppose Erlenborn's amendment. "Millions of women pay taxes into the federal treasury and we collectively resent that these funds should be used for the support of institutions to which we are denied equal access," Mink said during debate. Abzug noted that twenty-four of the thirty-four members of the American Association of Universities faced either formal charges or accusations of sex discrimination. Rep. Ed Koch (D–NY) said the Erlenborn amendment offered only "dribs and drabs," not full rights, and said women will not accept "the salami tactics being used by the Congress: that is to say, 'rights, a slice at a time.'"[68]

They lost this skirmish. The House passed the Erlenborn amendment in 1971 by a five-vote margin to exempt undergraduate admissions from Title IX.

Other parts of the larger education bill generated far more controversy: three anti-busing and anti-desegregation amendments, aid for schools attempting to desegregate, student aid distribution formulas, and ethnic studies.[69] After nearly a week of debate and fifteen votes on various amendments, the House passed H.R. 7248 in the wee morning hours of November 5 with 332 members in favor, 38 opposed, and 60 not voting.[70]

"Last night the House did violence to the Constitution and obliterated what progress has been made in human rights in the last decade," Mink said in written remarks submitted after the vote. She voted against an education bill for the first time in her seven years in Congress. "Blacks, women, all ethnic minorities, our children, and our college students—all the truly underrepresented groups in our society were placed in the rubble heap of this saddest day of my Congressional experience."[71]

But Green felt relieved and grateful. Nearly all her financial aid proposals remained in the bill and the only major concession was Erlenborn's change to Title IX. "I was really in seventh heaven," she said later. "I don't know when I have ever been so pleased, because I had worked so long, and it had been such a tough battle."[72] Still, she wrote to women's advocates, asking them to pressure the Senate to pass a version without Erlenborn's restrictions.[73] The Senate would reconsider the full education bill in 1972, when Bayh could try to improve Title IX.[74]

In her glass-half-full way of seeing the world, Sandler was sanguine. The damage was not as great as she expected.[75] By the end of 1971, WEAL, NOW, and individuals had filed complaints against more than 350 educational institutions under the executive orders.[76] Her speaking schedule grew. Her first year at PSEW, she attended at least thirty-two meetings and conferences.[77]

PSEW also attracted a powerful ally. Women at the Ford Foundation, the largest philanthropic foundation in the late twentieth century, organized a revolt in early 1970. They wanted women promoted to decision-making positions and more of the foundation's money going to programs benefiting women and minorities. And they didn't want to have to serve coffee.[78] Mariam K. Chamberlain, director of Ford's higher education program, arranged significant ongoing funding for PSEW, which also got money from Carnegie Foundation grants and others.[79]

In early 1972 Ann Scott moved to DC to be the sole employee in NOW's new legislative office.[80] Rep. Chisholm ran for president—the first Black woman to do so.[81] Already, though, signs suggested that feminists' early grace period might be ending. Conservative author and activist Phyllis Schlafly founded the Eagle Forum, with part of its agenda to oppose proposals by "radical feminists."

Bayh introduced his version of Title IX when the Senate took up the higher education bill again in February.[82] This time, he exempted military schools to avoid opposition from Sen. Thurmond. He reinstated coverage for undergraduate admissions to public universities that got stripped from the House version, but he left the exemption for private undergraduate admissions, deflecting opposition from the elite private universities.

"My view is that many of these exemptions will not be supportable after further study and discussion," Bayh said. His amendment required the commissioner of education to study sex discrimination and to recommend legislative remedies by the end of 1973, just as had been required for other forms of discrimination under parts of the Civil Rights Act of 1964. After that, he believed, most of the exemptions would be discarded. In the end, though, the House-Senate conference committee reconciling the different versions of the bill stripped out Bayh's requirement for a study on whether or not all the exemptions were warranted, so the exemptions never went away.

The topic of sports came up briefly for the last time during February debate on the bill. Bayh assured his colleagues that Title IX would not require coed locker rooms and that personal privacy would be protected. By implication, other aspects of the law would apply to athletics.[83]

On the Senate floor, he presented a masterful summation of data and entered into the *Congressional Record* an entire paper by Sandler.[84] If it weren't for nuns heading Catholic institutions, Sandler wrote, the number of female college presidents in 1970 would be fewer than the number of whooping cranes, who were declared "endangered" that year. "Less than 1% of our college presidents are women; perhaps we ought to declare women presidents as an endangered species," she wrote.

The Senate passed Bayh's amendment and the overall higher education bill. Separately, Congress passed the Equal Employment Opportunity Act in March 1972 to remove Title VII's exemptions for educators, public employees, and professional-level workers, a remedy included in Title IX's wording as well.

Campus activism for women's rights increased everywhere in the country in 1972. Women at the University of Kansas peacefully occupied a campus building for thirteen hours in February, demanding childcare, an affirmative action plan for women, an end to discriminatory employment practices, and more. Similar demonstrations disrupted St. Lawrence University in New York and American University in DC. Legislation to end sex discrimination in education began appearing in state legislatures.[85]

A House-Senate conference committee struggled to resolve the 246 differences between their versions of the Higher Education Act. By the time the conference committee took up the ten differences over Title IX, Congress had passed the ERA by large majorities.[86] Still, Erlenborn and Rep. Frank Thompson Jr. (D-NJ) again moved in the conference committee to exempt public undergraduate colleges from Title IX.

Green described the scene in a letter to a NOW leader.[87] She said she told Thompson "that it was incredible that he would vote for the Equal Rights Amendment in the House and then, behind closed doors in a Conference, try to have the official action of the Congress be one that would say to all undergraduate schools 'it is perfectly all right for you to discriminate in admissions policies against girls and young women.'" Fortunately, Green wrote, she held six proxy votes that defeated the attack. "This does point up the continuing battle that must be waged against those who somehow still believe the woman's place is 'pregnant, barefooted and in the kitchen.'!!!"

Conflicts over sections on busing and financial aid did not go as well for Green during ten weeks of negotiations.[88] At 5 a.m. on May 17, she walked out of the conference committee's final fifteen-hour marathon session.[89] The conferees settled on a bill that she could not accept.[90] Green threw her efforts into stopping the whole bill.[91] She wrote dozens of letters to college presidents, deans, student financial aid directors, and politicians urging them to help defeat the bill.[92] Green even circulated a memo from Duke University president Terry Sanford opposing the larger bill, in which he wrote, "As for doing away with bias against women, this is not real, for the Affirmative Action Program already offers more hope in this direction"—a statement Green surely didn't believe.[93]

The complex array of issues in the bill jumbled party-line voting. Seven of the thirteen women in the House voted to accept the conference report, including all three Republican women and Mink despite objections from the La Raza National Lawyers Association to the "unconscionable" limits on busing.[94] Chisholm and Abzug joined Green in the "Nay" votes for various reasons. The House voted 218–180 (with 34 not voting) on June 8 to approve the conference report.[95]

On June 23, five days after secret henchmen of President Richard Nixon burglarized the Democratic National Headquarters in the Watergate housing complex and started a political crisis that would force him out of office two years later, Nixon signed the Education Amendments of 1972.[96] The

New York Times devoted one sentence to Title IX in its coverage.[97] Hardly anyone noticed Title IX; there was no celebration party. Public attention focused much more on the drive to ratify the ERA, on ending the Vietnam War, and other controversies.

The opening 37 words of Title IX parroted Title VI, replacing "race, color, or national origin" with "sex": "No person in the United States shall, on the basis of sex, be excluded from participation in, be denied the benefits of, or be subjected to discrimination under any education program or activity receiving Federal financial assistance."[98]

Then came sixteen sections, subsections, and paragraphs of details and explanations, including a flaw that Title VI didn't have—exemptions. Title IX applied to vocational, K–12, and higher education institutions and programs; if they didn't comply with Title IX they could lose their federal funding. But Title IX did not apply to private undergraduate admissions. It also exempted existing single-sex schools, military schools, and schools controlled by religious groups "if compliance would violate the tenets of their faith."[99]

Title IX did not specifically define an "educational program or activity receiving federal financial assistance." That opened the door to desperate claims by conservatives later on that the law applied only to specific departments, not entire schools, or to specific schools, not districts, contradicting the broader intent expressed in congressional debates.

Sandler sent three thousand fat informational packets to the growing PSEW mailing list in July 1972. She stuffed the packets with materials, including separate papers about Title IX, the ERA, the executive orders, the Comprehensive Health Manpower Training Act and Nurse Training Amendments Act of 1971, and more.

She sent Green a consolation note: "Two and a half years ago when WEAL filed its first complaint (January 1970) only the Executive Order prohibited sex discrimination in education. Hearings on the Equal Rights Amendment had not yet been held. Title VII excluded educational institutions; the Equal Pay Act did not apply to faculty, and there were no provisions forbidding discrimination against women students. Thanks to you, women have indeed come a long way. Although there is still much to do, the first and hardest step—good legislation—has been taken. You have the gratitude of women today and tomorrow's women as well."

Green highlighted Sandler's words in yellow, added an asterisk, and asked staff to type them on a 4-by-6-inch index card. She wrote back to Sandler, "I must say that I am glad I played a part in each one of these legislative actions."[100]

The battles seem to have sapped some of Green's energy, though. She switched to the powerful House Appropriations Committee and stepped back from being Mrs. Education. Green retired at the end of 1974 and returned to Oregon.

In the months immediately after Title IX's passage, Sandler noticed controversy building around a topic that she and Green hadn't considered much—sports. She turned to Margaret Dunkle, the twenty-five-year-old research associate who joined PSEW in July 1972.

"Margaret," Sandler said in so many words, "I think athletics is going to be really important. Figure it out."[101]

4

Implementation
1972–1977

EVEN BEFORE TITLE IX, GIRLS AND WOMEN INCREASINGLY DEMANDED THE opportunity to play sports.[1] Some sued under state laws or the constitutional right to equal protection under the Fourteenth Amendment. Most of the pre–Title IX suits did not go well, though a few got high school girls onto boys' track, tennis, golf, and skiing teams because there were none for girls.[2] Countless other girls pushed but never made it to court.

Meg Newman straightened up from her crouch at shortstop on a spring practice day under gray skies.[3] The other players—all boys—who hoped to try out for the baseball team at Roslyn (New York) High School slackened their stances, too, wondering why the principal and another school administrator had come to the field. They'd come because of her—a girl on the field.

As an energetic, almost hyperactive girl growing up on Long Island, Newman really wanted to play team sports. Her high school offered just one sport for girls: tennis, an "individual" sport. She took the basketball that she'd learned to dribble in her family's driveway to the high school gym during recreation hours after school, but the boys there laughed and hounded her out. Whenever she could, she'd field baseball grounders and catch fly balls tossed by her father.

In 1971, as the baseball season approached in her junior year, Newman approached Tom Lynch, a nice teacher who also coached baseball. "I want to play," she told him. Lynch shook his head. That's impossible, he told her. But after talking with his wife and daughters, Lynch found Newman at school some days later and told her that if she wanted to play, she should try out.

Newman started practicing with the boys after classes, but before the tryouts officially began, the two school administrators showed up at practice. One walked with Coach Lynch toward her on the infield. Word had come down from state officials, the man told her: she wouldn't be allowed to play.

"This isn't right," she thought. "It's not fair." He took her gently by the elbow and escorted her off the field. Her teammates' eyes followed her exit.

Newman stuffed her glove next to some books in her backpack. Her parents would not be happy if she tried to fight this. The next day, though, she walked to one of the phone booths on campus and opened the glass-and-wood accordion door, stepping inside. She dialed an operator for information. "Could you give me the number for the American Civil Liberties Union?"

Coach Lynch appointed her the equipment manager and scorer so she could travel to games with them. Unbeknownst to administrators, he still let her play in team practices, which usually took place at a field a quarter mile away from the main campus. Before any legal action could start in her case, though, she graduated and moved on.[4]

Thousands of actions like these from girls and their parents started to pry open access to athletics before Title IX; the new law gave them a sturdier crowbar.

The number of girls playing high school varsity sports nearly tripled in the year before Title IX passed to 817,073 in its first year, 1972–73.[5] Many other girls didn't think of playing because they'd learned misogynist myths—that running could hurt their ovaries, that girls who liked sports were either homosexual perverts or heterosexually indecent, and other nonsense.

In colleges, increased numbers of women students in the 1960s contributed to a doubling of women in college sports in the second half of the decade. Responding to some of this pressure, men's sports started letting in token women, and leaders of women's athletics programs created more opportunities for women to compete against other women's teams.[6]

Women teachers of physical education created the Association for Intercollegiate Athletics for Women (AIAW) five months before Title IX's passage to provide varsity-style teams and coaching for female college athletes. AIAW rejected the "male model" of sports, with its exploitation of students and its history of corruption in the single-minded pursuit of winning. The women's model aimed for a more educational, egalitarian system of a "girl for every sport, and a sport for every girl," with broadly inclusive competitions. With that in mind, the AIAW restricted recruiting. It prohibited scholarships based solely on athletics and not academic criteria, setting up a clash with Title IX. If men got sports scholarships, women wanted them too, and they were ready to demand them.[7]

Eleven women tennis players and three teachers at two Florida colleges sued the AIAW in January 1973, claiming its scholarship ban violated the Fourteenth Amendment's equal protection clause.[8] AIAW leaders needed a lawyer to help sort things out. They found her by accident.

Margot Polivy welcomed AIAW president Lee Morrison to her law office in early 1973. Polivy had recently left the Hill after two years as Rep. Bella Abzug's administrative assistant (the equivalent of chief of staff) and opened a private practice in communications law, her specialty before her stint with Abzug. Morrison wanted to talk about Title IX. After much discussion they realized that Morrison had been referred to a lawyer named Carol Polowy, who was counsel for the American Association of University Professors, but she'd looked up Margot Polivy instead. By then it didn't matter. Thanks to the mix-up, Polivy served for a decade as AIAW's legal mother eagle.[9]

Men in athletics hadn't yet woken up to Title IX's implications, but women's advocates and HEW's Office for Civil Rights (OCR) tuned in quickly. Once Congress passes a law, the executive branch of government writes regulations to implement the law and then is responsible for enforcing them. For Title IX, those jobs fell to OCR, an office created within HEW in the mid-1960s to enforce Title VI of the Civil Rights Act of 1964, initially focusing on desegregating schools. Working with the Department of Justice, it had made such progress that unhappy Southern white legislators and other critics accused OCR of overreaching, of going beyond what the law allows or should allow. It's been a common refrain ever since among Republicans, in particular, as OCR's responsibilities expanded to enforce newer civil rights laws based on sex, disability status, age, and more.[10]

In the story of Title IX, OCR has been a character in itself, but with a bit of a Dr. Jekyll and Mr. Hyde personality, whiplashing back and forth when either Democrats or Republicans reclaimed the White House. OCR's politically appointed leadership at times made the agency a useful tool for change, and other times tried to neutralize or destroy it, depending on the administration. Even in the best of times, though, civil rights advocates always had to push OCR to do better.

Title IX's implementing regulations would have to answer fundamental questions. How would nondiscrimination be defined? Which actions or conditions would be lawful or unlawful? How exactly would they deal with violators? PSEW's Margaret Dunkle sent OCR some resources on equity in athletics in August 1972 and offered an informal litmus test for Title IX in general: "A rule of thumb that many women's groups use to determine if, in fact, a practice is discriminatory is to substitute the word 'black' for 'woman' and 'white' for 'man.'"[11] If a school provided uniforms for boys but not girls in athletics, isn't that a form of discrimination equivalent to giving uniforms to white but not Black athletes?

An October 1972 article in *Ms.* magazine by NOW's Ann Scott and the November issue of PSEW's newsletter alerted readers that the Title IX regulations should cover athletics. By the end of 1972, Ruth Bader Ginsburg published resources on equity in athletics and conferred with Dunkle and Sandler on the topic.[12] But women's advocates split on the issue of coed versus sex-segregated athletics. Many activists and OCR officers who came out of the civil rights movement long had fought the claim that separate education could be equal. Nonetheless, OCR quickly abandoned the idea of men and women together on most athletic teams, fearing only a few top women would qualify.[13]

Women's and other civil rights groups were starting to work together more, sometimes with difficulty. Scott, NOW's representative to the 130-group Leadership Conference on Civil Rights (LCCR), objected to the LCCR's failure to consult NOW on plans for a January 1973 dinner honoring two legislators for their roles in the civil rights movement even though they'd long fought against the ERA. LCCR chair Roy Wilkins replied that the Conference didn't consider their records on women's rights because the LCCR had taken no position on the ERA. Scott and NOW started a letter campaign to LCCR member organizations about "the indivisibility of human rights."[14]

At the LCCR's board meeting before the dinner, Scott asked the group to endorse the ERA. A majority agreed, "but not enough for consensus," so the dinner tribute would go on, Scott told feminist allies. NOW members picketed the dinner in protest. A few months later Wilkins asked Scott to chair a new committee to study how the LCCR could fight for equal rights for women. By April 1974 the LCCR had endorsed the ERA and instructed staff to lead a campaign to generate support for its ratification.

In public schools in Waco, Texas, at the Universities of Michigan, Minnesota, and Wisconsin, and elsewhere, women kept filing complaints about discrimination in employment and athletics under the Executive Orders, the Fourteenth Amendment, and then Title IX.[15] Athletics soon eclipsed employment and other topics in the public's consideration of sex discrimination in education, partly because of the sheer numbers of girls and women who wanted to play and also because discrimination in sports was easy to see and understand. Girls got a chance to play or they didn't. They got the same training, funding, and facilities as boys or they didn't. Men's athletics had a giant governance structure backed by immense amounts of money, a fact that journalists used to compare support for men's and women's programs.

Sports Illustrated highlighted inequities large and small in a series of articles in 1973 and 1974. One New Jersey high school, for example, provided ten sports for boys with eleven times the budget that it gave to three girls' sports. The $1.5 million annual operating budget of the National Collegiate Athletic Association (NCAA), predominantly for men's competitions, dwarfed that of the AIAW, which got by on $24,000 a year.[16]

With Title IX's passage, students had a new option for protesting sex discrimination. Previously, they could make informal complaints to school administrators or legal complaints in lawsuits. Under Title IX, they also could file a formal complaint with OCR alleging that a school violated

Title IX or its implementing regulations, which would have the force of law once they got through a lengthy process of public comment and more.

Title IX also gave education administrators new tools in the form of guidance from OCR on how to stop discriminating. Since the law's inception OCR has issued many "Dear Colleague" letters explaining how it interprets the law and its regulations. This guidance is not compulsory but lets schools know that OCR will assume they're complying with Title IX if they follow the guidance.

Issuing a Dear Colleague letter is faster and simpler than trying to amend the regulations themselves, giving OCR the ability to respond relatively quickly to questions or controversies. On the other hand, any Dear Colleague letter can be revoked just as quickly by the next administration. The political party that heads the executive branch calls the shots, influencing OCR's budgets, directing its focus, and determining the contents of Dear Colleague letters.

Under Presidents Nixon and Ford, both Republicans, OCR started getting complaints under Title IX but put them on hold until it finished creating its implementing regulations. Writing the implementing regulations for Title VI of the Civil Rights Act of 1964, which covers much more than education, took six months. For Title IX, it took three years. "To get Title IX regulations was like pulling teeth with your fingers," Sen. Bayh later said.[17]

A new legal champion for women targeted OCR over the delay and became the chief legal defender of Title IX for the next four decades—Marcia Greenberger.

Greenberger didn't plan to be a lawyer initially. She majored in history in college and aimed for a graduate degree in it. Her college advisor steered her away, saying she'd be wasting her time because most women don't complete a PhD. So Greenberger and two girlfriends decided to take the Law School Admission Test (LSAT). They gathered at Temple University in Philadelphia for the exam.

"What are you doing here?" men at the test site challenged the women before the test began. "Go home!" another demanded. "Get out of here!" In the fall of 1966, enrollment in law school qualified for a deferment from the draft and thus an escape from the Vietnam War. "If you get in," one man said, "somebody's going to have to go fight, and they could die!" But even years after that deferment clause ended, men continued to harass women who dared to take the LSAT, yelling things like, "This is a man's job!"[18]

Greenberger didn't know that law schools limited female admissions, and that overall only 4 percent of law students were women. Despite those restrictions, she got into the University of Pennsylvania Law School. The women in her initial cohort of more than two hundred students could be counted on two hands.[19] They and other women law students of their time encountered hostility and suspicion for being there. Professors singled them out with questions about rape cases. Missing a dorm curfew could get a woman expelled, but no curfews regulated the men. In her four years of college and three years of law school, Greenberger never had a woman professor.

The women's movement of the 1960s emboldened demands for change, so by the time Greenberg graduated cum laude in 1970 the numbers of women in law schools were on the rise. Title IX reflected that momentum and accelerated it.

Many law firms explicitly refused to hire women lawyers. They claimed that late-night work would be too dangerous, yet they required secretaries to work late.[20] At one of the first public-interest law firms in DC, the Center for Law and Social Policy, women interns and administrative staff revolted in 1971. They made four demands: hire some women lawyers; work on women's rights cases; stop underpaying women in the office and instead pay them commensurate with their skills and the complexity of their work; and don't expect the women to serve coffee. The center hired twenty-six-year-old Greenberger four months after Title IX passed, the only lawyer in Washington, DC, working on women's rights full-time. Her bosses asked Greenberger to see if there was enough work to keep a lawyer busy in a Women's Rights Project.

She immediately sought out Sandler and others for guidance about where to focus, the beginning of a long professional friendship. Sandler gave Greenberger enough for twenty-five people to work on full-time, if they could. Greenberger focused the Women's Rights Project on education, employment, and health issues.

Legal groups like Greenberger's also formed around the country in the

1970s to work on women's rights: the Women's Legal Defense Fund in DC (now called the National Partnership for Women & Families); Equal Rights Advocates in San Francisco; the California Women's Law Center in Los Angeles; the Northwest Women's Law Center in Seattle; the ACLU's Reproductive Rights Project (separate from its Women's Rights Project) in New York; and others in Philadelphia, Cleveland, Connecticut, and elsewhere. They took more of women's fights to court and increased the pressure on policymakers and legislators.

If women lawyers and Title IX provided the sticks to compel change, a separate proposed law offered a carrot. Feminists drafted legislation to offer federal funding to promote compliance with Title IX.

A handful of women looked around the room where they'd gathered in the early 1970s at the request of Arlene Horowitz, a twenty-six-year-old staff assistant to a House education subcommittee. She'd seen enough bills for special-purpose education programs that she came up with the idea for one herself.

"How much money?" one of them asked.

The bill they were drafting would fund programs to counter sex bias in educational materials, counseling, and other areas. One study found five times more boys than girls in the titles of children's books, and in their pictures, four times as many male animals as female ones.[21]

Horowitz initially called the small network of feminists around Capitol Hill in the fall of 1971 asking for help to flesh out the legislation. They were skeptical, but Horowitz persisted. If the bill only generated hearings on the subject, that still would help, she argued. A small group joined her in the effort: Sandler; Dunkle; Arvonne Fraser; Rep. Chisholm's aide, Shirley Downs; and a few others.[22]

At a meeting to hash out some language in the bill, they came to the part that would specify how much money Congress could authorize. They looked at each other. "Thirty million?"[23] Everyone laughed. "It'll never pass anyway," one said, so, why not dream big?

They recruited Rep. Patsy Takemoto Mink in March 1972 to sponsor the bill because of her seniority on the Subcommittee on Education. Mink wasn't the loudest agitator for women's rights in the House, but she was a strong feminist with personal experience of discrimination.

Entering the foyer of her family's southwest DC townhouse in early 1970, Mink picked up the mail and handed an envelope from Stanford University to her daughter Gwendolyn (Wendy). The high school senior had her heart set on attending Stanford. She ripped open the letter. Her face fell. In its rejection, Stanford said it limited women to 40 percent of undergraduate admissions. Wendy compared herself with that 40 percent, not with the men. "I'm not good enough," she thought to herself. She handed the letter to her mother.[24]

"Oh, my god," Mink cried, "it's a quota!" She remembered her own rejection by a dozen medical schools, some of them explicitly saying they limit women's enrollment. After graduating from the University of Nebraska, the best work she could find was as a typist. Switching strategies, Patsy applied to the University of Chicago Law School. It accepted her under its foreign-student quota, oddly, one of two women and two Asian Americans in a class of ninety. After graduation no Chicago law firms would hire her, a woman. She and husband John Mink and Wendy, then an infant, moved to her home state of Hawaii, where none of the white-controlled law firms would hire Asian Americans. She got involved in politics and voters elected her to Congress in 1964.

Mink introduced the bill as the Women's Education Act in April 1972 and reintroduced it the first week of 1973 as the Women's Educational Equity Act (WEEA). Arvonne Fraser got Sen. Walter Mondale (D-MN) to sponsor the Senate bill.

"Specific attention also needs to be given to minority females," Sandler noted in the October 1973 Senate hearings on WEEA. "Too often many of our minority programs have been aimed at minority males, and too often, our programs aimed at women have focused on white women. For example, textbook publishers have made a special effort to show pictures of blacks and other minorities in prestige positions: minorities now appear in books as doctors, judges, engineers. But these pictures and stories are almost exclusively limited to minority males."[25]

Title IX opened doors for girls and women, but WEEA was needed to make the room livable, she said.

Tennis superstar Billie Jean King drew attention to WEEA on the second day of hearings, November 9. Seven weeks earlier, an estimated 37 million people (roughly 17 percent of the U.S. population) had watched twenty-nine-year-old King defeat fifty-five-year-old former tennis pro Bobby Riggs in the much-hyped "Battle of the Sexes" before more than thirty thousand raucous spectators at the Houston Astrodome.[26] King had ten Grand Slam singles titles under her belt and a bunch more in doubles tennis. The event tapped the zeitgeist of girls and women demanding respect, men withholding it, and increasing battles over athletics for women.

Riggs rode into the Astrodome on a rickshaw pulled by five women he called his "bosom buddies." Four bare-chested men carried King in on a litter. Riggs gave King a giant Sugar Daddy sucker, a gift "for the biggest sucker in the world." King gave him a live baby pig in recognition of his pride in being a "male chauvinist pig." On the court, King won in three straight sets, 6–4, 6–3, 6–3, and took home a $100,000 prize (the equivalent of $640,000 in 2020).[27]

King carried the national glow from her victory into room 4232 of the Dirksen Office Building in DC to testify in congressional hearings in support of WEEA.[28] Sandler had coached her on the wording of her testimony. "By the time a girl reaches high school or college she is often well programmed to think of sports as extraneous," King said.[29] WEEA could fund programs to disrupt that brainwashing.

Mondale attached his Senate bill to the Elementary and Secondary Education Act extension in 1974, but Mink's version didn't pass the House. She urged women's advocates to lobby the conference committee for its retention in the final bill.[30] WEEA passed on August 21, 1974, and authorized up to $30 million per year in federal funding for WEEA programs.[31] Instead, Congress appropriated $6.27 million for WEEA's first year and $7.27 million for its second year—not what the advocates had dreamt, but still a success.[32]

Besides WEEA, feminist bills continued to flood Congress. In September 1973 alone, pending legislation included forty-one bills related to women that would amend or create civil rights laws and affect education, banking, housing, public accommodations, tax benefits, Social Security, family planning, abortion, childbirth, childcare, use of the honorific "Ms.," pensions, insurance, armed services, the minimum wage, cosmetics safety, flexible work hours, and Little League, among other areas.[33]

The upcoming Title IX regulations would include provisions for equal opportunities in competitive athletics, OCR made clear in February 1974.[34] Athletics directors and the NCAA could have embraced the societal movement toward equity and made sincere efforts such as splitting budgets or scholarship money equally between men's and women's programs, or fairly balancing game scheduling, supplies, and recruiting efforts, or providing equally qualified coaches. They did the opposite. To protect men's turf, they attacked Title IX.

The NCAA rallied member institutions to try and convince HEW to keep sports out of the regulations. PSEW countered by publishing the first national paper to examine sex discrimination against student athletes, Dunkle's twenty-one-page "What Constitutes Equality for Women in Sport?," in April 1974.[35] Dunkle routinely shared ideas and drafts with OCR staff, soliciting feedback. The paper explored a slew of models for equity in competitive athletics. Should teams be based on height and weight, not sex? Or could separate men's and women's teams compete alongside each other for their schools, using an Olympics scoring model that totals their scores to determine the winner in intercollegiate play? That might ensure equal investments and resources for all teams. Dunkle outlined the issues that needed addressing and laid the groundwork for OCR's regulations on athletics.

Ultimately, even women's advocates couldn't agree among themselves whether teams should be separated by sex.[36] WEAL and AIAW said yes, NOW said no. Sandler and others "spent endless hours with brilliant attorneys, policy wonks, athletic personnel, civil rights advocates, federal civil rights personnel, women's rights activists—all trying to devise some sort of a practical solution to the problem," Sandler wrote, "and yet every so-called 'solution' had some grievous flaws within it."[37]

The loose network of DC women's groups kicked into high gear in early 1974, agreeing to lobby OCR to include other specific provisions in the Title IX regulations. OCR adopted some, such as requiring that schools do a self-evaluation for sex discrimination, institute grievance procedures, and adopt various recommendations on athletics. But two years after Title IX's passage, OCR still hadn't issued the implementing regulations.

An integral part of the DC women's network, Greenberger used the legal tools of her Women's Rights Project in service of the broader coalition. She knew that the courts had ordered the Nixon administration to stop ignoring civil rights law enforcement thanks to a suit by the NAACP Legal Defense Fund on behalf of a Black father of six in Mississippi, John Quincy Adams, and others (*Adams v. Richardson*).[38] The courts ruled that while the government has a lot of discretion in how it enforces a law and who it goes after, it doesn't have the discretion to refuse to enforce a law altogether. Greenberger filed a similar suit in November 1974 on behalf of multiple women's groups and individual students to prod the government into finalizing the implementing regulations and enforcement mechanisms of both Title IX and the executive orders (*WEAL v. Califano*).[39] The court combined the *Adams* and *WEAL* cases. Advocates for people with disabilities joined in as plaintiffs, seeking enforcement of Section 504 of the Rehabilitation Act of 1973, which, following Title IX's example, had created a separate statute adopting Title VI's wording to outlaw discrimination based on disability.[40]

Greenberger won a negotiated settlement in 1977, but she returned the case to court again and again when OCR shirked its duty. The year that Greenberger first filed *WEAL v. Califano* to get the government to enforce Title IX, she gave birth to a daughter. Her girl turned sixteen before the case ended.[41] The case stayed alive that long not just thanks to Greenberger but also to a talented basketball player—Dorothy Raffel. The daughter of a WEAL president, Raffel first filed a Title IX complaint with OCR in 1974 because her junior high school offered a basketball team to boys but not girls. She served as a plaintiff in the *WEAL* case in high school, college, and even graduate school. When the government tried to get the case tossed in the 1980s, the court asked if any plaintiffs currently were being harmed. And there was Dorothy Raffel, pursuing a PhD and still being denied access to graduate-level basketball teams that provided professional networking opportunities for men students.

Widespread conflict around athletics in 1974–75 nearly derailed Title IX's implementing regulations as they were being developed.

Ellen Hoffman counted only five senators on the Senate floor with her and other staff on May 20, 1974. Her boss, Sen. Mondale, was away.[42] Sen. John Tower (R-TX) rose and quietly introduced an amendment to the

Elementary and Secondary Education Act to exempt from Title IX inter-collegiate sports that produce "gross receipts or donations"—just as the NCAA wanted. The few senators present passed it on a voice vote. If left intact, the amendment would obliterate Title IX in sports. Administrators could give as many resources as they wanted to any program, such as the football team, that took in even $1 in ticket sales, divvying up anything left to other athletic programs.

"Oh, my god," Hoffman thought. She hightailed it out to call Polivy, AIAW's counsel.

Women's advocates needed to act fast and behind the scenes. The last thing they wanted was a front-page debate about football, Hoffman cautioned.[43] That would agitate football fans and shift the focus away from ending sex discrimination. They had one last chance: the education bill to which Tower attached his amendment was headed for a House-Senate conference committee to iron out differences. They rallied women's groups over the next few weeks to urge committee members to cut the Tower amendment.

As the conference committee discussed the amendment, AIAW's Polivy huddled with Rep. Chisholm and a few others in the hallway outside the room. Sen. Jacob Javits (R–NY) stepped out during a break to consult with them. If he could propose an alternative to the Tower amendment, the conferees might let it go. He needed help wording an alternative. Quickly.

Holding a pen and paper, Polivy looked up and down the bare marble hallway, devoid of any writing surface. "Here," Chisholm said. She turned around and offered her back. Polivy scratched out what became known as the Javits amendment. It ordered HEW to publish proposed regulations for Title IX within thirty days (because it still hadn't produced anything besides leaked ideas) and said those regulations "shall include with respect to intercollegiate athletic activities reasonable provisions considering the nature of particular sports."[44] The Javits amendment made it clear that Congress *did* intend for Title IX to apply to athletics and created leeway to treat some sports, like expensive football, differently than others. Football uniforms, after all, cost more than a swimsuit. That made the amendment palatable for conferees.

OCR finally released proposed regulations for Title IX on June 18,

1974. Sandler took home a copy and made herself comfortable in the back yard so she could enjoy the summer before the heat arrived. She spent a whole pleasant weekend summarizing in plain English the serious defects in the proposed regulations and detailing how to submit comments about them. The direct advocacy in the analysis written and polished by Sandler and Dunkle couldn't come from PSEW, so this became "the WEAL analysis." Rep. Abzug inserted it into the *Congressional Record*, which made "the WEAL/Abzug analysis" accessible through libraries to readers across the country.

PSEW sent a summary to thousands of people on its mailing list, framing it as something to keep colleges informed about what women are demanding. Polivy said the draft regulations "could easily have been subtitled, '1,001 ways to discriminate against women and get away with it.'"[45]

Nearly ten thousand comments (instead of the usual ten to four hundred) poured in during the next part of OCR's "notice and comment" rulemaking process, 90 percent of them addressing athletics even though less than 10 percent of the regulations dealt with that area.[46] An overwhelming majority of the public comments called for equal expenditures for men's and women's athletics.[47] But that was too much for OCR to stomach; it stuck with the Javits amendment.

One of the people who could see most clearly the government's reluctance to implement Title IX was a government worker, twenty-seven-year-old Holly Knox, even before OCR had released its draft Title IX regulations or started taking public comments. She climbed aboard a bus taking women from DC to a rural retreat center in Virginia for a 1974 women's conference. Her bosses in the Education Office assigned her to attend. She happened to sit down next to Anne Grant, who volunteered as NOW's education committee chair. Their conversation turned to Title IX.

"You know," Knox warned Grant, "the government is not going to enforce this thing."

Four years earlier Knox had been assigned to write testimony to be given at Rep. Green's 1970 hearings by HEW deputy assistant secretary Peter Muirhead. She knew little about sex discrimination at that point. Sandler's WEAL complaints, which she read as background for Muirhead's testimony, blew her mind.[48] She wrote a passionate statement for Muirhead that endorsed amending Title VI and supported Green's goals, but administration officials made her change the ending to oppose Green's bill.

Two years later, as Title IX neared passage, Knox and Education Office staffer Mary Ann Millsap produced a 140-page report on extensive sex discrimination throughout education.[49] In any position from custodian on up, women made less than men. Most girls had no chance to play sports. Sexist stereotypes filled textbooks. A character in one primer said, "Look at her, Mother, just look at her. She is just like a girl. She gives up." Essentially, the government was funding a discriminatory system, they concluded.

During the long slog toward creating Title IX's regulations, Knox saw very little interest in the Office of Education to move things forward. On the bus, Knox told NOW's Grant, "You guys are going to have to set up advocacy here in Washington to put pressure on them."

Grant looked at her for a moment. "Why don't you do that? Why don't you get a grant and do that?"

"What? Me?" Knox sputtered. "I don't know anything about writing grants."

"Well, I'll help you. We'll help you."

Knox knew that NOW had created a new nonprofit arm, the Legal Defense and Education Fund, which could receive foundation grants. And not long before, Terry Saario of the Ford Foundation had initiated a brief meeting with Knox, saying she was looking to fund projects designed to attack sex discrimination in various parts of American education.

Knox thought, "Oh. Huh. Maybe."

She'd seen how Sandler promoted Title IX through PSEW and used that as a model. With grant-writing coaching from the NOW Legal Defense and Education Fund and from her boyfriend, Knox won a Ford Foundation grant to fund a project she called PEER—the Project on Equal Education Rights, sponsored by the NOW Legal Defense and Education Fund.[50] She quit her government job to lead PEER.

What Sandler and WEAL did in higher education, Knox and PEER did in K-12 education, tapping NOW's chapters and grassroots structures to empower parents and school employees fighting sex discrimination.

She fell in with the small group of women's advocates in Washington—

women like Sandler, Dunkle, Polivy, and Greenberger—who met informally to share information and strategies regarding sex equity in education.[51] Most were economically secure, highly educated white women. Of the twenty or so most active, nine had worked in federal agencies for more than three years.[52] They named themselves the Education Task Force.

While debate over Title IX's regulations continued, changes to Title IX itself came from the two legislators most responsible for the law—Rep. Green and Sen. Bayh. Controversy had been building over the prohibition of school resources for single-sex groups like Boy Scouts or Girl Scouts or college social fraternities and sororities. To head off potentially more damaging legislation, Bayh engineered passage of an amendment in December 1974: Title IX would not apply to these groups.[53]

Feminists also lost a champion at the start of 1975. NOW's Ann Scott died at age forty-five of breast cancer. Sen. Bayh and others eulogized her in a memorial service at All Souls Unitarian Church in Washington on February 17, 1975. Rep. Chisholm wrote in the program for the memorial: "In any struggle for the equality of humanity, there stand those individuals whose lives are examples of total commitment to the cause. Ann was such a person, constantly on the front line of battle for the espousal of equalitarian principles. We all are richer because Ann Scott lived among us."[54]

Sometimes the front line of battle for feminists in DC professional circles required absurd accommodations to sexist standards. Sitting in her sunfilled office at PSEW, Sandler answered a call from Margot Polivy, counsel for the AIAW. The White House had just invited her to meet that day with staff about the Title IX regulations; could Sandler go with her?

Sandler wanted to, of course, but she said, "Margot, I can't go to the White House. I'm wearing a pantsuit!" It was unthinkable, going to the White House in pants. Polivy said she was in the same boat, but they couldn't miss this opportunity. Each of them had a nice suit jacket hanging in their offices as backups. They devised a plan.[55]

Polivy and Sandler arrived early for the meeting in their nice blazers and pants. They asked to be shown to the meeting room so that they could confer with each other before the staff member arrived. When the White House representative joined them, they rose slightly out of their chairs and leaned across the table to shake his hand, never fully standing. The meeting went well. The staffer—a Black man with a new baby daughter at home—loved sports and seemed friendly toward Title IX. At the end, Sandler and Polivy asked if they could remain in the room for a few minutes to review notes. They leaned across the table again to shake hands in goodbye. They'd made it through the meeting without revealing their pants.[56]

Lobbying around the Title IX regulations shifted to overdrive in 1975. Public attitudes were changing in women's favor. A 1974 poll found that 88 percent of people favored equal funding for girls' and boys' sports in public schools. A widespread fitness craze in the mid-1970s inspired women and men to start jogging, playing tennis, and exercising. Sandler took up running and tried repeatedly to quit smoking.

When HEW sent the final regulations to President Ford on February 28, 1975, for his approval, Title IX advocates found them alarmingly inadequate.[57] Sen. Bayh blasted the regulations for violating "the spirit and intent" of Title IX.[58] Participants in the first Black Women's International Conference passed a resolution supporting Title IX.[59] Alerts sent out by NOW, PEER, the AIAW, and others urged people to contact the president, asking him to alter the regulations before releasing them to Congress. The women's coalition increased the frequency of its meetings to weekly, debating whether to renounce or accept the regulations.

Meanwhile, eight of the nation's most successful and popular football coaches flew to Washington and met for more than an hour with President Ford, who had been a star center on the University of Michigan's football team and coached the Yale University team while in law school.

The final regulations that Ford transmitted to Congress on June 3, 1975, didn't exempt football, as the coaches wanted. Lobbying by the women's Education Task Force got rid of some provisions that horrified them.[60] The final version allowed but didn't mandate separate athletics teams by sex if the sport is based on competitive skill. If a school chose separate teams, it could not treat them differently. Without separate teams, it would need to ensure that athletic interests were being met. The regulations adapted Dunkle's thinking into a "laundry list" requiring equal opportunities in eleven areas of athletics: accommodating interests and abilities, equipment and supplies, scheduling, travel allowances, coaching and tutoring, payment of coaches and tutors, locker rooms and playing facilities, medical and training facilities and services, housing and dining facilities and services, publicity, and financial aid. They also explicitly said that unequal spending by sex wasn't necessarily evidence of discrimination, but investigators could consider this as one factor when assessing compliance with Title IX.[61]

One thing remained before the regulations would take effect. An unusual 1974 law (later overturned) allowed Congress forty-five days to disapprove of new regulations. If legislators didn't act, the regulations would go into effect.[62] If women's advocates wanted these regulations, they would need to lobby for Congress to do nothing—to not disapprove of them. But were the regulations good enough to fight for? Time was running out for feminists to reach consensus on a plan of action.

In early June 1975, Sandler and Dunkle walked the five tree-lined blocks from their office on R Street to One Dupont Circle and took the elevator to the American Council on Education's eighth-floor boardroom.[63] Sandler counted representatives of twenty-four groups at the meeting called by the Education Task Force, including traditional education organizations and women's and Black civil rights groups such as the National Urban League and National Council of Negro Women.

The discussion was solemn and difficult. The "laundry list" of athletic criteria did not include scouting services and some other key parts of athletics programs. In the bigger picture, the regulations would lock athletics into a male-female split with no plan to evolve toward unified teams.[64] Should the women's coalition support or oppose the regulations?

Sandler could feel the opportunities slipping away. Don't let the perfect be the enemy of the good, she argued. Politics is compromise—achieving what's possible. She and others feared that there would be no Title IX enforcement for the foreseeable future if these regulations weren't accepted, further delaying action on discrimination complaints. The group decided to present a united front and urge Congress not to disapprove the regulations. The ACLU, which felt that separate athletics couldn't be equal and the regulations were too weak, distanced itself but agreed not to push Congress to disapprove the regulations.[65]

The meeting also helped them realize that to achieve greater impact, they needed to be more visible. Over the next few months the group changed its name from the Education Task Force to the National Coalition for Women and Girls in Education (NCWGE), representing a combined 3.5 million members in thirty organizations, with Dunkle as its first chair. What started as a friendly network evolved into what probably was the best organized women's coalition in Washington, Sandler thought. Participants so identified with the group that they referred to the coalition as "we" and their own organizations as "they" or "it." Decades later some described it as the most fun they'd had in their work lives.[66]

To convince Congress to let the Title IX regulations go into effect, the American Association of University Women and the League of Women Voters led trainings for NCWGE volunteers on lobbying techniques. Sandler and Dunkle printed up more than ten thousand buttons reading, "Give Women a Sporting Chance" or "God Bless You, Title IX."[67] Fourteen members of Congress including Mink, Chisholm, and Abzug invited House colleagues to a meeting on July 17 to talk about threats to Title IX.[68]

The House and the Senate saw at least nine bills and resolutions that summer to disapprove the regulations, exempt athletics from Title IX, or exclude "revenue-producing" sports. Congress held three sets of hearings in the forty-five-day window.[69] Chisholm, Mink, Abzug, Bayh, and others testified and lobbied alongside the women's groups.

NCWGE members stood outside hearing rooms to talk with legislators and their staff as they came and went. They roamed hallways handing out literature and buttons. They startled some House members by following them onto elevators to make their case.[70] Letters and telegrams poured in from educational associations, women's and student organizations, and unions with the same message—they would have liked stronger regulations but these were better than nothing.[71] The coalition's hustle and allies defeated all of these anti–Title IX measures as well as at least two others introduced later in 1975.[72]

Legislators bowed to pressure from "hundreds of women's rights lobbyists," the *Washington Post* reported in a front-page story. The perception made Polivy chuckle. "There were only about twenty-seven of us," she remembers, "but we were a talky bunch."[73]

One of the final votes came roughly a week before the regulations would take effect, during lengthy House debate on an amendment by Rep. Bob Casey (D-TX) to an appropriations bill. The Senate already rejected the measure, which would allow schools to separate PE classes by sex. At least twenty-eight newspapers and forty organizations opposed it, including the Leadership Conference on Civil Rights.[74]

During the House debate on July 16, Rep. Mink got word that her daughter Wendy, a graduate student at Cornell University, was critically injured in a head-on car crash in Syracuse, New York, that put her in intensive care with a punctured lung and broken ribs. Mink left immediately to be with Wendy. The House retained the Casey amendment by a one-vote margin, 212–211. But the Senate again decisively rejected the Casey amendment the next day, 65–29. Mink remained in Syracuse, where Wendy was out of intensive care and in fair condition. The House capitulated, wanting to finish the appropriations bill, and rejected Casey's amendment 215–178.[75]

Title IX's implementing regulations finally went into effect on July 21, 1975, three years after the law passed. OCR also issued final regulations for the provisions of the Public Health Service Act prohibiting sex discrimination in health training programs, nearly four years after its passage.

As chair of the new NCWGE, Dunkle lit three tall, tapered candles on a two-tiered frosted cake at a quickly organized Title IX birthday party on the evening of July 29. Rep. Chisholm beamed next to her as other House supporters gathered around. Bayh couldn't attend so they sent cake to his office, which made him very happy.[76] At PSEW, where Sandler jumped on any reason for celebrations with staff, she brought cake and presented each of them with homemade certificates for their parts in the battles for the regulations.

The 1975 regulations required schools to do a self-evaluation within a year, but few did more than go through the motions, if even that.[77] Each educational institution also had to designate a Title IX coordinator, notify students and employees on how to contact the coordinator, and publish grievance procedures for prompt and equitable handling of complaints.[78] Many schools virtually ignored those requirements.

As OCR finalized Title IX's regulations, it released a separate proposal that it not investigate *any* civil rights complaints.[79] Instead, the "Consolidated Procedural Rules for Administration and Enforcement of Certain Civil Rights Laws" would limit OCR to doing "compliance reviews" of educational institutions when it saw fit. OCR just didn't have the staff to do everything, President Ford's officials argued. By ignoring complaints, OCR could decide where to look for compliance with nondiscrimination laws. If it wanted to, OCR could prioritize inspecting schools serving predominantly low-income students whose primary language was not English and who were less likely to file complaints.

Civil rights groups of all kinds felt blindsided. OCR hadn't investigated a single complaint under Title IX in the law's three years; now it was saying it never would. "NOBODY IS HAPPY WITH THIS," Mink's aide, Susan Kakesako, wrote in a memo.[80]

The Leadership Conference on Civil Rights' 162 organizations demanded that HEW withdraw the proposed regulations.[81] The same day, the U.S. Commission on Civil Rights released a 673-page report criticizing the government for not enforcing antidiscrimination laws. Bayh got eighty of one hundred senators to sign a letter opposing OCR's plans.

Some OCR staff pitted civil rights groups against each other. They refused to investigate complaints filed by women or Spanish-speaking citizens, saying the *Adams* lawsuit compelled them to focus on racial discrimination.[82] At the same time, they said they couldn't do more to address discrimination based on race, national origin, or disability because they were overwhelmed by sex discrimination complaints pouring in.

Under months of pressure from civil rights advocates, OCR withdrew the proposed consolidated regulations in March 1976.[83] It agreed to conduct compliance reviews *and* investigate complaints of discrimination.

With the frenetic surge to finalize the Title IX regulations behind it, the NCWGE pursued a brisk pace of lobbying and educating to defend Title IX from continuing attacks and to promote other feminist legislation. Its core group of leaders leveraged their roles in multiple groups. Sandler alternated between representing PSEW and the National Advisory Council on

Women's Educational Programs (NACWEP), a presidentially appointed council created by WEEA that she chaired.[84] Knox spoke for PEER or as NACWEP's legislative committee chair. Dunkle acted for PSEW and as the first chair of the NCWGE.[85] Gleaves represented PSEW as well as the National Council of Negro Women's Commission on Higher Education.[86] PSEW reached peak strength in mid-1976 with a staff of eight employees, seven of whom worked full-time.

Orchestrating coalition agreements among the many groups in the NCWGE was challenging in a time before the internet, when high-priority documents were sent by bicycle messengers and the newest high-tech gadget was an IBM Selectric typewriter. Under a modified version of consensus and Dunkle's firm hand as coordinator, the NCWGE weighed in on legislation and policies in meetings with Cabinet secretaries, White House representatives, congressmembers, and more.

OCR sent out the first in a decades-long string of memos and Dear Colleague letters with guidance on how to comply with the Title IX regulations two months after they went into effect.[87] PEER created a chart so that parents, students, and educators could understand their rights; the left side listed bits of legalese from the regulations while the right featured translations in plain language. Dunkle wrote a 142-page manual, with input from Polivy, Sandler, OCR staff, and others, giving educational institutions detailed steps to comply with Title IX in athletics; HEW published it in September 1976.[88]

As more women demanded changes in athletics, more men freaked out. The NCAA sued HEW unsuccessfully in February 1976, claiming HEW exceeded its authority when it tried to regulate athletics.[89]

Women's activism on campuses grew, even if it didn't always produce immediate results. At Spelman College, a ninety-five-year-old historically Black college for women in Atlanta, Georgia, that had never had a Black woman president, students locked fourteen college trustees in a boardroom for twenty-six hours in April 1976 because trustees had picked a man to be the next president. Some six hundred students—roughly half the student body—spent a night in the hallways demanding the college's first woman president. They tied the meeting room doors shut with rope. Faculty and alumnae brought the students food. Finally, trustees agreed to meet with the protesters, who set them free. But Spelman didn't get a Black woman president until 1987.[90]

HEW invited NCWGE members and others to a "brainstorming session" in September 1976 on the supply of minorities and women for jobs in higher education. But women were an afterthought, attendees found. Neither the program nor any major speakers specifically addressed issues facing women. HEW distributed a working paper at the meeting that ignored the needs of women and discussed neither the double discrimination faced by minority women nor possible solutions. The whole premise of the "brainstorming" missed the point that discrimination, not "supply" of candidates, often was the problem for women seeking jobs. In 1974, 26 percent of women with PhD degrees were unemployed compared with 18 percent of men at that level of education.[91]

Throughout the 1970s, women's advocates had to defend Title IX from hostile legislation. The law itself and its implementing regulations weren't enough; they needed constant vigilance to protect Title IX from evisceration. A dozen or more congressional bills and proposals tried to weaken Title IX in 1976 alone.

In the long view, federal policy appears to change incrementally, but each new threat felt critical, requiring quick, creative, and persistent responses to protect Title IX.[92] The NCWGE played whack-a-mole, slapping down each one as best it could. Each swing required immense amounts of time, phone calls, meetings with each other and with government officials, engaging legislative allies, and rallying base members of pertinent organizations.[93]

The NCWGE also worked closely with Bayh, Mink, Chisholm, and others to make a few more alterations to Title IX in order to quell public controversies and head off potentially more damaging bills in the Education Amendments of 1976. They revised Title IX so schools could hold father-son or mother-daughter events as long as they offered "reasonably comparable" events to both sexes. School support for certain American Legion programs (Boys State, Girls State, Boys Nation, and Girls Nation conferences) would be exempt from Title IX. And Title IX would not apply to scholarships from single-sex beauty pageants.[94]

NCWGE members also poured efforts into portions of the Education

Amendments of 1976 to give states resources and mandates to battle sex discrimination in vocational education. Even though students in vocational programs more than doubled over a decade to 7 million in 1976, and those in postsecondary programs sextupled to 1.5 million, girls and women usually got shunted to lower-paying vocations. After the amendments passed, the NCWGE and allies rallied nearly six thousand people in all fifty states to HEW-run meetings about proposed regulations for the vocational education law. Their combined efforts got strong sex-equity language into the final regulations.[95]

The NCWGE had grown to fifty national organizations but some of its main congressional allies departed.[96] Mink and Abzug risked their House seats to run for the Senate in 1976 and lost. But voters did elect a potential ally as president, Democrat Jimmy Carter.

Title IX and its regulations are only as good as the executive branch's willingness to enforce them, and that hadn't been happening, for the most part. When Carter's people moved into OCR, they found two boxes containing around six hundred unanswered letters with Title IX complaints or questions left by President Ford's OCR. Files showed hundreds more Title IX cases open but stuck in limbo.

Title IX enforcement practically had to start from scratch.

5

Sexual Harassment
1977–1980

SHE ALMOST DIDN'T NOTICE THEM ANYMORE, ALL THE WHITE MEN STARING out from portraits on the walls of Yale University's halls. No darker faces. No female faces. But when Pamela Price entered Yale as a proud Black Nationalist with an Angela Davis–style afro in the freshman class of 1974, culture shock hit hard. It wasn't just the class differences, though those were huge.

Low, moat-like walls surrounded the stone residence colleges and many other Yale buildings, sending a subliminal message to "keep out." Somehow the school made Black students feel like foreigners, which alienated her. Black students got the message that they were at Yale only because of affirmative action, as though invisible asterisks were affixed to their records. Price could feel people assume that she was inferior because she was a Black person and assume that she wasn't serious because she was a woman. She knew that Yale had accepted Black students only because people fought and raised hell for their right to be there, to not be excluded. Price had seen worse; she would find her way through this too.

Since age eleven she'd been on a path of resisting white supremacy that distanced her from her middle-class family in Ohio. The assassination of civil rights leader Dr. Martin Luther King Jr. in 1968 shook Price to her core. Mr. Foster, who ran the neighborhood grocery store, taught the local youth some of the Black history and current events they weren't getting in school. He told stories about living in the South. From him, Price first learned of Black Americans' roots in Africa, and of the many tribes in their ancestry.

Cincinnati had no Black Panther party, but she took an interest in the Black Nationalists and through them learned more Black history. In the group's newsletter she read about activists being arrested or killed because of the FBI's Counterintelligence Program (COINTELPRO), though the full extent of COINTELPRO's disruptive and illegal activities wouldn't be known to the public for years. With FBI support, fourteen Chicago police staged a pre-dawn raid on a Chicago Black Panther Party household on December 4, 1969, firing eighty-two to ninety-nine shots compared with one gun shot from the sleepy residents.[1] A gunshot to the head at close range killed their twenty-one-year-old chairman, Fred Hampton. Another bullet killed twenty-two-year-old Mark Clark. Others were wounded. As with Rev. King's assassination, the killings changed Pamela Price.

To protest, she helped organize a sit-in at the public college preparatory high school that she attended and invited some Black Nationalists to speak. Officials at Walnut Hills High School kicked her out of school. Price's parents were furious at her, and terrified. Her mother, a teacher, and her father, a chemical engineer, were upwardly mobile African Americans trying to provide a better life for their children. Education was the lynchpin. They adamantly opposed her activism, afraid that their child would get killed on the streets of Cincinnati if she got further involved in the civil rights movement.

Angry, headstrong, and committed to fighting for change, Price ran away from home in January 1970 at age thirteen. She became a ward of the court and got placed in foster care, moving in and out of juvenile hall, foster homes, and group homes. An arrest at a demonstration tracked her into the juvenile justice system. But three Black women became her saving grace, providing guidance and foster homes.[2] One of them, educator Lorena O'Donnell, took Price with her to Connecticut when O'Donnell won a fellowship at Yale University. Price spent a semester at Wilbur Cross High School. After returning to Cincinnati, she chose to be emancipated from foster care at age sixteen.

The three women refused to lose track of her. O'Donnell brokered a meeting between Price and her parents in hope she would move back in with them. It didn't go well. For a while she lived with a boyfriend. When that fell apart, she was homeless for a brief and scary time. A teacher helped find her a place to stay. She stayed in Woodward High School as long as she could but needed to pay rent. In her senior year, Price dropped out of school and went to work in a linen factory.

Somehow, in all this, an application found its way to her from Yale University, perhaps because Lorena O'Donnell advocated for her or because she'd been a National Merit Scholarship finalist. This was ridiculous, Price thought—Yale would never let her in. She filled it out anyway and sent it in. Even though she wasn't attending high school, every now and then Price checked in with her school counselor. During a lunch break at the factory, Price called her.

"We've been looking all over for you," the counselor said. "You have been accepted to Yale College. We need you to come back and finish high school, so you can go to Yale." The university gave her a full scholarship.

In the early culture shock of being at Yale, the Black community grounded Price. She sang in the choir of the Black Church at Yale. She joined the group Black Students at Yale and the Umoja Extended Family (now Umoja Community) of Black students and town residents.[3] She started typing students' papers at night to make some money, and in her sophomore year landed a job at the Afro-American Cultural Center.

Before long, she could see that her work in class was as good as anyone else's—sometimes better—which vanquished any self-doubts about her abilities. Neither was she intimidated by the nearly three-to-one ratio of men to women students.

Price chose to major in political science. A student friend from Ghana gave her the Ashanti nickname Amma, which she adopted and used as an alias when writing some of her more provocative political articles for Black newsletters. Her inner strength as a Black activist and the alert, caring Black community around her proved crucial in what came next.

At the end of her sophomore year, Price fell sick. She requested extensions on the due dates for final papers in three classes. When she recovered, she went to political science professor Raymond Duvall's office on June 6 to hand in a term paper, "Tanzanian Development and Dependency Theory." To her surprise he opened the door and invited the nineteen-year-old in. Here's how Price remembers what happened next:[4]

Duvall stepped behind his small desk as Price followed him into the tiny, messy office, not decorated with much of anything but books cramming shelves and covering the desk surface.

"Have a seat," he said. Price handed him the paper and sat down in one of the two chairs taking up most of the space between the door and the desk. Duvall shuffled some papers.

"Oh, I see you didn't do very well on the final," Duvall said, not looking at her.

"Well, I was sick. That's why you gave me an extension. That's why I'm here to turn in the paper," Price said.

"I hope that this is an A paper."

"I hope so too," she said.

After a pause, Duvall slowly came around the desk. Price measured five feet two when standing. Looking up at him from her chair, she may have seen his face in shadow, the ceiling's fluorescent lights framing his head. His eyes averting hers, Duvall repeated, "I hope that this is an A paper."

"Okay, yeah, that's good. Me, too," Price said.

Duvall continued, "I really would hate to give you a C."

"Okay, that's fine," Price agreed. "I don't want a C. I'm not a C student."

Duvall sat in the chair next to her, very close. "I really, really would hate to give you a C," he repeated.

"I don't want a C," she said, confused about the conversation.

Finally, Duvall said, "Well, will you make love to me?"

With no frame of reference for this, Price at first didn't connect the question with the rest of the conversation. Her first and only thought was, "No." Trying to process this as if it were a reasonable question, all she could think was, "No. Right here in the office? No. What is he talking about? No," and her mind ticked off all the reasons for "No."

Out loud, she said matter-of-factly, "No. No, I'm not," as her mind churned over his strange request. "No. I don't think that's going to happen." Her head shook side to side. "No, I don't think that's a good idea. No. No."

After a lull, still oblivious, she said, "Well, can I leave now?"

"Yes, you can leave," Duvall said. She got up and squeezed between the chairs, his eyes following her. As she walked out the door, he added, "God, you have a really turn-on body!"

Duvall later denied Price's account.

She made her way down the stairs to the ground floor. "What's wrong with this man?" she thought. "There's something wrong with him." By the time she reached the base of the stairs, the meaning of it all hit her, and made her angry.

She went directly to work at the Afro-American Cultural Center and immediately told her boss, Khalid Lum, what had happened. "This professor just propositioned me. He offered to give me an A if I slept with him, and I think he's going to give me a C because I said, 'No.'"

Lum made her sit down right then and type out exactly what had happened—verbatim—in a complaint to be delivered immediately to a dean, Eva Balogh. He sent Kevin, a football player, with her to give it to the dean.[5] Given that there was a written statement and a witness to the delivery, the administration could not deny the complaint's existence. Price told Balogh that Duvall tried to extort sex for an A grade. Balogh said this kind of thing happens all the time and nothing could be done about it, Price remembers, though Balogh later said she simply advised Price to wait and see what grade Duvall assigned.

Duvall graded her paper a C and gave her a C in the course—the only C she received at Yale. The university had no grievance procedure for sexual harassment and did nothing about Price's complaint. She left for Tanzania soon after the incident on a planned junior year abroad, relieved to put the hostile weirdness of the university behind her and thrilled to be living in a Black nation that felt like going home.

Duvall moved that summer to a faculty position at the University of Minnesota.

Two months earlier, nineteen members of the Yale women's crew team marched into the office of Joni Barnett, head of women's athletics, on March 3, 1976, followed by a stringer for the *New York Times* and a photographer. The rowers stripped off their clothes to reveal "Title IX" or just "IX" written in Yale-blue markers on their backs and chests.[6]

"These are the bodies Yale is exploiting," their leader, Chris Ernst, read in a statement. "On a day like today the ice freezes on this skin. Then we sit for half an hour on the bus as the ice melts and soaks through our suits to meet the sweat that's soaking us from the inside. We sit for half an

hour with the chills . . . half a dozen of us are sick now," one with pneumonia. The men's crew took hot showers in their locker room located on
the banks of the Housatonic River, but the women had no locker room
or showers there. They waited on the drafty school bus to take everyone
twelve miles back to campus.

The Associated Press picked up the *Times* account and the story went
international, embarrassing Yale into installing better facilities.

The action was part of a growing feminist consciousness among Yale
students, especially since Ann Olivarius and six other students co-founded
the Yale Undergraduate Women's Caucus, attracting a hundred members
in September 1974.[7] While Pamela Price studied abroad in Tanzania, the
Women's Caucus developed a report on women's issues at Yale to be presented in 1977 to the Yale Corporation (its board of trustees). The report-
writing process was messy, with some conflict. The Council of Third
World Women wanted wording in the report critical of Yale's actions
toward minorities; the Women's Caucus included a disclaimer saying the
report "in no way pretends to address the special issues and problems of
Third World Women," and encouraged the Council to submit a separate
report.[8]

Five of the final report's twenty-three pages described three rapes by students and sexual coercion and assault by a teaching assistant. These problems were "not uncommon." Any woman brave enough to tell a professor
or dean received, at most, a word of sympathy. Without a formal complaint
process, the person they told didn't know that other students were complaining about the same perpetrator to other professors and deans. Individually, officials told each woman it was her personal problem to sort out.[9]

Their stories echoed a broader movement against sexual violence starting to catch fire.

Feminists in an audience of four hundred at Bay Path Junior College, in
Springfield, Massachusetts, refused to stay silent during a lecture by rape
apologist Frederic Storaska on April 26, 1975. On stage, Storaska advised
that women should appear to go along with a potential rape and try to out-
wit the rapist. Don't fight back, he said, contradicting the nascent women's
self-defense movement. Storaska's cottage industry as a self-designated
rape expert had put him on the lecture circuit in the 1960s. At this talk

in 1975 he had a book to promote, *How to Say No to a Rapist—and Survive* (Random House, 1975).

His dark hair cut fashionably low over his ears, the pudgy Storaska walked the stage, squatted, and gestured with his hands to make his points, the cowlick on his forehead bouncing. He advised women to see the rapist as a human being whose frustration turns to anger and rape when a girlfriend humiliates him, or she makes out with him but won't go all the way, or because society puts women on a pedestal, or the rapist had an emotionally distant mother—all scenarios in which he blamed women for the man's attack. Some people in the audience hissed their disapproval.

Women physically cannot fight off a man, Storaska claimed. If you feel you have to fight for your life, at least don't scream because that may make the rapist angrier. Better to let the rapist think you're into it so he lets down his guard and you can run away. Don't panic if a would-be rapist touches a breast, he said. "It doesn't fall off unless it's loose."[10]

Thirty or so women started chanting, "Rape is not a joke." Some of them stormed the stage and unplugged his microphone. A fight broke out; ultimately police arrested one woman.

Several college campuses canceled his scheduled talks. At other talks, like one at the University of Wisconsin-Milwaukee in November, women handed out flyers warning that Storaska had no evidence to back up his theories; they challenged him when he took questions.

The campus activism extended efforts to stop sexual violence that had been building for more than a century, led often by women of color. Black women—including a formerly enslaved transgender woman, Frances Thompson—testified to Congress in 1866 about gang rapes by white mobs in the Memphis Riots. Rosa Parks and other organizers campaigned in the 1940s and beyond to stop the raping of Black women by white men and false rape accusations by whites against Black men—both tools used to perpetuate white supremacist control.[11] In 1971, New York feminists held a public speak-out and conference about rape.[12]

As the women's movement evolved from consciousness-raising groups to concrete actions, feminists at the Universities of Iowa and South Florida, Fresno State University in California, George Washington University, and elsewhere founded rape crisis centers, taught self-defense classes, fought for rape-law reform, and organized annual Take Back the Night marches.[13] The number of rape task forces in NOW chapters blew up from fifteen to sixty-six by early 1974.[14] Even staid groups like WEAL in 1975 publicized that half of reported rapists were someone the victims knew.[15] Few rapes get reported; better data in 2017 showed that actually 80 percent of rapists are known by victims.[16]

Yale women joined a vigorous nationwide campaign by feminist and Black organizations in 1976 to free Joan Little. She killed a white jail guard in Washington, North Carolina, in self-defense after he held an ice pick to her head and forced her to perform oral sex on him. After a year of protests and publicity, a jury unanimously declared Little not guilty—the first U.S. woman acquitted for using deadly force to resist sexual assault.[17]

While attention to sexual violence grew, so did action against sexual misconduct that wasn't quite assault, most often in the workplace. Carmita Wood, a Black woman and administrative assistant for a Cornell University physics professor, became physically ill from the stress of fending off repeated sexual advances from her white boss,. She sought help in early 1975 from the university's Human Affairs Program, where three radical feminists (Lin Farley, Susan Meyer, and Karen Sauvigné) looked into her case. They found that every woman they knew had experienced something like what Wood reported, but virtually nobody talked about it. So they started an organization called Working Women United to address this, and connected Wood to a lawyer.[18]

Before they could change the problem, they first had to name it. They'd talked with Wood about "sexual abuse," "sexual intimidation," and "sexual coercion." They settled on "sexual harassment" in April 1975 because it covered a wide variety of conduct. Soon the press starting using the phrase.

Wood lost her case on appeal, but other desperate and courageous women filed six influential lawsuits between 1971 and 1975. The three Black and four white women complained of sexual coercion, assault, and retaliation by their men bosses—four white and two Black—and the employers who refused to stop them. Eventually, their cases established for the first time that Title VII of the Civil Rights Act prohibits sexual harassment.[19] That mattered to a lot of women—a 1976 survey of nine thousand working women found 90 percent faced some sexual harassment on the job.[20]

In Cambridge, Massachusetts, three feminists (Freada Klein, Lynn Wehrli, and Elizabeth Cohn-Stuntz) founded the Alliance Against Sexual Coercion in June 1976 and advocated political protest as well as legal action. The group prolifically published new research, resources, and analyses that placed sexual harassment at the nexus of capitalism, patriarchy, and racism: men targeted people they viewed as threats to their power, masculinity, or economic status.

At Yale, as the Undergraduate Women's Caucus collected stories of sexual harassment, some faculty names came up again and again as repeat offenders.

Ann Olivarius, co-founder of the Women's Caucus, approached a friendly administrator to see if something could be done about serial abusers. She and Sam Chauncey, secretary of the university, met almost weekly for months. In order to help, he told her he'd need the names of the accused faculty and of the students. Olivarius got the students' permission to share their names and stories. All this would be confidential, Chauncey assured her, but he broke that confidence.[21] Chauncey told music teacher and band leader Keith Brion that he'd been accused of rape, Olivarius said.

The Women's Caucus had heard three accounts of Brion raping students. Other Yale students said Brion locked his office door during music lessons, kissed their ears, and placed *Playboy* centerfolds on their music stands.[22] Many quit the lessons or the band to avoid him.

Brion started stalking Olivarius, she said. He tracked her down as she was cleaning dorm rooms to earn some money before graduation. Tall and thin, he pelted her with verbal threats. Then Brion's wife, LaRue, a secretary at Yale with access to Olivarius's records, found her in Yale's Branford College. She first begged Olivarius to back off, saying the students were lying and asking Olivarius not to hurt her family if she truly considered herself a feminist. When that didn't work, Olivarius recalled later, Mrs. Brion threatened her, saying she'd "fuck with" her academic files and interfere with Olivarius's applications to fellowships and graduate schools if she didn't stop.

Unnerved, Olivarius called Chauncey for advice. "I think I've got a problem," she said.

She did, Chauncey said, and he told her an alarming lie: Brion was about to have her arrested for libel, and Yale was backing him, not her, she remembers. "You better get a lawyer," Chauncey told her. Olivarius would go on to be a wildly successful feminist lawyer, but at the time she didn't know that you can't be arrested for libel.

She expected her parents to arrive in a few hours for graduation week. Frantic, Olivarius consulted one of her instructors, Catharine MacKinnon, who eventually became an eminent feminist legal theorist but at that time was a graduate student. MacKinnon pointed her to the sparse office of a new community-oriented law practice, the New Haven Law Collective, on the second floor of a commercial building overlooking the New Haven Green. No plush décor like you'd find at Canwe Cheatem & Howe. A large bank of windows in the dark brown brick façade illuminated desks scattered around the wood floor of a large, undecorated room, surrounded by a few smaller rooms.

Lawyer Kent Harvey listened to Olivarius's story, then called a Yale dean to discuss it. The dean yelled so loudly that Harvey had to hold the phone away from his ear.

"We have to figure something out. We have to," Olivarius pleaded. Not just for herself, but for all the women students being harassed or assaulted. Lawyer Anne E. Simon suggested they fight using offense rather than defense. But how? They tapped MacKinnon, who was finishing a law school dissertation that eventually became her groundbreaking 1979 book, *Sexual Harassment of Working Women*. The group adapted some of MacKinnon's thinking to an educational setting, which gave them a handle to open a new legal door.[23]

Simon took the lead on drafting a complaint arguing for the first time that unchecked sexual harassment in an educational setting constitutes sex discrimination, charging Yale with violating Title IX. It wasn't clear that individuals had the right to sue to enforce Title IX. The strategy was a gamble.[24]

Olivarius helped find other potential plaintiffs with assistance from the Undergraduate Women's Caucus. She gathered evidence and tried to poke holes in her team's draft legal arguments.

Senior Ronni Alexander agreed to tell her story. On a December day in her sophomore year, Alexander had been so dizzy it made her nauseated.

She couldn't focus, almost as if she were cross-eyed. She'd been getting out of a friend's car and whacked her head on the doorframe so hard it caused a concussion. Her friend brought her to the health center but had to leave. Alexander started walking unsteadily toward her dormitory.

Brion saw her on the way. He offered to drive her back to her dorm. Barely able to string together a coherent sentence, Alexander said, "Okay." She didn't like being near Brion. Her freshman year she'd quit taking flute lessons from him because he started touching her breasts while "checking her breathing." Another time he grabbed her, kissing and fondling her even though she told him to stop. But he was Yale's only flute instructor, and she dreamed of auditioning for Yale's Music School, so she restarted lessons her sophomore year.

On the way back to Alexander's dorm, Brion stopped at an apartment he kept near campus, separate from his family. He led her inside and laid her on the bed. "The sheets smell dirty," she thought. Then Brion raped her, she said. She didn't resist, didn't understand why, and didn't tell anyone from the shame. Soon after, though, she asked a student counselor what would happen if a professor forced a student into a sexual relationship. The counselor asked a dean, who said he would call the professor and student into his office to talk it through. Alexander said nothing. Brion raped her at least once more. Zombielike, she didn't resist, and blamed herself. Alexander took a Greyhound bus to Canada, where a friend talked her out of suicide. Eventually she returned to Yale, moved out of her dorm into an apartment, and gave up music.

When Women's Caucus members in her senior year approached her with other accounts about Brion, she agreed to file a report with Yale and joined the lawsuit that took her name, *Alexander v. Yale*. Besides Olivarius, other plaintiffs included Lisa Stone, who roomed with one of Brion's victims; Stone reported Brion to an English professor, whose only response was to sexually proposition Stone. A lone faculty member joined them— John (Jack) Winkler, a classics scholar, queer theorist, political activist, and Stone's thesis advisor.[25] Sexual harassment at Yale led to an "atmosphere of distrust" of male professors that undermined his teaching efforts, Winkler charged.[26] From the start, the plaintiffs decided they would not be anonymous. They were not ashamed.

Simon typed out a complaint on an electric typewriter with a carbon copy and filed suit on July 3, 1977, in U.S. District Court in New Haven. She wrote to Sandler's Project on the Status and Education of Women (PSEW) asking for Title IX information. The *New York Times* placed its story about the suit in the "family/style" section.[27] A Yale spokesman told the *Times* that faculty sexual misconduct is "not a major problem."

What hurt most, Olivarius said, was that the college she loved so much—"for God, for country, for Yale"—had turned on her and all the other women it claimed to support. At one point a Yale official tried to taint her integrity by suggesting to reporters that Olivarius was a lesbian and failing classes, neither of which was true. She started getting hate mail, threatening notes pieced together from cut-out letters in a style mimicking the Zodiac Killer's messages. Threats kept coming for years, especially in the wake of news reports on the suit, in all at least a hundred hateful messages. The sender would "slowly rape" her, one said; another would "cut" her "labia." Someone put human feces in her mailbox.

The Undergraduate Women's Caucus—now nearly two hundred members strong—learned of Price's complaint the year before and invited her to join the lawsuit. Price had never heard of Title IX, so she didn't instantly say yes. Her C grade and Duvall's misconduct bothered her, but more importantly, she could not abide Yale's treatment of Ronni Alexander. The woman was raped; Price felt she had to do something about it. She joined the lawsuit. From the start, *Alexander v. Yale* was about Title IX protection against rape (which the lawsuit called "coerced sexual intercourse") as well as behaviors lumped under the term "sexual harassment."

Simon added Price and another plaintiff to the suit: Margery Reifler, who said she'd been harassed by the field hockey coach.[28] The lawsuit asked for a formal grievance procedure to handle complaints of sexual harassment at Yale. A student petition for grievance procedures drew twelve hundred signatures.[29] The WEAL Fund helped bankroll the suit.[30] Marcia Greenberger's Women's Rights Project took the unusual step of asking to argue in person in support of the plaintiffs' right to sue under Title IX, an unsettled issue in the courts. The judge magistrate agreed; lawyer Margaret (Margy) Kohn traveled to New Haven and gave him a mini-tutorial on Title IX.[31]

The Yale women's lawsuit became the talk of campus and the town of New Haven. It generated national publicity, both supportive and derisive. The Women's Caucus organized campus discussion sessions and fundraisers. But when Ronni Alexander stopped by a bar popular with working women not long after she appeared on TV discussing the lawsuit, she was surprised to be met by cold, hostile faces. They seemed to think she was a weak, spoiled attention-seeker for talking about sexual harassment, something they all had put up with for years without publicly whining about it.[32] More than a few women students at Yale felt the same.[33] Still, the concept of sexual harassment being sex discrimination spread like wildfire among students.

The first ruling in the case came on December 21, 1977. District Court federal magistrate Judge Arthur H. Latimer affirmed for the first time that Title IX can apply to sexual harassment in education because "academic advancement conditioned upon submission to sexual demands constitutes sexual discrimination in education." And he recognized that the right to a private lawsuit exists in Title IX cases.[34]

But he dismissed Alexander because she had graduated and Reifler because she hadn't filed a complaint (even though Yale had no procedure for doing so). He dismissed Stone, Olivarius, and Winkler because they hadn't claimed personal exclusion from educational opportunities, and "no judicial enforcement of Title IX could properly extend to such imponderables as atmosphere or vicariously experienced wrong"—which years later became recognized as a sexually hostile environment.

That left Price, the only plaintiff who could move forward in the case. The decision pitted a lone Black woman student against a white man professor. She and Simon asked for class-action status representing all women students at Yale, but Latimer refused.[35]

Before this ruling, many of Price's friends trivialized the case as "those white women" or "those feminists." Now, their tone changed.

"I was subjected to the assumption of my inferiority as a black person as well as the assumption of my lack of seriousness as a woman," she said in a December 21, 1977, statement.[36] "This grade is a concrete expression of his racist and sexist appraisal of me as a person—in my case the one attitude is inherently linked with the other."[37]

The Council of Third World Women at Yale and the Afro-American Cultural Center helped turn out support.[38] The Women's Caucus released press statements and a fact sheet noting the racial overtones of the case and the double jeopardy of racism and sexism that women of color faced. Price loved that the lawsuit built bridges between Black and white activists, though extensive media coverage of the case largely ignored the issue of race. TV producers flew Price to Los Angeles to appear on a syndicated talk show.[39]

While Price awaited trial, the first books on sexual harassment appeared in 1978: *Sexual Shakedown* by Lin Farley of the Working Women United Institute, followed shortly by *The Secret Oppression: Sexual Harassment of Working Women*, in which Alliance Against Sexual Coercion members Constance Backhouse and Leah Cohen addressed overlapping discriminations.

Men accused of sexual harassment began fighting back by suing their accusers or employers who upheld the women's complaints. A professor sued Texas A&M University in 1978, for example, saying he'd been forced to resign under duress after an employee accused him of sexual harassment. An appeals court ultimately sided with the university.[40]

Sandler noticed the increasing attention to sexual harassment on campus. It radically reshaped her thinking. During her college years in the late 1940s and early 1950s, no one she knew spoke out loud about sexual coercion or rape. They whispered. Someone was (the speaker would pause for effect) "attacked." Even in the most egregious cases, they collectively blamed the victim. Sandler and her friends framed these incidents in ways they learned from a sexist society.

"Did you hear about" so-and-so? "They say she slept with eight men at a party!" "Oh! She must be a nymphomaniac!" In reality, a group had raped a drunken coed at a party. But men's behavior—of almost any kind—was the norm, and if women didn't like it, it probably was their fault, many believed.

When Sandler asked around about sexual harassment as she visited campuses in 1978 and 1979, it revived repressed memories of a groping orthopedist and an early boss who fired her after she refused his sexual advances.[41]

PSEW produced a seven-page paper on *Sexual Harassment: A Hidden*

Issue in 1978 and an eight-pager soon after, *The Problem of Rape on Campus.* In classic Sandler fashion, each listed more than a dozen actions to take to prevent or deal with sexual harassment or rape.[42] As President Carter's appointed chair of the National Advisory Council on Women's Educational Programs, Sandler commissioned a 1978 paper on Title IX's applicability to sexual harassment that set the standard for liability in higher education.[43] The PSEW *Sexual Harassment* paper prominently described the lawsuit against Yale as one to watch.

By the time the Yale case—now titled *Price v. Yale* but still often called *Alexander v. Yale*—came to trial in January 1979, Price had graduated and was in the middle of her first year at Boalt School of Law at the University of California, Berkeley. She missed three weeks of classes for the trial. Two of her professors supported her attendance and helped her catch up afterward, but an assistant dean warned her in advance that her absence from the third class would not be excused. "You know," he added, "I went to Yale."[44]

Price's pastor showed up every day to the second-floor courtroom of New Haven's federal district court building to support her during the two-week trial. Flyers urged spectators to attend because "This lawsuit is about: 1. Women fighting sexual harassment. 2. Women speaking out against sexual abuse. 3. Third World and white women standing together to say 'NO to racism and sexism.'" A multihued crowd of students and others rallied on the New Haven Green repeatedly during the trial. Students and faculty from Yale's law school came to watch the proceedings.

Judge Ellen Bree Burns, a Yale Law graduate, chose to conduct the trial as a tort suit, a claim of harm to one individual, instead of considering the broader harm to a group of people, as occurs in a class-action suit. She allowed only inquiries or evidence about Price's own experiences, not Yale's failure to comply with Title IX.[45] "If it was an individual thing, I wouldn't be here," Price told the media. "It's about more than the fact that Duvall propositioned me. It's about all women who are sexually harassed."[46]

Judge Burns announced her decision on July 2, 1979: there was no proof that the alleged proposition by Duvall happened; the C grade was deserved; and because Price had already graduated, Yale's policies no longer affected her.[47] "It's the same old story," Price said in a statement. "Where sex is concerned, black women's accusations are considered lies and white men's denials are believed. Unfortunately, the trial, which was presided over by a woman, was merely another manifestation of the racism and sexism pervasive in society and reflected in its laws."[48]

All five students agreed to appeal the decision minus Professor Winkler, who had left to teach at Stanford University in California. Two of the best feminist litigators in the country—Nadine Taub and Liz Schneider of the Center for Constitutional Rights—agreed to steer the appeal, with amici support from a slew of women's groups.[49]

Yale rehired and promoted Keith Brion, the band leader accused of raping Alexander and others.

Students at universities in at least six other states also organized to fight sexual harassment, inspired by the Yale suit and the movement against sexual harassment in general.[50] The American Council on Education held seminars across the country in 1979 on sexual harassment policy.[51] Secretaries at Boston University and Harvard unionized in 1979 and 1980, respectively, and won one of the first clauses about sexual harassment in a union contract. The Alliance Against Sexual Coercion created a handbook for establishing college grievance procedures, published a report on sexual harassment in Massachusetts high schools, and distributed two brochures in Spanish about sexual harassment.[52]

Inspired by *Alexander v. Yale,* around thirty University of California, Berkeley, students calling themselves Women Organized Against Sexual Harassment (WOASH) publicized thirteen complaints of sexual harassment by sociology assistant professor Elbaki Hermassi. The school had no grievance procedures or even a Title IX coordinator—clear violations of the law. In a 1977 survey, nearly 20 percent of undergraduate senior women and 7 percent of women graduate students reported enduring sexual remarks, touching, or propositions by professors.[53] Most of the harassment came from tenured professors, 94 percent of whom were white men.

WOASH reached out to Price at Berkeley's law school. In a daylong forum in March, WOASH announced its Title IX complaint, and Price exhorted between three and four hundred people in Pauley Ballroom to stand up against sexual and racial harassment in education.[54]

"I did not appreciate being called a liar" by Judge Burns, Price said at a joint press conference with a Black WOASH member in August 1979.[55] They both emphasized the impossibility of separating race and sex discrimination in their experiences. Hermassi harassed the WOASH member because, he told her, he wanted to "try" Black women, she said. "These incidents took place not only because I am a woman and therefore considered fair game in the eyes of Professor Hermassi, but also because I am a black woman."

The mostly white, middle-class members of WOASH had debated vigorously about whether or not to challenge Hermassi, a light-skinned Black Tunisian who was one of Berkeley's few faculty of color, when so many of the harassing professors were white. But Hermassi was being considered for tenure, a status that would make it even harder for anyone to challenge his behavior. Plus, some of his victims were women of color, so WOASH went ahead.[56] Outreach by at least one WOASH member drew some backing from the university's Black Women's and Chicana caucuses and the community's Third World Women's Alliance, which signed petitions and letters.

Leaflets designed like "Wanted" posters with Hermassi's picture appeared around campus. Anonymous activists broke into the building housing the sociology department and spray-painted feminist slogans and symbols in red on the office doors of four white men professors. The student senate resoundingly passed a resolution supporting the protesters' demands.[57]

Berkeley's chancellor suspended Hermassi, at that time already on sabbatical, without pay for one quarter. Hermassi resigned in the fall of 1980 before returning from sabbatical, abandoning a tenure review.

Soon after, two Black women employees in the Cashier's Office in Sproul Hall complained that they were fired for complaining about sexual harassment by the white man who supervised their work. Only a few WOASH members joined Price and others in protests on behalf of the Black employees. WOASH fizzled out as members returned to their studies or graduated.

For Price's appeal in the Yale case, Anne E. Simon, Nadine Taub, and New Haven Law Collective employee Phyllis L. Crocker traveled to New York for a mandatory mediation session before the court would hear arguments. Everyone around the conference table at the Second Circuit court-house had gone to Yale or its law school: the three women and, on the other side, Yale's attorney, representative, and the mediator. The three men called the women ungrateful for the privilege of attending Yale and said they should drop the suit, Crocker recalled. The women replied: *You just don't get it.*[58]

They officially argued the appeal on April 16, 1980, before three older white men in the Second Circuit of Appeals in New York City. By that time Yale had adopted a grievance procedure, though some found it inade-quate.[59] The appellate court backed Judge Burns's decision in favor of Yale on September 22. Alexander's claim that Brion's rapes killed her desired career as a flutist was "highly conjectural," they said, and Price hadn't proved anything in her case.

Within two years of *Alexander v. Yale* ending, though, the Universities of Minnesota and Wisconsin; the University of California, Santa Cruz; and Brown, Stanford, and Tulane Universities adopted formal sex discrimina-tion policies and grievance procedures, most of which were weak but at least a start.[60] Despite its "radical" reputation, Berkeley took years more just to appoint a Title IX Compliance Officer. It didn't create grievance procedures until 1986.[61]

Price was working as a student intern for a criminal defense firm in San Francisco in 1980 when one of her attorneys called to tell her they'd lost the appeal. "That's it. Title IX is dead," she thought. It will never be a use-ful tool to fight rape and sexual harassment.

But five years later, hundreds of colleges and universities had adopted grievance procedures.[62] It was just the beginning.

6

Enforcement

1975–1979

FAR FROM THE BIG-CITY CAMPUSES OF YALE OR BERKELEY AND THE WASH-ington, DC, halls of power, Fresno, California, considered itself "the best little city in the U.S.A.," but with a semirural vibe. Agriculture dominated its power structure. In the heart of California's breadbasket, rich white men who owned big farms in the Central Valley called the shots. The city's 413,000 residents were 65 percent white and 25 percent Hispanic. The president of its marquee institution—Frederic Ness of Fresno State College—left in 1971 to lead the Association of American Colleges. He, his wife, and their five daughters moved to DC, where he hired Sandler to lead the Project on the Status and Education of Women (PSEW).

But Fresno was no quiet backwater. Conflicts around anti-war protests and lack of support for ethnic studies marked Ness's tenure at Fresno State in the late 1960s. Though 42 percent of Fresno State's students were women, Ness left before women's activism joined the ongoing racial/ethnic organizing in the 1970s.

The artist Judy Chicago founded the country's first feminist art program at Fresno State in 1970. Women professors, who made up 18 percent of the college's faculty, created some women's studies classes at the college in 1971; two hundred students showed up.[1] They learned—likely through NOW and WEAL—about Rep. Edith Green's proposed "Title X," and a student called Green's office in 1971 asking her to come speak at the college.[2] As Title IX was being passed in 1972, the college became California State University, Fresno, and opened one of the nation's first women's studies programs. Fresno State was the first to offer classes in some topics, including Female Sexuality, Feminist Issues in Counseling, and Disabled Women.

In the athletics department, though, student Diane Milutinovich noticed that only men's teams got uniforms and shoes. The three women's teams—tennis, volleyball, and basketball—played in the white gym shorts used for PE classes. At least those were more sports than she'd been offered at Fresno High School. Milutinovich grew up in Fresno in a Serbian-American middle-class family, playing neighborhood games with her two brothers when they weren't helping their parents in their restaurant. Once she earned her degree in PE from Fresno State, Milutinovich took her first job teaching PE in tiny Perris, California, nearly three hundred miles to the south, as Title IX was being passed.

Her mother, Violet, bragged to friends, "Diane is teaching in Perris!" Their eyes would widen. "Oh! Paris!?" She'd savor it a moment before spelling the city's name.

In Perris, Milutinovich gravitated toward administration as a profession. She didn't like that the school hired more coaches for boys' teams and paid them better than the girls' team coaches. She didn't like that boys got better sports facilities and first dibs on any facilities they shared with the girls. The meticulous care of the baseball field and the neglect of the softball field irked her. But she figured there wasn't much she could do about it.

Then the Title IX regulations went into force in 1975. Milutinovich attended her first Conference on Women, Sports and the Law at the University of Southern California in 1976. Her packet of materials contained information on Title IX and athletics provided by PSEW, the ACLU's Women's Rights Project, and *womenSports* magazine. It also included articles by Title IX opponents like the NCAA and Sen. Jesse Helms, who warned that Title IX will kill football. From the start, the loudest opposition was always about football.

One afternoon in Perris, she walked out to meet the girls' team at the softball field. The grounds crew had turned on the sprinklers despite knowing the girls had practice. She'd had enough. Milutinovich filed a Title IX complaint with the Office for Civil Rights (OCR) in 1976 anonymously, hoping to protect herself from retaliation.

Generally, PE teachers tended to be politically conservative or apolitical;

they just wanted to do their jobs. Many of them were lesbians but would never dream of talking about it. Private lives were private lives, and the stigma was too great to be open about it; in many states, they could be fired for being gay or suspected of being gay. Straight women like Milutinovich sometimes were perceived to be lesbians because of their short hair or athleticism, whether they knew it or not. That increased the risk of being fired or harassed if they objected to anything such as inequities in athletics.[3]

Because of this risk and the relatively conservative politics of many women in sports, women's efforts under Title IX usually flowed separately from the young but growing movement for gay rights. Other streams carried movements for racial justice or for the rights of people with disabilities, though tributaries connected all of these and occasionally joined them into shimmering lakes that broadened the views of some in the women's movement.

One such lake formed in Houston, November 18–20, 1977, at the first and only National Women's Conference. Bernice Sandler came as a delegate from Maryland, one of two thousand delegates from every state and U.S. territory who were watched by nearly twenty thousand nondelegates packing the surrounding seats in the Albert Thomas Convention Center. She might have said hello to Ruth Bader Ginsburg, Reps. Bella Abzug and Patsy Mink, and many others during breaks between plenary sessions, where delegates considered twenty-six proposed planks for a National Plan of Action.[4] Federal funds not only paid for state conventions leading up to the national one but also subsidized travel to and from, so organizers were able to recruit diverse participants from an impressive cross-section of society in terms of age, race, ethnicity, class, and more.

The education plank they passed that Saturday called for eliminating discrimination in academic and sports programs in schools at all levels, expanding bilingual and women's studies programs, and removing racial and sexual stereotypes from textbooks. The eleventh plank, supporting ratification of the ERA, passed just before midnight after an hour of debate. A roar from the crowd carried into singing and dancing in the aisles, the people refusing to be silenced by the chair banging the gavel.

Sandler waved her "ERA YES!" sign above her mod print tunic, her smile beaming ear to ear.

For Sunday's sessions, three of the planks had been rewritten on the fly at the conference after disabled women, racial/ethnic minority women, and welfare rights activists expressed dissatisfaction with original drafts. Increasingly, some in the women's movement were speaking out about overlapping oppressions based on race, sex, class, and sexual orientation. Earlier that year in April 1977, for instance, the Combahee River Collective statement pointed out how neither the civil rights movement nor the white feminist movement dealt fully with issues facing Black women.

Asian, Hispanic, Native American, and African American groups that seldom collaborated on a national scale held all-night negotiations at the Houston conference to craft a plank that spoke individually to each group's problems and the "double discrimination" experienced by women in all these groups. The phrase "women of color" came out of the conference. When Coretta Scott King read the Minority Caucus plank at Sunday's plenary surrounded by delegates of color, Sandler may have been one of the many listeners moved to tears. Go forth from Houston, King said, as "a new force, a new understanding, a new sisterhood against all injustice that has been born here. We will not be divided and defeated again."[5] Someone started singing "We Shall Overcome," and everyone in the arena joined in, reaching for each other's hands.

But a rising movement of white, anti-feminist, Christian traditionalist women and men led by Phyllis Schlafly and her Eagle Forum co-opted some of the state conventions and tried to sabotage the national event. Schlafly was a smart, media-savvy, rabidly anticommunist author and activist married to a rich lawyer. She enrolled in law school herself after Title IX opened admissions to more women and would earn her JD in 1978, but that didn't stop her from trying to destroy Title IX and the ERA.

Schlafly built a network of conservative Catholics, Mormons, fundamentalist Christians, John Birch Society members, and white supremacists, though she denied these last two groups were involved. They managed to get approximately three hundred conservatives included as delegates to the National Women's Conference. They also organized a one-day rally across town, at the Houston Astro Arena, to compete for media attention. Their overflow crowd of fifteen thousand white anti-feminists plus less than a handful of Blacks included Ku Klux Klan members, Klan leaders told the press.[6] Schlafly warned that "women's libbers" and militant lesbians were destroying traditional families headed by men.

That clouded Sandler's thinking when delegates at the main Women's Conference debated the twenty-third plank of the National Plan of Action, on "Sexual Preference," affirming support for lesbians' rights. If delegates passed the Sexual Preference plank, Schlafly might parlay that into fearmongering to stop the ERA, Sandler and others feared. On the other hand, Sandler didn't like discrimination of any kind. But it bugged her—delegates were here to talk about women's issues. Why was this on the agenda at all?

Like many women's advocates, Sandler only gradually developed her understanding of the need to fight all forms of discrimination in order to realize all women's rights under laws like Title IX.

"Look around," a friend said. "A lot of the people here *are* gay. There are a lot of people in the movement who are lesbians."[7]

"Oh, yeah?" Sandler didn't think she knew any. "Like who?"

"Well, Margot's a lesbian," her friend said, referring to Margot Polivy, attorney for the Association for Intercollegiate Athletics for Women.

Sandler liked and admired Polivy. National Coalition for Women and Girls in Education (NCWGE) members had been to Polivy's house socially and for meetings. They'd met Katrina Renouf, with whom she shared her law practice and home, and some became Polivy's friends. But Polivy never talked to any of them about being a lesbian, she said later, simply because none of them ever asked, even into the twenty-first century.

In Houston, conservatives spoke against the Sexual Preference plank, but so did some feminists; one warned it would be "an albatross" to the women's movement.[8] Lesbians urged its passage, as did straight women who described the sting of having been accused of being lesbians themselves. Betty Friedan, who'd previously opposed the "lavender menace" of lesbians in the women's movement, surprised everyone by announcing her support for the plank. Sandler decided to vote for it too.

Once it passed, conservative delegates on the convention floor stood, turned their backs to the podium, and bent their heads as if praying. In the galleries thousands of supporters of lesbians' rights released balloons and waved signs saying, "Thank You, Sisters."

This crossover between the women's and LGBT rights movements, like most of the early crossovers between civil rights movements, developed separate from Title IX. Decades would elapse before Title IX started to address LGBT rights in the context of sex discrimination.

Sandler returned to work with a broadened appreciation for interlocking movements, but these seldom were addressed directly in PSEW's work. And PSEW was changing. Sandler lost her original work "family" as staff members moved on. An inflationary economy further reduced the staff. Margaret Dunkle moved to HEW as a special assistant on education legislation and she stepped down as chair of the NCWGE; she and Sandler remained lifelong friends. Francelia Gleaves took a job editing a newsletter for a Women's Educational Equity Act (WEEA) project at WEAL. Once she was gone, PSEW's "Minority Women" section in the newsletter shrank significantly. Another assistant, Arlene Fong Craig, took a government job, leaving PSEW with a small all-white staff by the end of 1979 and throughout the 1980s.

Sandler's own family crumbled too, specifically her marriage. When she first started filing complaints under the executive orders, Jerry had been so supportive. He taught her so much—even little things, like the etiquette of sending a thank-you after having a meeting with someone. But he seemed to change once she knew more than he did about the subject, when she became the recognized expert. He could handle the shifting status, she noted, as long as he was seen as the man behind the woman who had taught her everything. When she began to disagree with his dictates on strategy, though, he got furious. Bernice had never seen that before. And as she grew into more autonomous womanhood in the 1970s, she was asking him to change in ways he couldn't handle. There were certainly other cracks in the marriage. It probably would have fallen apart anyway, she believed.

Anguished but resolute, Bernice moved out, and eventually ended the marriage. She and Jerry divorced in 1978. The whole thing left her depressed. The depression scared her, enough to seek therapy. She tried hard, very hard, to not be depressed. Finally, she stopped fighting it.

Allowing herself to fully experience her feelings made them less frightening, even somehow reassuring. She turned a corner.[9]

Bernice bought a condo.[10] She started hiking again and got on a bicycle for the first time in thirty-five years. That, plus therapy and jogging and the work that she loved at PSEW, kept her going.[11]

The women's movement for equity in education was going strong. They'd shepherded the implementing regulations for Title IX out of OCR in 1974; now they demanded that OCR enforce the law. Milutinovich's Title IX complaint in Perris, California, fed into an early wave of complaints primarily addressing athletics and employment.[12] In Fresno, women filed three complaints against K-12 schools in 1976, two by custodians who got less pay, benefits, and promotions than men, and another by coaches who were paid a third less than what boys' coaches received.[13]

Milutinovich left Perris soon after filing her complaint to pursue a master's degree in PE Administration from California State Polytechnic University, Pomona. Not much changed in Perris. After her father died, she moved home in 1978 to live with her mother while writing her master's thesis and took some women's studies classes at Fresno State—something that didn't exist when she'd been an undergraduate.

For years, students and women coaches at Fresno State had been nudging politely for more support for women's athletics, without much progress. Even after administrators nearly doubled the budget for women's athletics for the 1975–76 year, it still lagged far behind the men's.

Advocates took their pressure up a notch in 1977. A student took the lead—senior and varsity women's basketball co-captain Meg Newman. Sports in California felt like paradise compared with the paucity of choices she'd had in high school or at her first college in New York. Yet, Fresno State prioritized the men's teams. The athletics director acknowledged that $416,000 went to men's athletics and only $22,000 to women's sports in 1975–76. The school offered eleven intercollegiate sports for men and six for women. Men got $183,000 in grants and scholarships compared with $4,000 for women.

Newman and her teammates saved some of the meager funds they received for meals on away trips so that they could buy team socks. Professional drivers transported buses of men to away games; the women's coach drove her car and had a player drive a school van for hours to get the women's teams to competitions.

With a cast on her broken right hand from a fall during practice, Newman typed a letter on a tiny portable typewriter on behalf of women athletes on multiple Fresno State teams. The group demanded more resources. At a coach's insistence she stressed, "It is our strongest desire to work with all of you." Yet, she added, "we emphasize that a lack of responsiveness would compel us to contact H.E.W."[14]

Administrators met with the students and claimed they couldn't afford anything more for women's sports.[15] "If there are limited resources, we'd like them distributed equitably," Newman told the *Collegian* student newspaper. Two months later she graduated and moved on. The student group didn't file a Title IX complaint.

Women ramped up sports activism at colleges of every kind once the Title IX regulations were approved. At Yale University, for instance, a one-page report by junior Abbe Smith described a similar sorry state of women's athletics. "Yale is certainly in direct violation of Title IX," Smith wrote. Two women coaches had filed a Title VII complaint about employment discrimination; students should complain under Title IX as soon as possible, Smith urged.[16]

Even when complaints were filed, though, most ended up in a black hole of government inaction.

There had been little progress against sex discrimination in education in the first five years of Title IX, leaders of the NCWGE testified in July 1977 before a House subcommittee on a bill to extend WEEA.[17] Teaching materials remained skewed: one study of textbooks found depictions of men in 147 jobs but women in only 23 jobs, if you don't count mother, queen, or witch. In 1976, less than 2 percent of high school principals and 10 percent of college full professors were women.

Two studies released by Holly Knox's Project on Equal Education Rights (PEER) showed how little OCR had done to enforce Title IX. Its first study in 1976 found that forty-one of fifty state education agencies violated at least one basic requirement of Title IX; four states violated all requirements the study measured.[18] In 1977's report, *Stalled at the Start*, PEER analyzed all 871 complaints about elementary and secondary schools sent to OCR from people in fifty states from June 23, 1972, through October 1, 1976. Employment discrimination led the types of charges (36 percent), followed by biased sports programs (22 percent), lack of access to courses (18 percent), and others; 40 percent of complaints listed more than one violation.[19] OCR "resolved" only 179 complaints—one of every five— usually through a process of sending a few letters back and forth with the school or district. Investigators visited the district in less than a quarter of cases. OCR never followed up with the few schools that promised to make changes.

On average, OCR took fourteen months to reach a resolution; some still were pending after years. More than a third of Title IX complaints from 1973 alone remained unresolved, though not because of a lack of staff, PEER pointed out. With more than a hundred staff people in DC and eleven regional offices, OCR received fewer than two Title IX complaints per investigator each year in 1973–76, on average. Even when counting the total caseload for discrimination based on race, ethnic origin, handicap, or sex, each investigator averaged just over six complaints per year.

Aside from complaints, OCR had conducted Title IX compliance reviews in only twelve of the nation's sixteen thousand school districts since the law passed.

"If government leaders, from the President on down, insist on results in enforcing the law, there will be results. HEW has the tools, it has the staff, and it has the law. All that is needed is the will," PEER concluded. With the publication of *Stalled at the Start*, PEER drew major news media attention to HEW's failure to enforce Title IX. The *Washington Post* featured the report on its front page.

The three-year "adjustment period" for higher education to comply with Title IX in athletics ended July 21, 1978, with a majority of colleges out of compliance, including Fresno State.[20] OCR received nearly a hundred complaints against more than fifty colleges and universities for sex discrimination in athletics.[21] Most athletic departments had used the three-year window as an excuse to make few or no changes. They were supposed to have fully equitable athletics programs by July 1978, but many claimed they thought they only needed a plan of action. Besides, they said, they couldn't figure out how to provide equal athletic opportunity in the areas delineated in OCR's 1975 regulations. What do "equitable" locker rooms look like, anyway? Spell it out for us, they told OCR officials.

Recalcitrant administrators "grossly overestimate the problem. They just want to find out how little they have to do to get over the line," Polivy complained. A PEER staffer said, "The law and the regulations are very clear about what has to be done. It's clear what comparability means. Those who say they don't understand just don't want to use their heads." Other civil rights regulations were not so different from Title IX's; this all wasn't entirely new.[22]

OCR proposed a more specific Policy Interpretation on December 11, 1978, to supplement sections on athletics in the 1975 regulations and allay any confusion.[23] If the share of funding for men's and women's athletics matched their proportions in the student body, a school would be considered compliant with Title IX; if not, OCR would examine the school under this and other criteria. The proposal generated more than seven hundred public comments by March.

An ad hoc coalition of outraged athletics administrators coalesced behind Duke University president Terry Sanford—who had fought to block Title IX from being passed in 1972—as their spokesman. He wrote to HEW on behalf of sixty-one college executives with his bright idea: Just trust us! "Voluntary compliance" and "leadership on campus" would make everything right, not regulations. Even Edith Green wrote to HEW secretary Harris supporting his plan.[24]

Throughout 1979 OCR met repeatedly with higher education officials, athletic directors, women's organizations, and others on the draft Policy Interpretation. OCR also put Cindy Brown in charge of a task force to develop the Title IX policy. A former OCR employee, Brown had been active in the NCWGE and the Leadership Conference on Civil Rights before returning to work at OCR. Brown's previous OCR expertise focused on racial issues and poverty, so she recruited AIAW's Polivy behind the scenes to give her many unofficial tutoring sessions on athletics.[25]

OCR sent her with a small team to eight Division I colleges and universities to assess how OCR's proposal might work. The college presidents wined and dined her, but they also positioned administrators at her elbow during her interviews. Handlers at the University of Richmond would not let her out of their sight. She had to escape to the women's restroom to hear the truth from the women's athletic director: the university treated men athletes like kings and women's athletics like they barely existed, the woman told her.[26]

While this was happening, the Supreme Court secured an important tool for women to enforce Title IX—the right to sue. Geraldine Cannon, a thirty-nine-year-old surgical nurse, had applied to medical schools at the University of Chicago and Northwestern University and been rejected by both because they refused to admit anyone older than thirty years. Cannon couldn't persuade them to reconsider, so she filed a complaint with OCR in April 1975. With no response other than an acknowledgment that the agency had received her letter, she sued three months later. Cannon argued that the age-limit policies discriminate because women interrupt their education and experience career delays more than men do. A federal appeals court ruled that only the government could enforce Title IX; but other women's suits produced conflicting court opinions.

The Carter administration filed an amicus brief when the Supreme Court agreed to review the case. The administration backed Cannon's right to sue, admitting that OCR didn't have the resources to respond to every sex discrimination complaint. In a 6–3 decision the Supreme Court upheld individuals' right to sue under Title IX on May 14, 1979, saying in part that Title IX's one enforcement penalty—cutting off all federal funds to an institution—was so drastic that it wasn't useful for an individual woman's complaint. Cannon could pursue her lawsuit. The universities soon agreed to settle with her.[27]

In Fresno, Milutinovich started coaching the Fresno State women's junior varsity basketball team while writing her thesis in 1978–79. The women coaches' frustration at the university's lack of athletics support boiled over in February 1979. Nine of them threatened to sue Fresno State for discrimination.

"They've been stonewalling us all along. The university isn't going to do anything until they're absolutely forced," said Basketball Coach Donna Pickel. This was no "bunch of radicals" waiting to "pounce on" the administration, Volleyball Coach Leilani Overstreet assured a student news reporter. "If that were true, we would have filed a complaint in

1975." In fact, "We don't want equality," she added. "We only want to be treated fairly."[28]

With men's athletics directors attacking OCR's proposed Policy Interpretation, women's leaders nationwide ramped up their own pressure, bombarding congressmembers with mail urging them to pressure OCR for strong Title IX regulations. Around three hundred people, many in T-shirts reading "Title IX, Hold the Line," chanted slogans with champion skier Suzy Chaffee at a rally across from the White House on Sunday, April 22, 1979, then marched up Pennsylvania Avenue to the Capitol.[29] NCWGE members wrote a Declaration of Women's Athletic Rights that volunteers hand-delivered to congressmembers. They criticized the Sanford proposal in hearings before the U.S. Commission on Civil Rights. In September the commission declared that football should not be exempted from Title IX.[30]

Sandler drafted a list of myths and facts about the athletics Policy Interpretation to counter allegations from Title IX critics. "Myth: HEW's athletic policies hurt minority athletes," one said. "Fact: Minority *women* athletes do not have the same opportunities for scholarships as their brothers do," which Title IX could change.[31]

The new Women's Sports Foundation organized a coalition of twenty-six national sports organizations representing 15 million people, urging quick finalization of the athletics Policy Interpretation.[32] But progress toward a final document limped along.

The long-standing *Adams* and *WEAL* lawsuits helped push OCR to the finish line. Though a court ordered OCR to hire 898 more employees and clear up its backlog of discrimination complaints by March 1979, in April 1,371 sex discrimination complaints remained. So Greenberger sued for contempt of court, which helped pressure OCR to finish the job.[33] HEW issued a final Policy Interpretation of the athletics regulations on December 11, 1979, under a new secretary, Patricia Harris, the first Black woman to head HEW.[34] But the contents of the Policy Interpretation had changed from the earlier draft.

OCR dropped the yardstick of equal per capita expenditures to assess compliance with Title IX; opponents had argued that it contradicted the Javits amendment, which allowed for reasonable differences. Men's and women's sports scholarships would need to be "proportionately equal" expenditures; other opportunities and benefits in athletics must be "equivalent" between sexes as measured in ways other than expenditures, OCR said. The document gave lots of details on what that meant. It added two areas (recruitment and support services) to the eleven areas in which it required equitable treatment in the 1975 regulations.[35] But if a school spends more money on men because, say, football uniforms cost more, that's allowed.

OCR considered but ultimately rejected requiring that schools split the number of players or athletics budgets 50-50 by sex. Instead, it adopted a relatively complicated compromise pushed by the NCAA and the Football Coaches Association that women's advocates had resisted.[36]

The new guideline said schools comply with Title IX's athletics regulations if they do one of three things, which became known as the three-prong (or three-part) test: (1) provide athletic opportunities that are "substantially proportionate" to the sex ratio of the student body (so, if women are 40 percent of students, they get 40 percent of player slots); (2) show a "history and continuing practice" of improving athletics for the underrepresented sex, or (3) show that the athletics program meets the interests and abilities of the underrepresented sex.

NCWGE leaders were relieved to have the new guidelines, if not entirely satisfied, knowing it was the best they could get at the time.[37] That year, women overtook men in college enrollment, and men's coaches started to regret the test's first prong; as women's proportion of students grew, so did the share of athletics they were entitled to have.[38] Men administrators claimed that feminists had pulled a fast one, pretending that the system hadn't come from them. Phyllis Schlafly even said Sandler had pushed for the three-prong test. Sandler wrote what she considered a "nasty note" to Schlafly saying that was not true: "I will be extraordinarily upset if you continue to say such things."[39]

Title IX advocates knew from experience that progress depended on OCR enforcing the new guidance. PSEW distributed sixteen thousand copies of a one-page summary of the athletics Policy Interpretation to encourage people to demand their rights.[40] HEW secretary Harris appointed friend and ally Cindy Brown to direct OCR for the last eight months of the Carter administration as the assistant secretary in the new Department of Education, which branched off from HEW to be its own department.

"These guidelines represent a step forward, no more, no less," PEER's Knox wrote. "An equal share for women is still a distant goal; let's get on with the journey."[41]

At Fresno State, advocates' steady pressure produced incremental change without filing a federal complaint. Women were 51 percent of the school's 15,257 students. They'd won equipment and staffing for women's volleyball and basketball on levels similar to men's teams, but on any day a men's coach could demand that a women's team give up scheduled gym time for his team's use, and he'd get his way. Each time something like that happened, women's coaches tried to bargain to get something else out of it for the women. In their annual program evaluations, they urged Fresno State to better comply with Title IX to avoid them filing a federal complaint.[42]

Nationally, girls in high school varsity sports zoomed from being 7 percent of athletes in 1971–72 to 35 percent in 1981–82.[43] Women's share of intercollegiate sports budgets grew from 2 percent in the early 1970s to 16 percent in 1978.[44] Too often women's advocates had to go to court to prod improvements. In the 1970s they won twenty-five of thirty-six major lawsuits over inequities in athletics.[45] In August 1980, OCR's backlog of 576 complaints included 124 about athletics at eighty institutions.[46]

Sandler gave this clear-eyed assessment: "The vast majority of institutions have not made all the changes we would like, but they have made some changes."[47] In talks and interviews she often said, "Things have gone from absolutely horrendous to only very bad."

For Title IX, things were about to get much, much worse.

Civil rights attorney Pauli Murray, NOW co-founder Sonia Pressman Fuentes, and Bernice Sandler circa 1977. *Schlesinger Library, Radcliffe Institute, Harvard University*

Sen. Birch Bayh with Rep. Shirley Chisholm at a 1971 conference in Albany, New York. *Indiana University Libraries*

Rep. Edith Green at home with her dog in 1973. *Oregon Historical Society*

Staff at the Project on the Status and Education of Women, Association of American Colleges, gather for a photo on the office's back steps in 1977. Bottom row: Francelia Gleaves, Debbie Martinez, Margaret Dunkle, and Kathleen Wilson. Middle: Kay Meckes, Connie Reid, and Bernice Sandler. Top: Arlene Fong Craig. *Schlesinger Library, Radcliffe Institute, Harvard University*

Rep. Patsy Takemoto Mink at a 1993 press conference introducing legislation on gender equity in education, with Rep. Cardiss Collins (behind Mink), Rep. Dale Kildee (left), and others. *By R. Michael Jenkins, in the* Congressional Quarterly Roll Call Photograph Collection, Library of Congress

Pamela Y. Price in the *Yale Banner* yearbook for the
class of 1978. *From* The 1978 Yale Banner *at Yale
University Library*

Pamela Price in 2017. *Sherry Boschert*

7

Backlash

1980–1990

PARTICIPANTS AT A NATIONAL COALITION FOR WOMEN AND GIRLS IN EDUcation (NCWGE) meeting in spring 1981 sat shell-shocked. Exhausted. Paralyzed. Sandler recognized it as a stage of grief.

They'd spent eight to ten years of their lives for hard-fought gains that were now targeted by the new ultraconservative administration of President Ronald Reagan and Republicans who'd taken control of the Senate in the 1980 elections. Social traditionalism, white male supremacism, and fiscal individualism combined in a surging movement against "government overreach" that appealed to people who resented civil rights laws for taking away some of their privileges. Backed by Phyllis Schlafly and others, they elected Reagan, whose campaign promised to eliminate the entire Department of Education for intruding on state and local decisions.

While Reagan publicly claimed he'd fight discrimination against women and minorities, his staff in the Office of Management and Budget openly made sexist and racist jokes. They called Title IX the "lesbians' bill of rights."[1]

His election solidified control of the Republican Party for at least the next four decades by those who do not believe government has a role to play in enforcing rules against discrimination, leveling the economic playing field, maintaining a basic social safety net, or building infrastructure. He engineered tax cuts and economic policies especially benefiting the rich and corporations. He cut social services. In 1986, six years into his two-term presidency, more than 30 percent of Black citizens lived in poverty.[2]

Reagan immediately began cutting budgets and dismantling civil rights programs. His Office for Civil Rights (OCR) didn't even spend $20 million of the funds appropriated to it by Congress in 1980–85. The budgetary hit to OCR continued under subsequent presidents of either party for decades. Full-time staff withered from 1,099 in 1981 to 563 in 2016, even though annual civil rights complaints in education grew from 2,887 to 16,720.[3]

On top of that, Sen. Bayh and nine other congressional allies to women lost their seats in the 1980 elections.

Over months, though, activists' numbness turned to anger. Younger members reenergized the NCWGE as many of its veterans stepped aside, worn out. Sandler sent staff instead of going to meetings herself but stayed on call to use her expertise where needed.[4]

Reagan tried but failed to abolish the Department of Education and several others. He cut their budgets. His budget proposals routinely ignored the Women's Educational Equity Act (WEEA). Congress inserted WEEA appropriations each year, but less and less over time. Reagan proposed rolling WEEA and Title IV of the Civil Rights Act of 1964 (which provides assistance to school districts to comply with antidiscrimination laws) and dozens of small grant programs into a single "block grant" to states. States generally chose not to spend federal money on educational equity; it was a backdoor way to attack civil rights in education.

"The president wants to send the girls back to the kitchens, the disabled back to the institutions, the Blacks back to the ghettos, and the migrants back to the fields, leaving the classrooms and playgrounds safe for the remaining students—little white boys," WEAL legislative director Patricia Reuss said.[5] Women's advocates activated their networks to block the proposal.

The National Women Students Coalition and sixteen other women's and higher education organizations sponsored National Title IX Awareness Week, starting October 5, 1981, with workshops and a petition to rally support for Title IX.[6] Backers sent thousands of letters and telegrams and called and visited members of Congress.[7] They crashed Republican congressional fundraisers to lobby Republican women in the House.

It worked; House members on the committee took WEEA and Title

IV out of the state block grants. They survived. When Republicans in the Senate introduced bills similar to earlier attacks on Title IX, the NCWGE and allies managed to fend them off, too, but it was hard.[8]

In two talks at Yale University in November 1981, Sandler shared "The News from Washington: Bad Times for Women in Education."[9] Reagan in 1982 shifted his first OCR director, Clarence Thomas, a Black man who opposed affirmative action, to head the Equal Employment Opportunity Commission, which was supposed to uphold affirmative action. Vice President George H.W. Bush led a Presidential Task Force on Regulatory Relief to identify "burdensome, unnecessary or counterproductive" federal regulations to eliminate, with a bullseye on Title IX.

Reagan jettisoned feminists in appointed positions except for WEEA director Leslie Wolfe, who had civil service status. Right before WEEA funding proposals were considered he transferred her and replaced experienced grant evaluators with fifty unqualified or anti-feminist ones— among them a dentist, a realtor, a cosmetics salesperson, and a genealogist. A woman tasked with reviewing applications for Title IX projects asked her panel moderator, "What is Title IX?"[10]

The NCWGE campaigned to save Wolfe's job, instigating news articles and hundreds of letters to Education Secretary Terrel Bell. House allies asked the General Accounting Office to investigate. On June 16, 1982, Sandler joined 150 members of the NCWGE on the Capitol steps to celebrate Title IX's tenth birthday with a high school marching band, balloons, cake, performances, and speakers, including Indianapolis 500 race car driver Janet Guthrie. Uniformed athletes delivered Title IX packets to congressional offices. PEER encouraged local events in supporters' hometowns.

Officials reinstated Wolfe as WEEA director. The Reagan administration wasn't invincible, Sandler noted; public outcry made a difference.

Reagan replaced Sandler and other members of the bipartisan National Advisory Council on Women's Educational Programs (NACWEP) with Republican women, all white but one, and made a Schlafly acolyte the executive director. Sandler, Knox, and others organized a Citizens Council on Women's Education to monitor and critique the council, copying a strategy from civil rights activists who had created a "shadow" council to oversee Reagan's conservative Commission on Civil Rights.[11]

National politics looked grim but Sandler could see progress. The Equal Rights Amendment (ERA) fell three states short of the thirty-seven needed for ratification by the 1982 deadline set by Congress. But five times as many women entered law school in 1981–82 than did a decade earlier.[12] The Supreme Court bolstered protections for working women, ruling in 1981 that Title IX covers employment (*North Haven Board of Education v. Bell*) and ruling in 1986 that Title VII prohibits both quid pro quo sexual harassment and sexually hostile workplace environments, with some limitations (*Meritor Savings Bank v. Vinson*).[13]

On the legal front, Title IX and other issues kept Marcia Greenberger's team so busy that she spun off from the Center for Law and Social Policy to co-found the National Women's Law Center (NWLC) in 1981 with Nancy Duff Campbell.

A call from twenty-two-year-old badminton player Rollin Haffer gave the NWLC the case that Greenberger hoped would finally end the ongoing argument that Title IX didn't apply to athletics. Led by the NWLC's Margy Kohn, *Haffer v. Temple University* was the first suit claiming sex discrimination in an entire college athletics program, filed on behalf of eight plaintiffs representing every women's team at the Philadelphia university.[14] Though 42 percent of varsity athletes there were women, they received only 13 percent of the athletic budget. A lot of the money went to football. Women received worse equipment, uniforms, scholarships, transportation, travel accommodations, facilities, you name it. Temple argued that athletics received no direct federal funding, so Title IX didn't apply. Greenberger's team dug up evidence to the contrary: federal work-study programs paid students to collect event tickets, and federal scholarships to student athletes freed up private funds for other athletics usage, they found.

District and appeals courts sided with Haffer, though several similar suits produced conflicting rulings.[15] If Temple appealed, Greenberger's carefully constructed case could have been decided by the Supreme Court, which would have put the issue to rest if it supported Haffer. But another case got there first and instead shut down Title IX in athletics: *Grove City College v. Bell*.

When President Carter's OCR had asked schools to resubmit statements saying they would comply with Title IX, twenty-two schools and districts

refused, including Grove City College, a private Christian school north of
Pittsburgh. Though students there received government grants and loans
for tuition, Grove City College officials argued that this was not direct
funding, so the school wasn't bound by civil rights laws. OCR moved to
cut off federal funds, and the college sued. When Reagan came to power,
though, the Justice Department showed little desire to defend Title IX
fully. It disagreed with Grove City College's assertion that Title IX didn't
apply to the college at all, arguing that if students received federal financial aid, then the school's financial aid office must comply with Title IX,
including the awarding of athletics scholarships. But that left the door wide
open for the theory that Title IX applied only to programs or departments
that directly received federal funds—an idea repeated by athletics administrators since the earliest days of Title IX, when they threw up any anti–
Title IX idea they could think of to see if it would stick.

The Supreme Court's 6–3 ruling on February 28, 1984, accepted those
limits to Title IX.[16]

As a result, Title IX prohibited sex discrimination in sports scholarships administered through financial aid offices but nowhere else in athletics.[17] In a sexual harassment complaint at Northeastern University, OCR
put the case on hold because the alleged harassment happened in the Economics Department in Lake Hall, which hadn't been built or renovated
with federal funds.[18]

Civil rights enforcement stalled. Several colleges cut women's teams.[19]
Courts dismissed at least eight Title IX lawsuits.[20] Greenberger kept *Haffer*
alive by amending the suit to claim discrimination under the Constitution's Fourteenth Amendment and the Pennsylvania ERA. OCR closed
or restricted sixty-five Title IX investigations, twenty-eight of them in
athletics.[21] The Reagan administration cut OCR's budget by a third.[22]

The *Grove City College* decision affected more than Title IX. Because the
law's first 37 words copied Title VI, as did the Age Discrimination Act and
Section 504 regarding disability discrimination, the ruling eviscerated all
those civil rights in education, narrowly limiting complaints based on sex,
race, color, national origin, age, or disability to only those departments or
programs directly receiving federal funding instead of applying nondiscrimination prohibitions to entire schools.[23]

That swath of destruction affecting all the civil rights laws may have been what saved them in the end. It compressed existing but scattered coalition work among the various civil rights groups into a focal point demanding attention from all of them. Before *Grove City College*, Reagan attacked civil rights in so many ways that he divided the energies of potential allies. Black groups fought proposed changes to the Voting Rights Act. Hispanic groups battled proposed immigration legislation.[24] Mostly white women's groups defended Title IX and abortion rights, though they also put considerable effort into public benefits and other topics affecting low-income women, a disproportionate share of whom were women of color.

These groups had supported each other in these issues while devoting most of their energies to their core campaigns. But *Grove City College* demanded a concerted effort to create a remedy the only way possible—through an act of Congress.

Greenberger and Kohn at the NWLC drafted a bill with Judith Lichtman of the Women's Legal Defense Fund that they and allies took to various congressmembers. Ralph Neas, executive director of the Leadership Conference on Civil Rights, led the campaign's strategic planning. By consensus they agreed not to try to improve on the civil rights laws, because that could spur hostile amendments or increase the risk of defeat. They were just trying to get back to what had been the status quo. The new bill—the Civil Rights Restoration Act—simply clarified that the "recipient" of federal funds in these laws would be defined as the entire educational institution.

"The major strategy is to keep all the protected classes together as much as possible and to oppose any and all amendments, friendly or unfriendly. We are showing a lot of self-restraint (for example, in not strengthening Title IX by amending Title VI)" to include the prohibition of sex discrimination, while also opposing hostile amendments against school busing, abortion rights, or anything else, Lichtman wrote.[25]

NCWGE leaders arranged press conferences, urged their members to contact Congress, testified at hearings, and accompanied sports celebrities to lobby senators for the Civil Rights Restoration Act. To stoke lobbying efforts for the Act, a relay race carried a torch from the Capitol through

Baltimore and Wilmington, Delaware, to NOW's annual convention in Philadelphia.

Greenberger studied hard the night before she escorted tennis superstar Martina Navratilova to the Hill, ready to answer any questions or refute concerns about the bill. The homework wasn't necessary, though; the senators were interested in only one thing. One after another pulled his tennis racket out and asked Navratilova, "Could you check my grip?"

On the other side, administration officials rallied opposing campaigns coordinated by Christian TV evangelists. They tried to divide the bill's backers, saying the administration might accept a modified bill that restored only Title IX, not the other civil rights laws.[26] Within three months of the *Grove City College* decision, a bill to overturn the Supreme Court's ruling passed the House but got blocked in the Senate.[27]

Title IX was on critical-care life support in 1987 when former Rep. Edith Green died on April 21 at age seventy-seven. None of the major newspaper obituaries mentioned one of her greatest achievements, Title IX.

Democrats regained control of both houses of Congress in 1987 and reintroduced the Civil Rights Restoration Act (S. 557). Women's advocates for years had fought off attempts to use the act to weaken Title IX by allowing schools to refuse to provide abortion services. The original 1975 regulations for Title IX required college campus health services to provide contraception and abortion services because that's what then secretary of education Caspar Weinberger felt was required under the Supreme Court's 1973 decision in *Roe v. Wade* that legalized abortion.

In 1987, though, Democratic leaders calculated that they finally could muster a veto-proof majority to pass a Civil Rights Restoration Act if it made abortion services on campus optional instead of a right. Some of the women's allies in the civil rights coalition went along with it because they were tired of waiting for the other civil rights laws to be restored. Whether women's advocates liked it or not, Congress would pass the act with wording allowing schools to refuse to provide abortion services, congressional leaders informed them.[28] Women didn't have the clout to stop them.

NOW declared to the end that its 175,000 members would not work for a bill that trades off one set of women's rights for another.[29] But Greenberger and Lichtman, facing the inevitable, worked night and day behind the scenes to mitigate the act's damage, getting friendly legislators to insert wording saying students could not be expelled, denied services, or otherwise discriminated against because they were pregnant or had an abortion.

Congress passed the bill in early 1988. Reagan vetoed it on March 16 but six days later the Senate and House overrode his veto.[30]

Greenberger never again accepted a strategy of just trying to regain a status quo in civil rights. Any compromise in that scenario would mean a loss of a previously protected right. Civil rights advocates must always try to push the envelope to expand rights, not just regain them, she urged anyone who would listen. Her new outlook bore fruit in the Civil Rights Act of 1991, which primarily aimed to overturn some very restrictive Supreme Court decisions limiting plaintiffs' ability to sue and get relief for employment discrimination under Title VII of the 1964 Civil Rights Act. The main purpose of the 1991 Civil Rights Act was to restore the status quo, but Greenberger and allies also pushed for the law to include giving women a right that other groups already had—the right to win money awards for damages in successful suits for sex discrimination at work. Though Congress added caps to the damage awards that applied to sex discrimination but not other forms of discrimination, women gained new leverage in fighting workplace discrimination under Title VII.

With Title IX back in force in 1988, Temple University settled the *Haffer* suit in September 1988 with promises of more athletic scholarship money and a monitored five-year program to improve women's athletics.[31] Rollin Haffer paid a price during the eight-year-long legal ordeal. Professors became unfriendly to her, Temple's football players tried to intimidate her, and she had trouble getting a teaching job after graduation. But she ordered a specialty license plate for her car that read "TITLE IX." Former PSEW staffer Margaret Dunkle also drove with a "TITLE IX" license plate in a different state. Sandler got one that read "WNDR WM."

Elsewhere, some women who took a less confrontational approach in athletics made incremental gains. At Fresno State, Diane Milutinovich had switched from coaching to be an administrator in the athletics department. She tried to go along to get along, giving her all to both the women's and men's athletics programs.

In her off-duty hours one weekend, she knelt and pushed a rolled strip of sod to flatten it, immersed in the smell of soil and sweat. Milutinovich took hold of one end and another volunteer grabbed the other. They pulled and tugged to stretch the green strip into place until its edges and corners aligned with the sod next to it. Dirt covered them and all the volunteers on the field at Bulldog Stadium. They just laughed at their mess.

Football Coach Jim Sweeney had put out a call for help: the field at Bulldog Stadium needed resodding but the university couldn't afford the installation. So they bought the sod and gathered volunteers on a Saturday—administrators including Milutinovich, men's and women's coaches, secretaries, everyone. They loved their Bulldogs.

She helped the athletics department in any way needed, such as resodding, working the concession stands, taking tickets, selling game programs, raising money. The athletic director promoted her to director of women's athletics in 1981. Part of her job was to know and uphold Title IX requirements. When anyone muttered that the law was a drain on the budget, she'd say, "The athletic budget is financed by taxes, gate receipts, and student funds, and I think half of that comes from women. But I would not like to see the men lose anything."[32]

She was the only woman in the room at most administrators' meetings. Milutinovich quickly realized that she had to be up on everything regarding men's sports—their budgets, what other schools were doing, and so on—in order for others to listen to her about women's sports. She developed a reputation as a know-it-all, but she had to be one. When Fresno State created an Athletic Corporation in 1982 (the only California State University with one), she also learned the intricacies of its white, male board, because all of the university's sports funding got channeled through the Corporation—another obstacle for women.

A month after OCR's 1979 Policy Interpretation convinced them that women's sports would be growing, NCAA members decided to start taking over women's competitions. The already weakened Association for Intercollegiate Athletics for Women (AIAW) folded on June 30, 1982.[33] The male model of athletics won out: intense and exclusionary competition, economic stratification, and less emphasis on academics. The system dwells in an artificially narrow zero-sum universe of winners and losers, where someone's gain is seen as someone else's loss.

In 1980 OCR issued an interim athletics manual for Title IX for investigators in its regional offices, and in 1982 released a follow-up memo with
further guidance.[34] Then came *Grove City College*, but just as Title IX
didn't change everything in athletics, neither did the evisceration of Title
IX. Popular support for women's athletics was higher than ever. Wom-
en won a record number of medals in the 1984 Olympic Games in Los
Angeles.[35]

At Fresno State, women's athletics didn't lose much in the 1980s despite
changes in policy, while the men's program gained. The university spent
$2.2 million ($5.6 million in 2020 dollars) to redesign the baseball stadium. Budgets for football and men's basketball skyrocketed.

Milutinovich stuck to her low-key strategy. In budget meetings with
senior management she'd ask, "Well, what are the men getting?" and try
to get something similar for women. Always, she had to contend with
the myth that revenue-producing sports were sacrosanct because they
funded the other sports. At Fresno State and nearly all other colleges and
universities, football, baseball, and men's basketball did generate revenue (via ticket sales and other means), but never so much as to even
cover their own expenses. Milutinovich knew better than to challenge
the "revenue-producing" line of thinking in her early years there, though.
Rock the boat, but not too much. Be a team player. At least California had
a state version of Title IX, so she still could point to legal imperatives to do
the right thing.[36] Sixteen states enacted laws similar to Title IX by 1985,
and more after that.

As long as things were moving in the right direction, Milutinovich was
okay with incremental progress.[37] Be reasonable, she urged her colleagues.
It's not like she was asking for things that some other women administrators were demanding—people like Donna Lopiano at the University
of Texas or Linda Estes at the University of New Mexico. She wasn't as
"radical" as them. Milutinovich would accept incremental change as long
as things moved forward. This "I'm not radical" strategy was also a favorite
of groups like WEAL and the Women's Sports Foundation.[38]

The collegial atmosphere in Fresno State's Athletics Department thinned
in 1987 when the director left and was replaced by a man less open to
women's sports.

Outside of athletics, Fresno State students held their first "Take Back the Night" march in 1980 to protest sexual violence. At Yale, a 1981 Take Back the Night rally featured minority voices including poet and play-wright Ntozake Shange, Dai Thompson of Differently Abled Women, and Gloria Anzaldúa, co-editor of a 1981 book that explored overlapping oppressions, *This Bridge Called My Back: Writings by Radical Women of Color.*[39] Take Back the Night became annual fixtures at many schools, sometimes drawing harassers.

At Princeton's first Take Back the Night march in April 1987, around thirty men met marchers with a sign reading, "We can rape whoever we want." Some shouted threats: "Get raped!" "Fucking beat them up!" "Take back the dykes!" One pulled down his pants, yelling, "You can suck my dick!" Two of the men drove a car into two of the marchers. Before the march, the university's provost had told Women's Center leaders in meetings that "Princeton men don't assault women. Princeton men are gentlemen." One of the marchers videorecorded the event on a camcorder; administrative denials wouldn't work this time. Newspapers all over the country publicized these attacks.[40]

The movements against sexual harassment and violence that mush-roomed in the 1970s grew into a towering presence in the 1980s that no longer could be ignored. An OCR memo in August 1981 made clear that Title IX covers sexual harassment (understood to include sexual violence) and offered guidance on grievance procedures, the handling of complaints, and how to conduct investigations, though it's unclear how much the memo was read outside OCR.[41]

PSEW's *On Campus with Women* shared dozens of news items about sexual harassment on campus.[42] The first legal symposium on sexual harassment convened in 1981 in Washington, DC.[43] Legal and academic journals published entire issues dedicated to sexual harassment. Social scientists increased research on the prevalence and perceptions of sexual harassment, but they rarely considered the effects on racial and ethnic groups, LGBT people, and other minority groups.[44]

Complaints to the Equal Employment Opportunity Commission (EEOC) about sexual harassment at work increased as Reagan cut EEOC's staff, so unresolved complaints doubled in the 1980s.[45] In schools, administrators often delayed addressing students' complaints of sexual harassment or assault until they graduated, then dropped the matter. Backlash lawsuits by faculty accused of sexually harassing students increased.[46] Phyllis Schlafly, testifying before Congress, blamed feminists for making "a Federal case out of the problem of bosses pinching their secretaries."[47]

In the fall of 1980, as the appellate judges were denying the *Alexander v. Yale* appeal, Pamela Price learned she was pregnant. During law school she'd fallen in love with a man who could be a lot of fun, but he was a complicated man who'd had a stressful childhood and carried a lot of personal baggage. In between the good times with him there were other times. He'd explode with anger. Eventually that escalated. He hit her. Price hit him back. They'd had a few physical fights. Once he threw her around an apartment.

She wasn't sure whether or not to have the baby as a single mother. She didn't want to marry the father or even live with him. On the other hand, she was on course to finish law school before the baby arrived and was set to do a fourth year at Berkeley to earn a second degree, this one a master's degree in jurisprudence and social policy. How hard could that be, compared with law school? She figured she could pursue her master's *and* take care of her baby.

The pregnancy made her physically miserable for much of her last semester in law school. At least it qualified her for student family housing in the low row houses used by the military in World War II that were converted to student use in nearby Albany. Price gave birth to a daughter in June 1981.

A few months after her baby's birth, they came home from church and met the father at Price's apartment. Neither of the adults was having a good day, Price recalled. They started arguing. His moods could escalate suddenly. She told him to leave. Instead, he flew into one of his rages and verbally threatened her. Price had more than her safety to consider; she had an infant. Price called the Albany Police. When they arrived the officers immediately started talking to him, not her. The police asked Price to step outside. Her daughter was still in the home. By this point the child's father wanted to leave. The police decided he should take the infant with him.

Price stormed back inside. "No, you can't take my kid! You cannot, nobody, *he* cannot have my baby. You cannot give him my baby." The police arrested Price and took her to Albany Police Station.

A friend picked her up when police released her late that night. The next day Price called the home of the father's mother, where she figured he would have taken the child. Sure enough, she had the baby, and Price fetched her home.

Price didn't have the close-knit Black networks that sustained her in New Haven. Berkeley had fewer Black students and no solid connections with the city's Black residents. Before her arrest, she had joined the Black American Law Students Association and, with local activists, co-founded the short-lived Bay Area Defense Committee for Battered Women. Price and other members had helped publicize and raise funds for Cassandra Peten, a local Black woman charged with killing her abusive boyfriend. They accompanied her to court, only to be disappointed when Peten's attorney convinced her to take a plea deal that sent her to prison.

Price refused to plead guilty and be punished for protecting herself and her baby.

It would be a couple months before her jury trial on a charge of resisting arrest. In the meantime, Price strapped her baby into a backpack and just kept going, graduating in 1982. She started working at the Bayview Hunters Point Foundation's Community Defenders office in San Francisco, doing criminal defense.

Jurors at her trial saw a Yale graduate with a law degree and a graduate degree from Berkeley being prosecuted on a flimsy pretext. They acquitted her. Afterward, they shared with her their reactions during the trial. "What the hell?" they thought. "Why are you trying to destroy this young woman?" they told her later. That's what district attorneys do, she replied, especially to Black women. And it's a reason people of color don't call the police.

The case behind her, Price walked away from civil rights and criminal defense work in 1984, disillusioned with the disconnect between law and justice. Besides, she had to provide for her daughter as a single mom. She moved to Berkeley and worked for small firms doing real estate litigation and legal malpractice defense. The work taught her the intricacies of civil litigation.

For many people of color in the 1980s, survival was the goal. The policies of Presidents Reagan and George H.W. Bush shifted economic gains to the rich and cut assistance to the poor. They weakened civil rights protections, giving discrimination greater leeway. They exacerbated racially disparate prison sentencing through practices such as imposing longer sentences for users of crack cocaine, who were more likely to be Black, than of powder cocaine, favored by white users. These policies fueled mass incarceration, especially of people of color in a burgeoning prison industrial complex.

Sandler's work was more stressful than it used to be, too, though not in a life-and-death way. Funding for PSEW diminished and Reagan's attacks on civil rights seemed never-ending. Even so, she finally quit smoking on her twenty-second try.[48] She regained her joie de vivre as time passed after her divorce. At a NCWGE meeting in August 1983, members asked each other who had contacted the *Washington Post* to generate a surprisingly positive editorial about Title IX. No one had. "Justice triumphs!" Sandler blurted.

She loved constantly traveling the country to speak, consult, and listen to faculty, staff, and students at colleges and universities. She conveyed what she learned to her staff of four to six white women who stayed at PSEW for most of the 1980s, with whom she grew exceptionally close. They celebrated together—birthdays, degrees earned, children born. They snuck out on shopping trips, lingered over lunch to process personal crises, and built lifelong friendships.

Attending an Aspen Institute seminar for nineteen executives (four of them women), Sandler noticed that women frequently got interrupted when they spoke. She started charting the gender of interrupters or those being interrupted. As pleasantly as she could, Sandler shared her findings with men in the class: men interrupted women twice as often as they interrupted each other, and in a qualitatively different way. Her chart couldn't be accurate, the men said. Surely, she had misunderstood. But the next morning, no one interrupted the women. The behavior was changeable! Now that Title IX barred most overt forms of discrimination against girls and women, she decided to do a paper on more subtle barriers to education.[49]

She and her staff named these less overt discriminations "a chilly climate," and in February 1982 published a twenty-two-page paper, *The Classroom Climate: A Chilly One for Women?*[50] Over the next eight years PSEW distributed close to 28,000 copies within higher education and got requests for 25,000 more.

The paper described thirty often unnoticed behaviors and their effects, drawing on research and anecdotes. Women were more likely to be singled out or ignored in class. Faculty (men and women, though most faculty were men) made eye contact more often with men students, engaged them in dialogue, and used a tone conveying interest rather than impatience. They waited longer for men to answer a question and picked men more often for course activities like field trips. Adult tutors working with elementary students were more likely to tell high-achieving boys that they were competent but tell high-achieving girls that the assignment was easy. Primary school teachers gave boys instructions on what to do and let them figure it out for themselves but showed girls how to do something, doing part of the work for them. They praised the intellectual quality of boys' work and criticized their lack of neatness but did the opposite for girls.

Even women in college rated scholarly articles higher if they believed men wrote them. They doubted their abilities more than men doubted theirs. During their college years, women showed a "surprising" decline in academic and career aspirations. The climate affected men, too, reinforcing negative views of women and hampering men's ability to relate to them as equals.

Plenty of disparities were not so subtle, like disparaging comments and sexual humiliation aimed, almost always, at women. One professor, for instance, interrupted a graduate student as she publicly discussed her work to ask if she had freckles all over her body.

The paper offered 114 recommendations for specific types of administrators, faculty, students, and professional organizations to help warm up the chilly climate.

PSEW followed that with a twenty-page paper two years later on similar problems in out-of-classroom environments such as lab teams and work-study jobs. A section of the paper discussed "Groups of Women Who May Be Especially Affected," including older, minority, or disabled women and the "double devaluation" they experience. Yet another paper in 1986 found similar treatment of campus women besides undergraduates: *The Campus Climate Revisited: Chilly for Women Faculty, Administrators, and Graduate Students.*[51]

The chilly climate papers were shared widely and reported in the media, but Sandler drew even more attention with a different topic—sexual assault.

The most disturbing stories Sandler heard on campus visits were of group rapes, usually at fraternities. Students at some schools told Sandler that gang rapes happened almost every week. Fraternity party flyers advertised the coming "gang bang" or "pulling train," which consisted of a line of men taking turns raping.[52]

By January 1985 she collected fifty confirmed episodes of "party gang rapes," finally settling on the term "gang rapes."

At Stanford, Duke, Brown, UCLA, Michigan State, and other universities, women were finding the courage to speak out about rapes, often without knowing about similar actions elsewhere. When they did speak out, other students frequently shunned and harassed them, and rapists seldom faced serious consequences from law enforcement or their colleges.

Prosecutors dismissed charges against one of two Sigma Phi Epsilon fraternity members at the University of North Carolina charged in 1987 with rape; the other pleaded "no contest" and received a two-year suspended sentence, probation, and a $200 fine. A Black psychiatrist trivialized a gang rape by eight men students at Missouri University of Science and Technology by claiming it was a "cultural behavior."[53] Occasionally, if rape accusations were upheld, the rapists might be required to seek counseling, or to read materials about rape and write an essay, or the fraternity would be barred from hosting parties for a time.

The media jumped when PSEW published the twenty-page paper *Campus Gang Rape: Party Games?* in November 1985.[54] "These women at these parties were being preyed on; it was being done very intentionally," Sandler told reporters.[55] Requests for her to speak on campuses spiked.

If the population of fraternities at that time constituted a state, it would be a very small state with about half the population of Vermont. "If, in a state that size, 50 confirmed gang rapes took place within two or three years, impartial observers might begin to wonder about the place," a University of New Hampshire official said.[56]

The gang rapes followed a clear pattern: A young woman drinks alcohol or takes drugs at a fraternity party, leaving her unable to protest effectively or at all against sexual assault. The men take this as assent or even an invitation; between two and a dozen of them rape her. They don't consider it rape, but she knows it is. She's unlikely to report it to police because of stigma (through blaming the victim) and the unlikelihood of prosecution. If she reports it to the college or university, there's little chance that administrators will support her or punish the men even though in most states the men committed a felony. Rape survivors were likely to doubt their own judgment, have trouble trusting again, and be slandered as liars if they spoke up. Many transferred or dropped out.

One woman who decided not to drop out found herself surrounded by her rapists as she walked to class one day; they were trying to intimidate her. At a separate large university, a student newspaper reported a fraternity gang rape; letters to the editor poured in, but most of them were indignant about the negative publicity the frat was receiving. Several dozen women dared to march along another campus's Fraternity Row with signs: "It's still rape, even when you're rich, white, and in a frat," one read. Frat members leaned out from windows and porches to taunt them with chants of "Gang rape. Gang rape," or "Let's rape her," and "I'll take that one."

The *Campus Gang Rape* paper offered 105 recommendations to address the problem, plus a page dispelling myths about rape and a list of resources.

The PSEW papers on sexual harassment and rape weren't perfect, of course. Sandler and her colleagues had their own blind spots. "Men can drink with their friends and not worry about being taken advantage of," the *Gang Rape* paper stated, not yet having the data on sexual assaults against men.[57] But the essential information in PSEW's papers overcame the flaws.

Any attention from college officials usually went to quid pro quo harassment of students by professors, not peer harassment. Fresno State had no Title IX coordinator known to students or faculty and no direct way for students to file a grievance about sexual harassment, both violations of Title IX. Complaints got lost in the bureaucracy until Fresno State appointed a

Sexual Harassment Designee for Students in 1985. Of the six cases investigated in spring 1988 by the designee, all of them alleged sexual harassment by male professors against five women and one man.

But the deck was stacked against students. Fresno State had no policy on professors "dating" students; administrators left it to "the professor's better judgment." It wasn't enough to report sexual harassment or even that the student told the professor "No." There had to be proof that they said "No"—perhaps a witness or a diary or a log. Often, the student felt there was no alternative but to drop out of a class or school. Lack of Title IX enforcement, in other words, denied them their right to an education.

Activists on multiple campuses tried many tactics to address the problem of sexual violence by students and faculty. They stenciled messages in school colors on campus walkways: "One Out of Every Five Women Will Be Raped." "A Woman Was Raped Here."[58] At Yale's first Rape Awareness Week in 1986, organizers taped a large X on campus sites where women were sexually assaulted. At one Michigan college, they took over administrative offices to protest a lack of attention to rape on campus. Issues of PSEW's newsletter, *On Campus with Women*, included dozens of items about conferences, talks, and materials about rape and new campus centers for sexual assault.[59]

In the first national survey of sexual aggression on college campuses, 27.5 percent of 6,159 women at thirty-two colleges and universities said they'd been raped or survived attempted rape.[60] Researchers concluded with a message that women in the anti-rape movement had been hammering for more than a decade: "Rape is much more prevalent than previously believed." Many studies in ensuing decades affirmed that a quarter to a fifth of women in college experience sexual violence.

Separate studies began to suggest that sex discrimination disproportionately targeted more vulnerable groups—people of color, people with disabilities, poor or immigrant students, LGBT students. Sandler's PSEW mentioned these convergences in its papers. Congress expanded WEEA's purpose in 1984 to also "provide educational equity for women and girls who suffer multiple discrimination, bias, or stereotyping based on sex and on race, ethnic origin, disability, or age."[61]

PEER created state-by-state "report cards" on progress in equitable education in 1979, 1982, 1985, and 1986, but they lacked tools to discern these overlaps. "Unfortunately, almost none of the available data are broken out by both race and sex and almost no information is available on the status of disabled women and girls," PEER reported. "It is virtually impossible, therefore, to provide a comprehensive state-by-state analysis of the status of women of color or of women with disabilities in education, thus limiting policymakers' ability to respond to many of the most pressing equity concerns facing women in education in the 1980s."[62]

Feminists—often led by women of color—increasingly grappled with the concept that overlapping oppressions create a set of problems that are more than the sum of the parts. Dividing feminist and antiracist work into separate channels, for example, marginalizes the experiences of women of color, for whom these are not discrete, entirely separable issues. That diminishes the likelihood that proposed solutions will help and puts antidiscrimination movements in competition with each other. In 1983 the first Black women's studies reader, *All the Women Are White, All the Blacks Are Men, but Some of Us Are Brave*, explored some of this thinking.[63] The next year, two more books built on multidimensional analyses of oppression: Audre Lorde's *Sister Outsider* and bell hooks's *Feminist Theory: From Margin to Center*.

Law professor Kimberlé Crenshaw put a name to the multidimensionality in 1989. She called it "intersectionality," a conceptual window that made it easier to see the multiple institutional barriers to fairness for society's most vulnerable people. Everyone will benefit, Crenshaw argued, by "addressing the needs and problems of those who are most disadvantaged" rather than trying to address one discrimination at a time, and by "placing those who currently are marginalized in the center."[64] She and others in the 1990s developed these ideas into a Critical Race Feminist Legal Theory that started to spread through academia and legal circles, gaining momentum in the 2000s.

In the broader society, though, entrenched organizations tended still to focus on one discrimination while acknowledging other types of discrimination. Sandler's PSEW, for instance, mentioned in its papers the multiple oppressions targeting vulnerable groups of women but never really centered them. The divisions of antidiscrimination work based on race, sex, age, LGBT orientation, disability status, and other factors remained. Ossified by omissions in the Civil Rights Act of 1964 and all the separate civil rights laws since, the different branches nevertheless formed coalitions and inspired each other.

Sandler sat near the back of a standing-room-only session at a conference on "The Constitution and Women" in 1988, the two hundredth anniversary of the Constitution's ratification. She'd had an exciting few days in Atlanta as one of the invited speakers. She'd met Coretta Scott King at a party for the speakers; the festive group even sang together, a memory she would cherish. Even the best conferences get tiring after a day or two, though. She felt lucky to have a seat as the current session got underway and latecomers kept coming in the door.

"Oh, my god," the woman next to Sandler said under her breath. "It's Rosa Parks." The diminutive Parks scanned the room. "Mrs. Parks!" The woman waved at her. "Please take my seat."

The elderly civil rights icon thanked her and settled into the chair next to Sandler, who sat tongue-tied. What could she say to thank Parks for all she'd done for civil rights? And for inspiring so many others like herself to fight for fairness? This was her chance. Would saying something be an imposition? Should she say anything at all?

She hardly had time to think about it when Parks's head nodded, then nodded again in a slow-motion roll that landed against Sandler's right shoulder. Parks fell fast asleep. Sandler sat very, very still for the next fifty minutes. The least she could do, she felt, was help Rosa Parks rest.

As the session ended, she gently moved her body to wake up Parks. It wasn't clear whether Parks knew she'd napped on her shoulder. Sandler said nothing, but she smiled.[65]

Sandler oversaw PSEW's release of two papers in 1987 and 1988 that included sections highlighting in more detail the increased rate of sexual harassment for subsets of women—Black, Hispanic, Asian American, Jewish, and physically heavy women. For the first time PSEW acknowledged that men also harass men, especially ones they think are gay. PSEW released the twelve-page *"Friends" Raping Friends: Could It Happen to You?* in early 1987, followed by the fifteen-page *Peer Harassment: Hassles for Women on Campus* in September 1988.[66]

Sandler's bosses were not happy with these subjects, Association of American Colleges (AAC) president John Chandler told Sandler. They'd rather she focus on college curricula, pedagogy, and women's studies. Sandler and her team stopped writing papers on rape and sexual harassment, but the issues didn't die.[67]

In November 1988, around three hundred students at the State University of New York at Binghamton staged a thirty-seven-hour sit-in to express concern about sex crimes and campus prejudice based on sex or ethnicity.[68] Thirteen months later, a man dressed in a hunting outfit rushed into a University of Montreal classroom in the engineering school with a rifle and yelled in French, "You're all a bunch of feminists!" He shot fifteen people dead, fourteen of them women, and injured twelve before killing himself.[69]

A phone call at work surprised Sandler in April 1990. The AAC's board of directors wanted her at an executive meeting underway that day. She climbed the narrow, carpeted stairs from PSEW's wing through the warren of halls to the boardroom. Perhaps this had something to do with her recent conversation with the president, she thought. You're traveling too much, he'd told her. Sandler had explained that it gave PSEW publicity, which helped sell materials and bring in revenue and grants. He didn't contradict her, so she figured that was that.

Sandler took a seat at the long oval table. You're being fired, they told her. AAC would take over PSEW and focus more on women's studies.

Had she heard right?[70] It felt Kafkaesque. She'd never had a job performance evaluation. Sandler knew that she generated more publicity, produced more papers, and met with more AAC members each year than the other half-dozen executives there combined (all men).

She could stay at AAC another year until June 30, 1991, the board said, under a grant to develop a prototype Chilly Climate Workshop. Sandler was sixty-three. It would be hard, if not impossible, to find similar full-time work at her level. The next week, her ninety-year-old mother, Ivy, became quite ill. Within three months, she died.

Her self-esteem battered, her heart broken, Sandler let people know about her dismissal when she visited campuses in her final year at AAC. Their outrage cheered her. One of them described to Sandler how she had called AAC's board chair to protest and was told that Sandler had worked there for a long time, was making a lot of money, and the AAC had to cut expenses. A lawyer that Sandler consulted called this age discrimination. She sued.[71] In the process of discovery, Sandler confirmed another suspicion—she was underpaid relative to the other executive employees.

A storm of angry letters and phone calls hit the AAC as word spread of Sandler's firing. Academics quit AAC boards and committees in protest; some started a campaign to get her reinstated. The AAC's leadership agreed to review its decision, then stuck to its dismissal.[72]

Sandler's attorney convinced her to accept a financial settlement. She wasn't allowed to discuss the amount, but she could smile. And there were other things to look forward to. She had a new grandchild—her first—with another on the way.

As the decade turned, WEAL dissolved in 1989, unable to maintain enough volunteers. PEER followed soon after. Rep. Patsy Mink returned to Congress after fourteen years away, rejoining the House Education and Labor Committee. A generation of students born after Title IX reached college age.

Sandler sent thank-you notes to the 116 supporters she knew of who'd written letters on her behalf. "It is the end of an era," she wrote.

8

Christine, Jackie, Rebecca, Nicole, Alida, LaShonda

1991–1999

PAMELA PRICE STARTED A NEW ERA OF HER OWN IN 1991. SHE OPENED HER own litigation practice in Oakland. The next year, she married for the first time—to Vernon Crawley, affirmative action officer for Marin County, California.[1] They formed a blended family with her daughter and his five children. As a lawyer, Price was successful enough that she later bought an Oakland building, where she painted the office walls purple. She stood out in meetings and courtrooms, with a colorful flair for fashion down to her shoes and fingernails.

Price expected to do much the same kind of work she'd done at other firms—real estate litigation and legal malpractice defense. A Georgia teenager named Christine Franklin helped change the course of her work.

In 1986 North Gwinnett (Georgia) High School economics teacher and coach Andrew Hill began asking Franklin, a sophomore, about her sexual experiences with her boyfriend. He started calling her at home and forced kisses on her in the school parking lot. In 1987, he interrupted a class and asked the teacher to excuse Franklin; Hill took her to a private office and raped her, Christine later said, and he raped her on two other occasions after that.[2]

Other students had complained to multiple school officials about Hill's harassment. Christine told her mother, who told school and district officials. The school's band director urged Christine to keep things quiet to avoid negative publicity. The Franklins complained to the Office for Civil Rights (OCR); Hill and the principal left the school, which adopted a grievance policy, so OCR was satisfied. The Franklins sued the school district in 1988 and demanded something unusual under Title IX—$11 million to compensate for Christine's suffering.

Before *Franklin v. Gwinnett County Public Schools*, the most a plaintiff could expect under Title IX was a court order for the school to do better, and only if the plaintiff was still in school. But financial claims don't expire when students graduate, and big money means real consequences.[3] Title VI allows damage awards, and so should Title IX, the National Women's Law Center (NWLC) and twenty other organizations argued in an amicus brief in support of *Franklin v. Gwinnett*.[4]

Gwinnett officials disagreed, and the George H.W. Bush administration backed them.[5] Franklin was twenty-two years old and married by the time the case reached the Supreme Court. On February 26, 1992, it ruled unanimously that courts could order monetary awards under Title IX for harm done.[6] Eventually, Gwinnett settled with Franklin out of court for an undisclosed amount.

Title IX lawsuits spiked; there were twenty-four court decisions alone from the end of 1992 to 1995.[7] The *Franklin* case caught Price's attention. So did a controversy involving a different Hill—not Andrew, but Anita, who focused national attention on sexual harassment during the U.S. Senate's consideration of a Supreme Court nominee.

President Bush nominated Clarence Thomas, Reagan's former OCR and Equal Employment Opportunity Commission (EEOC) director, for an opening on the Supreme Court in 1991. Stories emerged from former employees who said he sexually harassed them. The Senate Judiciary Committee had no intention of letting them speak at his confirmation hearing.

Women in the House of Representatives started making one-minute speeches on October 8 demanding that the Senate delay the nomination vote. Five of them, including Rep. Patsy Mink, spontaneously marched over to the Senate to demand that the women be allowed to testify. News photos showed the group ascending the Capitol steps. Senators finally agreed to let a Black law professor, Anita Hill, testify but they refused the testimony of three others who could attest to Thomas's harassment of EEOC employees.[8]

Television coverage of Hill's testimony on October 11, 1991, riveted the nation. Members of the all-white, all-men Senate panel called Hill a liar, a lesbian, and a nymphomaniac; no one on the panel (not even Democrats) defended her.[9] Thomas, a Black man, during his testimony angrily denied Hill's allegations, attacked his accusers, and cast himself as the victim of racist political harassment.[10] The hearing was a "high-tech lynching for uppity Blacks," he said. The Senate rushed the process to a vote, confirming Thomas 52–48 to a lifetime seat on the Supreme Court over the vociferous objections of women across the country.

Callers deluged their elected representatives' offices with angry, tearful accounts of sexual harassment that happened to them or their daughters. A letter in the *New York Times* signed by sixteen thousand Black women "in defense of ourselves" protested the racist and sexist treatment of Hill by Thomas and the discriminatory system behind him.[11] A record number of complaints poured into the EEOC about workplace sexual harassment.[12] The month after Thomas's confirmation, Marcia Greenberger and other women's advocates got Congress to pass the Civil Rights Act of 1991, allowing women who sue for sexual harassment at work to win financial damages, as workers who faced racial discrimination could do. Before that, someone who harassed a woman of color at work could avoid paying for damages by saying the harassment was based on sex, not race; white women couldn't win damages at all.

Accusations of harassment in government, the military, and education forced some senators to resign or not seek reelection. Voters elected an unprecedented twenty-eight women to Congress in 1992, which became known as the Year of the Woman, though women still were only 10 percent of Congress.[13] Voters also replaced President Bush with Democrat Bill Clinton. Before the decade ended Clinton would be impeached for lying to Congress in an investigation of his own sexual harassment of an intern.

After Anita Hill's testimony, potential clients inundated Pamela Price with stories of sexual harassment.

In California, Berkeley Unified School District refused to remove a white music teacher who sexually abused two preteen, mixed-race sisters, their mother told Price. It started during Christmas break from school in 1987. The mother, Patricia H., and the music teacher, Charles Hamilton, had been dating. They all took a trip together to play in the snow at Lake Tahoe—Patricia H., twelve-year-old Jackie, ten-year-old Rebecca, and

Hamilton. A couple weeks after they returned, Jackie came to her mother, upset. A naked Hamilton had climbed into bed with her in their Berkeley home and rubbed against her, she said. Before that, at Tahoe, he forced her to handle his genitals and made nasty comments to her.[14]

Patricia confronted Hamilton. He denied doing anything in Tahoe; he "stroked" and "tickled" Jackie in Berkeley, he admitted, but alcohol and cocaine impaired his judgment, he said. Patricia stopped seeing him.

Her daughters could not avoid him at school, though. Hamilton taught in Berkeley's only high school and rotated through some of its other schools. Patricia tried unsuccessfully to get district officials to help. She sent Jackie to live with relatives in Minnesota in August 1988 to attend eighth grade there.

Patricia went to the Berkeley police, who charged Hamilton with misdemeanor sexual molestation but dismissed charges when he agreed to get substance abuse counseling and psychotherapy. The school district put him on leave and the state ultimately suspended his teacher credentials for three months.

The younger child, Rebecca, said Hamilton hadn't molested her, but the fifth grader became a different student at school. She had earned healthy report cards until then. Suddenly she was easily distracted, unorganized, and falling behind in homework, her teacher said.

On July 20, 1990, Patricia found a note that Rebecca had left for her: "Mom, Charles did sexually abuse me can we talk about it through letters." Hamilton had molested her around ten days before they all went to Lake Tahoe, Rebecca told her. Police declined to file charges. Over the next two years Jackie returned from Minnesota, tried commuting to school in a neighboring city, then enrolled in Berkeley High and couldn't take music classes because Hamilton was there. Her behavior and grades got worse. Sometimes she ran away from campus when Hamilton was there, or didn't go to school at all. A therapist described her behavior as symptomatic of post-traumatic stress caused by sexual molestation.

"They are both afraid of him," Pamela Price said when she sued the Berkeley district on behalf of the family in November 1992, Jackie's senior year.

It wasn't a question of whether or not Hamilton had abused the girls; the district attorney and state already concluded he had. Title IX isn't about assigning guilt or punishment anyway; it's about addressing conditions that unfairly block or disrupt the educations of students because of their sex. By leaving Hamilton in school, Berkeley had tolerated a hostile environment, the suit alleged. The family paid the price in psychological harm, lack of access to a normal education, and the costs of transferring in and out of other schools, programs, and counseling, Price said.

She escorted Patricia H. and Jackie into the marble-lined foyer of a tall steel-and-glass building to the Harrison Street offices of the lawyers defending the school district, a block from Oakland's Lake Merritt. They rode the elevator to the thirteenth floor. Ushered into a meeting room, they sat opposite a handful of men in suits (all white except one Black lawyer) who would be taking Jackie's deposition in the lawsuit against Berkeley Unified.

The deposition turned sour quickly. One of the men started asking Jackie about her attraction to boys. Price knew instantly where this was headed: blaming the victim, manipulating personal history to claim she's a slut or that what happened was consensual. It plays into widely held myths of girls and women, especially Black women, as promiscuous and vengeful liars. It's a major reason so few people report sexual assault.[15] Price remembered her own harsh deposition in *Alexander v. Yale*; she vowed never to let that happen to her clients.

"Excuse me?!" she interrupted immediately. "Really? Are you really asking that question?" Everyone looked at her. "You really think she's going to answer *that* question?"

"Well, yes," one of the lawyers said. "She has to answer that question."[16]

"No, she doesn't," Price said firmly. "The federal rules provide protections. She does not have to answer that question and she's not going to answer that question." The California Evidence Code also prohibits questions about the plaintiff's sexual conduct or reputation in civil lawsuits over sexual harassment and assault.[17]

From the other end of the table another man pushed back, essentially declaring, "Well, I'm going to ask her the same question, and I'm going to insist on an answer."

Price stood up. "No. We're not having this." She started gathering her notepad and other items. "We're going to call the judge. And we're not answering any questions about this." She turned to her clients. "Come on. Get up. We're leaving." As she escorted Patricia and Jackie out of the room, Price shut the door behind her so hard that it barely held onto its hinges.

She did call the judge. The insinuating questions stopped.

Women's groups including the NWLC submitted a brief supporting Price's suit.[18] Price shocked her lawyer friends by filing a motion for summary adjudication (an initial ruling by the judge), a tactic usually pursued by defendants. Plaintiffs' lawyers didn't do that! "Well, I do," Price replied. She convinced Judge W.H. Orrick—a Yale graduate well aware of Price's role in *Alexander v. Yale*—that Title IX deserved a standard similar to the Supreme Court's 1986 decision confirming that Title VII prohibits sexually hostile work environments. He ruled on July 21, 1993, that a "reasonable student, having experienced such an assault, would be intimidated and fearful of Hamilton's presence at her school, so much so that her fear would interfere with her ability to learn." It was the first time a court said students could seek damages for hostile educational environments due to sexual harassment under Title IX. The lawsuit could proceed. Other cases soon also backed hostile-environment protections under Title IX.[19]

Berkeley had no chance after that, Price believed, but more time passed. Jackie spiraled downward. Berkeley agreed in September 1994 to a $1.8 million settlement in *Patricia H. v. Berkeley Unified*. The district admitted no wrongdoing and kept employing Hamilton.[20]

Public consciousness of sexual misconduct and of Title IX swelled over the next decade, and Sandler rode that wave. A *People* magazine story in December 1990 carried several accounts from victims of date rape. A seven-part series in *USA Today* focused on campus crime. The June 3, 1991, cover of *Time* magazine blared, "Date Rape." Some schools took baby steps forward: Brown University, for instance, made sexual assault a violation of the student conduct code; previously, student survivors of assault simply were told to call a lawyer.[21]

Sandler brought her materials and publications on these topics with her when she left the Association of American Colleges and landed at the Center for Women Policy Studies. As a keynote speaker at the First

International Conference on Sexual Assault on Campus in Orlando, Florida, she talked about peer harassment and gang rape.[22] Duke University appointed her to a task force to create "a reasonable sexual harassment policy."[23]

In 1986, after student Josoph Henry raped and murdered eighteen-year-old freshman Jeanne Clery in her dorm at Lehigh University in Bethlehem, Pennsylvania, her parents discovered that over a three-year period there had been thirty-seven other violent crimes at the university that school officials had kept quiet about. Public outcry pushed Congress to pass a law in 1990 requiring colleges and universities that receive federal funds to track and disclose crime on or near campuses. The law, known as the Clery Act, joined Title IX as an important tool for campus activists.[24] Congress amended the act in 1992 to require five basic rights, especially for survivors of student-on-student violence: equal opportunity for witnesses in hearings, equal notification of outcomes, mandated notification by the school of counseling services for complainants, options to go to the police, and possibilities to change classes or housing to avoid one's attackers.[25]

Students continued organizing against sexual violence around the country, mostly on a local level. Anonymous women attending Brown University wrote a list on the library bathroom walls with the names of students who raped them. Janitors scrubbed it off repeatedly; each time, the list reappeared, growing to thirty names written in multiple bathrooms on campus. Administrators agreed to create a new dean for women's issues, start mandatory freshman seminars on date rape, and compile information on how to file a complaint about sexual harassment or date rape into one brochure instead of it being scattered in several publications.[26]

The Stanford Rape Education Project surveyed 2,400 students and found that one in three women and one in eight men reported having been pressured into having sex against their will. A task force said the university's use of the criminal-law standard of evidence ("beyond a reasonable doubt") made it nearly impossible to discipline sexual assaulters. It recommended appointing an overseer. Some grumbled about the cost, but the "position of sexual-assault coordinator is much more important than a lot of other bureaucratic positions we have at this university," junior Minal Hajratwala told the *New York Times*.[27]

Police arrested thirteen students in a series of protests demanding that the University of Minnesota restore a sexual violence program and expand services, which the school did in February 1990. When Brigham Young University officials responded to an assault on a female student by advising women not to walk alone on campus at night, a committee of women organized a rally of three hundred people and made a counter-proposal: require all men, not women, to have escorts after 10 p.m. to make sure they don't assault anyone.[28]

"The biggest problem we face is that the universities are more concerned with their image than with the welfare of their students," one student leader said at NOW's first national Young Feminists Conference.[29]

Democrats in Congress including Rep. Mink introduced the Violence Against Women Act in 1991; it passed in 1994 after lobbying by thousands of women's advocates, securing $1.5 billion over six years for a National Domestic Violence Hotline and state programs to address domestic violence, sexual assault, and stalking.

Academic research on sexual harassment and assault grew, continually reporting high rates on campuses, and not just in postsecondary schools. In a survey of 179 students in fifth through eighth grade, nearly a third reported experiencing some form of sexual harassment in school. The survey asked students what the penalty should be; all wanted stronger measures than the school was using.[30]

At least twenty states enacted laws against stalking in the first half of 1992, with more on the way.[31] By 1993, marital rape finally was a crime in all fifty states.

Media attention mushroomed, with many books—including Sandler's first one, in 1996—as well as films, plays, and pop songs addressing sexual harassment and assault.[32]

But a rising backlash criticized the growing movement against sexual violence as "victim feminism," "politically correct" policing of "ordinary" behaviors, and a threat to free speech. The backlash was increasing, Sandler said in one of her campus talks, "partly because we have made a lot of progress, but also because of the growing realization that women are not merely wanting better jobs for women. Women want to change the institutions. They want to change the world."[33]

Orders for Women's Educational Equity Act (WEEA) funded publications about gender-based violence grew.[34] WEEA funding had dwindled to $500,000 in fiscal year 1992. The National Coalition for Women and Girls in Education (NCWGE) enlisted Mink's help; Congress reauthorized WEEA as part of reauthorizing the Elementary and Secondary Education Act and bumped funding initially to $2 million and then $4 million in 1996—minor amounts in the grand scheme of things but better than nothing.[35]

In the early 1990s the OCR issued a slew of pamphlets and formal guidance letters related to employment, student counseling, athletics, and pregnant or parenting teens, but nothing on sexual harassment since mentioning it in a 1981 memo. The National Women's Law Center (NWLC) in 1996 organized a NCWGE meeting with the secretary of education, which Sandler attended, to demand immediate and comprehensive sexual harassment policies from OCR.[36]

OCR did provide some guidance in the settlements of its investigations of sexual harassment complaints, which circulated among academic administrators. Evergreen State College in Olympia, Washington, violated Title IX, for example, by requiring "clear and convincing" evidence in a claim of sexual harassment. "The evidentiary standard of proof applied to Title IX actions is that of a 'preponderance' of the evidence," OCR's regional director wrote to the college president on April 4, 1995.[37]

The "preponderance of evidence" standard is the norm for civil laws including Title IX. If the allegations are more likely than not to be true, they are accepted as having happened. This standard of evidence is less rigid than the standard used under criminal law—"beyond a reasonable doubt"—which is designed to give the accused extra protections before the state can impose severe punishment. The "preponderance" standard is less onerous than "beyond a reasonable doubt," but so are the potential penalties that apply in civil law compared with criminal cases. Some schools including Evergreen State College tried to create a middle ground—"clear and convincing" evidence—but, for no logical reason, applied this tough-to-prove standard only to sexual harassment and assault, not to other kinds of student violations.

In the backlash against the application of Title IX to sexual assault, some critics and even a few feminists argued that all sexual assaults should be handled by police and criminal law, ignoring the abject failure of the criminal justice system to hold rapists and harassers accountable, and confusing Title IX's purpose of ensuring the victim's equitable access to education with a criminal justice goal of determining the accused's guilt or innocence.[38]

Mounting pressure moved OCR to hold a series of meetings with groups representing students, teachers, school administrators, and researchers on sexual harassment in education. It issued draft guidelines in 1996 that drew approximately eighty public comments, not an unusual number for similar documents. The final guidance on sexual harassment of students issued by OCR on March 13, 1997, said complaints under Title IX would be upheld if the offending conduct is "sufficiently severe, persistent, or pervasive that it adversely affects a student's education or creates a hostile or abusive educational environment." Schools would be held responsible if they "knew, or in the exercise of reasonable care, should have known" about the harassment.

OCR reiterated that schools must designate at least one Title IX coordinator—preferably more than one, in case the coordinator is a harasser—and must have effective policies and procedures to eliminate all types of sex discrimination. The document also discussed when schools may be required to pay for professional counseling or other services to remedy the effects of harassment.[39]

OCR did not, however, explicitly discuss in its 1997 guidelines the level of evidence required in sexual harassment complaints despite earlier endorsing a preponderance of evidence. It simply mentioned obliquely that "legal standards for criminal conduct are different" than those used by OCR for civil complaints.[40]

Sandler's unpaid relationship with the Center for Women Policy Studies soured in a mismatch of expectations. She was used to being a free agent; the center expected greater integration with its work. Disagreements over finances related to the materials that she brought from her previous job led her to sue, resolved by a settlement.[41] Sandler departed in 1994 for the unpaid title of senior scholar in residence for the National Association for Women in Education (NAWE), where she worked on a Chilly Climate Guidebook. NAWE dissolved in 2000 from lack of funding.

She monitored news accounts of sexual harassment in education and wrote to offer her services, drumming up paid work as a consultant or expert witness. By the end of 1995 she'd been involved in cases at seven universities.[42] When the Supreme Court in 1996 ordered state-funded military schools to admit women, one of her letters landed a three-year contract.[43] The Citadel, The Military College of South Carolina, tapped Sandler's expertise to create an "assimilation" plan for women cadets, a sexual harassment policy, training program, pregnancy policy, and more. She and others in the anti–sexual violence movement started shifting some of the focus from potential perpetrators to the training of bystanders as potential interveners to prevent or stop a sexual assault.[44]

A trip to Emory University in 1997 was typical of her many consulting visits: Sandler met some faculty for breakfast, then conducted a workshop for graduate students on sexual harassment, and then another for faculty on effective teaching strategies to warm the "chilly climate." Later she gave an open lecture and went out for a "fabulous" dinner with a few faculty, leaving at 6 a.m. the next morning. Wrote one host: "What energy! I want to be just like her when I grow up!"[45]

Sandler had seen mixed progress in Title IX's first twenty-five years on the issues that first engaged her. The numbers of graduate degrees awarded to women each year increased anywhere between ten- and twenty-four-fold, depending on the field.[46] Women poured into faculty positions after Title IX but still got bunched in the bottom ranks, she noted in multiple talks and interviews. The proportion of women among full professors hadn't budged in a decade.

Most of the gains in graduate education, employment, and athletics went to middle-class or upper-class white girls and women; fewer gains went to girls and women of color or the poor, the NWLC reported in a "Title IX at 25 Report Card on Gender Equity." The nation's grade average: C.[47] The NCWGE issued its own twenty-fifth anniversary report card, giving a D+ grade for progress on eliminating sexual harassment in education. Harassment at younger ages especially targeted girls of color and girls with disabilities, so our education systems especially were failing these students by this metric.[48]

For Title IX's twenty-fifth anniversary on June 23, 1997, Rep. Mink and sixty-four co-sponsors introduced a resolution acknowledging progress but adding that "there is still much work to be done if the promise of Title IX is to be fulfilled." Mink's letter to colleagues said she "helped to craft Title IX" in 1972, and "I certainly consider Title IX one of my most significant accomplishments." Though technically true in that all thirty-seven members of the 1972 House Education and Labor Committee could make that claim, her words perhaps gave the misimpression that she authored Title IX instead of Rep. Edith Green and Sen. Birch Bayh.[49]

An OCR fact sheet in January 1999 touted the "Impact of the Civil Rights Laws" in removing barriers to educational opportunity based on race, gender, disability, or age, all neatly compartmentalized. The race section didn't mention sex. The gender section didn't mention race. Intersectionality hadn't made much of an inroad at OCR.

Pamela Price became an educator. She and her husband developed a course on sexual harassment and liability prevention and presented it at conferences, to human resources departments, and to police and sheriff's departments, part of a growing industry of consultants and courses on the topic. Many school districts still didn't have Title IX coordinators or grievance procedures, she found. Some didn't even know about Title IX.

"With so little knowledge and no experience in enforcing the law, *it is still 1977 in most parts of America*," she wrote.[50]

Price tilled some new legal ground with Nicole M., a young client and student at Martinez Junior High School in California. Pervasive peer harassment had plagued Nicole from the time she started there in September 1991. Boys repeatedly made lewd remarks about her figure; one touched her breasts in class. The principal suspended the boy for one day and moved Nicole into different classes, then placed one of the worst offenders in her class. He kept harassing her. Nicole no longer felt safe; she transferred to another district in 1992.

Price sued the school district and individual officials in December 1993 for failing to help Nicole, in *Nicole M. v. Martinez Unified School Dist.*[51] It's difficult for school personnel to regulate adolescents, Martinez officials replied in a rewording of the "boys will be boys" trope. Besides, requiring districts to ensure acceptable teen behavior would unleash a flood of lawsuits. Judge Marilyn Hall Patel, the first woman on the Northern California District Court, disagreed. In one of the first court judgments to say so, she ruled in April 1997 that Title IX applies to peer sexual harassment. The lawsuit could proceed.

Price also represented two San Francisco City College students, Catherine M. and Stephanie G., who hoped to be photographers. Their photography professor, James Doukas, repeatedly sexually harassed them, the 1994 suit claimed. Each of the women fled City College, forced to abandon their education, and sued both Doukas and the City College district. The district finally concluded that Doukas had an extensive history of sexual harassment and fired him. In fighting the lawsuit against the district, though, the hostile and relentless questioning by City College's lawyers gave the plaintiffs nightmares.

A San Francisco Superior Court judge dropped City College from the suit in January 1997, saying district officials responded to the women's complaints, news media reported.[52] Price said City College got off on a technicality: sexual harassment still was an unsettled area of law, and the court said the women should have pursued remedies through the California Department of Fair Employment and Housing before suing. In any case, City College demanded that her clients pay $40,000 in attorneys' fees. At one point, Price recalls, a woman lawyer for the college asked one of the plaintiffs to take out her wallet. "How much money do you have in your wallet?" she said. "We'll take that." Price's clients had nightmares about that lawyer for years.

While Price appealed the Superior Court ruling, hoping to keep the suit alive, the U.S. Supreme Court decimated twenty years of jurisprudence regarding sexual harassment and gutted Price's cases with its 1998 ruling in *Gebser v. Lago Vista Independent School District*.[53]

Fourteen-year-old Alida Star Gebser was in eighth grade when teacher Frank Waldrop started making sexually suggestive comments to her and others. That led to kissing and fondling her, then he "instigated sexual relations" (started raping her), often during class time, although never on school property. Gebser knew this wasn't proper but didn't know what to do. Lago Vista had no anti harassment policy or procedures for reporting sexual harassment. Students complained about Waldrop's comments, but the principal never told the district's Title IX coordinator. A police officer found Waldrop raping Gebser and arrested him. Alida and her mother, Alida Jean McCullough, sued for damages. The case wound its way to the Supreme Court.

In a 5–4 decision, the court again confirmed that financial damages could be granted to individuals for sexual harassment under Title IX but set two criteria: a school official with the authority to do something about it had to have "actual knowledge" of the discrimination, and the official had to have deliberately failed to respond appropriately.

The *Gebser v. Lago Vista* tests made it much harder to hold schools responsible for sexual harassment of students under Title IX than for harassment of employees under Title VII. Title VII presumes that an employer is responsible for sexual harassment unless it can prove that it acted reasonably by offering good, well-publicized procedures that the employee failed to use. *Gebser* flipped that for Title IX: a school is presumed *not* to be responsible for sexual harassment on campus unless a student can prove otherwise.

Even worse, *Gebser* gave schools a legal incentive *not* to know about sexual harassment, to make filing a complaint difficult or opaque enough that they could turn a blind eye while claiming that if they only had known, they would have acted. And if they did get notice, almost any action would be sufficient, no matter how ineffective, because at least they tried. They'd never *deliberately* allow harassment to continue!

Because Gebser hadn't reported the harassment and assaults, the district couldn't be held liable, even though there was no apparent method for her to report it. Even if Gebser had reported it, the court's criteria rule out the employees that students are most likely to report to—teachers or counselors. The onus is on the victim to find the right person high enough in the chain of command—a principal or superintendent, likely—who could do something about the problem. Gebser lost her case, and a precedent was set.

In Price's case on behalf of Catherine M. and Stephanie G., the appeals court dropped San Francisco City College as a defendant, citing *Gebser*.[54]

The alleged harasser, Doukas, agreed to pay $375,000 in a 1999 settlement, then declared bankruptcy. Price filed a claim in bankruptcy court. A few years later, Doukas inherited a family trust when his parents died; through Price's court action, Catherine M. and Stephanie G. at least got their settlement from him.

A jury trial started in Price's other case, *Nicole M. v. Martinez Unified School Dist.*, in September 1998, nearly five years after Price filed the suit. Based on jury instructions derived from *Gebser*, the jury exonerated the district and all its officials after district administrators testified that they take allegations of sexual harassment very seriously and never intentionally would allow it to happen. They had, after all, suspended one harasser for a day and let Nicole change classes, though that didn't stop the harassment. "That 'deliberate indifference' was just impossible. It was so high" a bar to meet, Price said later.

Less than a year after *Gebser*, another major case sent Price's practice spinning. Conflicting legal opinions about whether Title IX prohibits student-on-student sexual harassment brought the issue to the Supreme Court in a case called *Davis v. Monroe County Board of Education.*

Ten-year-old LaShonda Davis couldn't get away from her harasser, G.F. They shared a double desk in their fifth-grade class at Hubbard Elementary School in Forsyth, Monroe County, Georgia. Starting in December 1992, he tried to grab her breasts and genitals. He chased other girls in the schoolyard and told them and Davis that "I want to get in bed with you," or "I want to feel your boobs," and other lewd comments. The harassment escalated for five months, most of it directed at Davis.

LaShonda told her teachers and her mother, Aurelia, after each of these incidents. In all but one instance, Aurelia called and visited the teachers or principal, demanding protection for her daughter. LaShonda and a group of girls asked their teacher for permission to go to the principal's office to report G.F., but the teacher refused, saying the principal will call if he wants them. Nothing changed. The district had no Title IX coordinator.

LaShonda, once an eager, star student, couldn't concentrate or sleep well. She developed signs of depression and feared going to school. Her formerly high grades fell. Home from school one day, she approached her mother.

"I don't know how much longer I can keep him off me," she said.

G.F. placed a doorstop in his pants during a PE class and mimicked sexual thrusts at LaShonda. Irate, Aurelia once again called the principal. "I guess I'll have to threaten him a little bit harder," the principal said. The school disciplined G.F. for striking a white girl student, but LaShonda was African American. It took three months of complaining by LaShonda and her mother before officials moved G.F. to a different seat. The harassment continued. Aurelia kept calling and meeting with teachers and the principal. She insinuated herself into a school board meeting, demanding action. She contacted a state school accrediting agency and a local social service agency. Still, nothing changed. In April, G.F. sexually rubbed his body against LaShonda in the school hallway.

Then LaShonda's father found a suicide note.

Aurelia called the local sheriff, who arrested G.F. The boy pled guilty to sexual battery in May, at the end of the schoolyear. The school district failed LaShonda but also failed G.F. by neither educating him to act responsibly nor holding him responsible.

The Davis family filed a Title IX complaint and then sued the school board, the superintendent, and the principal in 1994 for creating a hostile environment and interfering with LaShonda's education. They lost the first round. Verna Williams, a Black attorney at the NWLC, and her colleagues represented Davis through appeals and before the Supreme Court. They put Sandler on retainer as an expert witness. The court provided a bittersweet victory.

In a 5–4 decision, the Supreme Court affirmed in *Davis v. Monroe County Board of Education* that Title IX covers peer harassment and plaintiffs could sue for damages.[55] And it agreed that Monroe County officials had received "actual notice" of sexual harassment and been deliberately indifferent, so the suit could proceed. The justices didn't discuss how the school's response to harassment of Black students differed from its response to harassment of white students.[56] But the Supreme Court weakened Title IX by fashioning a definition of actionable sexual harassment more stringent in education than in employment. Under Title VII, the harassment must be severe *or* pervasive enough to create an objectively hostile environment. Under Title IX after *Davis*, the sexual harassment must be severe, pervasive, *and* objectively offensive—all three—and deprive the student of educational opportunities.

The tougher standards set by *Gebser* and *Davis* made lawsuits for sexual harassment in education much harder to win.

The school board settled with the Davis family out of court in 2001, when LaShonda was in college.[57] Research began to uncover the extent of the problem in K-12 schools. More than two hundred workshops on sexual harassment in middle schools in the South in 1996–2000 revealed pervasive, intense sexual harassment affecting students in all racial, socio-economic, and other subgroups.[58]

After each Supreme Court decision, OCR warned school officials that they still had to take "reasonable steps" to prevent and manage sexual harassment under Title IX. In 2001, it revised the 1997 guidance on sexual harassment to clarify that *Gebser* and *Davis* apply only to private lawsuits for monetary damages, not to OCR's more expansive administrative enforcement of Title IX.[59]

In the judicial system, a slim ray of hope remained in the wording of the *Gebser* and *Davis* decisions—that plaintiffs might be able to sue individual school officials. "Unless and until individual school administrators are held *personally* liable for either failing or refusing to do their job, nothing will change," Price wrote.[60]

Ten years after opening her law practice, Price regularly had a waiting list of 50 people seeking help, sometimes as many as 120. One client who suffered discrimination at work as a prison nurse got rejected by about fifty lawyers before Price took on his civil rights case and won a jury verdict.[61] She had better success suing for sexual harassment in employment than in education.[62]

Sexual harassment cases were hard work—exorbitantly expensive to prepare and try, requiring sacrifices of time and effort. Critics labeled the plaintiffs as troublemakers and Title IX as a "windfall for lawyers," evoking a laugh from Price.

Price lost too many student cases after *Gebser* and *Davis*. As the owner of a small law practice reliant on fees instead of the foundation grants or donations that support larger groups like the NWLC, she couldn't afford to keep losing. Price stopped taking most Title IX cases. It's hard to tell how many other lawyers also may have shied away from student sexual harassment and assault cases because of the hurdles placed by *Gebser* and *Davis*.

9

Athletics

1992–1999

FRESNO STATE'S ATHLETIC DIRECTOR, GARY CUNNINGHAM, LOOKED SOMberly at the employees of his department. He'd gathered them in August 1993 in the large conference room of the Duncan Athletic Building next to the football stadium. They'd read news about NOW's lawsuit against the entire California State University system over athletics. And now the Office for Civil Rights (OCR) was investigating, criticizing how they treated men better than women.

Changes are being forced on the athletics department, he told them. He wasn't happy about it. "Some people are going to benefit," Cunningham said. "And some people are going to suffer."

Diane Milutinovich heard just as clearly the words that Cunningham didn't say. He didn't say, "Title IX is the law, and we've been too long trying to comply. We're going to do our best not to drop any sports, but we might have to." He didn't say, "You know, this is the right thing to do. I have daughters." He didn't say, "Think of it like a family. You have two kids—one's a football player and one's a tennis player—and then you have a third kid. You don't starve the third kid. You divide the pie evenly."

No, she heard the message that they no longer were one team. He drew a line between "us" and "them"—the men's teams that would "suffer" and the women that would benefit. The athletics director sets the tone for everyone in the department to follow, Milutinovich knew. That gave the men license to complain. Coaches Lindy Vivas and Margie Wright countered their accusations, everyone's voices rising. "Don't engage," Milutinovich said quietly to the women on either side of her. The meeting was spiraling out of control. Someone was going to say something they'd regret.

"Do not yell back," Milutinovich kept saying. "We can fight this another way."

Part of Milutinovich's duties in 1991 as an associate athletic director and the senior woman administrator was to keep the department informed about Title IX. By some metrics, Fresno State was doing better than the average university. If anyone asked, Milutinovich would tell them that the university had made progress but had a ways to go toward equity.

Vivas and Wright didn't always like Milutinovich's impulse to keep an even keel, to stick with a tactful tone. Milutinovich had what they called "the fairness gene," always trying to find the equitable approach for women *and* for the men, even if the men didn't reciprocate.

Resentments over Title IX had been bubbling beneath the surface like carbonation pumped into a bottle of Coke. Cunningham could have gently twisted off the top, poured out the contents, and waited for the bubbles to fizz away so everyone could share the Coke.

Instead, he shook the bottle.

They'd turned a corner to a darker place, Milutinovich realized. She walked to her car in the August heat and drove a mile to the McDonald's on Shaw Avenue. They had a pay phone. She pulled out her address book, dropped in some coins, and dialed a friend who recently started seeing a therapist. "What was that lady's name?" she asked. Milutinovich called her right then and got an appointment for the next week. She'd never seen a therapist before. She would see this one for the next fifteen years.

Fresno State athletics always took on an outsized importance to residents of the area because there are no major professional sports teams in the large San Joaquin Valley, California's fertile agricultural area. Most Fresno State students come from the valley and tend to stay there after graduating, so many alumni live nearby. Some sports fans follow the local minor league baseball or ice hockey team, but much of the community's athletics boosterism over the years has identified with Fresno State.

Every high school in the area fielded football teams; Fresno State played against the "big boys" in NCAA Division I football and its other sports. Not only was that a point of pride but it meant more money. Fresno State could offer more athletics scholarships and field more teams because the NCAA reimbursed institutions based on the number of scholarships given, the number of sports offered, and graduation rates. What Fresno State lacked but that larger, powerhouse NCAA schools had were TV contracts and the revenue that came with them. Nonetheless, the school won four football championships in its conference in the 1980s. Fans often filled thirty thousand or more seats in the football stadium or sold out the near-ly ten-thousand-seat Selland Arena downtown where men's basketball played. The winning softball team drew more spectators than any other Division I softball program. Fresno State was in the top third of three hun-dred or so NCAA Division I athletics programs based on how all its teams did in championship competitions.

If Fresno wanted to be "the best little city," it needed Fresno State teams to win, the thinking went. The school gave sports fans in the San Joaquin Valley teams to root for, and Fresno State officials tapped that enthusiasm in a symbiotic relationship that helped them pour money and ambition into the athletics program. For the men, at least.

The school added and improved men's facilities but not women's. Schol-arships and playing opportunities for women still lagged those for men. Progress for women's athletics stalled, so Milutinovich initiated informal conversations with OCR.

Part of the resistance, she felt, had come from Fresno State's president since 1991, John Welty. Previously at Indiana University of Pennsylvania, he oversaw athletic cuts that left seven teams for each sex but took an unfair portion of playing slots from women in order to maintain the huge football roster. Gymnast Dawn Favia led a group of athletes who sued under Title IX. Because of the university's cuts, it didn't meet prongs two (a continu-ing history of expanding women's opportunities) or three (meeting the interests and abilities of women athletes) of OCR's three-prong athletics test for equitable participation. So, to comply with Title IX, the university had to meet prong one—offering playing slots proportional to each sex's share of enrollment. Courts ordered the university to restore two women's teams. Financial difficulties are no excuse for discrimination, intentional or not, the court ruled.[1]

Tensions in athletics departments almost everywhere flared as many men resisted change, while girls and women who'd grown up under Title IX got tired of waiting for equity. Schools spent the 1980s putting their elite men's sports on financial steroids and then budgets tightened. Athletics directors often scapegoated Title IX for any threat to football and raided funding for "minor" men's sports to maintain football's supremacy.

The NCAA picked its first female president, Judy Sweet, and conducted its first study on the status of women in NCAA athletics, then ignored the report's recommendation to increase scholarships for women.[2] It did, however, encourage colleges to meet prong one of Title IX's three-prong test (proportionality), and it promoted "emerging sports" that had been varsity sports for women until the NCAA consumed the Association for Intercollegiate Athletics for Women a decade earlier. Most of these were more familiar to higher-income, white girls—rowing, ice hockey, team handball, water polo, synchronized swimming, archery, badminton, bowling, and squash. In comparison, at large universities 83 percent of Black women with athletic scholarships played basketball or ran track.[3]

OCR didn't offer much help toward athletics equity under Presidents Reagan or Bush. A 1991 pamphlet reiterated responsibilities under Title IX but OCR rarely checked on schools and when it did, a school's promise to do better usually sufficed. Courts repeatedly declared schools in violation of Title IX that OCR had deemed in compliance.[4]

After voters replaced Bush in the "Year of the Woman" election in 1992, President Bill Clinton picked lawyer Norma V. Cantú, formerly with the Mexican American Legal Defense and Education Fund, to head OCR. Cantú appointed a national coordinator for Title IX in athletics in 1994.[5] OCR settled eighty Title IX complaints that included inequities in participation opportunities during Clinton's first term and conducted compliance reviews at 44 of 1,200 NCAA colleges and universities during his eight years as president.[6]

Fresno County students and employees alone filed 112 Title IX complaints with OCR from 1988 to 2017. Most reported discrimination in athletics (37 percent), sexual harassment (18 percent), or employment (12 percent).[7]

In January 1992 OCR notified four California universities including Fresno State that it would conduct Title IX compliance reviews. On top of this, someone sent a formal complaint to OCR in April 1992 charging Fresno State with twelve violations of Title IX: eleven for athletics discrimination and one for sexual harassment in athletics. Then California NOW (CalNOW) sued all twenty schools in the California State University system in February 1993, charging them with violating Title IX and state education codes requiring equal opportunities in athletics.[8] The proportion of women athletes at the state universities had shrunk from 36 percent in 1978 to 30 percent in 1993 even though women had become a majority of students.[9]

Given Title IX's twenty-year history and the high level of guidance from OCR on athletics over the years, any sex discrimination in athletics most likely is intentional, the Supreme Court had said in *Franklin v. Gwinnett*.[10] A lawsuit by gymnast Amy Cohen and other students at Brown University showed the lengths that schools were willing to go to maintain discrimination.

The students filed a class-action lawsuit in 1992; women were 48 percent of Brown's students but got only 37 percent of athletic opportunities. Brown didn't lack for funds but spent most of its sports budget on men.[11]

The university fought for six years and spent nearly $2 million on the suit despite multiple court decisions against it, trotting out every cliché of an argument in the nationally watched case. The application of the three-prong test constituted reverse discrimination, its lawyers said, and women just weren't as interested in sports as men. In a last-ditch effort, Brown asked the Supreme Court to review the case, but it declined. A lower court approved a remediation plan in 1998 that included a mandate to maintain women's share of athletic opportunities with 3.5 percent of their share of enrollment at the university.

Sandler sent Cohen Title IX buttons and thanked her for the landmark suit.

During the six years that *Cohen v. Brown University* was pending, NCAA colleges added 1,162 new women's varsity teams. Women learned to file class-action claims to make sure the suits outlasted their individual graduations. More colleges were willing to negotiate after *Franklin* imposed the risk of financial awards for damages. Besides the *Brown* case, women won or received favorable settlements against Auburn, Cornell, the Colorado

State Universities, California State University at Fullerton, the Universities of California at Los Angeles, Massachusetts, Oklahoma, Texas at Austin, and others.[12] Courts repeatedly emphasized that equality and justice are essential, not luxuries, and mandated by Title IX.

At home with her mother one night in 1993, Milutinovich heard the phone ring at 10 p.m.[13] It was the mother of one of the women's basketball players. The team was in Provo, Utah, for a weekend of conference games at Brigham Young University.

"He went off his rocker," she told Milutinovich, referring to Coach Bob Spencer. Her daughter had called home, feeling uneasy because the coach kept the players up late at night and said sexually "inappropriate" things. Milutinovich thanked her. Fresno State already had suspended Spencer for fifteen days in 1990 after a university investigation determined he sexually harassed a woman assistant coach the previous season.[14] Milutinovich caught a plane to Utah in the morning with the athletics director's approval.

She told Spencer she was there to look over BYU's softball facility. Milutinovich stayed in the players' hotel, came to their games, and hovered close by when she could. When Spencer went off to do some recruiting, she spoke with the players. She started documenting the coach's behavior and informed her boss.

Word spread that the university wouldn't renew Spencer's year-to-year contract. He announced his retirement in March after twelve seasons. Spencer blamed Milutinovich, acquaintances told her, and said he'd get a gun and shoot her if he could. Milutinovich reported him to campus police, who banned Spencer from campus for a year. That didn't stop him from coming to women's basketball games the next year, making players and the new coach feel uneasy.

Athletics Director Gary Cunningham called a meeting of the head coaches, one of many about Title IX issues, but this time without Milutinovich or any other administrators, which made some of the women coaches nervous. Most of the women sat on one side of the president's conference room while the men sat on the other.

Discussion turned to word that OCR soon would release the findings of its Title IX review, and Fresno State would have to make changes. It didn't take long for three of the men to get loud. The whole thing was Softball

Coach Margie Wright's fault, they believed. Someone told them (though incorrectly) that she'd filed the Title IX complaint. They bashed Title IX and what the women were "doing to" Fresno State.

"You don't care about men's sports!" one of them yelled to the women in the room.

"That's not true," a woman responded. They weren't going to sit there and take being yelled at. A coach directly across from Volleyball Coach Lindy Vivas accused the women's teams of taking all the money the booster club had raised for *his* team, apparently not understanding that athletics funds from boosters and the university go into one pot, to be apportioned equitably. Vivas gave her standard argument that taxpayer-funded institutions aren't allowed to discriminate and must treat all students fairly. That set him off; the coach started yelling at her.[15]

"Well, you know what?" Vivas said. "I don't have as much as you, but you know what? Really, if you need *more* money, you can have all that we have. You know, go on. You can have it. I don't care."

He pushed up out of his seat and leaned over the long conference table toward her, his mouth running. He looked as if he might slug the five-foot-four Vivas. She stood up too, even while thinking, "Don't do anything. Diane told you, don't do anything."

Wright shouted, "This is ridiculous!" A couple other coaches piped up with, "Yeah, c'mon," and "Knock it off." No one said, "Sit down, Bob," or intervened with the aggressor. The meeting soon ended.

Not long after, a friend from out of state visited Vivas, a pastor on his way to officiate a wedding near Yosemite. She asked him to go with her to the sporting goods store. They drove to the Herb Bauer store on Blackstone Avenue. The counter clerk unlocked a case and pulled out a couple of handguns. Vivas turned each one over in her hand, feeling the weight and the grip.

"There's no back door to my office," she told him. "If one of these guys gets enraged and goes off the deep end, they could come blasting in there, shooting all the women. I wouldn't be able to escape." It was illegal to keep a gun in her desk at work. She didn't care.

"I don't think you should do this," he said.

"Are you kidding?" Vivas said. "I will not go down as a sitting duck in my own office."

"I don't think you should do this," her friend said gently, again and again. "I don't think you should do it."

They drove back to Vivas's house with no gun. She didn't tell Milutinovich until years later. Mad as a hornet, Milutinovich gave Vivas a piece of her mind, listing all the repercussions she could have faced if she'd gone through with the plan.

Around the country, men in "minor" sports started suing in unsuccessful attempts to block Title IX, blaming the law for cuts to their teams instead of objecting to the bloated programs for football, men's basketball, and baseball that schools protected.[16]

NCAA colleges and universities had cut fifty-three men's wrestling teams in the four years between 1984 and 1988, when the *Grove City College* decision neutralized Title IX, and cut fifty-five teams in the four years after the Civil Rights Restoration Act revived it. In 1982–92, schools also cut thirty-nine men's gymnastics teams, but that was less than half the eighty-three women's gymnastics teams eliminated.[17] Clearly, Title IX was not to blame for cuts to these "minor" men's sports, though that didn't keep men from claiming so.

Wrestlers, in particular, had powerful friends such as Rep. J. Dennis Hastert (R-IL) and Sen. Paul Wellstone (D-MN), both former wrestlers. A high school teacher and wrestling coach who served as president of the National Wrestling Coaches Association before entering politics, Hastert went on to be the longest-serving Republican speaker of the House from 1999 to 2009. He also sexually abused at least four boys when he coached in high school; authorities imprisoned him in 2015 for having lied about bank fraud to pay hush money to one of the survivors over the years.[18]

In the 1990s Hastert used his position to aggressively attack Title IX, introducing legislation, demanding government investigations, and holding multiple congressional hearings.[19] His crusade relied on his unwillingness to admit the real problem. Schools spent more on men's Division I sports than on women's mainly because of football, the NCAA's executive director testified in 1992, and 93 percent of all NCAA football programs sported deficits. Substantial increases in Division I-A football budgets dwarfed any new spending on women's sports.[20]

Lawsuits that blamed women's sports for cuts to men's wrestling, swimming, and other sports failed, but "minor" men's teams kept filing them. Men lost every one of those cases but kept banging their heads against a wall, filing similar unsuccessful suits for over a decade and a half. Courts recognized that cutting men's teams isn't sex discrimination if men overall still had disproportionately greater chances to play or better facilities and services.[21]

In October 1993 what became known as the CalNOW Consent Decree settled NOW's lawsuit and locked all California State Universities into strict goals and timetables to correct disparities in athletics within five years. By 1998–99, Fresno State and the other twenty-nine schools could have no more than a 5 percent difference between the proportion of women among enrolled NCAA-eligible undergraduates and their share of athletic opportunities or scholarships. The proportion of funds allocated for athletic expenses had to be within 10 percent of women's share of NCAA-eligible undergraduates—greater leeway that was meant to accommodate higher costs for football.[22]

Separately, OCR revealed the findings of its compliance review of Fresno State and tasked the university with creating a plan to comply with Title IX. Some Fresno State Bulldogs fans grumbled, but not everyone. "Our poor old slowpoke and laggard Fresno State" had eighteen years to level the playing fields for men and women but four athletics directors in that time provided more promises than action, *Fresno Bee* columnist Jim Wasserman wrote. "And then—pow!—when the feds swoop in and ask what the heck planet they've been on since the Ford administration, they resort to what guys traditionally do when caught: whine like *they're* the victims."[23]

Fresno State gave OCR an inadequate action plan to resolve the compliance review, kicking off months of back-and-forth letters that tried OCR officials' patience. In April 1994 they cited the university for non-compliance in eleven athletic areas. Women were 54 percent of full-time undergraduates but received only 27 percent of athletic opportunities and inferior selections of sports, facilities, recruiting funds, practice times, and medical services.[24]

"There is a coalition of citizens of Fresno that is bird-dogging what we're doing," an OCR regional spokesperson told the press. "And if you look at when the law was passed, it's understandable."[25]

Pat Shelton of OCR's San Francisco office welcomed Fresno State's President Welty, Milutinovich, and two other officials to a negotiation session. Welty, a short man, looked even smaller shaking hands with Shelton, a relatively large woman. He had asked Milutinovich to accompany him knowing that only she could feed him Fresno State's Title IX information on demand. The four of them dove into the nitty-gritty of athletics inequities at the university, going over them one by one.

Courtesy cars, for example. Local dealers loaned Fresno State some free cars for coaches' official use. The dealer reaped publicity and community goodwill. But, Shelton pointed out, Fresno State gave seven cars to the men coaches and three to women coaches.

"Yes," Welty said, but the department paid the other women coaches a stipend to use their own cars for team purposes, "so, it's no big deal."

Shelton looked at him. "Well, you're going to take three of those cars from the men and give them to the women," replacing those men's cars with stipends, she said. Welty's ears burned red. "Since it's no big deal, John."

The bird-dogging coalition of Fresno citizens pressured the school with a guerrilla press conference in the spring of 1994.

One of Fresno State's PE teachers unlocked the chain-link gate to the softball field, a compact stretch of grass wedged between beige one-story athletics offices and the tennis courts, near the student dining hall. Milutinovich was out of town; Fresno State's women coaches avoided the field around noon to avoid retaliation if they were seen to be part of this protest. In trooped forty to sixty women and news reporters for a press conference called by the new Title IX Equity Coalition of Fresno County.[26]

Representatives of NOW, the American Association of University Women, the League of Women Voters, the National Women's Political Caucus, and Fresno County Women Lawyers stepped across the spongy grass to the mound. Speakers waved the media's attention to the meager bleachers that could seat a few dozen fans, the lack of lights for evening games, how the facilities were inaccessible to people with disabilities, and the nonexistent dugouts, locker rooms, and even bathrooms.

Then they pointed to the northwest. Beyond view of those on the soft-ball diamond but visible in the mind's eye of everyone present sat the baseball stadium, a state-of-the-art facility with everything the softball field didn't have, for a team that had won only two conference titles in the previous ten years. The softball team in that time won seven conference titles, made seven College World Series appearances, and were runners-up in three NCAA tournaments, building a fan base that usually led the nation in softball attendance.[27]

Women demanded accountability on a national level too. Rep. Cardiss Collins and Sen. Carol Moseley Braun, two Black members of Congress from Illinois, introduced the Equity in Athletics Disclosure Act with fifty-two co-sponsors in the House, including Rep. Patsy Mink, and five co-sponsors in the Senate. Passed in 1994, the act requires federally funded institutions of higher learning to compile and make public annual data reports about their intercollegiate athletics departments.[28] Data in elemen-tary through high schools would remain opaque, but the act cast some light on Title IX compliance at colleges and universities.

Already facing the CalNOW mandates, Fresno State agreed to a Cor-rective Action Plan with OCR in 1994 to build a proper weight room for both sexes, a softball stadium, and four women's locker rooms in a new North Gym annex. The plan created a Gender Equity Monitoring Committee at Fresno State with Milutinovich and Softball Coach Margie Wright as two of its eleven initial members.[29] "This will go a long way toward providing equitable opportunities for male and female student ath-letes," Milutinovich told the press. The men coaching track told women athletes out of spite not to use the new locker room for women's track and tennis because, they argued, men didn't have their own dedicated track locker room, even though men's teams overall had much more.

In 1996 racial and ethnic minorities became the majority of students at Fresno State.[30] Nationally, athletics policies and budgets increasingly would affect students of color as their proportion of the population increased.

Wendy Hilliard, president of the Women's Sports Foundation and the first African American woman to compete internationally in the Olympic sport of rhythmic gymnastics, addressed an argument increasingly being raised against Title IX when she testified at congressional hearings in 1995.

"There are those who would stoop to allege that supporting gender equity is supporting racism," she said. Limiting the size of football, basketball, or track programs, where high proportions of Black men played, penalized minorities in order to add sports like golf and lacrosse that cater to white women, the argument went.[31]

That kind of thinking perpetuates "minority ghettos" in athletics without addressing "the real problem of discrimination and lack of encouragement of minorities in other sports," Hilliard countered. "It is ridiculous to suggest that gender equity efforts should stop until sport integration occurs. Such a position results in pitting two victims of discrimination against each other: women and racial minorities . . ."

Title IX controversies in athletics were so common, they spilled into popular entertainment. A character named Gil in the 1995 film *The American President* catches the ear of the president (played by Michael Douglas) at a Christmas party. "Mr. President, militant women are out to destroy college football in this country," Gil says.

"Is that a fact?" the president says.

"Have you been following this situation down in Atlanta? These women want parity for girls' softball, field hockey, volleyball . . ."

"If I'm not mistaken, Gil, the courts ruled on Title IX about 20 years ago."

"Yes, sir, but now I'm saying these women want that law enforced."[32]

Despite men's sports advocates pushing Congress and OCR to weaken Title IX, Congress kept the Title IX regulations as they were. OCR reiterated support for the three-prong test in a January 1996 Dear Colleague letter and policy clarification, emphasizing once again that a school need only meet one of the prongs, not all. Nothing in Title IX requires a school to cut men's athletics; in fact, regulators favor adding playing opportunities for women rather than cutting men's teams, OCR said.[33] It already had updated its manual on Title IX and athletics in 1990, and the following year distributed a pamphlet summarizing schools' Title IX obligations. In a 1998 letter, OCR further explained that athletic scholarships should be awarded to the two sexes within 1 percent of their proportions in athletics, not their proportion in the student body.[34]

Flailing, some Title IX opponents resorted to personal attacks.

Fresno State's softball team climbed onto the bleachers on a spring day in 1995, tossing their near-uniform ponytails behind them as they settled onto benches facing Coach Wright, Milutinovich, and Jeannine Raymond, the university's human resources director. On paper, she also was the part-time Title IX coordinator, though the school didn't publicly identify her as such until 1996. "You need to come hear from the players themselves," Milutinovich and Wright had told her.

Bullying by the baseball team hurt, the players told her. Even in class, they said things like, "You're nothing but a bunch of dykes on spikes." Maybe they were jealous of the softball team's record, or maybe they didn't like that administrators cut the baseball squad from thirty-five to thirty players in order to give more women a chance to play without shrinking the football team. It didn't matter why the baseball players were harassing the women—it had to stop.

"You just need to turn the other cheek," Raymond said. She talked some more but no one heard much else, stunned silent. Raymond later denied making the comment, but that's what Milutinovich and Wright heard.[35] They did not confront her, too appalled by the wrong turn this had taken.

They talked with the team after Raymond left. "That's wrong," Milutinovich said, shaking her head slowly back and forth.

Acceptance of LGBT people was growing in U.S. society but homophobia remained strong, and being called a lesbian carried stigma. Several times in the 1980s, vandals either damaged or destroyed the Fresno State gay and lesbian student group's booth outside the Student Union. Religious conservatives targeted the campus LGBT community in talks and articles that some considered "hate speech."[36]

Homophobia especially persisted in sports. A women's basketball coach at a Pennsylvania college declared she would not permit lesbians on her team; a reprimand made her back off. Some parents of star basketball recruits received anonymous letters saying certain college coaches were lesbians.[37]

"As more and more straight women claim their right to play, homophobia has become increasingly prevalent on the courts and fields, and in the locker room," Lucy Jane Bledsoe wrote in 1997 in the *Harvard Gay & Lesbian Review*. "Women's sports promoters are working hard to clean the dyke image off the face of women's athletics." She added, "No woman would have a place on the team today if it weren't for the lesbians—and straight women who were not afraid to be called lesbians—who fought long and hard for that place."[38]

Milutinovich decided that if anyone insinuated that she's a lesbian, she would neither confirm nor deny it. That way, she hoped, both straight and gay students might feel comfortable coming to talk to her about anything. Besides, if people get to know you before they apply a label, then the label won't matter, she believed.

The door to Milutinovich's office hung open, as usual, on October 26, 1995. It seemed like everyone else in the building had their doors open that afternoon, too, with radios in every office loudly tuned to KMJ, Fresno State's partner station that broadcast men's competitions. The day before, KMJ talk show host Ray Appleton alerted listeners that he'd be talking Thursday about problems in the Fresno State Athletics Department, who's causing them, and why. He didn't say that seven coaches had paid him a visit, urging him to attack. He claimed he'd deeply researched the topic, but he hadn't.

At 1 p.m. Appleton's voice boomed out of Athletics Department offices, enveloping anyone walking down the hallway.

"Title IX is an evil little beast" being pushed by Milutinovich and Coaches Wright and Vivas, he said in a three-hour tirade. "This is not about making the playing field level," he said, but about greed and personal power trips. He implied that they misused athletics funds for personal gain. "Orders have been given by Milutinovich" about things she has no right to decide, said Appleton.[39]

Milutinovich marched over to the office of Scott Johnson, public relations director for athletics. Radios blared Appleton's voice out his open door, but Johnson wasn't in.

Callers to the talk show overwhelmingly agreed with Appleton's disgust for Title IX, except two. One woman mocked Baseball Coach Bob Bennett for "crying over the fact he doesn't have a weight room. Come on! The girls don't even have a dressing room. They have to sit out in the grass to have a team meeting." A man who had coached high school girls' teams said the "vindictiveness of the calls" and ignorance of the discrimination against female athletes discouraged him. "It's blowing me away to hear the identical arguments and things that I heard 17 years ago."

"I know more," Appleton hinted to another caller. "I mean, I've got the dirty little secrets" about Milutinovich, Wright, and Vivas, which he threatened to reveal unless "everybody comes together and works this out." He didn't utter the word "lesbian" but told listeners, "You've probably heard some of the dirtier stories as well, correct? . . . Because it's out there, but it's been one of those little closeted dirty things that nobody's wanted to talk about."

Milutinovich made a point of eating dinner that night at her brother's upscale restaurant, The Lime Lite. Many of Fresno's movers and shakers regularly dined there. She wanted them to see that she was not cowed by Appleton's attack. On the contrary, Milutinovich and Wright sued Appleton for defamation. During the discovery process, a witness reported hearing Scott Johnson tell Appleton that "if you get rid of Diane you don't have to worry about Margie or Lindy."

Neither Johnson nor any of the seven coaches (six men and one woman) who instigated Appleton's attack received even a reprimand.

In June 1997, nearly two years after Milutinovich and Wright sued KMJ radio and Ray Appleton for defamation, the women won approximately $60,000 in an out-of-court settlement, nearly all of which went to their legal expenses. Appleton had to read a carefully worded statement on the air acknowledging that the university said some of the statements he'd made about Milutinovich and Wright "were inaccurate."[40] Everyone loves a winner, so when the women's attorney threw a party to celebrate, all the Fresno bigwigs came.

A cold rain poured all night and Sunday morning of opening day at Fresno State's new $3.5 million softball stadium in February 1996. Milutinovich, the facilities crew, everyone connected with the stadium arrived early to get ready for the double-header against the nation's number-one team, UCLA. "Will the fans come?" she wondered.

The sun broke through three hours before game time. A standing-room-only crowd of 5,427 filled the stands. Even before the first pitch, the team felt like winners. Now they had top-of-the line facilities, the first softball stadium on a college campus. They lost the first game to UCLA but won an upset in the second.

Colleges and universities from all over the country started calling Fresno, asking for the architectural plans to the stadium. They'd been through losing Title IX battles or were trying to avoid one by building a smaller version of Fresno's softball stadium.

For Title IX's twenty-fifth anniversary in 1997, the National Women's Law Center used newly available data thanks to the Equity in Athletics Disclosure Act to file complaints against twenty-five colleges about athletic scholarships, generating coverage in some major newspapers. OCR investigated, cleared eight of the charges, and got commitments over the next year and a half from the other seventeen to increase funding for women's scholarships.[41]

Thirty of OCR's forty-one compliance reviews in 1994 through 1998 focused on athletics, even though sexual harassment dominated among the reasons for Title IX complaints. Athletics ranked fifth among reasons for a complaint but was most likely to prod a school to agree to make changes (in 67 percent of cases). OCR received more than three times as many complaints about sexual harassment. It produced commitments to change in only 16 percent of the complaints; among the rest, OCR dropped some complaints or decided that no changes were required, and shunted the remainder to the Equal Employment Opportunity Commission (EEOC) or other agencies.[42]

The National Coalition for Women and Girls in Education (NCWGE) co-sponsored an event with President Clinton and the Jackie Joyner-Kersee Youth Center Foundation to mark Title IX's twenty-fifth anniversary.[43] Clinton thanked former senator Birch Bayh, who attended the June 17, 1997 event, for his leadership on Title IX. The president announced an initiative to get all federal agencies that run schools (such as the Defense Department—the largest "school district" in the world—and the Departments of Agriculture and Energy) to issue Title IX regulations, something the NCWGE had pushed for since the 1970s. By summer 2000 all twenty-nine of the pertinent agencies had issued regulations.[44]

The Education Department's report, *Title IX: 25 Years of Progress*, and subsequent fact sheets took a glass-half-full view of gains made since the law passed. Similar proportions of girls and boys were taking algebra, geometry, and calculus classes. The number of girls playing high school sports had increased eightfold and women in intercollegiate athletics had

quadrupled by 1996–97, though high school boys had 24,000 more varsity teams than did girls. Women's college athletics operating expenditures
grew 89 percent from 1992 to 1997, but men's swelled by 139 percent.[45]

On the other hand, teachers and administrators in K-12 schools didn't
understand Title IX or California's sex-equity laws well, a study of eighty
state compliance reviews in 1994–98 found. Many hadn't implemented
sexual harassment policies, though California laws had required them
since 1992.[46]

At Fresno State a one-page flyer posted in athletics facilities in 1998
listed a dizzying nine people that students could call if they felt they were
being sexually harassed, none of whom was identified as the Title IX
coordinator.[47]

When the softball team won the national championship in 1998—the
first-ever NCAA Division I championship for any Fresno State team—the
trophy deepened the jealousy and resentment in some men. But women's
sports were more popular than ever. The U.S. women's hockey team won
its first Olympic gold in 1998 and got its photo on the Wheaties cereal
box.[48] In 1999, 40 million people watched on television as the women's
national soccer team won the World Cup for the second time, beating
China before a record crowd of ninety thousand at Pasadena's Rose Bowl.

Fresno State calculated that it had spent $8.9 million by December 1999
to improve athletics facilities since the CalNOW Consent Decree.[49] The
school added soccer and equestrian teams for women and cut men's swimming and water polo. It chose not to cut its 110-man football squad, double
the size of NFL rosters.[50]

Administrators wrote to OCR in April 1999 saying Fresno State athletics complied with Title IX through prong two—a steady and continuing
pattern of improvement. By 2001 women were 52 percent of the school's
athletes, so OCR closed its file on the Corrective Action Plan. CalNOW
supported or filed complaints against seven colleges and three high schools
over a fifteen-year period, but mandatory monitoring of state university
athletics under the consent decree ended in March 2000.[51]

All that was left for Fresno State was voluntary compliance with the law.

10

Retaliation

2000–2010

Coach Wright and one of her softball players stopped by the Athletics Department's Business Office one April day in 2000 to check on some paperwork.

"What's this?" the student asked, brow furrowed.

A three-by-four-feet butcher-paper sign draped the wall with five-inch hand-drawn letters: "Ugly Women Athletes Day." Below it someone had drawn stick-figure bodies topped by photos of the heads of Associate Athletics Director Scott Johnson and Media Relations Director Steve Weakland, cut from a Fresno State media guide. The two men and staff were sharing a potluck lunch. Everyone got quiet.

Oh, one of the women in the office explained, they'd overheard Weakland a few days earlier cracking "jokes" with Johnson, saying he thinks all women athletes are ugly. The staff decided to mock them with the poster and an Ugly Women Athletes Day lunch.

No one considered how this would affect students, even though everyone in the department had watched a mandatory video that year about sexual harassment. When the softball team heard about the banner at practice soon after, two players marched to the Business Office and yanked it down.

Milutinovich had just returned from lunch and settled into her office when one of the women from the Business Office popped in. "Do you know what the softball team did?" she said, complaining about the students taking the poster. Milutinovich walked out to the field to hear the team's version of events. You're right, she told them—the banner and the "luncheon" were offensive. "They were wrong. I agree with you all. But you know, you should have asked that it be taken down, and not taken it, because it wasn't yours to take." She and Wright walked a small group of players back to the Business Office to return the crumpled banner and apologize.

Milutinovich had barely returned to her office when a commotion drew her back to the hallway. The man who coached women's tennis screamed at the softball players. "Who do you think you are?" The women in the Business Office had worked hard on the banner and you had no right to take it, he shouted.

"Hey, hey!" Milutinovich raised her voice. "It's not right for you to be yelling at them." She moved between him and the players. "Go mind your own team."

The whole thing poisoned the team atmosphere for the softball players, Coach Wright said. Fresno State reprimanded four coaches and administrators for Ugly Women Athletes Day.

Nationally, Title IX became an issue in a presidential campaign for the first time in the 2000 election, particularly with regard to how the law applied to athletics. Reporters asked candidates if Title IX had gone too far. Part of the Republican Party's higher education platform called for a "reasonable" approach to Title IX "without adversely affecting men's teams."[1] Republicans regained the White House and controlled the House of Representatives; the Senate teetered between Democrat and Republican majorities.

When President George W. Bush took office he picked two Black men to oversee Title IX: Education Secretary Roderick R. Paige, a former football coach, dean, and superintendent, and Office for Civil Rights (OCR) director Gerald Reynolds, former president of a conservative think tank opposed to affirmative action. Title IX advocates prepared to defend the law once again.

Rep. Mink asked the General Accounting Office to report on Title IX's impact, reminding everyone of the progress made in admissions, athletics, and equitable financial aid.[2] She defended the Women's Educational Equity Act (WEEA) from the latest attacks by the conservative Heritage Foundation, which claimed "boys, not girls, are being shortchanged by the current system."[3] Congress reauthorized WEEA as part of late

2001 education legislation and appropriated nearly $3 million per year for it in each of the years 2001–2006, but this would be the last decade of WEEA. Funding dropped to $1.8–$2.4 million in 2007–10 and then ceased altogether.[4]

Sandler worried about the new Republican majority. Now a senior scholar at the Women's Research and Education Institute, she frequently traveled to campuses to consult or speak. She feared Title IX attacks ahead but took comfort in "knowing that there is much that cannot be readily changed, and that there are many good people who are working so that the gains of many years will not be lost," she wrote in a January 2001 holiday letter to family and friends.

Those gains came more easily to some women than others.

Britt King stood in Milutinovich's office doorway one day. "Diane, I'm kind of getting tired of this," said King, the women's basketball coach and the first Black head coach in any sport at Fresno State. She flew home the night before from a recruiting trip. The flight was delayed, so it was close to 1 a.m. when she got into the Ford Expedition that she'd parked at the airport—one of the athletics department's courtesy cars, though no signage indicated that. A few miles toward home, a police officer pulled her over for "driving while Black." She asked why she'd been stopped. The cop said he saw her car cross the dotted line in the center of the road. He seemed to assume that a Black person in an expensive car like that must be doing something wrong.

This wasn't the first time she'd been stopped in a Fresno State car. A few weeks earlier a cop pulled her over after a late practice; when he approached and saw her dressed in Fresno State gear he claimed her brake light was out. But when King took the car to a shop, they said the brake lights were fine.

Milutinovich walked King over to Athletics Director Al Bohl's office. Maybe he could make a call downtown, or somehow intervene to stop the harassment?

Bohl didn't see a problem. It's not a big deal, he said. He'd grown up poor and felt discriminated against, but he didn't let it get in his way.

"Well, Al, there's a big difference," Milutinovich said. "You could change being poor. She's Black and she can't change that. She's a woman and she can't change that. Nobody knows whether you grew up poor or not." Bohl shook his head. You're just going to have to deal with it, he said.

Perhaps Milutinovich shouldn't have been surprised. Some of the white men coaches for years had put racist and sexist hand-drawn cartoons and holiday letters on their office doors and in everyone's mailboxes, with only a rare, mild objection from higher-ups.

People of color on Fresno State's faculty had increased in two decades from 9 percent of employees to 26 percent in 1997; women now were 41 percent of faculty. Of the university's eighteen thousand students, 51 percent were people of color and 56 percent were women. Like most places, the school did not track data by sex *and* race, just sex *or* race.

Athletics tended to be whiter, though, and more accessible to suburban, economically privileged students. Nationally, 36 percent of Hispanic sophomore girls played interscholastic sports in high school compared with 52 percent of non-Hispanic white sophomore girls in 2001–2002, a survey of federal data showed.[5] The sports that colleges had been adding for a decade to comply with Title IX—soccer, lacrosse, golf, rowing, equestrian—weren't ones that most urban high schools had the space or money to accommodate. Title IX generated more athletics scholarships for women, but they predominantly went to the "best" athletes who had a head start, many of whom honed their skills in costly pay-to-play sports clubs.[6]

"When you increase scholarships in these sports, you're not going to help people of color," concluded Tina Sloan Green, director of the Black Women in Sport Foundation. "But that's not in their line of interest. Title IX was for white women. I'm not going to say black women haven't benefited, but they have been left out."[7]

A 2003 study supported her "benefited but left out" assessment. The number of women of color in intercollegiate athletics increased 955 percent from 1971 to 2000, and their athletic scholarship assistance grew from less than $100,000 to $82 million. Clearly, Title IX had helped many women afford college or start an athletics career, but these numbers should have been better. Women of color now were 25 percent of college students but only 15 percent of athletes, the Women's Sports Foundation reported. The study also exposed the myth that Title IX hurt men athletes of color. Men of color were 22 percent of students and also 22 percent of athletes. Both men and women of color were underrepresented in a majority of sports—men in fourteen of twenty-five sports, women in twenty of twenty-five—and overrepresented in basketball, football, track, and a few other sports.[8]

Title IX also benefited another group that still got pushed out of athletics—pregnant women. Fresno State's trainers drafted a 2001 policy excluding pregnant students immediately from athletics practice and competition, in line with a 1999 NCAA policy change. Milutinovich wrote to the NCAA and explained to her colleagues that the NCAA rule was biased, paternalistic, and violated the law. It allowed no input from physicians and acknowledged no differences in potential risks to the mother or the fetus in, say, the second month of pregnancy compared with the sixth or eighth month.[9]

"No one ever told her to get pregnant," one Fresno State trainer said to some women athletes. "She shouldn't have gotten pregnant," a coach said, ignorant that Title IX prohibits discrimination because of pregnancy or parenthood. Fortunately, Fresno State's legal counsel blocked the draft policy that tried to exclude pregnant athletes.

Most colleges had no formal policies on pregnant athletes in the early 2000s. Some women who feared being pushed off the team hid their pregnancies as long as possible, potentially endangering themselves and their babies. Others who told coaches they were pregnant lost scholarships instead of being offered the same kind of accommodations made to athletes temporarily sidelined by injuries. At least one woman successfully sued her college for revoking her scholarship and denying her "medical redshirt" status that would qualify her for an extra year of NCAA play.[10]

Sports channel ESPN broadcast a report about blatant discrimination against pregnant athletes in *Outside the Lines: Pregnant Pause* on May 13, 2007, that generated additional news coverage. OCR responded with a Dear Colleague letter reminding schools that they must treat pregnancy or childbirth the same as any other temporary disability. The NCAA eventually issued a model policy on pregnancy written by two women experts on Title IX and pregnancy.[11]

President Welty appointed Scott Johnson athletics director at Fresno State in January 2002, ignoring written objections from Milutinovich,

Vivas, and Wright about Johnson's hostility toward strong women and women's sports. When Johnson quickly "reorganized" the department in a way that ultimately eliminated only Milutinovich's job, he blamed budget pressures for the changes. Through an appeals process she met with a university vice president and deconstructed the alleged reasons she was let go. "That sounds spurious," he agreed. She couldn't wait to get home and crack open a dictionary. People in her circles didn't use words like "spurious."

The university reassigned her to be director of the Student Union in August 2002—anything but athletics. The woman who replaced her as Fresno State's senior woman administrator in athletics and the next woman in that post both admitted to knowing next to nothing about Title IX.[12]

For Title IX's thirtieth anniversary in 2002, the National Women's Law Center (NWLC) filed complaints against thirty colleges and universities that allegedly shortchanged women in athletics scholarships by a collective $6.5 million.[13] The 2002 "report card" on equity issued by the National Coalition for Women and Girls in Education (NCWGE) graded higher education on areas of progress since Title IX passed: math and science, B-; athletics, C+; treatment of pregnant and parenting students, C+; sexual harassment, C. Adequate improvement, but not impressive.[14]

Alumni of Yale and Marquette Universities joined the National Wrestling Coaches Association in suing the Department of Education that year, claiming that prong one of the athletics test (proportionality) is unfair to men. Sandler reminded everyone that women's advocates in the 1970s simply wanted everything split down the middle; the NCAA and football coaches came up with the more complicated three-prong test.[15] "The underlying complaint is still against Title IX itself," Marcia Greenberger told the *New York Times*.[16] An appeals court dismissed the wrestlers' suit in 2004.[17]

At a June 2002 Senate hearing where five speakers praised Title IX for its thirtieth anniversary, Education Secretary Paige gave more ominous remarks. He announced the creation of a Commission on Opportunity in Athletics to review Title IX and find "opportunities to ensure fairness for all athletes"—code for appeasing dissatisfied men. Multiple employees of the NWLC stationed around the room handed out press releases headlined, "NWLC to Bush Administration: 'Hands Off Title IX.'"[18]

From the start Paige's commission focused mainly on men. Commission members came predominantly from colleges with big football programs; no one represented elementary or high school sports. Most of them seemed to have little understanding of Title IX.

Bayh testified at the commission's first hearing, a two-day event in a downtown Atlanta hotel in late August. "Equality of opportunity. Equality. That shouldn't really be a controversial subject in a nation [that] now for 200 years has prided itself in equal justice," he said.[19] The commission held three more public hearings, in Chicago, Colorado Springs, and San Diego, where both Milutinovich and Fresno State president Welty testified.

As usual, Title IX opponents argued that the law "went too far," required quotas, and made men the victims—as if saying the same things over and over for decades somehow made them true. The law's supporters clarified that 72 percent of colleges and universities that added women's sports teams between 1992 and 2000 did so without cutting men's teams, and schools added more men's teams overall than they eliminated.[20]

Over time, football gobbled more and more resources.[21] Reduce the salaries of the many dozens of football and men's basketball coaches who made more than $1 million a year to $200,000 a year (still higher than 99 percent of faculty) and each college could add three to six sports, Smith College economics professor Andrew Zimbalist testified at a commission hearing.[22]

Around the time of the commission's first hearing, Rep. Mink contracted chicken pox and quarantined herself. Two days later she was admitted to a Honolulu hospital; viral pneumonia put her in intensive care. Mink died on September 28, 2002, at age seventy-four surrounded by family.[23]

Multiple talks and interviews in the months before her death featured Mink discussing Title IX for its thirtieth birthday, as someone there at the beginning. She and House colleagues wrote Secretary Paige urging him to require athletics data on sex equity from the nation's sixteen thousand high schools; Paige declined, saying that would be "quite burdensome."[24] Mink gave the keynote address at the eighth annual NCAA Title IX Seminar in spring 2002.[25] NOW honored Mink but embellished history when it gave her a Woman of Vision award in part "for her leadership in passing Title

IX."[26] The Women's National Basketball Association also honored Mink at center court during the All-Star Game halftime.

Speaking on the House floor in June to recognize the law's anniversary, Mink repeated that Title IX was "one of my most significant accomplishments as a Member of Congress," carefully chosen words that were accurate yet magnified her role in Title IX's birth.[27]

With her words fresh in their minds and Title IX under attack by Paige's commission, seventy-two representatives rose in the House over a three-day period to deliver memorial tributes to Mink after her death. Forty referenced her connection to Title IX: Mink was a co-author, or *the* author, or the mother of Title IX, some said. One colleague proposed renaming WEEA after Mink, which would have been appropriate. Instead, a joint resolution of Congress renamed Title IX itself the Patsy Takemoto Mink Equal Opportunity in Education Act.[28] Before long, uninformed internet posts solidified the legend that Mink authored Title IX.

In a tribute inserted into the *Congressional Record*, Sandler praised Mink for helping Rep. Green lay the groundwork for Title IX, for defending it from attacks after it passed, and for being the mother of WEEA. The catalog of materials available for purchase from WEEA's programs that week showed a diverse legacy, Sandler said. In addition to publications such as *Lifting the Barriers: 600 Strategies That Really Work to Increase Girls' Participation in Science, Mathematics and Computers* were materials about working with immigrant students, Native American or Latina women and girls, women of the South, Cuban American women, girls with disabilities, single mothers, "and yes, even materials for providing equity for boys," she noted.[29]

Outside the Title IX commission's final meeting in January 2003, rain fell on college students organized by NOW and the Feminist Majority Foundation who marched and chanted "Save Title IX" in front of the Washington, DC, hotel.[30] The commission's nonbinding report, released on February 26, suggested changing Title IX guidance to stop colleges from cutting men's teams but said little about the discrimination women athletes still faced.

Two commissioners—former Women's Sports Foundation president Donna de Varona and soccer star Julie Foudy—publicly disseminated a minority report objecting to the commission's rushed, slapdash process and faulty conclusions. The press gave extensive coverage to both reports, producing a firestorm of public objections, even one from NCAA president Myles Brand. "Title IX is not broken, and it does not need to be fixed," he said.[31]

The outcry tempered OCR's response. Instead of acting on the commission's controversial recommendations, OCR published a Dear Colleague letter on July 11, 2003, essentially leaving Title IX regulations as they were. It again clarified that nothing in the law requires cutting men's teams and that OCR disfavors that strategy. Meeting any prong in the three-prong test complies with participation requirements, OCR reiterated, and private funding of teams is allowed but doesn't change a school's Title IX obligations for fairness.[32]

Milutinovich and a few others held a press conference on October 9, 2002, in the lobby of the Piccadilly Inn diagonally across from Fresno State's campus sign and next to a Marie Callender's restaurant. She set up easels and poster boards with charts explaining Fresno State's finances. Milutinovich had filed complaints with the Equal Employment Opportunity Commission (EEOC), the State of California, and OCR for discrimination and retaliation by Fresno State, the first steps toward a lawsuit.

Her attorney and another from Equal Rights Advocates blasted Fresno State's claim that budget constraints forced it to cut her job. Since signs of a possible budget deficit emerged in 2001, the department had increased the football coach's salary, paid $250,000 to participate in the Silicon Valley Bowl, and spent more than $150,000 to repair luxury suite windows. The department's 2002–2003 budget projected a $264,000 surplus. It also added six new positions and reinstated two of the three that Johnson had cut—just not hers.[33]

The reorganization was for budget reasons alone, President Welty told reporters.[34]

Milutinovich asked her attorney, Rayma Church, to meet with Volleyball Coach Lindy Vivas the next month. When Vivas's contract expired at the end of 2002 the best she could get was a two-year renewal, though coaches for football, baseball, and basketball all got five-year contracts. Johnson added performance goals for scheduling, attendance, and winning that no other coach had to meet. It looked like a setup to push Vivas out. Milutinovich and Church would meet Vivas at her house after work, sometimes until 11 p.m., team-writing responses to her supervisor's emails to make sure her rebuttals were accurate and to build a paper trail in case she needed one. They stated and restated information carefully.

Fresno State opened its new Save Mart Center arena in November 2003. After just one volleyball match there instead of the expected thirteen per season, Johnson shunted the team to the smaller, much older North Gym. That would make it hard for Vivas to recruit and thus hard to meet the performance clauses in her contract. She filed a complaint with OCR in May 2004.[35] Seven months later, Fresno State declined to renew her contract. The school kicked out the winningest volleyball coach in its history who had been honored three times as Western Athletic Conference Coach of the Year. It hired a man who had never coached Division I women athletes to replace her. He slogged to a three-year record of 18 wins and 71 losses.

Both Milutinovich and Vivas had good legal cases, Church felt, but she cautioned them. Every time Fresno State officials needed to do something related to women's athletics, they could do one of three things: (A) the right thing, (B) the neutral thing, or (C) the wrong thing. Fresno State always chose C, as far as Church could see. If her clients got overly hopeful that the university might do the right thing, she reminded them: pick C.

A few weeks later, Church's senior partner in the firm, James D. Emerson, called her into his office. "You shouldn't be doing these cases," she remembers him saying. It's bad publicity. The firm could lose important clients. Fresno is a small town. Church refused to back down, so her colleagues dissolved the firm's legal partnership and pushed her out. Church moved back to Missouri to be near family and practiced law there but stayed in touch with Milutinovich and Vivas.

Everywhere they turned, other lawyers told Milutinovich and Vivas they had worked for the university and couldn't take their cases due to conflicts of interest. Deadlines approached for Vivas to sue or let it go. Milutinovich suggested they attend an American Association of University Women luncheon featuring Dan Siegel, a civil rights attorney from Oakland. They convinced him to represent them both.

With Milutinovich out of the athletics department, the women's share of the budget dropped from 24 percent to 20 percent in 2005. Fresno State inflated the number of women participating in track and women's equestrian; there were so many women on the equestrian team (ninety-six in January 2003) that each student could ride maybe two hours a week. "These aren't real opportunities for women—they just look that way," Milutinovich said in public testimony.[36]

Johnson moved Softball Coach Margie Wright out of her office of twenty years to a remote room out past the track-and-field coaches. He reduced softball's budget, slashed maintenance at the stadium, and cut the marketing budget, Wright said. That made it harder to draw fans and recruit players. Wright was the winningest coach in NCAA Division I softball history. Administrators were determined to make her life miserable so she'd quit, another coach testified later.

Wright and Vivas were the only two coaches of Fresno State's Tier 1 teams of either sex to go to the NCAA tournaments, and the only two not to get raises or five-year contracts, Milutinovich wrote to OCR's San Francisco office in 2004.[37]

OCR officials informed Fresno State they would investigate complaints from Milutinovich, Wright, and a woman swimmer.[38] In October 2004 Milutinovich sued Fresno State for Title IX violations and for firing her in retaliation.

Two months before Athletics Director Scott Johnson pushed Milutinovich out of athletics in 2002, he hired Stacy Johnson-Klein (no relation) to coach women's basketball. Johnson-Klein was on the "home team," he told her—code for being straight—and got more pay and a longer contract than the other women coaches, from whom she kept a distance. President Welty hosted her wedding at his fancy campus house; the athletics department posted wedding photos on its website.[39] Johnson had a hit list of presumed lesbian coaches and administrators he wanted to fire; he referred to Milutinovich, Vivas, and Wright as lesbians, dykes, and atheists, Johnson-Klein later said.[40]

Provocative images of tall, blond Johnson-Klein saturated Fresno-area billboards, posters, articles, TV commercials, and magazine covers. She wore form-fitting dresses in cheesecake poses, stomped her four-inch heels courtside in a pink fur poncho, and posed in a revealing halter-top with the Bulldog mascot.[41] She also was an excellent game coach, in Milutinovich's opinion. A team that had five consecutive losing seasons went 21–13 her first year. Game attendance grew 798 percent. Season ticket holders increased from 66 to 4,500.[42]

Soon, though, the behavior of some men in the department turned toxic toward her. Johnson grabbed her breast as they rode through a car wash, she said. He urged her to visit his lakeside cabin without their spouses. He told her that a big donor would like to go "one-on-one" with her. New associate athletic director Randy Welniak started hounding her with sexually tinged comments about her clothes and looks.[43]

Johnson-Klein complained to administrators in 2004 about inequities between men's and women's basketball, pointing to unfilled vacancies for her assistant coaches, lack of a certified trainer, and more. In January 2005 she asked Johnson to stop Welniak's harassing comments. Instead, the university started "investigating" her. Within three weeks it suspended her, and then fired her on March 2. She called Milutinovich for advice, who helped find her an attorney.

In another "pick C" move, Fresno State officials posted its 380-page investigation report online, accusing Johnson-Klein of financial misdeeds, mistreatment of some players, and having asked a player to give her some painkiller medicine. It virtually guaranteed that Johnson-Klein wouldn't be hired anywhere else. So, she sued.

Johnson-Klein was out of a job, but so was Athletics Director Scott Johnson. He abruptly retired after the men's basketball coach quit under pressure because of hundreds of NCAA rules violations, but Johnson got paid for many more months, to the end of the year.[44]

Late on a Friday afternoon while many schools were on 2005 spring break, Bush's OCR quietly issued guidelines developed without any public comment to make it easier for athletics programs to comply with prong three of the three-prong test (meeting the interests and abilities of women athletes). Two-thirds of the 130 athletics programs OCR investigated from 1992 to 2002 had used prong three to comply with Title IX. Under the new guidelines, schools could now email the surveys used to assess student interest in sports, and non-responses could be counted as a lack of interest.[45]

Quick and loud outcry from many organizations representing women, education, athletics, and civil rights advocates pointed out the methodological flaw: unanswered emails don't indicate anything other than no response. The U.S. Senate Appropriations Committee demanded a more detailed report from OCR, which displayed its sloppy reasoning. The NCAA urged OCR to rescind this latest clarification and essentially told its member schools to ignore it. Congress then passed a bill in late 2006 requiring email surveys of athletic interests to be considered only with other findings regarding Title IX compliance.[46]

In the courts, a 2005 Supreme Court decision turbocharged the Fresno State women's lawsuits—*Jackson v. Birmingham Board of Education.*[47]

Roderick Jackson, a Black man who coached high school girls' basketball in Alabama, pushed his school and district to fix disparities between the girls' and boys' teams. Boys practiced in a nice gym, girls in a ninety-seven-year-old building with slick floors, plywood backboards, and wrong-sized courts and hoops. Colleagues told him, "You better hush your mouth. You're making problems for yourself," he said.[48] The Birmingham Board of Education took away his secondary coaching job; Jackson sued for retaliation while he continued teaching health and PE.

The National Women's Law Center guided the appeals to the Supreme Court. A Leadership Conference on Civil Rights coalition of 180 groups filed a brief supporting Jackson, including the NAACP, the American Jewish Congress, the American-Arab Anti-Discrimination Committee, and the National Gay and Lesbian Task Force. Even the Bush administration sided with Jackson.

The Supreme Court ruled that Title IX prohibits retaliation even against someone who is not the direct target of sex discrimination but who protests it. In November 2006 the school district agreed to pay for Jackson's financial losses and keep him as a coach, settling the case.

Preparing for trial of Milutinovich's suit, her attorneys deposed Fresno State president Welty in February 2006. Milutinovich noticed a subtle change after that. Her bosses at the Student Union seemed more distant.

"I'm going to be fired," she told her attorneys. No, no, they assured her: "They're not that stupid, to fire you a second time."

Pick C. Fresno State dumped Milutinovich in July 2006.

During Title IX's thirty-fifth anniversary year, 2007, men's sports advocates sued the Education Department in an attempt to weaken the law, this time calling their group Equity in Athletics and using arguments that already had been rejected in *Cohen v. Brown* in the 1990s. An appeals court rejected this suit too.[49] The conservative Pacific Legal Foundation again asked OCR to rescind the three-prong test in 2007, but OCR declined. These kinds of lawsuits and campaigns finally tapered off after more than three decades of failure to stop Title IX in athletics, but plenty of educational institutions still didn't offer equitable athletics programs.

Title IX was popular: a solid 82 percent of a thousand adults surveyed said they supported Title IX in a 2007 poll by the NWLC, Greenberger testified before twelve U.S. representatives on June 19, 2007.[50] Yet, OCR conducted only one compliance review in athletics in the previous five years under President Bush, she said. And coaches—who have the easiest access to evidence of inequities—filed just 8 percent of the 416 athletics complaints in the prior four years because they feared retaliation. Half of coaches' complaints reported retaliation.

Volleyball Coach Lindy Vivas sued Fresno State in February 2006, alleging retaliation for her whistleblowing on Title IX violations, and discrimination based on her gender, marital status (she was not married), and perceived sexual orientation. With not much else happening in the hot Fresno summer, on June 4, 2007, news media converged on the boxy eight-story county courthouse with the honeycombed concrete façade for a five-week trial.[51]

Milutinovich testified, wearing a "IX" pin on her lapel. Coach Wright testified about the "dykes on spikes" incident, Ugly Women Athletes Day, and more; she then got threatening calls on her office phone. Campus security told her to drive a different route home every night. Johnson-Klein described on the witness stand the many homophobic comments made by athletics administrators, and how Scott Johnson had told department officials to make Vivas's life miserable.

Supporters packed the courtroom for the jury verdict. One of them, former Fresno State coach Donna Pickel, had brought her laptop each day of the five-week trial to send out summaries to a network of athletics advocates. "LINDY WON! LINDY WON! LINDY WON! POINT! GAME! MATCH!!!!!!!" her message read that night.

Before the trial Fresno State had offered Vivas $15,000 to drop her suit. The jury awarded her $5.85 million.[52] Jurors told Vivas and her lawyers that they'd created a nickname after hearing Fresno State's top five officials testify. They called them "the fabulous fibbing five." Milutinovich and other Vivas supporters headed for The Lime Lite restaurant, converging in the long bar until Vivas walked in. Cheers and applause erupted from thirty or so allies raising glasses.

Fresno State offered Milutinovich $3.5 million a few months later to drop her suit. She probably had the strongest case among the lawsuits by her, Vivas, and Johnson-Klein. She probably could get more through a trial, she reasoned, but that wasn't guaranteed. The university appealed the Vivas verdict, so it wasn't over yet, and who knew what would happen in the Johnson-Klein trial?

"Pigs get slaughtered," her brothers told her. She didn't want to be greedy.

She figured $1.2 million of the offer would go to her lawyers and $1 million to taxes, leaving her with $1.3 million. Milutinovich was fifty-nine years old, near the end of her career; she just needed enough to live on and feel vindicated. Plus, she wanted to spare her family the stress of a trial.

At a press conference in the courthouse with her mother and two brothers looking on, Milutinovich announced the settlement, which included giving her the title and privileges of associate athletic director emeritus, without any confidentiality clause so she could talk about the case. Her five-year struggle showed the importance of standing up for fairness, she said: "Hopefully, when you do that, you'll leave it better for those who come after you."[53]

Word already had gone out: *Let's meet up at The Lime Lite to celebrate.*

At Stacy Johnson-Klein's trial soon after, there was no dispute that she had asked one of her student basketball players for a Vicodin pill to get through some shoulder pain left from a car accident. The coach called it a "poor decision" and said she'd taken one pill.[54] But the same year that Fresno State suspended Johnson-Klein, locked her out, separated her from her team, publicly announced her firing, and issued a press release accusing her of multiple misdeeds, Fresno State cut a different deal with Men's Basketball Coach Ray Lopes. He had 457 NCAA violations. He made prohibited recruiting calls, knew about his players' drug use but failed to address it, and may have helped a player avoid questioning about a murder. Administrators paid Lopes through the end of the season, giving him a severance package and no public reprimand.

After Johnson-Klein's nearly nine-week trial, everyone expected the jurors to deliberate for days. A quick decision would favor the university, lawyers predicted. Milutinovich was home when the call came after just four hours: the jury had finished and soon would deliver its verdict. She phoned one friend after another, driving her SUV to the courthouse. Dozens of supporters crowded the narrow second-floor hallway, hugging and talking into cell phones.

One who wasn't there but was following the trial closely was Rayma Church, the former attorney for Milutinovich and Vivas who got pushed out of her firm and moved to Missouri. Church had flown in on her own dime months earlier to assist with jury selection in Vivas's trial and help prepare Vivas to take the stand. Church realized that she missed Fresno. She moved back after Vivas's trial and practiced employment law independently until her old firm—which had struggled without her—asked her to come back on her terms.

Church felt too anxious to join the crowd for Johnson-Klein's verdict, so she went for a drive in her six-year-old Ford Explorer Sport truck. As she pulled back into her office parking lot, her cell phone rang. Church pushed the stick shift into park before answering. On the other end, Vivas laughed with gusto.

"What? What?" Church said.

Overwhelmed and ecstatic at the quick verdict, Vivas finally got two words out: "Nineteen million." Jurors awarded Johnson-Klein $19.1 million, one of the largest jury verdicts in history to that point against an institution for any kind of discrimination.[55] Church walked from the truck and pulled open the side door of her office building. The whole staff of her firm lined both sides of the hallway, clapping. She met up soon after with everyone else at The Lime Lite.

Within a few years plaintiffs won millions in similar suits at multiple universities around the country.[56]

Judges reduced the Vivas and Johnson-Klein jury awards and the university appealed, eventually settling for a total payout of nearly $18 million in just these three cases ($5.4 million in the Vivas case, $3.5 million to Milutinovich, and $9 million to Johnson-Klein and her lawyers), compared with $2.8 million paid out by the entire California State University system in the previous five years.[57] Settlements with several other women coaches and secretaries in less public complaints of sex discrimination over the same decade cost Fresno State approximately another half a million dollars.[58] A state university insurance system covered most of the payouts.

Both President Welty and the university system chancellor received raises. Neither ever admitted any wrongdoing.

Milutinovich, Vivas, and Johnson-Klein never worked on the college level again.

It's a form of retaliation not covered by Title IX. "No one can force them to hire you," Milutinovich said. Many women coaches, including at the Universities of Iowa and Minnesota-Duluth, also lost their jobs; some sued under Title IX but couldn't work again. When men coaches lost their jobs, they got recycled with second and third and fourth chances.

Coach Margie Wright, who hadn't been forced out, remained in Fresno State athletics. Mediation of her Title IX complaint in 2008 brought around $605,000 in pay and increased benefits, a renewable five-year contract, and some improvements for the softball program. She retired in 2012 after winning more games than any Fresno State coach in history, and returned in May 2014 to throw out the first pitch when the school renamed the softball stadium the "Margie Wright Diamond."[59]

Separate from the lawsuits, Milutinovich's Title IX complaints to OCR went forward, with a twist. A consultant hired by Fresno State convinced OCR to transfer the complaints to its Seattle office instead of San Francisco to avoid potential bias. Milutinovich called the best-known Title IX activist in the Pacific Northwest for advice—Herb Dempsey.

Dempsey chose Title IX compliance monitoring as his hobby when he retired from teaching and law enforcement in the 1990s. He called and wrote to schools and OCR, when needed, whenever and wherever he saw athletics inequities. Once word got out about his doings, girls and parents from all over the country asked for his help. He communicated with a small army of gadfly fathers—dubbed "dadflys" by *Sports Illustrated*—who fought for their girls just like the fathers of the 1970s who initiated most of the early sex-discrimination lawsuits in athletics.

A white, balding grandfather with a pugnacious penchant for verbal jousting, Dempsey filed nearly a thousand Title IX complaints by 2007 and was involved in roughly two-thirds of OCR athletics cases in Washington State over a decade, he estimated.[60] "Everybody has biases," said Dempsey of Battle Ground, Washington. "But when you use my tax money to enforce your bias, and when your bias is a sexist pig's bias, then you and I are going to a barbecue pit!"[61]

Computer technology made his project easier. Dempsey would "fly" over a school using Google Earth. If the baseball field had lights but the softball team didn't, or if the boys played on groomed fields while the girls played in a bog, he initiated contact. Not everyone appreciated his stream of complaints to OCR. They clogged up the pipeline and delayed federal consideration of bigger, better-researched cases with potentially stronger impact, some staff at the NWLC felt. An inadequately funded and staffed OCR couldn't handle it all.

Dempsey saw his and the NWLC's work as complementary. At the current rate of progress, it would take another 131 years for sports opportunities to be split fairly between boys and girls, he calculated using National Federation of High Schools data. He took a NWLC complaint letter, replaced particulars with blank spaces, and used it as a template that he shared with the dadflys.

At Fresno State, OCR eventually used Milutinovich's Title IX complaints to require forty-five remediation actions in athletics that would take years to complete. They didn't close the case until 2016.[62]

Probably 80 percent of colleges and universities had enough compliance problems in 2008 that they violated Title IX, one consultant estimated.[63] OCR issued another Dear Colleague letter on September 17, 2008, clarifying criteria defining a sport: activities like cheerleading that promote and support other sports don't qualify.[64]

In the 2008 presidential campaign, Democrat Barack Obama promised to strengthen Title IX enforcement and said he'd support a bill to require high schools to report athletics data.[65] He won the election but the bill didn't pass. On April 20, 2010, his OCR formally withdrew the controversial 2005 clarification that had weakened prong three of the three-prong test by interpreting non-responses to emailed surveys as lack of interest in athletics.[66]

As the nation grappled with a severe economic recession, college football spending showed no signs of abating. About a hundred coaches at schools in the NCAA's Football Bowl Subdivision made $1 million or more per year.[67] Base pay averaged $267,000 to coach a men's sport and $98,100 for a women's team in 2010; benefits and other resources widened that disparity. Most of the 1,100 intercollegiate coaches surveyed said they received no formal training on Title IX and relied on the media for their knowledge of the law, an unpublished study found.[68] The intentional ignorance bred into the system made both willing and unwitting discrimination more likely than it should have been.

On the K-12 level, Title IX helped revolutionize girls' sports, but less so for urban children or communities with people of color or immigrants, the Women's Sports Foundation reported in 2008.[69] In the suburbs, girls and boys played sports at close to the same rate: 50 percent and 54 percent, respectively. But only 35 percent of city girls played a youth sport compared with 51 percent of city boys. Few athletics programs anywhere offered opportunities for kids with disabilities.

Urban girls regularly had to play under unpaid or barely paid coaches, scrounge to buy uniforms, and arrange their own transportation to competitions, the *New York Times* reported. Urban girls—who were more likely to be girls of color, immigrants, or from economically disadvantaged families—still struggled with challenges that all girls had faced at Title IX's creation.[70] The Title IX revolution in athletics hadn't reached everyone equally.

11

Sexual Assault

2000–2010

THE SHADOWS OF GEBSER AND DAVIS HAUNTED COURTHOUSES IN THE NEW century. The weakening of Title IX in the courts made complaints to the Office for Civil Rights (OCR) a more important option for sexually harassed students when schools failed to help them.

While most of any attention to Title IX in the 2000s revolved around athletics, the movement against sexual harassment and violence in all sectors of society built momentum, enough to generate more organized pushback from alleged perpetrators and the conservative groups that championed them. The inaction or even obstructionism of educational institutions became more apparent as survivors of sexual violence and harassment called out the policies that protected perpetrators and failed survivors. Student survivors increasingly highlighted the institutionalized discrimination, not just the harmful actions of the perpetrators.

OCR's 2001 Dear Colleague letter, published in the final days of the Clinton administration, updated the 1997 Title IX regulations around sexual harassment to reflect Gebser and Davis and reemphasized administrators' responsibility to prevent and deal fairly with the problem.[1] "If harassment has occurred, doing nothing is always the wrong response," it read—a pretty low bar to clear but indicative of what was (or wasn't) happening on many campuses. A 2002 study illustrated the potential harm of responding ineffectively to even one rapist: 120 of 1,900 college men said they'd done things that met definitions of rape or attempted rape, and 63 percent of those said they did it more than once, with an average of six victims each.[2]

Bush administration appointees shelved the OCR 2001 guidance on sexual harassment shortly after his inauguration, though, removing it from the website.[3] They considered it "not more official than a brochure," one staffer said, though the public mostly didn't know this.[4]

The 2001 guidance didn't explicitly discuss using the "preponderance of evidence" standard to assess reports of sexual harassment, but it emphasized that Title IX's civil procedures appropriately differ from legal standards used in criminal investigations. OCR in the 2000s did clarify more than once that schools must assess sexual harassment complaints based on a preponderance of the evidence, not stricter criteria like "clear and convincing" evidence or the criminal-law standard of "beyond a reasonable doubt" that make it likely a victim's educational rights will not be protected. OCR echoed its 1995 letter to Evergreen State College in letters to Georgetown University and the University of Virginia criticizing their policies for expecting "clear and convincing" evidence.[5] "This raised concerns that it was more difficult than it should be for the University to hold students and employees responsible for acts of sexual harassment," an OCR official wrote in 2004.[6]

Most colleges and universities did not say which standard of proof they used for student disciplinary cases in 2002 and 2004 surveys. Of the 20 percent that did share that information, 81 percent used a preponderance of evidence.[7]

As awareness of sexual violence grew, research expanded to investigate institutional responses. More survivors pushed for justice, and the media paid closer attention.

One study in 1999 found that colleges and universities used a variety of definitions of sexual assault, did little preventive education, and inconsistently met their reporting obligations under the Clery Act.[8] More than a third (36 percent) of colleges didn't report crime statistics in ways required by the Clery Act, according to a 2002 study funded by the Department of Justice. Salem International University in West Virginia, which had documented sexual offenses on its campus, never included them in its Clery Reports and agreed in 2005 to pay $200,000 in federal fines. LaSalle University in Pennsylvania paid $87,500 in 2007. The government fined Eastern Michigan University $350,000 in 2008.[9] But the Department of Education deserved some of the blame—it didn't publish a handbook explaining the 1990 law's provisions until 2005.

Other research since the 1980s had revealed obstacles on the personal level that hindered attention to the problem of sexual misconduct: many young men and women didn't recognize their experiences as sexual harassment or rape, even when it met legal definitions, or felt afraid to seek help when they did recognize it.

Tufts University student Wagatwe Wanjuki helped her very drunk boyfriend stumble across the green expanse of the President's Lawn on campus in Medford, Massachusetts, trying to get him safely back to his place. "It's all your fault!" he yelled at her, angry that he'd been kicked out of a bar hosting an off-campus student event.

He was just being belligerent, she thought. She'd learned to accommodate his belligerence. Still, it hurt that he blamed her.[10]

The daughter of strict immigrant parents from Kenya and the Bahamas, Wanjuki had little social independence before she arrived as a freshman at Tufts in 2004 and, like most college students, jumped into exploring her freedom. Her parents had done their best to give her the confidence of belonging in rich, white America, moving the family to white suburbs and sending her to a private all-girls preparatory high school on scholarships. She won another scholarship to Tufts, a predominantly white, private university near Boston. Wanjuki struggled academically the first year in part because she didn't know how to ask for help, hadn't needed to ask for it before. Taking summer classes kept her on track with her cohort, though.

She started dating her boyfriend her sophomore year. It was weird, how he took her silence for consent. It felt like he "took" sex from her. And sometimes they clashed. In one argument, he told her to leave but she didn't leave fast enough. He called the cops. When they arrived, he falsely told them she wasn't a Tufts student, and they arrested her. That changed the dynamic between them. She knew he always had the option of calling police. They both were Black, but the police would believe him over her.

At a Halloween party at his fraternity a month later, one drink that may have been spiked with a date-rape drug sent Wanjuki into a near-blackout. She woke up the next day at his place and became aware they'd had sex, though she'd been in no shape to consent. A tiny voice in her head whispered, "That's rape. You should call the cops." But she didn't think the police would help. And she couldn't tell her peers; they would think she's crazy. It seemed easier and somehow more respectable to keep dating him, to try to make it a relationship.

It wasn't easy. He was good at isolating her, criticizing her to other people so they stopped talking to her. He broke into her emails and deleted everything. She struggled again academically and kept to herself. But her senior year, Wanjuki joined a peer education group that facilitated discussions about healthy relationships. She started to accept that a lot of what was going on wasn't okay.

That night at the bar in December 2007, wildly drunk, he threatened to kill her. Everybody heard. The bar staff kicked him out. Still in a caretaking role, Wanjuki left the event early and went with him, worried he might pass out and suffocate on his own vomit before he made it home. But when he shoved her and hurt her arm, something snapped awake inside her.

"I'm done," she thought. "I'm totally done" with him.

Traumatized and struggling, Wanjuki dropped out before finals. Tufts put her on academic probation—she was not allowed to return until the spring semester of 2009. She called the Tufts victims' advocate and, with her encouragement, reported the ex-boyfriend to Tufts police. That went nowhere. In spring 2008 she filed a detailed complaint through Tufts' generic adjudication process for student misconduct. That, too, went nowhere. From the start, it seemed to Wanjuki that administrators were more concerned about him than her and acted like she was a jilted ex-girlfriend seeking revenge. Tufts officials decided most of the abuse happened outside their one-year deadline for reporting, so they didn't need to act. They offered Wanjuki no help, academic or otherwise, she said. She moved home. He graduated on time.

Returning to Tufts in spring semester 2009 proved emotionally and mentally tougher than Wanjuki expected. She found it hard to concentrate.

In her first women's studies class, she got to know a classmate who eventually revealed that she too had been sexually assaulted. But she'd reported it right away, submitted to a rape evidence collection kit, done everything "right" to make her case, and Tufts still did nothing, she said. "Oh," Wanjuki realized, "this is a systemic problem."

They started a campus chapter of Students Active for Ending Rape (SAFER), through which they learned of Title IX. After unproductive meetings with Tufts administrators in which the students asked for more survivor-supportive policies, they organized a huge "town hall" during finals week, where sexual assault survivors spoke spontaneously. "I walk past my rapist every day on campus," one said, then choked up and ran out.

Wanjuki's grades suffered, so she started summer classes at Tufts to catch up. About halfway through, a letter came: Tufts was expelling her for academic reasons, it read. The university rejected her appeal. She moved home again with her parents in New Jersey.

Wanjuki was an unemployed Black woman with no college degree, no health insurance, and immense tuition loan debts during the worst economic recession since World War II. Depressed, anxious, and adrift, she bought an 89-cent internet domain name—RapedAtTufts.info—and, in the early years of social media, started blogging about her ordeal. Race, sex, and socioeconomic class influenced how she'd been treated by police and by Tufts, Wanjuki believed. She opened a Twitter account, @rapedattufts.

That caught Tufts' attention. Before long, Tufts changed its policy to extend the statute of limitations for reporting rape. In 2010 Wanjuki filed an anonymous Title IX complaint with OCR against Tufts. Slowly, she rebuilt her life, enrolling in community college in 2011 with the help of financial aid and then a scholarship. That gave her the confidence to finish her degree at Rutgers University, ten years after she first enrolled at Tufts and still facing crushing debt.

All over the country, activists tried multiple ways to change campus policies. A Harvard University–sponsored report recommended requiring "sufficient independent corroboration" of sexual violence complaints before conducting investigations, a policy that left victims in the lurch since sexual assaults often happen in intimate spaces with no witnesses or evidence. An anonymous Harvard student complained to OCR in June 2002 with the help of attorney Wendy J. Murphy. After months of OCR investigating, Harvard retracted its "corroboration" requirement; OCR accepted its revised policy as compliant with Title IX.[11]

Other activists created organizations. Walk a Mile in Her Shoes became a popular event on college campuses starting in 2001. Men, especially from fraternities, signed up to walk a mile in high heels and receive anti-violence materials on the premise that it built empathy and potentially reduced dating violence, sexual assault, and stalking. On the contrary, a 2015 study suggested, Walk a Mile in Her Shoes reinforced gender inequalities and did not address the gendered abuse of power at the root of most sexual violence.[12]

SAFER, a chapter of which Wanjuki helped start at Tufts, originated with Columbia University students in 2000, providing data and training in campus organizing to help students reform their college's sexual assault policies; it converted to a national nonprofit organization in 2004.[13] Tarana Burke in 2006 founded the nonprofit Just Be Inc. and its "Me Too" program to support younger Black victims of sexual harassment and violence.[14] Students at Spelman College, a historically Black women's college, in 2006 complained of sexual assaults by students at the adjacent historically Black men's college, Morehouse, which led to a documentary film by Spelman graduate Laura Holman Rahman about sexual violence at historically black colleges and universities, *Broken Social Contracts*.[15]

Still others fought "gag rules" or non-disclosure agreements commonly imposed by colleges and universities on students as part of sexual harassment investigations; officials typically blamed the Family Educational Rights and Privacy Act for their overly suppressive policies designed to protect college reputations as much as student privacy.

S. Daniel Carter of the nonprofit Security on Campus successfully filed complaints against Georgetown University, the College of William and Mary, and others for violating the Clery Act and Title IX through gag orders and by giving investigation results to accused perpetrators but not to complainants.[16] (In the neutral terminology of Title IX proceedings, someone filing a complaint about sexual assault or harassment is the "complainant," the accused perpetrator of the assault is the "respondent" to the complaint, and the educational institution is the "recipient" of federal funding and as such is required to protect victims' access to education.) Congress amended the Clery Act in 2008, explicitly requiring institutions of higher education to disclose the results of disciplinary proceedings for sex offenses and violent crimes to complainants and respondents alike—such a basic tenet of fairness that it's hard to imagine today why they wouldn't.[17]

Even when assault survivors didn't know about Title IX—a common problem—some still protested injustice. Laura Dunn contacted a news reporter to describe how the University of Wisconsin delayed action for ten months after her 2005 report that a crew team member and others raped her, then botched the investigation. S. Daniel Carter saw the story and emailed Dunn about her rights, which is how she first learned about Title IX. Ultimately, OCR found "insufficient evidence" that Dunn's university wasn't prompt but required it to set goals for timely handling of complaints.[18] Dunn later got a law degree and founded the nonprofit SurvJustice to provide legal assistance to sexual assault survivors.

Some outcomes were worse. A few days after Penn State University decided to withhold her rapist's degree for only a year, Angela Tezak overdosed on sleeping pills and needed five days of hospitalization; she dropped out and eventually transferred. Megan Wright dropped out of Dominican College in New York State after being gang-raped and suffering flashbacks while the college essentially did nothing, waiting for police to investigate. She suffocated herself at home with a plastic bag in 2006. Two years later the college agreed to appoint a Title IX coordinator (something they'd been required to do for more than three decades) and paid a state fine of $20,000 for fraudulent crime statistics. OCR faulted at least three other schools in 2004–2007 for delays in sexual assault investigations.[19]

A case-control study of 2,005 women who'd been physically or sexually attacked found they were 50–70 percent more likely than non-abused women to develop gynecologic or chronic stress-related or central nervous system problems including headaches, back pain, vaginal bleeding or infections, sexually transmitted diseases, pelvic pain, painful intercourse, urinary tract infections, appetite loss, abdominal pain, and digestive problems. Another study of 304 women found higher risk for significant depression, anxiety, and poor sleep in those who'd been sexually assaulted.[20]

Sexual violence, plus betrayal by the institutions that were supposed to help, clearly hurt victims and by extension their ability to stay in school. Like sex discrimination in athletics, though, the problems festered despite decades of movements to stop them. Partly because the people holding power refused to acknowledge that the assaults were happening or made weak efforts to address them, and partly because there seldom were repercussions if they just ignored the problem. They blamed women for mis-interpreting "normal" sexual behavior and lying about assailants' actions. Another factor was the persistent belief that these were isolated incidents. The broader society didn't yet realize the ubiquity of sexual assault.

That started to change as major media exposés revealed epidemics of sexual assaults in the U.S. military, the Catholic Church, and the Boy Scouts of America.[21] The few campus assaults that drew headlines often featured popular sports programs.

Two former players in the powerhouse women's soccer program at the University of North Carolina sparked ten years of legal battles when they filed a Title IX lawsuit in 1998 alleging a sexually hostile environment under Coach Anson Dorrance. The university paid $355,000 to plaintiffs and agreed to revise its sexual harassment policy.[22]

The national TV talk show *The Jane Pauley Show* invited Bernice Sandler to be a guest in November 2004 for discussions about coaches who sexu-ally abuse their athletes.[23] She'd been serving on a new Centers for Disease Control and Prevention advisory board for the National Sexual Violence Resource Center and published her second book in 2005, *Student-to-Student Sexual Harassment, K-12: Strategies and Solutions for Educators to Use in the Classroom, School, and Community*, co-authored with Harriett M. Stonehill.[24] On top of her campus trips to give talks, Sandler got a few calls almost every month from students, staff, or faculty wanting to consult about athletics inequities, sexual harassment, or hostile environments. One Arizona woman called fifteen to twenty times for advice at various stages after being raped at a party.

Scandal enveloped the University of Colorado at Boulder when Lisa Simpson sued in 2004 for the mishandling of her report of rape by five football players and recruits. An appellate court criticized Colorado Uni-versity's "official policy of showing high school football recruits a 'good time' on their visits" without sufficient supervision, so that "the likelihood of such misconduct was so obvious that Colorado University's failure was the result of deliberate indifference." The school settled Simpson's Title IX lawsuit three years later for $2.85 million.[25]

College students who scored higher on measures of racism, sexism, homophobia, ageism, classism, and religious intolerance were more likely to accept rape myths, 2006 research showed.[26] And members of all-men groups like sports teams and fraternities that tolerated rape myths were more likely to sexually assault someone than men students as a whole, a 2007 study reported.[27]

Assault survivors who caught the news media's attention tended to be white women, perhaps because of the media's penchant for focusing on attractive, young, straight, able-bodied white women. Surveys suggested that more marginalized groups experienced higher rates of sexual assault but they faced added barriers to being heard and getting help, seldom making the news.

At one major university, students complained to administrators of racial stalking by a white man professor who targeted Japanese women because "he believes they are submissive" and wanted "sex slaves." Their demands were modest: counseling for the professor to get past his need to sexually subordinate women, and HIV counseling. Officials denied he was an "agent" for the university, saying his behavior was "private," outside the university's reach. When students tried to warn incoming freshmen about him, the professor and the university threatened them with legal action for defamation and invasion of privacy. A book chapter that described the case kept the students and the school anonymous to avoid repercussions for the students.[28]

National media and internet coverage of gang-rape allegations against Duke University lacrosse team members in 2006–2007 handed sexual assault deniers a victory they exploited for years to come. Crystal Mangum, a Black college student and single mother of two, told police she'd been hired as an "exotic dancer" and then raped and sexually assaulted by three white lacrosse co-captains at their off-campus house. After an investigation, a grand jury indicted them. But the local district attorney hid the fact that DNA evidence from the medical exam didn't match that of the three players; defense attorneys took the unprecedented step of getting the North Carolina State Bar to charge him with concealing evidence and being too outspoken about a case. The district attorney dropped the rape charges; at Mangum's request, he pursued the remaining charges until he had to hand off the case to the state attorney general so that he could defend himself before the state bar.

Mangum never got her day in court. Attorney General Roy Cooper dropped the remaining charges and unilaterally declared the players "innocent." He never charged her with making false accusations, but the media coverage merged with the widely accepted myth that women lie about sexual assault. Media commentators brandished the Duke lacrosse case to counter any allegations of sexual assault anywhere. Two far-right extremists launched their careers by vocally defending the lacrosse players—Republican political advisor Stephen Miller and white nationalist Richard Spencer.[29]

The overlapping influences of gender, race, and class in the Duke case seldom drew nuanced discussion in mass media. But recognition of the layered and intersecting effects of race, sex, class, sexual orientation, and other factors was growing. Public recognition of the experiences of women of color facing discrimination because of the interlocking effects of race and gender became more visible, for example.

Counterintuitive to many white feminist leaders, women of color were more likely than white women to consider themselves feminists, according to research in 2003 by the Center for the Advancement of Women. But many women of color felt detached from the mainstream feminist movement because it long had neglected issues of greater importance to minority communities, such as gun violence.[30]

During three years in the late 2000s, three foundations organized a series of gatherings of diverse women leaders (especially women of color) from academia, grassroots organizations, and national groups in what they called the New Women's Movement Initiative. Organizers asked participants to work through their differences in age, race, ethnicity, geographic location, economic status, sexuality, and so on to reach consensus on a new agenda for the women's movement. That agenda must be based on a "social justice feminism," participants decided, one that forges a link between theory and action. That action must work from the bottom up, supporting leadership from society's least empowered to dismantle structures propped up by intersecting discriminations, wrote Kristin Kalsem and Verna L. Williams, the former National Women's Law Center (NWLC) attorney who argued the *Davis* case in the Supreme Court and then taught law at the University of Cincinnati.[31]

As those concepts began to gain traction in social change movements, OCR fielded a diverse array of discrimination complaints. OCR director Stephanie Monroe noted that "a significant number of students are still subjected to sexual harassment" when she re-released OCR'S 2001 Title IX guidance with a Dear Colleague letter on January 25, 2006. She alerted officials that OCR would be conducting compliance reviews related to sexual harassment in schools.

For most of the decade, though, other issues occupied OCR, on top of athletics. Boy Scouts of America policies excluding gay or transgender people and atheists led some schools to stop providing meeting space on campuses. Congress passed a 2002 law saying that schools can't keep Boy Scouts off campus if they let other "patriotic" groups use school facilities. OCR sent Dear Colleague letters in 2006 and 2009 to get schools to follow that rule.[32] (Scandal later engulfed the Boy Scouts in 2012 when records revealed the organization had hidden from the public its knowledge of 7,819 scout leaders accused of sexually assaulting 12,254 victims over a seventy-two-year period. Facing hundreds of lawsuits, the organization declared bankruptcy. By July 2021 more than 84,000 people claimed they were sexually abused as Scouts; the organization agreed to pay $850 million to those victims.)[33]

Conservative idealogues framed harassment complaints as overreactions trying to squelch free speech, so OCR distributed a Dear Colleague letter in July 2003 saying civil rights regulations do not constrain First Amendment rights. Another Dear Colleague letter on April 24, 2004, reminded schools of their Title IX responsibilities, motivated by an OCR review of selected schools showing some *still* hadn't instituted Title IX's most basic provisions: designating a Title IX coordinator; disseminating the coordinator's contact information; implementing a nondiscrimination policy; and adopting grievance procedures.

Single-sex classrooms and schools became a hot point. Despite a federal report concluding that single-gender education may violate Title IX, the Constitution, and state constitutions, OCR in 2004 under President George W. Bush adopted somewhat vague rules under Title IX allowing single-sex education in public schools.[34] Quickly, plans sprang up for several hundred single-sex programs "with no end in sight," Sandler wrote in a 2007 article. "This is the most dangerous attack on Title IX . . . because these programs typically reinforce stereotypes . . . [and] with very rare exceptions, single-sex programs and classes in public schools almost always shortchange girls."[35]

Growing concerns about bullying led to a ten-page OCR Dear Colleague letter in October 2010. Sections on sexual and gender-based harassment reminded educators that under Title IX they must fight bullying of people of any sexual or gender orientation and should make it clear that educators "could not require the student to confront" the harasser.

For Title IX's thirty-fifth anniversary in 2007, the American Association of University Women's Lisa M. Maatz refocused attention on the problem of sexual harassment at a congressional subcommittee hearing.[36] Citing the results of an AAUW 2001 study, Maatz shared that 80 percent of high school students reported being sexually harassed—one in four of them "often." So did 62 percent of college students.[37] Because OCR never sanctioned schools as long as administrators agreed to change, and because the Supreme Court made lawsuits so difficult, they incentivized schools to ignore the problem unless someone filed a complaint, which few survivors did, Maatz said. Congress could repair the damage done by the *Gebser* and *Davis* decisions, she argued. It needed to pass legislation so it's not harder to prove sexual harassment in schools than in the workplace.

Congress didn't do that, but the Supreme Court shored up one of the other tools students relied on. Parents of an elementary school student being harassed by peers had sued under both Title IX and the Constitution's equal protection clause. Lower courts said they couldn't do that, but the Supreme Court ruled in 2009 that plaintiffs can sue for sex discrimination in education under both Title IX and the Fourteenth Amendment at once.[38]

An estimated 6,450 students at twenty-six colleges were sexually assaulted during a six-month period in 2008, based on Department of Justice data, but the schools reported only twenty-five cases that led to campus disciplinary proceedings. OCR had fewer staff than ever before in fiscal 2009 (582 full-time employees), even though complaints of discrimination in education had increased 27 percent since 2002.[39] But locally, women agitated for change and more schools started programs they hoped might prevent sexual violence or assault.

Dozens of Yale freshmen fiddled with miniature red "Stop" signs as an actor and actress took their places on stage in the fall of 2008. "Raise your Stop sign when you think any of the behavior you'll see crosses a line," organizers instructed audience members. Part of Yale's orientation for new students, the "Sex Signals" play staged a rape to start discussions about boundaries.[40]

Student Alexandra Brodsky couldn't believe her eyes. Plenty of people never lifted their "Stop" paddles. Afterward, organizers divided the audience into discussion groups led by students. Brodsky grew increasingly uncomfortable. Her group talked about the play as if the truth about violence was unknowable, as if every opinion was equally valid.

"Well, she let him touch her boobs, so that means that everything that happened afterwards was fine," one guy said. Brodsky snapped. She went off on him, verbally rebuking him for sexist, harmful assumptions. She startled the other students. It was her first week at Yale.

"Ugh," she thought to herself. "I guess I'm going to be *this* girl in college."

That semester, she also became the other "girl"—the one assaulted and stalked by another student. Yale officials discouraged her from taking formal action even though she had a written admission of guilt from him. Don't tell anyone, they advised, to protect *her* "reputation." She didn't know about Title IX. She wanted him to stay away from her. They persuaded the man to transfer out of the small English seminar they shared and leave her alone. Brodsky found that the campus seemed to shrink as she learned to avoid places where he still lived and frequented, and even more so as friends told her of assaults by other men. They didn't want to go to areas where their assailants might be, or even near the offices where they'd reported the violence and were told, "Clearly, he just loves you. That's why he's doing this."

Brodsky grew up in affluent Westchester, New York. She played sports all her life. As a white person of privilege she entered Yale comfortable in the institution, but the university's hushing of her complaint showed that the campus was not hers, which hurt worse than the violence. She couldn't imagine how the experience might shake someone who didn't naturally feel at home in a space of power and privilege.

Waves of Yale women campaigned to stop sexual harassment and violence in the 2000s, through Take Back the Night events, articles in major magazines, and more.[41] Someone filed a Clery Act complaint against Yale in August 2004 for leaving campus-adjudicated sexual assaults out of its reports, listing only those referred to police. Yale expanded its reporting in 2007 but the Department of Education cited Yale on May 23, 2011, for failing to disclose crime statistics.[42]

In 2004, fraternity men stole four T-shirts featuring artwork by Yale sexual assault survivors—displayed in a Clothesline Project that was part of Take Back the Night events—then photographed themselves wearing them. The next year, fraternity pledges stole twenty of forty-eight Clothesline Project T-shirts. Frat brothers made pledges march through campus in 2006 and other years chanting, "No means yes! Yes means anal!"[43]

When a racist article in a student satire magazine in April 2006 used gross stereotypes casting Asian American students as sexually submissive "gold-diggers" (women) or having "no game" (men), fifteen racial and ethnic student groups at Yale endorsed a statement by students Christine Hung and Annette Wong deploring the racism.[44]

Nearly thirty years after Ann Olivarius initiated *Alexander v. Yale*, her daughter Chase entered Yale in September 2006. A second daughter, Kathryn, enrolled in 2007. They both threw themselves into the diverse and stimulating communities centered around the Yale Women's Center.[45] Each served a year on its board, spending much of their time in the meeting rooms in the basement of Durfee Hall on the Old Campus, next to Durfee's Sweet Shoppe.

Before long, Chase knew three women who'd been raped. She'd seen sexist flyers posted in residence hallways for fraternity parties: "Bro's and ho's," one advertised. Another showed a cartoon of a girl bending over, her ass bare, with the pedophilic headline, "Champagne and schoolgirls." Her second semester, 150 Yale Medical School students signed a letter protesting sexual harassment on campus that included eight sexual assaults.[46] Administrators said they'd review their policies.

In front of the Women's Center in January 2008, soon after Kathryn joined the board, Zeta Psi fraternity pledges gathered with signs reading, "We Love Yale Sluts." Frat brothers posted photos of it on Facebook.

Furious emails flew among the students most involved in the Women's Center and its supporters.

"This time we sue!" Chase insisted.

The Women's Center board denounced the stunt in the *Yale Daily News* and criticized Yale administrators for failing to tackle "the systemic nature of this problem." The issue infused dining hall conversations and lit up online discussion forums. Some commenters called women who were offended by the signs "cunts" or "whiny bitches."[47] Chase wanted to escalate and confront. Kathryn argued for dialogue; the controversy gave Kathryn an opening to talk to fraternities and first-year students about sexual harassment. Women's Center board members—around half of them women of color and diverse in terms of class, sexual orientation, and geographical origin—met repeatedly with administrators.

They never did sue; no attorney would take the case. A Yale task force investigated the Zeta Psi incident and published an insipid report two years later.[48]

As the fall 2009 semester started, someone leaked an anonymous email circulated among men's sports teams and fraternities that ranked fifty-three freshman women by appearance in a "Preseason Scouting Report." Administrators disciplined no one.[49]

But when a Yale lab worker sexually assaulted and strangled graduate student Annie Le days before her wedding in September 2009, it was clear that the protests of recent years had changed the tone of conversations, Kathryn noticed. While *People* magazine reported it as a freak, crazy crime, students talked about it as gender violence.

On a Wednesday in October 2010 at 9:30 at night, approximately thirty-five men from Delta Kappa Epsilon (DKE) fraternity led a line of twenty or so blindfolded pledges in a march outside the Women's Center. Their hands on the shoulders of the man in front of them, pledges chanted to a sea shanty–like tune, "My name is Jack. I'm a necrophiliac. I fuck dead women and fill them with my semen," and "No means yes! Yes means anal!" Women's Center board members convened immediately. They insisted the *Yale Daily News* run a story about the "hate speech" and its "active call for sexual violence." They also posted a video of the chanting men on YouTube and emailed it to a list of groups including sororities.[50]

By the next morning it was the talk of the campus. Thousands of students and alumni signed petitions calling for university action. DKE leaders apologized on Friday, and the Women's Center board wrote, "We do not think that the fraternity brothers intended to incite violence; more likely, they neglected to consider how their words would impact our community." Three days later a *Yale Daily News* editorial shocked and angered nearly everyone by chastising the Women's Center board for overreacting with a "radicalism" that wasn't "the right kind of feminism." Yale put reprimands in the files of DKE leaders and barred the fraternity from campus events and resources for five years.

After the DKE incident, a friend mentioned to Alexandra Brodsky that some students were considering filing a Title IX complaint against Yale. "Yes, yes, yes!" Brodsky said. "I'm on board." She'd started taking a class at the law school on sexual rights and learned about Title IX. Brodsky quietly helped recruit other students to the complaint, meeting in each other's apartments to make a plan.

Sixteen Yale students—women and men, students and recent alumni—filed a twenty-six-page complaint with OCR on March 15, 2011, describing seven years of campus sexual harassment and violence. University inaction produced a hostile educational environment, they said. From the start they agreed not to release the complaint's text publicly or discuss individuals' stories in it, to protect the participants still on campus, some of whom were stalked. When OCR wrote back agreeing to investigate, the group held a press conference on March 31.

"After an attempted assault my freshman year, I left school and was hospitalized for two days because I was ill from stress. When I came back I got a D on an exam—up until that point I had been a straight-A student," one complainant wrote. "I stopped taking courses I thought he would be interested in, stopped hanging out with groups of mutual friends and refrained from participating in organizations he was a part of. I suffered panic attacks when I ran into him."[51]

Unless Yale applied consequences for sexual assault, the problem would continue and victims would continue to lose access to education, several complainants told the press. "Plagiarism is something people are expelled or suspended for, but there seems to be a near-infinite tolerance for rape," said Presca Ahn. Six students of color described the intersectional aspects of the Title IX complaint in the *Yale Daily News*, enumerating cases of harassment and violence against women of color at Yale.[52]

Elsewhere, sexual assault survivors approached news reporter Kristen Lombardi when she lingered at a journalism conference after her talk about reporting on the Catholic Church's cover-up of a pedophile priest. They told her stories of campus cover-ups. That inspired a yearlong investigation by Lombardi and two other reporters at the Center for Public Integrity, which published multiple articles it then compiled into a hundred-page report in 2010, *Sexual Assault on Campus: A Frustrating Search for Justice*.[53] They surveyed 152 crisis services programs, interviewed fifty experts and thirty-three current or former student survivors, and assessed ten years of Title IX complaints, Clery Act complaints, and lawsuit documents.

National Public Radio jointly broadcast the findings. Only one-twentieth of the 20 percent of college women who were sexually assaulted reported it; those who didn't report it blamed themselves, or didn't think they'd be helped, or didn't identify what happened as sexual assault even though it met the definition. Nearly half of those who reported said they unsuccessfully sought criminal charges, then felt betrayed by campus procedures. They all encountered procedures discouraging them from pursuing a complaint, which rarely led to OCR investigations because students didn't know their Title IX rights. Colleges commonly pushed mediation even though federal guidance said they shouldn't because of the trauma and power imbalances in assault cases. Victims' reports of sexual assault seldom resulted in penalties for perpetrators.

As groundbreaking as the Center for Public Integrity's stories and report were, they framed the issue almost solely as a matter of punishing perpetrators, nearly overlooking Title IX's primary purpose of ensuring equitable access to education. That kind of punishment-and-justice outlook conflated Title IX's aims with criminal justice.

Complaints kept coming about colleges ignoring or mishandling sexual assaults. Some schools still claimed to be confused about how to comply with Title IX when managing sexual harassment or assault. OCR rarely ruled against schools for mishandling sexual assaults when it did investigate, the Center's report noted.

OCR director Russlynn Ali pledged to do more.

With President Obama's blessing, she gathered with Vice President Joe Biden and Education Secretary Arne Duncan at a news conference at the University of New Hampshire on April 4, 2011, coincidentally a few days after the Yale students' press conference. OCR announced a new nineteen-page Dear Colleague letter, a short backgrounder, and a two-page flyer, "Know Your Rights: Title IX Prohibits Sexual Harassment and Sexual Violence Where You Go to School." Every related OCR guidance since 1981 had used the phrase "sexual harassment" to cover the gamut from unwelcome sexual comments to violent sexual assaults; this one also explicitly named "sexual violence" as a problem, so no institution could claim ignorance. Like the many Dear Colleague letters and guidance documents before, it tried to give educational institutions the more specific guidance they said they needed to comply with Title IX and put them on notice that OCR would pay more attention.

"Today we are strengthening our response to sexual assault in schools and on college campuses," Biden said.[54]

12

Acceleration

2011–2014

In 1972 Congress carved a set of tools for girls and women who already had been demanding fairness in education when it passed Title IX. Barely more than sturdy poles at first, these rough instruments helped them steer on the flowing waters of the women's movement. OCR's Policy Interpretation of 1979 honed one pole of Title IX's regulations into a more effective shape, after which women paddled furiously toward equity in athletics. With the Dear Colleague letter of 2011, survivors of sexual assault now had a set of oars. They rowed—hard—into a churning confluence of rivers that accelerated flow in a number of social justice movements—against sexual violence, racism, police brutality, and ever-widening economic inequality, and for LGBT rights and humane treatment of immigrants and refugees.

Large demonstrations and marches against the U.S. invasion of Iraq in 2003 didn't stop the war but helped galvanize people to stand up against rising hate crimes against Muslim Americans. Marches for immigrant rights starting in 2006 urged passage of a federal DREAM Act (Development, Relief and Education for Alien Minors) and broader policy reform, led mainly by undocumented Latina, Black, and Asian women who disproportionately identified as LGBT. Two thousand people gathered in Manhattan, on September 17, 2011, and thrust class oppressions and the obscene economic divide into global consciousness with a two-month occupation of Zuccotti Park—dubbed Occupy Wall Street—that inspired copycat demonstrations worldwide.[1]

In 2009, Bay Area Rapid Transit police officers responding to reports of a fight held an unarmed Black man, Oscar Grant, face-down on a con-crete station platform in Oakland. One of the officers, a white man, then shot and killed Grant. After the killing, Pamela Price and other lawyers assisted attorney John Burris in the many lawsuits that went on for years. The grainy cell phone video of the shooting was the first shared widely in a new era of social media exposing police killing people of color. The shooting of unarmed Black seventeen-year-old Trayvon Martin in Febru-ary 2012 in Sanford, Florida, and the 2013 acquittal of his white vigilante killer sparked protests around the country. Three women—Alicia Garza, Patrisse Cullors, and Opal Tometi—started a Black Lives Matter move-ment that from the beginning focused on intersectional discrimination and was led mainly by young, college-educated Black women who predomi-nantly identified as LGBT.[2]

Student sexual assault survivors participated in these sociopolitical cur-rents and fed their concerns about sexual violence into other movements for change. They had no manual to guide them; some parts of being an activist confounded them.

Alexandra Brodsky never knew quite what to say when people approached her to confide that they, too, had been sexually assaulted. She wasn't prepared to be their therapist or social worker at age nineteen; she still isn't. After the Yale complainants' press conference, messages deluged them from students at many schools and alumni going back decades. They hadn't really thought of campus sexual assault as a national issue. They were consumed by the problems right in front of them.

OCR's 2012 report on Yale detailed some of those problems. Yale desig-nated Title IX coordinators among existing staff, adding this to their other job responsibilities, but virtually no students or staff knew who they were because Yale didn't tell them. The coordinators were unclear about their responsibilities. Students were confused by Yale's use of two grievance procedures, both of which advantaged the alleged perpetrator. Yale signed an agreement with OCR to fix these and other deficiencies, but Brod-sky kept hearing stories about Yale administrators silencing and shaming sexual assault survivors.[3]

Complaints to OCR about four-year colleges and universities mishan-dling sexual harassment and assault had started increasing in 2006 and began accelerating in 2010.[4] The 2011 Dear Colleague letter provided many more specifics by which students could judge whether or not their school met its legal responsibilities.

The Dear Colleague letter reiterated some earlier OCR messages that shouldn't have needed repeating. Every school must designate an appropriately trained Title IX coordinator, disseminate notice of nondiscrimination policies, and publicize grievance procedures. Sexual harassment includes sexual assault. Athletics departments shouldn't oversee sexual violence complaints against athletes because of conflicts of interest. Only the "preponderance of evidence" standard is appropriate to address sexual assault under Title IX because it's the only standard that provides equal rights for complainants and respondents. Approximately 61 percent of higher education institutions already used the preponderance standard, according to a study conducted shortly before the Dear Colleague letter.[5]

The letter also clarified areas of potential confusion: Sexual assault is defined as "physical sexual acts perpetrated against a person's will or where a person is incapable of giving consent." Schools must investigate student sexual assaults even if they occur off campus. A single instance of sexual violence is severe enough to create a hostile environment. Mediation is never appropriate after sexual violence.

In case anyone still doubted the need to act, the letter noted that public high schools reported 800 rapes and 3,800 sexual battery incidents in 2007–2008 alone. Colleges and universities reported 3,300 forcible sex offenses in 2009. Everyone knew these were the tip of the iceberg. Only 4–8 percent of sexually assaulted college students reported it to campus officials, and only 2 percent to police.[6]

The problem remained that most students didn't know about Title IX.

But sexual assaults became a more common topic of conversations. In 2012 many campuses screened *The Invisible War*, a documentary about rape in the military.[7] In August, a video of high school boys in Steubenville, Ohio, raping an unconscious girl went viral.[8]

Over the next two years, Title IX would become associated in the public's mind primarily with issues of sexual harassment and assault, much as Title IX was with athletics in the 1970s, and for some of the same reasons.

The immense numbers of girls and women who were affected amplified preexisting movements demanding equity for victims of discrimination, and strong resistance from men who didn't like the changes that were happening intensified public attention.

A mutual friend introduced Brodsky to Amherst College student Dana Bolger, who'd been protesting on her campus after being raped and stalked. A dean encouraged Bolger to put her education on hold when she reported the rape. "Get a job at Starbucks or Barnes and Noble, and come back after he's graduated," he told her. Not knowing her rights, she took his unethical and illegal advice. Soon, though, a friend connected her with the Victim Rights Law Center—the first nonprofit law center solely focused on helping U.S. sexual assault victims, starting in 2003—who told her how Title IX applies to sexual assault, not just sports.

She'd lost a semester. Back at Amherst, Bolger joined a student-run survivors' support group. She and Sonum Dixit, Kinjal Patel, and Nancy Yun Tang started *It Happens Here* in spring 2012, a print and then online magazine about rape at Amherst. She worked an internship at the National Women's Law Center (NWLC) that summer. In June a twenty-one-year-old man killed himself after being raped as a student at Amherst, leaving a suicide note that *It Happens Here* reposted from The Good Men Project's website with the family's permission.[9]

Those developments caught significant attention, but nowhere near the level generated by an October 2012 article in the *Amherst Student* newspaper—an unprecedented, lengthy account by Angie Epifano of being raped by a student and mistreated by administrators, including being forced into a psychiatric ward. No one up to that point had described publicly in such detail the effects of campus sexual assault and the betrayal by people who were supposed to help. Her story crashed the paper's website, drawing more than a hundred thousand views the first day, millions eventually, and generating national media coverage.

A week later, Bolger and Jisoo Lee published a photo project showing eleven Amherst survivors (or their stand-ins) holding signs with words that people said to them when they revealed they'd been raped: "If you didn't want to have sex with him, why were you sitting on his bed two weeks before?" "Was he drunk? Well, that's not as bad." And from a dean, "You never took your case to trial, so you don't actually count as a rape survivor."[10]

Messages poured in from all over, ranging from eighteen-year-olds who said they'd just been raped to eighty-year-olds who never told anyone about their college rape until then. One note came via Twitter direct message from students at the University of North Carolina (UNC), Chapel Hill, asking to talk with Bolger.

Annie Clark expected support when she sought help from a UNC official after being violently raped by a stranger in 2007. The administrator she met with told her, "Rape is like a football game, Annie, and if you look back on a game, what would you do differently in that situation?" Rape is not like football at all, Clark said. "Well, were you drunk?" the woman asked. All Clark heard was blame, blame, blame.

That inspired her to devise a student advocacy project her senior year: she installed "comment" boxes around campus where students could anonymously report being sexually assaulted and pick up pamphlets listing resources.[11]

In spring 2012, Andrea Pino-Silva dropped her anonymous letter in one of the boxes.

The twenty-year-old sophomore had gone to an off-campus party with friends and started dancing with an attractive white guy with blue eyes and brown hair whom she didn't know. She wasn't drinking, but the rest is harder to remember. He pulled her into a bathroom and violently assaulted her. By the time Pino emerged, aching and confused, her friends were gone. She walked back to her dorm alone. The next morning there was blood in her bed. She thought it was her period. More than a week later she tried to run the Tobacco Half Marathon and bled again. Pino started asking her friends what happened that night. It took her months to fully recognize she'd been raped. In vivid nightmares Pino tried to pry the rapist's hands off her neck, waking to bloody scratches on her skin.

Meanwhile she struggled mentally and academically. Research in 2015 showed that most survivors of rape, sexual assault, or abuse suffer a drop in their grade point averages and are more likely to leave school for lack of support.[12] Pino asked for a temporary medical withdrawal from some classes. An administrator granted it but ridiculed her: perhaps she wasn't good enough to handle UNC courses. Later Pino would be diagnosed with depression, generalized anxiety disorder, and post-traumatic stress disorder.

She dropped out of two classes and doubted herself. She also dropped her anonymous report into one of the boxes Clark created.

In a feminist political theory class in fall 2012, Pino learned for the first time about Title IX and *Alexander v. Yale*. It rocked her world. Pino had worked her butt off to get to UNC; she and other students deserved the education that the brochures promised instead of being abandoned to fear school, fail classes, or drop out after sexual assault.

She had met Clark briefly her freshman year. Pino messaged Clark, then in Oregon, via Facebook: "Can I talk to you about something?"

Their conversations gave Pino the courage to come out publicly about the assault. Nine more rape survivors at UNC contacted her. Pino set up meetings with the dean of students and the vice chancellor, just as Clark had met with the chancellor four years earlier. From what they could see, the administration would ignore or delay doing anything until a new batch of students with no institutional memory cycled through.

"The same stuff that's going on here is going on everywhere" but no one is connecting the dots, Pino said to Clark. The two started researching everything they could about Title IX and related laws. Pino tweeted to Bolger; they and Clark talked on Skype. Bolger connected them with Brodsky. The UNC women saw Epifano's essay about Amherst and reached out to her. They tracked down Title IX activists from the 1970s. They tried the NWLC and Legal Momentum but didn't have the money for lawyers. The project consumed them.

Clark sat up in bed at four o'clock one morning with an epiphany. "Couldn't we also do a Clery Act complaint? There's no statute of limitations," she wondered. That makes sense, Pino agreed, but neither knew whether anyone had done that before. More research ahead.

Pino paced the red-orange brick pathways crisscrossing the vast lawns of the UNC campus quadrangle, wishing she could avoid the call she had to make. Her mother answered the phone.

Pino lived in two worlds, between her Cuban American family and culture and the UNC environment. Even when she'd named her assault and rape to herself, she couldn't bear to tell her parents. She was their hero, the first family member in college. They found out because they saw a column she wrote about it for the student newspaper. On top of all this, she'd been figuring out over the past year that she's a lesbian, another tough topic to discuss.

"I need to let you know that we've been working with a reporter at the *Daily Tar Heel*," Pino told her mother. "We're going to have a press conference." They had filed a complaint against UNC, and the federal government had agreed to investigate it. How people might react was unpredictable. "It could be small. It could be big. I don't know. But it's going to happen."

Her mother worried. Could she lose her scholarship? "I don't know," Pino said. "I don't know what it's going to cost me." What mattered more was trying to make her school safe for anyone coming after her.

Her mother's parents had fled Cuba for Florida before the revolution. Her father immigrated from Cuba. Pino grew up in inner city, blue-collar Miami, "Little Havana," where school officials didn't offer much support for a smart, opinionated Latina skeptical of authority figures. When she enrolled in some community college courses on top of her high school classes, a white professor accused her of cheating because there was "no way" a sixteen-year-old like her could write such excellent papers.

Pino threw everything she had into being a model high school student. When UNC accepted her, it was a dream come true. The assault turned her life upside down. She stopped wearing high heels or dresses. She stopped running. Pino dropped her major because it required night classes. She didn't feel safe on campus, not just because of the assault; it seemed clear that UNC officials would not protect or help her.[13]

This was the hardest part for many college assault survivors—betrayal by the institutions they loved, the schools that were supposed to support them. Nearly half of students who reported rape or attempted rape also were betrayed by their schools, whether they realized it or not, research found. Since at least 2008 University of Oregon psychology professor Jennifer J. Freyd and associates had been studying "institutional betrayal" and found it was associated with additional harm—worse trauma symptoms, more reports of anxiety and depression, and greater interference with education.[14]

Clark, Pino, and two other UNC students filed a thirty-four-page complaint with OCR on January 17, 2013, for themselves and sixty-four other anonymous victims. Former associate dean of students Melinda Manning joined the complaint. She'd quit UNC after being pressured by higher-ups to understate the number of sexual assaults on campus, she said. During her time there, at least a hundred students came to her reporting sexual assault; as far as she knew, no perpetrators got expelled, and some assaulted repeatedly.[15]

The complaint alleged violations of Title IX, the Clery Act, the Campus Sexual Assault Victims' Bill of Rights, the Family Educational Rights and Privacy Act, Titles VI and VII of the Civil Rights Act of 1964, and Title II of the Americans with Disabilities Act.[16]

Once OCR took their case, the students called the press conference. "We are here to put a face to our national movement," Clark said.

UNC officials denied responsibility. "The allegations are false. They are untrue. And they are just plain wrong," the university's lawyer said. But Pino did not lose her scholarship.

After the UNC press conference, vandals broke into Pino's residence hall, spray painting large penises and hostile messages everywhere. Someone left a knife near her room. Anonymous haters tweeted: "You deserve to die. Fuck you and your cult of victimhood."[17] One man told Clark in person, "Bang bang, bitch. Die." The abuse echoed harassment dumped on Ann Olivarius of *Alexander v. Yale* and thousands of other students who'd stood up for their rights under Title IX since the 1970s.

For Title IX's fortieth anniversary in 2012, the ACLU publicized its picks for the nine most influential actors in Title IX history, including Bernice Sandler, the *Alexander v. Yale* plaintiffs, and others. Pamela Price and *Alexander* lead attorney Anne E. Simon joined hundreds of supporters at a San Francisco luncheon in June 2012 when Equal Rights Advocates honored Price at its annual fundraiser. In her practice, Price won large awards in the 2000s for sexual and/or racial discrimination against clients who worked for the California prison system (multiple cases), Amtrak (which she argued before the Supreme Court), the City of Oakland, Contra Costa

County, and more. One suit managed by Price and an associated attorney prompted the California Department of Corrections to implement a state-wide policy to address sexual harassment of female officers by inmates.[18] In the 2000s she joined the board of the Lawyers Committee for Civil Rights in San Francisco and for a time served as interim executive director.

Other celebrations of Title IX's fortieth anniversary recognized the law's legacy in athletics. Sandler and Marcia Greenberger stood smiling in the spotlights at center court at the NCAA Women's Basketball Championship in April 2012. The NCAA honored them and four other Title IX advo-cates in a halftime ceremony, praising the activism that enabled so many women's "firsts" in sports.

The basic lack of knowledge about Title IX by many educators still floored Sandler, though. On February 8, 2012, the day that the Penta-gon announced that women could serve closer to the frontlines of battle, the Dallas Independent School District bused five thousand fifth-grade boys—but no girls—on a Black History Month field trip to watch the new film *Red Tails* about the Tuskegee Airmen. Emails obtained by reporters showed that no principal or administrator discussing the trip ever ques-tioned the appropriateness of excluding girls. Sandler's takeaway: schools of education need to do more to teach future educators about Title IX than just mentioning it in courses on law.

Media coverage of Title IX's fortieth anniversary favored celebratory narratives that glossed over political and cultural struggles and cast dis-crimination as a relic of the past, researchers noted. It largely ignored intersectional discrimination in Title IX's story. Although girls' athletic participation in high schools grew from 294,015 in 1972 to nearly 3.3 mil-lion in 2013—definitely something to celebrate—a smaller percentage of Black girls played sports in 2002 compared with 1972: 27 percent versus 35 percent. In higher education, the gap between white and Black wom-en's athletics participation widened in Title IX's lifetime.[19] From an inter-sectional vantage point, Title IX was failing.

Twenty Black women connected to athletics gathered in Harlem that June for a private discussion on "What's Not Being Said About the Title IX Anniversary," hosted by the Schomburg Center for Research in Black Culture. They agreed that the law mostly benefited white women athletes

and administrators, the *New York Times* reported.[20] A few days earlier, at
a similar discussion—this one public—in Washington, DC, to mark Title
IX's fortieth anniversary, a panel of four athletics experts cited the lack
of understanding of intersectional discrimination. "We've stayed at the
1970s thinking that it's one way, it's gender inequality, and that's all," said
Dionne L. Koller, director of the Center for Sport and the Law.[21]

Intersectional discrimination was starting to draw more attention.
Minority students faced harsher discipline and were taught by less experienced and lower-paid teachers. They had less access to rigorous high
school curricula compared with white students, OCR reported in 2012.[22]
Sexual assaults were at least twice as likely to target students of color or
LGBT students than white or non-queer students, a University of Michigan study reported. In addition, multiracial women were sexually harassed
five to thirty-two times more than any other cisgender racial group, wom-
en or men, the Centers for Disease Control and Prevention found in a 2011
study.[23]

Student activists in the movement to support sexual assault survivors
typically learned about each other from conventional media or connected through digital media. Spontaneous uprisings by survivors churned in
non-hierarchical collaborations. Someone started an invitation-only Facebook group called IX Connection for student survivors that drew eight
hundred or so members from around the country. Brodsky and Bolger
noticed Wagatwe Wanjuki's blog, *RapedatTufts*. They reached out, bringing her into the younger activists' networks. Students and faculty at the
University of California, Berkeley, and Occidental College in Los Angeles
read about the North Carolina complaint and contacted Pino and Clark.

Wanting some way to help the many who asked for advice, Brodsky and
Bolger enlisted multiple survivors to create a website sharing resources
for legal action, campus organizing, and self-care. They thought of it as a
one-time project when the Know Your IX site launched in spring 2013.
Simultaneously, Bolger, Brodsky, Wanjuki, and others began organizing
actions to pressure the Education Department's OCR under the name ED
Act Now.

They sweated in the July 2013 heat outside the bulky horizontal concrete of the Education Department headquarters in Washington, DC. A

few dozen students who recognized each other from profile photos on Facebook chanted, "Two, four, six, eight, no more violence, no more hate! Three, five, seven, nine, schools need to follow Title IX!" They took turns using the bullhorn, telling their stories to participants and the media. "Stand up for justice," Wanjuki said. "Don't let other students go through what I went through."[24]

Wearing tank tops and T-shirts with their schools' logos over skirts or shorts, the protesters brought cardboard boxes filled with 115,471 signatures from an online petition demanding tougher, faster enforcement of Title IX and the Clery Act. Education Department officials had agreed in advance that someone would meet with ED Act Now leaders after the event, but protesters were surprised when Undersecretary Martha Kanter came outside to accept the boxes of petitions. She invited them to come in from the heat and meet with Education Secretary Arne Duncan.[25]

They'd been even more surprised the day before when officials from the White House called organizers, inviting them to talk with members of the vice president's office and the Council on Women and Girls. Seven protesters changed into nicer clothes after the rally and headed to the Justice Department. They were six women, including three women of color (Wanjuki, Kate Jae Sun Sim, and Suzanna Bobadilla) and three white women (Brodsky, Bolger, and Laura Dunn) plus queer activist John Kelly, all of whom had attended elite colleges. When security wouldn't let in two of the women of color—both children of immigrants whose names didn't match ID cards exactly—the rest of the group refused to start the meeting without them. After a delay, officials agreed to admit them. The meeting was tense. The students felt betrayed by their government. Those who don't act against violence, they told officials, are complicit in violence. Asked for policy requests, ED Act Now made several, and followed up with multiple phone discussions.[26]

Brodsky and Bolger's Know Your IX (KYIX) took on a life of its own in the following months. Students contacted them for more information. Legislators sought their advice on crafting legislation. But the young activists could see the beginnings of a backlash. They'd need a real organization to deal with all that, they decided. Someone from the nonprofit group Advocates for Youth heard Bolger speak, offered to be their fiscal sponsor, and coached them on raising enough funds for Bolger to be KYIX's sole full-time staff after she graduated in December 2013. KYIX would give students tools and training to organize on their campuses and then carry their concerns to policymakers.

Pino and Clark wanted to offer more of a direct service. Students around the country asked them for help after learning of them through other survivors or media coverage of their January 2013 press conference at UNC. Clark and Pino began coaching students on how to file their own Title IX complaints. A front-page photo of them in a *New York Times* story about the growing activist network in March 2013 opened a floodgate of emails, social media messages, and phone calls to them.[27]

They teamed with Berkeley assault survivor Sofie Karasek and Occidental College faculty Danielle Dirks and Caroline Heldman to co-found End Rape on Campus (EROC) as a voluntary organization in 2013. They would walk survivors through every step of filing and publicizing OCR complaints, if that's what they wanted, and try to connect survivors' stories with the bigger picture. EROC emphasized that this was a ubiquitous, systemic problem. Students at Swarthmore and Occidental, for example, filed their complaints at the same time and mentioned each other at press conferences.

Pino took a semester off and moved in with Clark in Oregon. Clark quit her job, their attention entirely focused on the national movement against campus sexual assault. On one wall of their home pink stickers dotted a large map of the United States, denoting places students had reported sexual assaults: Ohio State, Texas A&M, Appalachian State, University of Tulsa, and dozens more. Stacks of papers covered desks and tables with Title IX studies and reports. They survived on savings and odd jobs.[28]

Many other activist groups popped up, mainly on individual campuses and mostly ephemeral. Dartmouth Change. Our Harvard Can Do Better. Faculty Against Rape. Students applied red tape to spell out "IX" on their mortarboards at graduations.

Pushed by women's advocates, Congress inserted some provisions in its 2013 reauthorization of the Violence Against Women Act to bolster parts of the 2011 Dear Colleague letter, which didn't have the force of law. Section 304, the Campus Sexual Violence Elimination Act (Campus

SaVE), amended the Clery Act so that colleges and universities must provide sexual violence prevention training to incoming students and new
employees that is culturally relevant, responsive to community needs,
and includes diverse communities and identities. The training must also
include bystander intervention options. The bill added three new categories of crimes to be reported in Clery Act data—domestic violence, dating
violence, and stalking—and two new categories of bias to identify hate
crimes: gender identity and national origin.[29]

OCR's work in other areas continued, of course. A Dear Colleague
letter and pamphlet in June 2013 reminded educators of their Title IX
responsibilities to help pregnant and parenting students finish their educations. Only 51 percent of young women with a child before age twenty
achieved a high school diploma by age twenty-two, OCR's materials noted.[30] Fresno, Madera, and Tulare counties had some of the highest teen
pregnancy rates in California, but nearly two years after OCR's reminder
only seven of twenty-two school districts there had support programs for
pregnant or parenting teens. Pregnant girls often got shunted to continuation schools or independent study.[31]

Around the time that OCR and the Department of Justice released a
Dear Colleague letter on January 8, 2014, reminding schools that race discrimination when disciplining students violates Title VI, multiple reports
and statements by the NWLC, Black Lives Matter, and others called attention to biased application of "zero tolerance" policies that fed girls of color
into a school-to-prison pipeline.[32] Another OCR Dear Colleague letter
on May 14, 2014, clarified that civil rights laws apply to public charter
schools too.[33]

But the campus sexual assault problem drew much more federal attention.

"We need to keep saying to anyone out there who has ever been
assaulted—you are not alone. You will never be alone," President Obama
said at a January 22, 2014, news conference launching a high-level Task
Force to Protect Students from Sexual Assault. It had ninety days to develop
recommendations for decreasing assaults and improving school responses.[34]

Soon after Obama's announcement Bolger's phone rang. Tina Tchen,
director of the White House Council on Women and Girls, called to con-
gratulate her and thank her for her work. Four of the federal task force's five

objectives matched demands from the ED Act Now petition six months earlier. Bolger rapidly emailed her activist friends; they'd had no idea the task force was coming. Soon they had their second meeting with White House officials, as the task force conducted twenty-seven "listening sessions" with student activists, parents, administrators, and more.

OCR finally agreed to student advocates' top demand, releasing an initial list in May 2014 of fifty-five colleges and universities in twenty-seven states under investigation for mishandling sexual assaults. When Pino and Clark mapped the fifty-five schools, it nearly matched the map they'd created on the wall of their home in Oregon. They estimated they'd had a hand in two-thirds of the complaints being investigated.

Not Alone, the White House Task Force's twenty-page report released on April 29, urged schools to conduct "campus climate surveys" to better understand the extent of sexual violence at their institution. The report set goals such as trauma-informed training so that administrators understand unique aspects of sexual assault: victims often blame themselves, for instance, and neurological changes after trauma can leave memories fragmented and make it seem like they're lying. Insensitive questions can cause more damage.

The same day, OCR released guidance documents fleshing out the task force report, further clarifying legal responsibilities under the 2001 and 2011 Dear Colleague letters. The schools received forty-six pages of Q&A guidance and a two-page flyer available in five languages titled "Know Your Rights: Title IX Requires Your School to Address Sexual Violence." A toolkit included a sample climate survey, a checklist for sexual misconduct policies, and more. The Obama administration also launched a new website, NotAlone.gov, a one-stop shop of guidance materials, sample policies, and resource lists.

Social media amplified the movement against sexual violence like never before. After a man who wanted to kill sorority sisters slew six people and himself near the University of California, Santa Barbara, the hashtag #yesallwomen drew thousands of posts by women describing the harassment, threats, and violence they've faced. The #notallmen hashtag emerged like a collective defense mechanism, redirecting attention to men instead of listening to women's experiences.[35]

Emma Sulkowicz, a multiracial student at Columbia University, started carrying a blue 50-pound, extra-long twin mattress everywhere they went on campus in September 2014. (Sulkowicz identifies as a nonbinary person, using the gender-neutral pronouns "they" and "them.") The mattress was just like the ones in dorms, like the one on which Sulkowicz said white student Paul Nungesser sexually assaulted them. Sulkowicz and two other students reported assaults by Nungesser to the university. He denied the charges and said his mother raised him to be a feminist. University hearings found him not responsible for one assault, dismissed another after the complainant felt overwhelmed and stopped cooperating, and found him responsible for groping the third student. He appealed; the complainant graduated, and the decision was overturned. The university denied Sulkowicz's appeal.

Twenty-three students and alumni who survived sexual assault at Columbia filed a hundred-page complaint with OCR for the school's alleged failure to protect their educational rights.

"Mattress Performance (Carry That Weight)" was Sulkowicz's performance art project that served as a senior thesis in visual arts. They would carry the mattress until Columbia removed Nungesser from campus or graduation, whichever came first. Student allies stepped up to help in "collective carries." Sulkowicz carried the mattress across stage during graduation ceremonies in 2015. Nungesser sued Columbia for allowing the project, framing it as harassment under Title IX, but lost the first round in court. He and the university settled privately in 2017.[36]

Advocates at more than a hundred colleges in October 2014 carried their own mattresses or pillows to publicize the problem of campus sexual assault. They created an organization called Carry That Weight that eventually merged with KYIX. In the inevitable shake-out of multiple, like-minded young organizations, KYIX and EROC absorbed some groups and carried on while others folded.

The Obama administration launched a major public awareness campaign on September 9, 2014—"It's On Us"—seeking to get men more involved in preventing campus sexual misconduct.

A new Yale scandal hit the *New York Times* front page that fall when the provost unilaterally reduced sanctions against the School of Medicine's

Chief of Cardiology, Michael Simons, for sexual harassment.[37] Brodsky, then a second-year student at Yale Law School, encountered sexism among students during her law school orientation the year before, just as she had during undergraduate orientation years earlier. One student informed her specifically where she ranked in attractiveness among the first-year women as judged by a group of men in the class. Another man told her not to get so worked up in conversations about sexual assault because, he said, it wasn't personal.[38]

She walked over to the Blue State coffee shop one day to meet a national journalist, a Yale alumna, who'd asked her to provide some background on this new era of Title IX activism. Why, the woman asked, couldn't Brodsky's generation just muscle through in the wake of violence the way that her generation—and she herself—had done? Closer in age to the *Alexander* plaintiffs than to Brodsky, she could have been one of the students and alumni who said the same to Ronni Alexander in the 1970s. Brodsky and her friends heard this too many times from older women. It saddened her that these women didn't believe they deserved better, and angered her that they resented the younger women for knowing that they did.[39]

The current activists faced many of the same old challenges. Brodsky and Bolger wore heels to one meeting about proposed OCR regulations. An older attorney pulled her aside afterward. "Why are you wearing heels?" she asked. Sandler had feared being discredited if she didn't look "feminine" enough because she wore pants to the White House; Brodsky's mentor feared they wouldn't be taken seriously if they looked too "feminine."

Wearing a bright pink suit jacket over a white turtleneck and black pants, Sandler bounded from her seat on the dais among eight other inductees into the National Women's Hall of Fame in October 2013. She smiled ear to ear as a Hall co-president draped a wide purple-and-white ribbon holding a large medal around her neck.

"Title IX is not just a women's movement. It is not just a feminist movement," Sandler said to the audience of hundreds in Seneca Falls, New York. "It is a worldwide revolution which will take generations to fulfill."

Now in her eighties, Sandler still traveled to colleges to meet with campus leaders and the latest generation of students. On a trip to Fresno State in November 2014 to give a lecture, she spent more than an hour talking with women's studies students and faculty who were trying to improve campus policies concerning sexual assault. One point of dissatisfaction for the students: administrators had set up a committee that didn't include anyone from the two student groups that had worked on the issue for decades—the Fresno State Women's Alliance and People Organized for Women's Empowerment and Representation (POWER). Sandler coached the women's studies group on Title IX and getting their voices heard. It was one of her final consultations before stepping back from public commitments in 2015 owing to declining health at age eighty-seven.[40]

She joined her hosts the next evening at a ceremony inducting Milutinovich into the Fresno Sports Hall of Fame for her Title IX advocacy.

Title IX remained much needed in sports. The NWLC in 2010 filed complaints about athletics inequities in twelve school districts nationwide that prompted yet another unsuccessful lawsuit in 2011 by the conservative Pacific Legal Foundation trying to rescind the three-prong test. Washington, DC, schools agreed in October 2013 to increase sports opportunities for girls after separate complaints by the NWLC and Title IX gadfly Herb Dempsey.[41]

Dempsey and his loose network of retirees, calling itself Old Guys for Title IX, submitted mass complaints about athletics discrimination against at least 1,558 colleges and universities in 2013 and 1,545 in 2014 alone. OCR dismissed them, saying the Old Guys didn't have "standing" to represent students, or demanding proof from Dempsey that schools didn't meet prong three instead of asking schools to show that they did meet Title IX requirements. The discrimination may have been real, but unless the complaints came from students, parents, faculty, or staff, they'd be rejected.[42]

The 2011 Dear Colleague letter specifically advised against allowing athletics departments to oversee complaints of sexual assault by athletes, but three years later 20 percent of 440 four-year colleges and universities surveyed still did so, a U.S. Senate subcommittee reported.[43]

Sexual assault survivors in and outside of athletics forced the issue into the sometimes harsh glare of media spotlights.

Audrie Pott, a sophomore at Saratoga High School in Northern California, survived being sexually assaulted by student athletes at a 2012 party but was emotionally crushed when photos of the assault spread on social media. She killed herself eight days later. The documentary *Audrie & Daisy* included her story. Another documentary made the rounds of campuses: *It Happened Here*, which profiled Wanjuki and four other sexual assault survivors.[44]

Rolling Stone magazine published an explosive account of an alleged gang-rape at a University of Virginia fraternity house in November 2014, but had to retract the story five months later because of faulty reporting, providing new fuel for critics aiming to discredit rape allegations in general. Rape accusations against star quarterback Jameis Winston at Florida State University, Vanderbilt University football players, and other athletes consumed the sports world, none so much as the scandal at football-crazy Penn State University.[45] Leaders fired iconic Football Coach Joe Paterno (who died in January 2012) and President Graham Spanier as police uncovered evidence they'd tolerated signs of child abuse by Assistant Coach Jerry Sandusky. A court convicted Sandusky on forty-five counts of molesting ten boys and sent him to prison. The Department of Education eventually fined Penn State a record $2.4 million for Clery Act violations; a local jury ordered the university to pay $7.3 million to a coach who'd been fired after he blew the whistle on Sandusky. The university ended up paying $93 million to thirty-three people sexually assaulted by Sandusky.[46]

In these first few years of intense activism after the 2011 Dear Colleague letter, a new generation of students learned of Title IX, if at all, solely as a sexual assault law. But another application of Title IX soon generated additional headlines because of a growing backlash against protections for transgender students.

Margie Wright, Diane Milutinovich, and Lindy Vivas at a 2008 Women's Sports Foundation reception in Beverly Hills, California, before the presentation of the "Billie Awards," named after Billie Jean King. © *Rayma Church*

Yanna List, Suzanna Bobadilla, Alexandra Brodsky, and Wagatwe Wanjuki (left to right) deliver signatures on petitions at the first ED Act Now protest, 2013. © *S. Daniel Carter*

Andrea Pino (left) and Annie Clark under their map of college campuses with complaints of sexual assault, 2013. *Thomas Patterson / The New York Times / Redux*

National Women's Law Center co-founder Marcia Greenberger waves to the crowd during halftime in the finals of the 2012 NCAA Women's Basketball Final Four, Denver, Colorado. © *Chris Humphreys—USA TODAY Sports*

Transgender student Gavin Grimm speaks at the 2018 Transgender March in San Francisco's Dolores Park. *Pax Ahimsa Gethen*

Pop diva Lady Gaga joins hands with student sexual assault survivors on stage at the 2016 Academy Awards after performing the theme song to *The Hunting Ground*. *Patrick T. Fallon / The New York Times / Redux*

13

Critical Mass
2015–2016

When Sandler's third grandchild was born in 1994, she sent gifts featuring the loveliest, frilliest clothing she could find, elated to have a granddaughter after two beloved grandsons. "So much for being free of stereotypes!" she wrote in a holiday letter.[1]

Approaching adulthood, JJ no longer identified as her granddaughter but as a transgender man, throwing Sandler for a loop initially. She didn't really understand it, so she turned to bibliotherapy and read what she could about it.

Even more confusing to Sandler, over several years, JJ's self-understanding evolved to identify as nonbinary, neither exclusively woman nor man. Sandler had pet nicknames for all her grandchildren—"my best oldest grandson," "my best youngest grandson"—but she couldn't call JJ her best granddaughter anymore. She switched to "my best gender-neutral grand-child." She did her best to use their new name, JJ, and preferred pro-nouns (they/them/their instead of she/her/hers), but old habits died hard. Sandler felt grateful that JJ was going through this now instead of thirty or forty years earlier, when undoubtedly it would have been much harder for them.

Like so many other U.S. liberation movements, struggles for civil rights for people who don't fit straight, cisgender norms grew more visible and organized in the 1960s and 1970s, though the term "transgender" didn't come into wide usage until the 1990s. Early transgender activists Sylvia Rivera and Marsha P. Johnson were seventeen and twenty-three years old, respectively, when they participated in the 1969 Stonewall Inn rebellion in New York City, one of a number of militant protests popping up across the country against police harassment that accelerated the gay rights movement. The next year Rivera, a Puertorriqueña, and Johnson, a Black woman, founded STAR—Street Transvestite Action Revolutionaries.[2]

In the 1990s and 2000s, broader understanding of the transgender experience increased with the development of "queer" as an identity, feminist intersectional theory, the internet, and other factors. Writers explained the difference between biological sex (as determined by male or female sex organs or, for intersex people, some combination) and gender, the socially and culturally constructed characteristics assigned to women and men, including standards of dress, grooming, public interactions, and so much more of day-to-day life. Both sex and gender are distinct from sexual orientation—the sex or gender of the people to whom one is sexually attracted. Eventually, lesbian, gay, and bisexual organizations started adding "transgender" to their names. Major Hollywood films, books, TV shows, and academic research explored transgender topics.

The Office for Civil Rights (OCR) first addressed Title IX's application to discrimination against queer students in its original guidance on sexual harassment in 1997, which addressed sexual orientation. The guidance seemed to split hairs and confused many when it said Title IX does not prohibit discrimination against people based on their sexual orientation but conduct of a sexual nature can violate Title IX regardless of the sexual orientations of the people involved.

In its 2001 revision of the 1997 guidance, OCR clarified that "gender-based harassment, including that predicated on sex-stereotyping, is covered by Title IX if it is sufficiently serious to deny or limit a student's ability to participate in or benefit from the [educational] program." So, for instance, schools could be responsible for dealing with students who ridiculed a boy who they deemed too effeminate to the point that his grades suffered. And transgender students grabbed a lifeline when OCR wrote in its 2001 guidance that "it can be discrimination on the basis of sex to harass a student on the basis of the victim's failure to conform to stereotyped notions of masculinity and femininity."

Transgender students definitely needed that lifeline. The first large survey of transgender adults, covering 6,456 respondents in 2011, and a follow-up study of 27,175 in 2016 reported some of the problems transgender people face. A majority said they experienced discrimination in schools, on the job, and elsewhere.[3] A separate 2015 study found 82 percent of transgender youth felt unsafe at school and 44 percent had been physically abused. Five national organizations collaborated on an online guide with tips for administrators, teachers, and parents to improve the school environment for transgender students.[4]

In 2003 San Francisco became the first school district to allow transgender students to use facilities—such as bathrooms and locker rooms—corresponding with their gender identity. When controversy developed around transgender student Cinthia Covarrubias running for prom king at Fresno High School in spring 2007, some students were unperturbed: "It's not like the stereotype where the king has to be a jock and he's there with the cheerleaders anymore. We live in a generation now where dudes are chicks and chicks are dudes," one student said.[5]

Four schools contacted the Washington Interscholastic Activities Association (WIAA) in early 2007 asking for guidance in responding to transgender students who wanted to participate in binary sex-segregated athletics or cheerleading activities. None of the country's state high school activity organizations nor the NCAA had policies on transgender athletes. The WIAA adopted International Olympic Committee rules for participation, but these essentially blocked almost all postpubertal transgender high school students from competitive sports. "The policy is not perfect," said a spokeswoman for the National Center for Lesbian Rights, "but if something's not out there, we can't work to make it better."[6] It was a start.

JJ didn't tell anyone in high school besides their brother about their transgender identity; they came out as transgender later, as a student in the supportive community of the University of California, Santa Cruz. After graduation JJ started working in K-12 schools in Northern California as an instructional assistant and then substitute teacher, in addition to doing part-time work in theater as a stage manager. School colleagues dissuaded them from talking about pronoun use—from revealing their transgender self. For unrelated reasons JJ left education to pursue stage managing full-time.

A few years earlier, a high school sophomore named Gavin Grimm asked his principal at rural Gloucester High School in Virginia to support his gender transition by requesting that teachers use male pronouns when referring to him; a few weeks later, he asked permission to use the boys' bathrooms. Grimm had been teased since kindergarten for associating with boys; he told friends in eighth grade that he's transgender, then told his family. He had short hair, wore boys' clothes, was receiving testosterone shots, and had legally changed his name. He didn't raise any eyebrows when he used men's restrooms off campus. He started using the boys' restrooms at school in the fall of 2014 until some parents complained to the school board.

After two volatile public meetings, the board adopted a policy limiting sex-segregated restroom access to students "of the corresponding biological genders." A nonvoting student member of the board, Campbell Farina, said she wasn't hearing much common sense in the discussions. "How would you all feel if this was a question of race? It's the same thing."[7]

Grimm and the American Civil Liberties Union (ACLU) sued in 2015, saying the policy violated Title IX, OCR guidance, and the equal protection clause of the Constitution.

The issue was a manifestation of what former OCR director Martin Gerry (1975–76) called the "latrine theory" of opposition to civil rights. White people argued against Title VI of the Civil Rights Act because it would lead to Black and white students sharing school bathrooms. In testimony for the ERA before the Senate Judiciary Committee in the 1970s, Sandler strategically played the role of the "bathroom expert" among witnesses—hardly her strong suit but necessary testimony to counter alarmist fears that the ERA would lead to men and women sharing public bathrooms. She reminded senators that men and women, boys and girls already shared bathrooms at home and on airplanes, and the world had not fallen apart. Foes of Title IX regulations in the 1970s claimed they couldn't house women in men's dorms because they'd have to share bathrooms; Sandler suggested they alternate dorm floors. Some of the strongest opposition to Section 504 in the 1970s and the Americans with Disabilities Act in the 1980s revolved around the cost of making bathrooms accessible.[8] And now this.

OCR director Catherine Lhamon came better prepared to deal with questions of transgender people's rights than some other public servants, having written a substantial paper while at Yale Law School on Title VII's application to transgender persons. In a question-and-answer guidance primarily addressing single-sex K-12 classes, OCR clarified on December 1, 2014, that students must be allowed to attend the classes that matched their declared gender identity.[9]

Conservatives who deemed this a violation of their religious beliefs or another attack on "traditional" families opposed treating transgender students according to their gender identification, as did people who objected to government enforcement of civil rights. For school administrators, this was an advanced Title IX topic for the many schools that hadn't yet implemented even fundamental requirements of the law more than forty years after it passed.

OCR once again had to repeat some Title IX basics in an April 2015 Dear Colleague letter reminding schools that they must appoint a Title IX coordinator. A 2016 review by the Feminist Majority Foundation found only 23,000 Title IX coordinators nationwide when there should have been more than 100,000. OCR also sent a *Title IX Resource Guide* to Title IX coordinators that recapped their responsibilities. The American Association of University Women organized a "Title IX Delivery" project that inspired more than seven hundred activists to meet with K-12 Title coordinators in twenty-nine states to hand-deliver the *Title IX Resource Guide*.[10] A separate 2016 Dear Colleague letter addressed persistent inequities in vocational education, now called Career and Technical Education.

With battles over transgender students' use of bathrooms heating up in Virginia, South Dakota, Oregon, Texas, Tennessee, Wisconsin, Maine, and Ohio, OCR issued its most controversial guidance since the 2011 Dear Colleague letter on sexual harassment and assault.

"It has come to the Education Department's attention that many transgender students . . . report feeling unsafe and experiencing verbal and physical harassment or assault in school, and that these students may perform worse academically when they are harassed," OCR and the Department of Justice wrote in a May 13, 2016, Dear Colleague letter to K-12 administrators. Accompanying the letter were nineteen pages of questions and answers with examples of policies and emerging practices to uphold these students' access to education.[11] "Our guidance sends a clear message to transgender students across the country: here in America, you are safe, you are protected and you belong—just as you are," Vanita Gupta, head of the Justice Department's Civil Rights Division, said in a press release.

By then at least thirteen states, hundreds of school districts in four more states, and the District of Columbia prohibited discrimination in schools on the basis of gender identity. But twenty states led by Texas sued over the 2016 Dear Colleague letter, and a federal district judge in Texas blocked it with a nationwide injunction.

A district court judge rejected Gavin Grimm's lawsuit in spring 2016; the Fourth Circuit Court of Appeals disagreed in August and supported his right to pursue the case. As Grimm headed into his senior year, the Supreme Court granted an "emergency stay" to leave the school district policy in place until it could hear the case, making it a focal point of transgender struggles nationwide.

Advocates on Fresno State's staff helped a transgender student of Aztec/Nahuatl heritage become one of the first on the campus to change his name on a student identification card, to Alex Love. They worked with the university to improve bathroom access. When the nearby, conservative Clovis Unified School District refused to adopt a gender-neutral dress code that year to accommodate transgender and nonbinary people, students protested by swapping clothes.[12]

Anti-trans activists claimed that transgender girls in girls' bathrooms or locker rooms endangered other girls' privacy or even their safety. But data suggested the transgender students joined girls and women as the ones in danger. One of the largest surveys of campus sexual assault—and the first to use gender categories beyond a man/woman binary—found in 2015 that 12 percent of more than 150,000 undergraduates at twenty-seven universities reported experiencing nonconsensual penetration or forced sexual touching. It was an even bigger problem for certain students—19 percent of women and 22 percent of transgender, genderqueer, questioning, or gender nonconforming students. In the larger category of sexual assault or misconduct, the 23 percent prevalence rate among women matched multiple previous reports that showed the problem affected every one in four or five college women.[13]

Critics of OCR's efforts to enforce Title IX with regard to sexual assault dovetailed with Republican politicians issuing racist dog whistles. Many intentionally ignored the law's decades-long history and the lengthy stream of Dear Colleague letters from OCR to criticize President Obama directly for imposing "new," "burdensome" rules in the 2011 Dear Colleague letter. It didn't matter that OCR under both Democratic and Republican administrations had spelled out that Title IX is governed by civil, not criminal, procedures, or that courts and OCR had been telling schools they must deal effectively with sexual harassment and assault since *Alexander v. Yale* in 1977. Because more white men were facing consequences for rape on campus, they blamed the Black president.

They broadcast the myth that women commonly lie about sexual assault (even though rates are similar to false accusations for other crimes, 2–8 percent). They demanded that campus processes for sexual assault accusations use standards of evidence favoring the respondents, despite the Association for Student Conduct Administration endorsing the preponderance of evidence standard as the only one that treats "all students with respect and fundamental fairness."[14]

The National Coalition for Men (around since the 1970s), the Foundation for Individual Rights in Education (FIRE, founded in 2009), the Fraternity and Sorority Political Action Committee (founded in 2005), and other custodians of patriarchy blamed Title IX instead of the perpetrator's actions when schools sanctioned someone for sexual assault. Sometimes schools did screw up an investigation in ways unfair to complaint respondents, but Title IX foes faulted the law's regulations instead of the school's failure to follow the regulations. Many criticisms by complainants and respondents alike—that they weren't notified about investigations or results, or they were left out of the process—raised similar themes that the regulations already addressed, if only schools would follow them.

OCR for the first time found in 2016 that a college violated Title IX in this respect by discriminating against a student who'd been expelled for alleged sexual assault at Wesley College in Delaware. The college failed to give him and three other students accused of sexual assault some of the rights guaranteed to both complainants and respondents under Title IX.[15]

Alleged perpetrators filed seven lawsuits over "due process" in campus sexual harassment cases in the twenty-one months after the 2011 Dear

Colleague letter. They filed another seven in 2013 alone, some genuinely believing they hadn't been afforded the rights they deserve and others likely suing as a bargaining chip to negotiate a return to campus. That grew to forty-five in 2015 and—after FIRE publicly recruited plaintiffs in 2016—to seventy-eight in each of 2017 and 2018.[16]

Mothers of students who'd been expelled or suspended for sexual misconduct founded Families Advocating for Campus Equity (FACE) and Save Our Sons (SOS) in 2014. Title IX enforcement created a hostile environment for men, they claimed, backed mainly by anecdotes and emotions, not data. In the real world, only four of eighteen investigations for sexual misconduct at the University of Michigan in 2017 held the alleged perpetrator responsible, for example, and only one got expelled; none was suspended.[17]

Many in the backlash against holding perpetrators accountable rushed toward mandatory-referral laws that would require all reports of campus sexual assault to be referred to police. They co-opted feminist terminology from decades of trying to get police and prosecutors to take gender violence "seriously." Campus rape was so serious, they argued, that even campus proceedings should incorporate criminal-law standards—standards well known to disadvantage victims. At least seven states introduced mandatory-referral bills in 2015–17.[18]

A 2015 survey by Know Your IX (KYIX) and the National Alliance to End Sexual Violence found that 88 percent of sexual assault survivors believed fewer victims would report to either schools or the police under mandatory-referral laws.[19] Groups disproportionately abused by police (people of color, immigrants, LGBT, or low-income people) justifiably may fear police involvement, inhibiting their willingness to report.

Calls for criminalization of Title IX proceedings came at a time of increasing public protests against a racist criminal justice system that let police stop motorists for "driving while Black" and kill unarmed Black people with impunity. After the killings of Oscar Grant and Trayvon Martin, the fatal police shooting of eighteen-year-old Michael Brown Jr. in Ferguson, Missouri, in 2014 launched more than a hundred street protests around the country in the next week alone.[20] More protests and campaigns for reform of police and prison systems followed videos or news accounts of police killing Eric Garner, Freddie Gray, Michelle Cusseaux, and many others.

The civil processes of Title IX gave students another option besides criminal law, one that offered survivors support to stay in school.

To counteract the backlash against Title IX, eighty organizations representing women, the LGBT community, and minority groups signed a July 13, 2016, letter to Education Secretary John B. King Jr. defending OCR's enforcement efforts. OCR's guidance didn't introduce anything radically new, they pointed out, but clarified existing rights under Title IX and reminded schools that complainants and respondents get the same due process rights. Among the many signatories were the National Women's Law Center (NWLC), NAACP, KYIX, End Rape on Campus (EROC), Anti-Defamation League, National Council of La Raza, and Human Rights Campaign.[21]

At least three conservative organizations sued the government in 2016 saying the 2011 Dear Colleague letter was invalid because it hadn't gone through a full "notice and comment" rulemaking process used when adopting "new" regulations, even though it was no different in that respect from all the previous Dear Colleague letters. The Republican Party platform for the 2016 elections faulted Democrats for using Title IX to foist "a social and cultural revolution upon the American people by wrongly redefining sex discrimination to include sexual orientation or other categories" such as gender. The Republicans pledged to institute OCR policies that would punt any cases of campus sexual assault to courtrooms requiring the criminal standard of evidence "beyond a reasonable doubt," negating survivors' rights under Title IX civil law.[22]

Discontented white men who saw themselves as victims of change found a pop hero in a psychology professor at the University of Toronto who echoed these sentiments. After Canada added gender identity and expression to its Human Rights Act, Jordan B. Peterson posted a three-part YouTube series called "Professor Against Political Correctness," reviving the conservative hysteria of the early 1990s that used that phrase.[23] Following in the footsteps of the rape apologist Frederic Storaska in the 1970s, Peterson hit the lecture circuit. His book *12 Rules for Life: An Antidote to Chaos* (Random House Canada, 2018) sold more than a million copies in its first four months. The feminine is chaos, he said; the masculine is order. That's why men are in charge. And other nonsense.[24]

Survivor advocate networks spent huge amounts of time and energy fighting mandatory-referral bills and other anti-IX legislation, mostly successfully. Even survivor supporters needed educating. Two of the activists' main friends in Congress, Senators Kirsten Gillibrand (D-NY) and Claire McCaskill (D-MO), both former prosecutors, were willing to listen to survivor advocates and back off from mandatory-referral bills. Democratic 2016 presidential candidate Bernie Sanders hadn't read the proverbial memo when he told an interviewer that student rape is a "very serious crime" that must always be investigated by police.[25]

KYIX's second executive director, Mahroh Jahangiri—a sexual assault survivor, Muslim, and daughter of Pakistani immigrants—took the role in 2016 when Bolger left for Yale Law School. Jahangiri already had worked with KYIX for two years and was excited to make a critique of the racist, sexist criminal justice system more explicit in their work. Too many people still didn't understand why people don't go to the police and why school procedures need to provide an alternative. They didn't understand intersectional discrimination, or how mandatory referrals to police could increase danger for people from vulnerable groups.

Jahangiri and KYIX's wider team members, many of them women of color, guided the group to become perhaps the first Title IX organization to embrace abolishing policing, prisons, and punitive campus discipline. Under her leadership, KYIX actively built ongoing relationships with movements against state violence. It focused on supporting people who experience sexual harm without relying on a racist policing system. KYIX helped defeat every state or federal mandatory police reporting bill for sexual assault that it actively opposed, she said. Jahangiri led KYIX's campaign to help block California legislation proposing mandatory minimum criminal sentences for sexual assault, a bill generated by outcry from many survivor advocates after a Stanford student spent only three months in a county jail for raping an unconscious woman behind a dumpster in 2016.

At the time these stances by KYIX weren't typical of the movement against sexual violence, but they converged with a growing prison-abolition movement as Black Lives Matter, especially, opened more eyes to racist police and prison brutality. And Title IX, as always, offered a different, essential mechanism to help people who are assaulted or otherwise discriminated against regain access to education.

Jahangiri moved on from KYIX in 2017, then she too went to law school, this time to Harvard Law, where still only 23 percent of full-time faculty were women. Her first job after graduating: a fellowship to work on sexual violence by police officers.

Pamela Price entered electoral politics for the first time in 2014, running for the California State Assembly on a platform of reducing funding for prisons, supporting civil rights, boosting funds for education, and helping small businesses. She wanted to accelerate change. She came in third in the primary election, missing a spot on the final ballot, and learned why only a privileged few have the capacity to run for office. It takes tremendous resources and time commitments that most people can't afford. Her law practice suffered. Her marriage struggled too; Price and her husband entered divorce proceedings in 2016 and ended it in 2018.

The San Francisco Bay Area's National Lawyers Guild honored Price in April 2016 as a "Champion of Justice" for her role in Title IX history and her career as a civil rights lawyer. The tribute meant more to her than many of the awards she'd won. These folks were giants, she felt—radical, unapologetic advocates for justice—practicing law the way she always strived to practice it. At the same time, she felt disappointed to learn that she was the first Black woman to receive the award.

In 2016 she won election (and later reelection) to the Alameda County Democratic Central Committee for the 18th Assembly District—the Democratic Party's local organization—by a record number of votes. The same day, Democrats nationally picked the first woman to be a major party candidate for president, Hillary Clinton.

The Black Lives Matter movement spread through campuses as students joined national protests over police killings and challenged racism at their schools.

A 2016 essay by Yale student Briana Burroughs described being physically and verbally harassed as a Black woman by fraternity members and athletes in Yale's dining halls, frat houses, and on New Haven streets.

Harassers called her "ghetto Black bitch," fondled her, screamed at her, or spanked her—and each time it happened, she was alone and bystanders did nothing. She urged classmates to denounce racism and misogyny, especially in fraternities.[26]

Campus anti-racism protests inspired a scathing 2016 report by Yale's Senate of the Faculty of Arts and Sciences: Yale praised inclusion while enabling a climate hostile to female and minority faculty and graduate students, it said.[27] Minorities composed 42 percent of Yale's undergraduates but only 17 percent of faculty. For comparison, Fresno State's faculty in 2017 were 42 percent racial and ethnic minorities, and a majority women.

In response to increasing racist incidents at the University of Missouri–Columbia, the football team in November 2015 refused to play until the president of the system resigned. Missing the next game would have cost the system $1 million, so the president resigned. In a copycat move, the University of Minnesota football team borrowed that strategy the next month, declaring it would boycott its bowl game if the university didn't reinstate ten students (including team members) who'd been suspended after complaints of sexual assault. Two days later the university released the investigation report, providing disturbing details of the assault. The team ended its boycott.[28]

At the K-12 level, the NWLC again reported discrimination especially against girls of color in school sports in a 2015 report entitled *Finishing Last.* Girls in general still received significantly fewer opportunities than boys to play sports in school, but the gap was more frequent and severe for girls of color in a severely segregated U.S. school system. More than 42 percent of public high schools were either at least 90 percent white or 90 percent minority students. Forty percent of heavily minority schools and 16 percent of heavily white schools had large athletic "gaps" in which boys got 10 percent or more playing slots on teams than did girls.[29]

Academics and activists, often led by women of color, increased attention to excessive punishment and the school-to-prison pipeline targeting K-12 minority students. Black boys were three times more likely to be suspended from school than white boys, but Black girls were nearly six times more likely to be suspended than white girls, studies showed. American Indian/Alaskan Native girls were three times more likely, and Latinas nearly twice as likely to be suspended compared with white girls. The disparate treatment started as early as preschool.[30]

The NWLC published an online toolkit in November 2016 with advice on identifying school policies that unfairly punish girls of color and how to demand better from schools. Alexandra Brodsky, then a fellow at the NWLC after graduating from law school, helped produce an April 2018 report that zeroed in on discriminatory dress codes; NWLC released a follow-up report in September 2019. Local and national news coverage of the issue inspired parental organizing and student protests. A lunch walk-out at one high school shamed administrators into reevaluating the dress code. Students at another school organized a "head wrap clapback," asking everyone to come to school wearing head wraps, bonnets, and do-rags (also known as durags) to protest being punished for wearing head wraps even though the student handbook didn't prohibit them.

A 2019 NWLC report also highlighted the lack of attention from schools to the mental health challenges facing Latina students, one in seven of whom in Philadelphia had attempted suicide.[31]

End Rape on Campus (EROC) launched its "Centering the Margins" initiative, offering resources especially to support survivors from margin-alized groups most affected by sexual violence—women of color, LGBTQ students, immigrants, low-income students, people with disabilities, and others. Not once, though, did any journalist ask Andrea Pino during her time with EROC for her perspective as a Latinx survivor.[32]

At its annual meeting, the Association of Title IX Administrators (ATIXA) drew a standing ovation with its October 2016 statement affirm-ing "the essential truth that Black Lives Matter" and recognizing "the per-niciousness of systemic racism, and the intersectionality of various forms of hatred and oppression." Title IX administrators were seeing more reported incidents involving intersecting discriminations, one of its executives said. A Black gay male student may be harassed for behaving in ways the harass-ers considered inappropriate for a Black man, for instance, or a female student might be harassed if others think that her dress or behavior doesn't fit cultural expectations for women.[33]

Some critics of Title IX enforcement asserted without evidence that the recent surge in sexual assault complaints comprised a racist trend to falsely accuse men of color. They never talked about the women of color being assaulted, though. The truth is, nobody really knew the racial makeup of Title IX complainants and respondents because schools usually concealed any identifying information to protect privacy. At least one academic, lawyer Nancy Chi Cantalupo, called for new legislation to require schools to report anonymous demographic data for research purposes, perhaps by amending the Clery Act or the Civil Rights Data Collection survey.[34]

Wagatwe Wanjuki, who had spoken out about intersectional discrimination and Title IX controversies many times since her case at Tufts University, started the blog *Fuck Yeah, Feminists!* and quickly drew sixteen thousand followers.[35] OCR found Tufts in violation of Title IX in 2014 after others complained that the university mishandled sexual assaults. Tufts students started an unsuccessful petition asking Tufts to give Wanjuki an honorary degree to make amends for its earlier treatment of her.[36]

Her freelance essays appeared on mainstream and feminist sites and social media. She blogged against calls to criminalize campus assault complaints and challenged conservative newspaper columnist George Will's June 2014 claim that women lie about sexual violence because "victimhood" has become a "coveted status that confers privilege." "Where's my survivor privilege?" Wanjuki tweeted in response, sending the hashtag #survivorprivilege trending. "Was expelled & have $10,000s of private student loans used to attend a school that didn't care I was raped." She also tweeted, "The #survivorprivilege of being too scared to leave my dorm for fear of running into my perp."[37]

She formed a short-lived organization—Survivors Eradicating Rape Culture—with Harvard Law graduate and assault survivor Kamilah Willingham, another Black woman. Wanjuki tossed her gray Tufts sweatshirt into a barbecue grill and set it on fire, live-streaming the protest on social media to symbolize the anger generated by institutional betrayal. Their #JustSaySorry campaign urged schools to apologize to survivors who'd been failed by bad policies. Each week they burned some memento and live-streamed it—the Tufts rule book, Willingham's Harvard sweatpants, and her admissions letter to Harvard Law.[38]

Andrea Pino and Annie Clark left Oregon and drove all over the country helping student survivors file complaints, sometimes sleeping in their car and washing up in fast food restaurant bathrooms. For a while they landed in a 500-square-foot studio apartment in Los Angeles, working a coffee shop job and freelance gigs to survive. Being near Hollywood made sense at the time. A film crew had been following them for nearly two years, shooting footage for a documentary.

A national spotlight hit EROC with the 2015 release of *The Hunting Ground*, a documentary about the epidemic of sexual assaults on campuses. The film featured many campus activists but particularly focused on Pino and Clark, in part because their activities provided a more cinematic storyline. Their connection to a big-name college helped tell the story too.

Like the elite colleges that fought hardest against Rep. Green's version of Title IX in 1971, the most famous institutions failed spectacularly in this latest Title IX controversy. "The Ivy League schools are the worst" in dealing fairly with sexual assault "because they are the most arrogant and they think no one can tell them what to do," one national expert on college sexual assault told the filmmakers.[39]

Besides showing in theaters, the film screened at more than a thousand schools, community centers, and government offices. Pino and Clark hit the road again, appearing at many of the screenings. The White House, OCR, the Justice Department, and some state legislators also hosted screenings. So did the NCAA. CNN aired the film nationally in November 2015.

EROC's team found a fiscal sponsor and enough funding to pay several staff (including Pino and Clark) minimal salaries. They had no office the first year, working from home or anywhere with free Wi-Fi when on the road. When Pino and Clark moved to Washington, DC, they'd occasionally host weeklong staff meetings at their home, talking late into the night, drinking wine, and braiding each other's hair.[40] On Pino's twenty-first birthday she helped Swarthmore College students file a complaint.

Hearing story after story of assaults from the people who sought them for help burdened them with vicarious trauma. At the same time, connecting with other survivors felt empowering.

"It's the only way I get up in the morning," Pino told Clark as they drove to see another survivor. "I would have given anything to have had someone who believed me, someone who supported me."[41]

Nearly 30 million viewers watched as pop diva Lady Gaga quietly started singing the theme song to *The Hunting Ground* onstage at the Academy
Awards in February 2016. Alone at a white piano, dressed in an elegant
white pantsuit before pitch-black curtains, she struck a chord. "Till it happens to you, you don't know how it feels," she started. She did know how
it feels, having survived sexual assault herself.[42]

Pino, Wanjuki, and others waited silently in the dimness behind the
curtains, an eclectic group with one thing in common. They all held
hands—a Harvard Law graduate, a Texas Republican, a corporate CEO,
a tenor at the National Cathedral, and others, a greater number of Black
and brown people than usually graced the stage of the Oscars.[43] Gaga built
to an anguished crescendo, pounding on the piano keys as the curtains
rose behind her. The fifty young people emerged from silhouettes. As
they raised their linked hands, the audience could see messages written
on their forearms: "It happened to me." "Survivor." "Unbreakable." And
most common: "We believe you."

For Pino, it was an out-of-body experience. The stage crew gave them a
standing ovation in rehearsal. Actors approached them, offering hugs and a
"Thank you." But she regrets that the film didn't make evident how many
of the assault survivors were LGBT students. "What would it have meant if
I was a visibly queer Latina in *The Hunting Ground*?" she wondered. Would
it have helped some young queer Latina to see herself represented there?

The film also didn't show the messy parts of the "hero's journey." None
of her panic attacks made it to the screen. Nor activists' general lack of
health insurance. Or her coming to terms (still) with her queerness and
how to talk about it with her family and Cuban community, some of whom
believed the rape had made her queer, though she knew that wasn't true.

Pino made sure EROC's website included information in Spanish. With
Clark, she edited a book of essays, *We Believe You: Survivors of Campus
Sexual Assault Speak Out* (Henry Holt, 2016), sending them on another
string of trips to promote it. After some health problems Pino transitioned
out of EROC. She finished her college degree, interrupted by the sequelae
of sexual trauma and her years of activism, three years after she normally
would have graduated. The week before her senior finals, she traveled to
Capitol Hill to talk to senators about issues important to assault survivors.

Pino went to work for the National Center for Lesbian Rights and eventually back to school aiming for a PhD.

In attempts to prevent misunderstandings leading to sexual assault, at least eight hundred colleges and the state of California adopted "affirmative consent" policies in 2015, requiring students to obtain consent from an awake, sober partner before having sex. "'No means no' is better than 'No means yes,'" legal scholar and former *Alexander v. Yale* team member Catharine MacKinnon acknowledged, but "consent" is a criminal-law concept that worried her when applied under Title IX because it "puts the victim on trial" and doesn't account for coercion that can look like consent.[44]

Despite all the publicity and studies about sexual assaults on campus, more than two-thirds of college and university presidents did not believe that sexual assault is prevalent at American colleges and universities, a 2015 survey found.[45] By mid-2015, OCR was investigating 140 complaints of sexual assaults at 124 colleges and universities and 41 at K-12 schools.[46] By June 2016, there were 246 OCR investigations for sexual assault at 195 colleges and universities (plus another 68 for sexual harassment).[47]

Survivor advocates and the media created online tools so people could track the surge in complaints and compare information. Volunteers launched the Academic Sexual Misconduct Database in February 2016 with documents and outcomes from public cases of academic sexual misconduct. The *Chronicle of Higher Education* started a "Title IX Tracker" of OCR investigations in June 2016. The anti-IX group Title IX for All also launched a website monitoring lawsuits by alleged perpetrators of sexual misconduct, the "Title IX Legal Database."

KYIX in 2015 mentored 250 new campus activists, published the first toolkits for high school students and alumni on their Title IX rights, and launched its first IX Activist Bootcamp trainings for college students. KYIX and EROC testified before Congress, gathered tens of thousands of petition signatures to successfully campaign against potentially harmful legislation, and more.

A corporate industry of consultants mushroomed to help colleges handle Title IX responsibilities. After the 2011 Dear Colleague letter, the NCHERM Group (formerly the National Center for Higher Education

Risk Management) doubled its staff, for example, and founded the Association of Title IX Administrators.[48]

The movement against sexual harassment and assault on campus seemed
to have reached a critical mass, such that it never again could be ignored.

Familiar sexual harassment scandals blew up in fall 2016 at Harvard,
Columbia, Princeton, and Amherst, where various men's sports teams were
caught circulating emails and social media messages filled with misogy-
nistic, racist, homophobic, and lewd comments about students. This time,
administrators responded by organizing campus discussions and canceling
or suspending teams and some players.[49]

Baylor University ousted its football coach and demoted President Kenneth Starr in spring 2016 amid a highly publicized scandal over alleged
rapes by football players. Starr, best known for doggedly pursuing sexual-
misconduct charges against President Bill Clinton in the 1990s, resigned
from the law school faculty three months later. At least ten sexual assault
survivors sued Baylor for enabling the rapists and mistreating survivors.
Baylor's first full-time Title IX coordinator, hired in 2014, resigned in
2016. Another Title IX employee sued the university, claiming retaliation
when she tried to investigate reports of sexual assault.[50] Other football
rape cases tarnished Indiana, Vanderbilt, and Michigan State Universities
that year.[51]

Even the "father of Title IX" faced a reckoning. A woman journalist
tweeted in 2016 that former senator Birch Bayh groped her in a car in the
1990s. Bayh did not respond to the accusation. He died three years later at
age ninety-one.

Vincent Macaluso, who had mentored Sandler when she first starting
filing complaints of sex discrimination, was ninety-four when he died of
congestive heart failure on November 8, 2016—the day Americans elected
a president who proudly trumpeted every kind of discrimination Macaluso
fought against. Republican Donald Trump had a known history of racist
behavior, sexually harassing women, demonizing immigrants, and mock-
ing the disabled. In a close election, he won anyway.

One might assume Macaluso died of a broken heart from Trump's election. But the last piece of political information he heard was a poll pre-
dicting that Hillary Clinton's odds of winning were 99 percent. He died

happy, believing that the United States had its first woman president, his wife said.

Instead, Trump became the forty-fifth president of the United States. He quickly aimed a wrecking ball at civil rights laws, including Title IX.

14

Backlash

2017–2020

"Hey fam," the December 2016 email blast from Know Your IX (KYIX) read. "It's been a tough month." Not only did Republicans retake the White House, but they retained control of the House and Senate.

KYIX's suggested action items reflected the extent of anticipated sociopolitical damage and the multifaceted challenges ahead: Support undocumented students by demanding that your school become a sanctuary campus (expecting increased deportations). Sign petitions, call the White House, and donate to help Indigenous young people protesting at the Standing Rock Reservation to block the Dakota Access oil pipeline (in the fight against climate change). Support KYIX's work with the American Civil Liberties Union (ACLU) in Gavin Grimm's Supreme Court case to protect transgender students. And if you're thinking of filing a Title IX complaint with OCR, you might want to talk to a lawyer (because filing lawsuits—as problematic as they are—may now be more productive than appealing to the Office for Civil Rights (OCR).[1]

Unlike some feminists' dejected paralysis after Reagan's 1980 election, women and allies mobilized almost immediately to resist Trump's discriminatory agendas.

Approximately 4 million people in U.S. cities and towns—and another million around the world—took to the streets for the Women's March the day after Trump's inauguration in what was described as the biggest single-day demonstration to that point in history. Activists had challenged the initial white organizers of the march to be more inclusive. Within days they put women of color and LGBTQ people in charge, bringing an explicit, public commitment to combatting intersectional discrimination.[2]

Bernice Sandler and a friend laughed as the million marchers surrounding them on Washington's streets brought movement to a standstill. Not just the size of the crowd but the diversity thrilled her. And the signs! "So bad, even introverts are here." "My pussy is not for grabs." "Love trumps hate." "Brown is beautiful." "I can't believe I still have to protest this shit." Sandler's distinctive white bobbed hair, large glasses, and immense smile caught the eyes of some around her. A few young feminists recognized her and squeezed their way over to chat. Older women who spotted her said hello, recalling they'd met her in Cleveland or Seattle or another city.[3]

After the march, thousands of voters called their senators to try and block Trump's nomination of billionaire Republican donor Betsy DeVos to be secretary of education. DeVos favored using public dollars to fund private, for-profit, and religious schools. She had nearly no experience with public education and refused to commit to fighting discrimination when asked at her confirmation hearing. On February 7, 2017, after an all-night series of opposition speeches by Democrats, Vice President Mike Pence cast the tie-breaking vote in the Senate, the first one ever needed to confirm a cabinet nominee.[4]

DeVos cut 13 percent of Education Department workers her first year, mostly from OCR and the Office of Federal Student Aid.[5] She also narrowed the reasons to investigate school districts. When OCR investigations did produce resolution agreements with educational institutions, though, the terms usually were good enough that Obama's former OCR director, Catherine Lhamon, said she would have signed off on them.[6]

Two weeks after taking office, DeVos rescinded OCR's 2016 Dear Colleague letter on transgender students' rights.[7] That led the Supreme Court to cancel oral arguments scheduled for March in Gavin Grimm's Title IX case, returning it to the Fourth Circuit Court of Appeals for reconsideration. But separate federal courts the next year supported two other transgender high school students' rights to use gender-appropriate bathrooms. The Supreme Court in May 2019 declined to hear an appeal of one of them.[8]

Grimm's case seemed to come to a close in late 2019, five years after the school district blocked him from boys' bathrooms. A three-judge panel of the Fourth Circuit upheld the earlier district court ruling that school policies segregating transgender students from gender-appropriate bathrooms and denying them name changes on school transcripts are unconstitutional and violate Title IX. Judges denied the school district's petition for a rehearing by the full Fourth Circuit Court.[9] Grimm was more than a year past high school graduation. But opponents of transgender rights persisted in his case and others.

Conservatives introduced more than a hundred bills in twenty-nine states in the first five months of 2017 to reduce the rights of LGBTQ people in areas like adoption and commerce; six bills passed.[10] Trump's attorney general, Jeff Sessions, rescinded guidance that applied Title VII to protect transgender workers.[11] On the other hand, Hawaii in 2018 became one of sixteen states that ban discrimination in schools based on sex, including sexual orientation and gender identity or expression.[12]

With federal support for transgender rights and the rest of Title IX unlikely, KYIX in 2017 created a State Policy Playbook for Ending Campus Sexual Assault containing resources to help students strengthen policies in their states. Its new Campus Organizing Toolkit boosted local actions.

Spelman College students, who'd been complaining about rapes by Morehouse College men since at least 2006, got even more organized in 2014–17. They protested administrators' inaction against sexual assaults through a #SilenceIsViolence vigil, town halls about sexual violence, an anonymous @RapedAtSpelman account on Twitter, and other actions. Activists plastered flyers across the adjacent campuses of Spelman and Morehouse the morning of November 8, 2017, their headlines reading "Spelman Protects Rapists" and "Morehouse Protects Rapists," with names of alleged perpetrators, their affiliated organizations, and the hashtag #WeKnowWhatYouDid. More than seventy Spelman faculty signed a letter of support for the action.[13]

Students at Howard University occupied the school's administration building for nine days in March and April 2018 demanding a variety of changes. The sit-in ended after university officials agreed to overhaul sexual assault policies, create a food bank, consider freezing undergraduate tuition, reconsider letting campus police carry weapons, and more.[14]

Inspired by activists posting reports of racial discrimination at schools and colleges on the social media app Instagram, students at the University of Denver and Loyola University did the same in spring 2020 for sexual assault, harassment, and administrative bungling. Similar to the students thirty years earlier who wrote the names of rapists on bathroom walls, they posted anonymous descriptions (to protect survivors from harassment) that reached millions instead of people at just one campus. Anonymous posts on several Instagram accounts in June 2020 reported more than a hundred incidents of sexual assault and harassment in at least twelve junior and senior high schools in one Maryland district, often naming alleged rapists. District officials called police to investigate.[15]

At the 2019 "big game" between the UC Berkeley and Stanford University football teams, security personnel escorted a group of students out of Stanford's stadium because they hung a banner reading "40% of Stanford Women Experience Unwanted Sexual Contact," based on survey data for their university.[16]

OCR declared UC Berkeley in violation of Title IX and announced a resolution agreement in March 2018 after investigating the 2014 complaint by End Rape on Campus (EROC) co-founder Sofie Karasek and others. A 2015 lawsuit by Karasek and two other women produced a novel ruling by the U.S. Court of Appeals for the Ninth Circuit in January 2020 that could shape similar suits in the future. Though the plaintiffs didn't meet the stiff criteria for proving the university was deliberately indifferent *after* they reported being sexually assaulted, the court said their suit could proceed on the claim that the university's handling of campus sexual violence *before* the attacks put them at greater risk for assault, thus violating Title IX.[17]

The ruling raised an interesting possibility that harkens back to the 1992 Supreme Court ruling in *Franklin v. Gwinnett*. Title IX's then-twenty-year history and extensive guidance from OCR on how to provide equitable athletics meant that any sex discrimination in athletics most likely is intentional, the court stated. If OCR could maintain consistent guidelines for managing sexual harassment and assault, perhaps someday Title IX violations in this area also could be presumed to be intentional, opening the door to more costly repercussions for violators.

News media investigations and lawsuits around faculty sexual misconduct already have led to some historically huge payouts by universities accused of turning a blind eye to the harassers they employed.

UC Berkeley paid $1.7 million to one employee and $80,000 to a doctoral student. UC Santa Cruz agreed to pay $1.15 million to a student survivor; UC San Francisco paid $150,000 to another. The UC system fired fewer than half of the 57 employees found to have sexually assaulted students, colleagues, or patients, a *San Francisco Chronicle* analysis found.[18] California State University campuses hit state taxpayers and insurers for another $440,500 in payouts for five sexual harassment claims on four campuses in 2014–17.[19]

Those amounts were peanuts compared with the $500 million that Michigan State University agreed in 2018 to pay to settle claims by at least 250 girls and women against sports doctor Larry Nassar for sexual assault and harassment. The Education Department then fined the university a record $4.5 million for Clery Act violations. A judge sentenced Nassar to 40–175 years in prison on top of 60 years for child pornography charges.[20]

Dartmouth College agreed to a $14 million settlement of a class-action suit by nine students alleging fifteen years of faculty misconduct in one department.[21] Claims that sports physician Robert E. Anderson sexually abused eight hundred or more students, mostly men, over decades cost the University of Michigan $10.7 million by October 2020, with more likely to come. Hundreds of people, again mostly men, came forward in 2018–21 reporting decades of abuse by Ohio State University athletics doctor Richard Strauss that some students had discussed with university employees as far back as 1979. Investigations revealed at least 127 rapes and around 2,200 instances of fondling by Strauss, who died in 2005. About four hundred men sued Ohio State for not stopping him. The university agreed to pay nearly $47 million to settle suits by 185 of them, with other suits ongoing in 2021.[22]

The University of Southern California announced that it would pay almost twice as much as all those settlements combined—$1.1 billion— to hundreds of former patients of campus gynecologist George Tyndall.

Lawsuits charged Tyndall with sexual molestation and racial harassment over decades and accused the university of doing nothing to stop him. The March 2021 agreement settled three sets of lawsuits with the largest payment for sexual misconduct to that date. Prosecutors charged Tyndall with thirty-five felonies; he has denied the charges.[23]

When it came time once again to take stock of Title IX's impact for its forty-fifth anniversary in 2017, the National Coalition for Women and Girls in Education reported both great improvements and glaring deficiencies.

The number of women earning doctorates in STEM fields had increased tenfold by 2013, but only 24 percent of full professors in STEM were women, it said. The proportion of women in nontraditional Career and Technical Education programs (that lead to better-paying jobs than traditionally "female" subjects like cosmetology) had grown from nearly 0 to 28 percent in 2013.[24]

In athletics, high school girls were 42 percent of athletes in 2015–16 but still numbered fewer than the total of boys in high school sports in 1972. More concerning, girls in schools whose compositions were 90 percent or more minorities received 39 percent of the playing opportunities that girls in heavily white schools had. There still was no federal legislation requiring high schools to release data on athletics participation and expenditures, as postsecondary institutions had to do. In colleges and universities, men got 42,258 more playing slots than women did despite being a minority of students. By 2017, colleges and universities had spent $2 billion less on women's athletics than men's over the previous twenty years, the Women's Sports Foundation estimated.[25]

Single-sex education exploded after 2000, with more than a hundred all-girl or all-boy public schools and more than a thousand coeducational K–12 public schools having at least some single-sex programming by 2011–12. Two popular consultants—Leonard Sax and Michael Gurian—spread what many experts considered quack theories that influenced these programs. Teachers should speak softly to boys, for instance, but yell at girls because of alleged hearing differences. The ACLU, in particular, put great efforts into interrupting discriminatory single-sex classes that received little public oversight. In Wood County, West Virginia, boys could move around freely but girls had to stay in their seats, for example; boys got to play outdoors as rewards after tests but girls got stickers.

The National Women's Law Center (NWLC), among others, remained a Title IX watchdog for pregnant and parenting students. When a Georgia college in 2015 refused to excuse absences for a student's medically necessary bed rest, the NWLC convinced the college to let her make up work and to change the school's policies.

But the NWLC was about to go through one of the biggest changes in its history, just as the Trump-era backlash was taking hold. Marcia Greenberger and NWLC co-founder Nancy Duff Campbell decided to step down in 2017 after forty-five years at the helm. In that time they had built a formidable feminist law firm and helped improve the lives of millions of girls and women. The National Women's Hall of Fame inducted Greenberger in 2015, nominated by Bernice Sandler.

The NWLC's board of directors transferred leadership of the organization's sixty-plus team members on July 1, 2017, to Fatima Goss Graves—a Black graduate of Yale Law School who'd worked at the NWLC for more than ten years in multiple leadership roles.

"Women and girls are facing unprecedented assaults on their rights and economic security," Goss Graves said in a statement. "To meet these challenges, our work must be inclusive, with a particular focus on the experiences and interconnected threats facing LGBTQ people, women of color, immigrant women, and low-income families."[26]

Meanwhile, the Trump administration ramped up its attacks on Title IX and other civil rights laws.

Candice Jackson, DeVos's interim OCR director, ridiculed sexual assault survivors, telling the *New York Times* in July 2017 that sexual assault "accusations—90% of them—fall into the category of 'we were both drunk,' 'we broke up, and six months later I found myself under a Title IX investigation because she just decided that our last sleeping together was not quite right.'" The *Washington Post* called for Jackson's resignation because "someone who doesn't think sexual assault on campus is a real problem in the first place is not qualified" to sort through legitimate questions about applying Title IX to campus assaults.[27]

Though she later apologized for the comment, Jackson and her OCR staff collaborated over at least a four-month period with three groups that claimed campus men were being persecuted by the college-rape "hoax": Stop Abusive and Violent Environments (SAVE), Families Advocating for Campus Equality (FACE), and the National Coalition for Men Carolinas (NCFMC).[28] More than a hundred survivor advocates demonstrated outside the Education Department building in Washington on another wilting July day when DeVos met with these groups. Survivors' "Dear Betsy" campaign urged her to "help end rape culture, don't perpetuate it." They got a single, chilly meeting with DeVos.

Students protested at George Mason University, in Arlington, Virginia, when DeVos announced on September 8, 2017, that she soon would dismantle the 2011 Dear Colleague letter. OCR director Jackson replaced the 2011 letter and its 2014 Question-and-Answer Guidance two weeks later with "interim" guidelines on managing sexual misconduct (though these were as permanent as any previous Dear Colleague letter).[29]

A huge outcry from Title IX advocates pleaded with DeVos to return to fairer guidelines. Alexandra Brodsky co-authored one letter signed by 145 Yale alumni including former OCR director Lhamon and the NWLC's Goss Graves.[30]

DeVos continued on her path of destruction, the next month rescinding seventy-two policies related to the civil rights of students with disabilities. OCR's new case processing manual in March 2018 made it easier to close an investigation or dismiss a complaint, allowing the shutdown of more than 1,200 civil rights investigations inherited from the Obama administration.[31] In December 2018, DeVos officially canceled the 2016 guidance that had discouraged unfair discipline of students of color.[32]

The gears of women's coalitions built over decades came together quickly to coordinate intergroup and intergenerational responses to DeVos's Title IX regulations. The NWLC and its network of established groups (the American Association of University Women, Equal Rights Advocates, and others) included the newcomers (KYIX, EROC, SurvJustice) in meetings and weekly phone calls. Even though KYIX saw its work as fighting for civil rights, acceptance came slower from broader coalitions of civil rights groups, some of which saw KYIX simply as sexual assault movement activists. KYIX didn't yet belong to the Leadership Conference on Civil and Human Rights, for instance, and didn't have the resources to pursue membership, with just one full-time staff member and far-flung teams of student organizers paid small stipends.[33]

NWLC staff recruited a nationwide stable of lawyers to advise (and sometimes represent) women, bisexuals, and transgender people facing sex discrimination of many kinds, and announced the Legal Network for Gender Equity in early October 2017. San Francisco–based Equal Rights Advocates started another national network of attorneys and activists to train hundreds of lawyers on helping sexual assault survivors through Title IX, calling it the Initiative to End Sexual Violence in Education.

"If the OCR won't defend Title IX," ERA's executive director, Noreen Farrell, told journalists, "we will."[34]

The courage of student sexual assault survivors who went public spread to other sectors of society. More women spoke up about harassment in every industry and all parts of life.

Journalists at the *New York Times* and the *New Yorker* uncovered decades of sexual harassment and rape allegations from multiple actresses against Hollywood movie mogul Harvey Weinstein, for instance. White actress Alyssa Milano tweeted on October 15, 2017, "If you've been sexually harassed or assaulted write 'me too' as a reply to this tweet."

Millions did on various social media, using the hashtag #metoo—more than 12 million in the first twenty-four hours on Facebook and 19 million on Twitter within a year—demonstrating the pervasiveness of sexual harassment and assault. Activists of color pointed out that a Black woman, Tarana Burke, had originated a "me too" campaign in 2006 in her work with young survivors; Milano and others then amplified her voice.[35]

Almost immediately, women in nonprofit organizing, law, politics, and entertainment began meeting to plan and fund a network of lawyers for gender equity cases in employment, calling itself Time's Up. An open letter to Hollywood's sexual violence survivors from the Alianza Nacional de Campesinas—penned by co-founder Mónica Ramírez and published in *Time* magazine on November 10, 2017—expressed solidarity from seven hundred thousand women farmworkers who'd been fighting sexual assault in the fields. Time's Up decided to focus on helping low-income women and flow its funds, initially $14 million, through the NWLC.

Leading Hollywood stars wore black and brought Time's Up activists including Burke, Ramírez, and domestic worker advocate Ai-jen Poo as their "plus ones" to the 2018 Golden Globes awards show, broadcast to millions.[36]

Approximately 2 million people hit the streets again in cities across the country for the second Women's March in January 2018 to show resistance against Trump's policies.[37]

Five years after Andrea Pino, Annie Clark, and the others filed their complaint against the University of North Carolina (UNC), OCR ruled on January 25, 2018, that the university violated Title IX and other laws. OCR found UNC was too slow to respond to complaints and didn't maintain appropriate policies and grievance procedures, among other deficiencies. UNC officials agreed to make some changes.

Clark left EROC's executive director position soon after that. All the vicarious trauma of EROC's work over the years took a heavy mental toll on both Clark and Pino. They went separate ways.

All hours of the day and night, they'd received hundreds of emails from survivors needing help. They'd spent countless hours hearing their stories, being virtually by their sides in each step of responding, moving toward healing, and reclaiming their educations. Clark recently had spent considerable time helping a young woman in Alabama; when she killed herself, it hit especially hard.

With Clark's departure from EROC's staff, all the originators of EROC and KYIX had moved on, though most stayed engaged as advisors or board members. EROC grew to a 2018 annual budget of $683,000 with five full-time staff, and sought six more employees that August.[38] But in late 2019 its board abruptly suspended and then let go all employees but one, its announcement referring obliquely to alleged mismanagement and financial difficulties. When the dust settled, EROC carried on, led for the first time by a Black woman, Kenyora Parham.[39]

The Education Department validated Clark and Pino's 2013 complaint again in 2019 by finding UNC in violation of the Clery Act.[40] It fined UNC $1.5 million in June 2020 and imposed three years of monitoring.

"With this, my chapter of student activism closes," Pino tweeted that day. "It's on all of us to make Carolina better. Let's keep going."

Media investigations and government reports also brought more public attention to sexual misconduct in K-12 schools and in graduate programs.

A yearlong investigation by the Associated Press in 2018 revealed a "hidden horror" of seventeen thousand sexual assaults by K-12 students against their peers over a four-year period, with attacks beginning as early as ages five and six and increasing in frequency up to about age fourteen.[41] OCR investigations of complaints about K-12 sexual assault and harassment led to 222 resolution agreements with schools from fall 2012 to fall 2018.[42]

Chicago Public Schools had no Title IX coordinator in 1999–2018 and ignored or neglected students experiencing sexual violence, a *Chicago Tribune* investigation found, exposing once again how too many education officials casually ignored Title IX's most basic requirements. OCR launched investigations of the district's response to 2,800 complaints of peer harassment or assaults and 280 complaints of adult-on-student sexual misconduct in more than four hundred schools in 2012–18. When Chicago administrators didn't cooperate, OCR tried a new tactic. Instead of the "nuclear option" of withholding all federal funding—the only sanction described by Title IX—OCR selectively blocked $4 million in funds for a larger grant to assist Chicago magnet schools and threatened to withhold $11 million more. Chicago officials sued, claiming OCR denied it due process before revoking the grants, but agreed to a resolution agreement in September 2019, promising significant systemic changes.[43]

On the other end of the educational spectrum, a two-year report by the National Academies of Sciences, Engineering, and Medicine in 2018 called for colleges, universities, and research centers to move beyond Title IX and treat sexual harassment as a cultural problem, not just a legal one. Faculty or staff harass 20–50 percent of women students in these three disciplines, and some 58 percent of women faculty experience sexual harassment, the report said. It called for institutional changes. Treat sexual misconduct as seriously as research misconduct, for instance, and diffuse faculty power by assigning each graduate student to a group of mentors instead of to a single faculty advisor holding power over the student's career.[44]

Clearly, sex discrimination still plagued graduate programs nearly five decades after Bernice Sandler smacked into institutionalized discrimination in her graduate program and field.

For Sandler's ninetieth birthday on March 3, 2018, purple, white, and blue helium balloons surrounded scores of family and friends who braved an icy windstorm to celebrate with her in the ballroom of the Woman's National Democratic Club in Washington, DC. JJ wore a dress, and Sandler, her white silk turtleneck with the brocaded collar under a red satin jacket. Icing on a giant cake read, "Happy 90th Birthday Bunny, Godmother of Title IX."

A younger Sandler shared her story that spring on stage at Yale's Hopper Cabaret, yet it wasn't actually her. Yale senior Rora Brodwin became Sandler for three nights in a white turtleneck under a blue-and-white striped dress shirt. Sandler couldn't attend, but much of the rest of the family was there for Brodwin's one-act play *Bunny, Godmother of Title IX*, her senior thesis in American Studies that dramatized the lead-up to the law's passage and its ramifications since. Brodwin affectionately called Sandler her "great aunt" to convey the connection between them; Brodwin's grandmother was Sandler's favorite cousin.

"There are things that I want to say to Bunny that I have not said," Brodwin told the audience, slipping in and out of character. "I want to say, 'Bunny, I was sexually assaulted, which is a great loss of power for my body, for my mind," and "because of you—because of *you*—there were systems in place, there were people in *this institution*, who could give power back to me. . . . I would be a different person if you had not created that strength and authority on which I rested." Yale's Title IX Office funded a restaging the next semester for faculty and staff.

By 2019 Yale had twenty-three Title IX coordinators listed on its website. They heard 115 complaints of sexual assault, intimate partner violence, or stalking in calendar year 2019, not counting greater numbers of harassment and other forms of sexual misconduct. At Fresno State, with roughly double the number of Yale's students (24,403 versus 12,458), complaints of sexual misconduct, dating or domestic violence, and stalking totaled seventy-five in fiscal year 2019–20, again not counting the sexual harassment and other misconduct complaints.[45] Fresno State didn't appoint a full-time Title IX coordinator until 2018. In general, experts say, higher numbers of reports don't necessarily reflect more assaults and other misconduct, but may indicate a better understanding of the Title IX process and a greater willingness to report, perhaps because more people know that filing a report is an option or there's a greater belief that reporting will be helpful, not harmful.

The influence of the movement against sexual violence also showed up in previously unexamined corners of American culture. Disney amusement parks changed a robotic scene in the Pirates of the Caribbean ride in 2018 from one showing women tied up and waiting to be sold to one depicting men and women pirates auctioning off stolen goods. Another scene of leering pirates chasing women became angry women chasing pirates.[46]

When President Trump nominated conservative appellate court Judge Brett Kavanaugh, a graduate of Yale and its law school, for an open seat on the Supreme Court in 2018, multiple women came forward accusing Kavanaugh of sexual harassment and assault in high school and at Yale. KYIX, then led by Sage Carson, facilitated a nearly round-the-clock presence on Capitol Hill in the weeks leading up to his confirmation, including a new cohort of high school sexual assault survivors called IX High. A letter from 250 law professors nationwide objected to his nomination; KYIX co-founders Bolger and Brodsky drafted a similar letter signed by hundreds of Yale Law alumni.

Bolger, then in her third year at Yale Law, and others placed signs around Yale: "#metoo," and "We believe Dr. Christine Blasey Ford," one of Kavanaugh's accusers. Kavanaugh followed Ford's dignified testimony at his Senate confirmation hearing with his own display of tearful, angry, snarling victimhood, much like Clarence Thomas's demeanor at his confirmation hearing twenty-seven years earlier. It seemed a tour-de-force performance of what increasingly was recognized as DARVO, an acronym coined by Professor Jennifer Freyd representing a common response by people accused of sexual assault: Deny, Attack, and Reverse Victim and Offender.[47] She named the strategy in order to change it, or at least people's responses to it.

Bolger organized a bus carrying a hundred Yale Law students to DC to protest Kavanaugh's nomination. A chorus of women in the Senate's gallery chanted "Shame! Shame!" as senators confirmed Kavanaugh by one of the slimmest margins in history. The year before, Trump had pushed another conservative onto the Supreme Court—Justice Neil Gorsuch—after Republicans stalled a vote on President Obama's nominee for nearly a year.

The month after Kavanaugh's confirmation, November 2018, voters elected a record number of women—one hundred—to Congress. They made the 116th Congress the most diverse in history, with 126 women including 43 women of color. Democrats retook control of the House of Representatives.

More locally, Pamela Price challenged the incumbent district attorney of Alameda County, California, in the 2018 primary election as a reform candidate, attracting support from Black Lives Matter co-founder Alicia Garza, former congressman Ronald Dellums, activist Angela Davis, and others.[48] Of all the awards she's received over decades, one of the most meaningful to her came that year—the Pauli Murray Trailblazer Award, from the African American Policy Forum. Price lost the DA primary election but drew impressive support for a relative newcomer. She then immediately jumped into the fall 2018 race for mayor of Oakland and placed third.[49] Each race took a toll of time and money. Price had to rebuild her law practice after every campaign, but by 2020 her business was recovering. She won reelection to the county Democratic Party Central Committee on a slate of "People-Powered Progressives."

Progressives had little say in the federal government. DeVos launched a "Notice and Comment" period in November 2018 for proposed changes to the Title IX regulations—the first regulations changes in four decades. Unlike all the intervening nonbinding guidance and Dear Colleague letters, this lengthy rule-making process would give DeVos's changes the force of law. Her rules went easier on students accused of sexual misconduct and reduced the responsibilities of educational institutions.[50]

Among DeVos's proposed changes, schools could limit the number of employees empowered to receive complaints. Imagine if DeVos's rules applied to earlier times: if Pamela Price hadn't delivered her complaint about a professor's sexual coercion to exactly the right dean, or if Alexandra Brodsky hadn't complained to exactly the right person about a student sexually assaulting her, Yale would not have been responsible for follow-up. Coaches would have been allowed to turn a blind eye to sexual assaults by athletes. Under another DeVos proposal that schools only be responsible for what happens on campus, Price could not have helped her client Patricia H. because the music teacher who sexually abused Patricia's two daughters didn't do it at school. The Education Department estimated that the changes could save schools $286–$367 million over a decade because they'd investigate fewer complaints.[51]

Lawyers' groups didn't always agree with survivor advocates in criticisms of the proposed rules. The American College of Trial Lawyers endorsed using the clear-and-convincing standard of evidence that the new rules allowed instead of the "preponderance of evidence" that was standard for civil procedures. The ACLU disagreed with that and other parts of the proposed regulations but approved of requiring a live hearing and cross-examination, which most survivor advocates opposed as potentially retraumatizing for the complainant.[52]

More than 124,000 comments about DeVos's proposed regulations poured into the Department of Education, more than ten times as many as Sandler and all her allies generated for the original Title IX regulations in 1974. Most of them challenged DeVos's revisions. OCR would have to spend more than a year responding to them all before the regulations could be finalized.

Sitting on the broad, tan couch in the living room of Sandler's Washington condo in late 2018, JJ offered Sandler some M&Ms candies—one of Sandler's favorite treats. Sandler always took a packet with her on planes and ate the contents before takeoff in case the plane crashed and it was her last meal. JJ was between jobs and able to visit Sandler often in the latter part of 2018, treasuring time with their grandmother. JJ knew that each packet of M&Ms really could be the last meal.

Sandler had been diagnosed with multiple myeloma, a blood cancer, something she referred to with resignation. "Most people don't know what they're going to die of," she said. "Now I know." On January 5, 2019, Sandler died in home hospice care.

Family, friends, and former colleagues gathered one more time in the Woman's National Democratic Club on June 26, 2019, for a celebration of Sandler's life and legacy.

"We know that Bunny Sandler did more for Title IX than any member of Congress," said Rep. Eleanor Holmes Norton, who had served as the first woman (and first Black woman) chair of the Equal Employment Opportunity Commission (EEOC) and instituted the EEOC's first guidelines against workplace sexual harassment under Title VII in 1980. "If you look at the history of the civil rights laws—the 1964 Civil Rights Act, which was my great privilege to administer, the 1965 Voting Rights Act, the 1968 Fair Housing Act—you will not be able to find a single individual that you can say, 'But for that person I'm not sure we would have gotten so far.'" Sandler was that person for Title IX.

Sandler loved being the center of attention and knew about plans for the memorial before she died. "Sounds like fun," she said. "I wish I could be there."[53]

On every table, guests received cards colorfully decorated with a drawing of a bluebird—a symbol used by suffragists in the early 1900s—and featuring the slogan "Uppity Women Unite." Affixed to them were some of Sandler's final stash of Title IX buttons, to take home and wear in her honor. Next to them were packets of M&Ms.

Death swept the country nine months later as a potentially deadly virus never before seen in humans sped around the world, starting in late 2019. By spring 2020 tens of thousands of sick and dying patients with coronavirus disease 2019 (COVID-19) overwhelmed hospitals in New York and other cities around the world. Many schools, colleges, and universities closed, sending everyone home to sequester and try to finish the school year on hastily created remote-learning classes streamed live via computers. UNC and some other schools welcomed students back in the fall but quickly sent them packing when COVID-19 predictably spiked.

Among approximately 321,000 known infections in students, staff, and faculty at more than 1,700 colleges and universities by mid-November 2020, at least eighty people died, including four or more students. These were undercounts; many schools tested only those with symptoms. Willingness to release data varied by campus.[54]

Many schools tried to let football play on in spite of the pandemic—usually the only sport allowed to play, which seems a clear Title IX violation that no one addressed. And the potential harm of the violation cut both ways: Why should men athletes get to play but not women? Why should men athletes be endangered by greater virus exposure but not women?

Coronavirus spread to dozens of football players and coaches, endangering lives and postponing or canceling at least eighty-one games by November 21, 2020. More than five thousand cases of coronavirus were linked to more than ninety athletics departments at universities competing in the NCAA Division I Football Bowl Subdivision, representing the largest, most competitive football programs. These again were undercounts; dozens of programs refused to release infection data.[55]

In the midst of the pandemic, athletics departments slashed men's minor sports teams but rarely football, often blaming coronavirus-constricted budgets. Fresno State and multiple other universities announced they also would cut some women's teams, leaving men with a disproportionate share of playing slots. Women athletes fought back, suing Fresno State and the University of Iowa. Threats of lawsuits convinced others to reinstate some women's teams, including Dartmouth College, East Carolina University, the College of William and Mary, and Brown University. What's remarkable is not that women's teams won these skirmishes but that administrators still thought they could ignore Title IX requirements.[56]

The NCAA used the pandemic as an excuse to backtrack on a new policy requiring student athletes to tell schools if they've been investigated, disciplined, or convicted for "sexual, interpersonal or other acts of violence." It created the policy under public pressure after a USA Today investigation found that athletes expelled or otherwise disciplined for sexual misconduct commonly transferred schools and returned to competition without the new community knowing that history. Athletes were less than 3 percent of students but made up nearly 9 percent of those found responsible for sexual misconduct; football players were less than 1 percent of students but more than 6 percent of those disciplined for sexual misconduct. After COVID-19 hit, the NCAA said that for the next two years it would not sanction athletics departments that turn a blind eye to players' sexual misconduct.[57]

When three women track-and-field athletes sued the NCAA, saying its lack of rules in this area enabled a renowned high-jump coach to sexually abuse them, the NCAA argued it has no legal obligation to protect student athletes. The NCAA employed nearly sixty workers to investigate and sanction players for nonviolent infractions like bad grades and smoking marijuana, but it refused to create penalties for sexual assault.[58]

The pandemic exacerbated long-standing gender inequities for working women, especially women of color and low-income employees. With schools closed, children were home and their care fell mainly to women. Faculty women wrote significantly fewer papers than men, received harsher evaluations from students, and juggled higher teaching loads and service roles.[59]

In the midst of the pandemic, a Minneapolis police officer knelt on George Floyd's neck for more than eight minutes during an arrest on May 25, 2020, suffocating the unarmed Black man. A video of the killing (witnessed and recorded by a teenage girl, Darnella Frazier) sparked more than 4,700 Black Lives Matter street demonstrations over the next forty-four days in all fifty states, in more than 2,500 cities, suburbs, and rural towns. That alone made Black Lives Matter likely the largest protest movement in U.S. history, involving an estimated 15 million to 26 million people, or 4–8 percent of the U.S. population. Protests continued in some locations for many months over Floyd's death and new episodes of police violence against Black men and women. Unlike the settings of earlier Black Lives Matter protests, nearly 95 percent of the counties that saw protests were majority white, and nearly three-quarters had white populations greater than 75 percent.[60]

More than ever, white people started to grapple with institutional racism and intersectional discrimination that had been obvious to people of color for so long.

These protests, along with others since Trump's election—the Women's Marches and demonstrations against climate change, gun violence, Trump's policy of separating refugee children from parents, and more—accounted for a dramatic increase in popular resistance. One in five Americans said they'd protested under Trump. Nineteen percent of them were new to protesting.[61]

Social justice movements looked inward, too. At least forty-six mostly state-based coalitions against sexual assault and domestic violence signed onto a June 2020 statement admitting that their movement—especially its white leadership—failed to listen to Black feminist liberationists and other colleagues of color. The movement had ignored community-based, transformative justice approaches created by Black, Indigenous, and people of color leaders, instead promoting "false solutions" emphasizing policing and imprisonment.[62]

Conservative forces were gaining traction, however, on the issue of transgender rights. Anti-transgender forces branched out from suing about bathrooms and PE locker rooms to sue about transgender girls playing competitive school sports, arguing that they have a physical advantage and take playing slots away from cisgender girls. Idaho became the first state to ban transgender athletes from playing on sports teams for girls and women.[63] DeVos's OCR threatened in spring and summer 2020 to withhold federal funding from six Connecticut school districts and the Connecticut Interscholastic Athletic Conference if they allowed transgender girls to compete. The ACLU intervened to represent the transgender athletes.[64]

The conservative-majority Supreme Court surprised many in June 2020 when it ruled 6–3 that Title VII prohibits employment discrimination based on sexual orientation or gender identity, discrimination that had been legal in twenty-one states. These new workplace protections for gay or transgender employees raised hopes of future court rulings to protect transgender rights for students.[65] Sure enough, by August 2020 two appeals courts and a federal judge in Idaho cited the Supreme Court decision in three rulings supporting the rights of transgender students—including Gavin Grimm—under Title IX and the Constitution to use gender-appropriate bathrooms or play on sports teams that match their gender identity.[66]

But the biggest hit to Title IX in this century came in May 2020 when the DeVos OCR finalized the new Title IX regulations, which went into effect August 14, 2020. The bulk of their 2,033 pages responded to 124,196 comments that comprised "a torrent of criticism from universities, advocacy groups, survivors of sexual assault and campus leaders," the *Washington Post* reported.[67]

The new regulations narrowed the definition of sexual harassment, adopting phrasing from *Davis* that was stricter than definitions of workplace sexual harassment under Title VII or definitions used for racial and other harassment. Unwelcome conduct had to be so severe *and* pervasive *and* objectively offensive that it interrupts education. Plaintiffs in lawsuits had to prove the schools were "deliberately indifferent," the regulations said, a tougher test than showing that they knew or should have known about sexual misconduct.

Students could be represented by attorneys; too bad if the other side couldn't afford one. The school had to provide a written notice to complaint respondents (the alleged perpetrators of sexual misconduct) that they are presumed innocent but not to complainants (the alleged victims) that they are presumed to be telling the truth. If someone submitted a statement or texts or emails as evidence but didn't want to endure cross-examination, that evidence would get discarded.

Many provisions made the processing of sexual conduct complaints more like a courtroom than a campus civil procedure, but only for sexual misconduct, not any other kinds of student misconduct.

"#TitleIX is not a replacement for the criminal (in)justice system, and we have never wanted it to be," Andrea Pino objected in a tweet. "Every student has the right to a safe, equal education, and the threat of sexual violence makes that impossible." Wagatwe Wanjuki took a wide-angle view in her tweets: "The Title IX changes by Betsy DeVos are a part of the right-wing crusade to eradicate civil rights in education as we know it." In the *Atlanta Journal-Constitution*, the NWLC's Fatima Goss Graves and Derrick Johnson, president of the NAACP, wrote, "All these changes would particularly hurt black women and girls, who face even higher stakes when reporting sexual harassment. . . . Both of our organizations have stated, again and again, that an attack on Title IX is an attack on all civil rights."[68]

Advocates' efforts won a few helpful modifications in the final version. A school could ignore off-campus sexual misconduct at, say, a house rented by student athletes, as DeVos proposed, but must address misconduct in "locations, events or circumstances" in which the school substantially controlled students and activities. Colleges and universities had to allow live cross-examinations but only by representatives for the alleged perpetrators, not by the alleged perpetrators themselves, and this could be conducted in separate rooms via communication technology. Schools could use either the preponderance or clear-and-convincing standard for evidence, but advocates gained a provision that the same standard must apply to students and faculty. They also got "rape shield" protections inserted, so that a survivor's sexual or mental health history could not be used to victim-blame or humiliate the complainant.[69]

"Our fight continues, and these rules, which we believe cannot withstand a fair review by the courts, will not be the final word," Alexandra Brodsky tweeted. "The ghost of Phyllis Schlafly may still roam the halls of the Department of Education, and bend Secretary DeVos's ear, but such outdated and dangerous views cannot be allowed to dictate modern public policy."

Multiple lawsuits tried to stop the revised Title IX regulations, including suits by NWLC, eighteen state attorneys general, Equal Rights Advocates, New York school boards, and the ACLU for KYIX and other groups. By March 2021 three remained alive.[70]

DeVos became the most-sued secretary of education in history, with at least 455 lawsuits by October 2020 against her and the department over a period of less than four years (compared with 356 in eight years under Obama). She lost more than won in court.[71] But when the new Title IX regulations went into effect, the men's rights group Save Our Sons declared victory and disbanded, posting a goodbye message on its website.

Trump and the Republican Senate rapidly appointed his third Supreme Court justice after eighty-seven-year-old Justice Ruth Bader Ginsburg died in September 2020. Judge Amy Coney Barrett's one previous ruling on a Title IX case, a unanimous opinion she wrote for a three-judge panel, allowed a man to sue Purdue University after he'd been found responsible for sexually assaulting a classmate and suspended for a year. Barrett reasoned that OCR's efforts to enforce Title IX could be evidence of bias against men. "By Judge Barrett's logic," Brodsky blogged on the Public Justice website, "the only way to avoid the appearance of discrimination against men is to ensure their impunity."

Weeks later, though, voters dumped Trump in a close election, choosing Democratic President Joe Biden and Vice President Kamala Harris—the first woman, person of color, Black person, and person of Indian descent to be vice president. Harris would serve as the tiebreaker in a Senate evenly divided between Democrats and Republicans; the Democrats narrowly retained control of the House. A record 643 women ran for Congress, and the 117th Congress sworn in January 2021 was 27 percent women, also a new record. Women of color held 9 percent of the 535 seats in Congress plus three non-voting seats as delegates from U.S. territories and districts.[72]

Biden, a strong supporter of Title IX when he was Obama's vice president, in March 2021 started the long process of undoing Trump's changes to the Title IX regulations, especially those around sexual harassment and assault. It would take years, but the momentum shifted back toward equity.

His secretary of education, Miguel Cardona, affirmed in June 2021 that Title IX covers gay and transgender students, referencing the Supreme Court's 2020 decision in *Bostock v. Clayton County* protecting transgender workers under Title VII of the Civil Rights Act.[73] And the Supreme Court acted one last time in Gavin Grimm's case, after Virginia's Gloucester County School Board asked it to reconsider the appeals court's 2020 support for Grimm. The Supreme Court turned them away without comment. Grimm finally had won.[74]

"At last, my victory feels final," he wrote in the *Washington Post*. "But I shouldn't have had to fight this hard."[75]

Conservative state legislators proposed more than 110 anti-transgender bills in the first half of 2021, an unprecedented onslaught targeting transgender children and young adults. Thirteen passed by mid-June.[76] The struggle was far from over.

15

Fifty Years

BERNICE SANDLER ONCE NAIVELY THOUGHT THAT SEX DISCRIMINATION IN education would disappear within a couple years of Title IX's passage. Two years later, she extended that to five years. Then ten. Finally, she realized the process would take more than her lifetime.

And here we are, after her lifetime.

The tool she helped create—Title IX—boosted the women's movement and the movement against sexual violence, profoundly reshaping society for the better. Title IX's benefits reach some girls more than others, but a growing understanding of institutional and intersectional discriminations suggests we may be on the cusp of a new era that realizes Title IX's promise for all.

Fulfilling Title IX will require additional profound changes in society. There are signs that some are underway.

Thanks to Title IX, women in higher education consistently increased their numbers, becoming a majority of college and university students in 1979, a majority of law students in 2016, and a majority of new medical students in 2017.[1] Decades of graduates infused faculties, law offices, and every sector of society with women's talents and perspectives. By 2018 women held nearly half of full-time faculty jobs in higher education—Sandler's original dream job—yet they still were bunched in the lower ranks. Only a third of full professors were women.[2] Nearly half of undergraduates but only a fifth of faculty were people of color in 2021.[3]

Why haven't women reached parity with faculty men after a half-century of Title IX? Sexism and racism in academia became more subtle after civil rights laws, including Title IX, outlawed the most egregious practices, but institutionalized barriers still block women's advancement, such as lack of childcare and policies built around men's lives. From 2011's Occupy Wall Street to more recent campaigns for a universal basic income, more people are challenging a growing economic divide propped up by centuries of financial discrimination that make marginalized groups less able to access education and more vulnerable to crises. Fallout from the coronavirus pandemic offers a reckoning, highlighting how women of color and other women handle more than their share of the caretaking work on campus and at home, for instance, leaving less room for research and other work important to their careers.

Nearly a decade of Black Lives Matter—the modern intersectional iteration of the racial civil rights movement—has helped society confront entrenched racism with new vigor, even among supposed allies. After the 2015 unmasking of a white part-time professor (Rachel Dolezal) who posed as a Black woman, other exposés revealed more white academics impersonating people of color, including at least five in 2020 alone.[4] Separately, the National Organization for Women's white president, Toni Van Pelt, resigned in August 2020 citing health concerns after several years of controversy about the racial climate in NOW. Former vice president Gilda Yazzie, an Indigenous American, had sued NOW claiming she suffered retaliation for raising concerns about racist harassment; fifteen former NOW staff and interns complained of a toxic environment, and nearly a dozen members and staff described people in some NOW chapters heckling and disparaging women of color.[5]

In education, the biggest and most stubborn Title IX controversies in its first fifty years, after the initial wave of concerns related to employment and college admissions, arose from areas saturated with archaic notions of gender roles: sports and sexual misconduct.

High schools accommodated more than ten times as many girls in athletics by 2017 but still fewer than the number of boys playing sports at Title IX's inception in 1972, while the number of boys in athletics increased. Women grew to 57 percent of college and university students but still got only 44 percent of NCAA athletics opportunities in 2018. That's a vast improvement from their 15 percent share before Title IX, but why do we tolerate the ongoing disparity?

White women filled 69 percent of those NCAA team positions in 2018, far above their 53 percent proportion among students as a whole.[6] Head coaches of women's teams are almost all white (85 percent) and mostly men (59 percent). Until we design athletics systems that deal with intersectional discrimination involving race, sex, and other factors, Title IX will unfairly favor some groups over others.

Generations of girls have grown up under Title IX learning the strength of their bodies and minds and expecting to be heard. One of the treasures this gave us is the Women's National Basketball Association (WNBA), whose players were among the first professional athletes to speak out in a unified fashion for social justice. Since 2016, many WNBA teams have worn warm-up shirts supporting Black Lives Matter, taken a knee or other stance in protest against racism or gun violence, and held media blackouts to change WNBA policies suppressing political messaging.[7]

We might have even more of these badass athlete activists if schools gave girls and women their fair share of athletic opportunities. They rarely do. Reports mandated by the Equity in Athletics Disclosure Act (EADA) showed that in 2018–19 Yale University sported a 6 percent gap between women's proportion of all students and their proportion of students who played on at least one sports team; Fresno State's participation gap was 9 percent. Rare is the school that gives girls or women their fair share of athletics. Why do we tolerate the continuation of an unnecessarily complicated three-prong system to evaluate Title IX compliance in athletics that is routinely gamed to shortchange girls?

The late Justice Ruth Bader Ginsburg, when asked when there will be enough women on the Supreme Court, famously answered, "When there are nine." Because, she reasoned, "there'd been nine men, and nobody's ever raised a question about that."[8] Perhaps when girls and women get more than their proportionate share of playing slots as often as men do, we might consider Title IX athletic procedures to be fair.

Money would seem to be a simpler solution. If we apportion a school's athletics budget based on men's and women's share of enrollment, no one legitimately could call that sex discrimination. Then men could decide among themselves whether to spend their share on football or make room for other sports and stop blaming women for their choices.

People who benefit from big money in what's now the big industry of college sports haven't been willing to accept the idea of equal budgets, though. Both Yale and Fresno State had roughly twice as many men in head coach positions as women in those positions, their 2018–19 EADA reports showed; they paid head coaches of women's teams significantly less than head coaches of men's teams—a total of $64,000 less at Yale and $500,000 less at Fresno. Yale spent half a million dollars less to recruit women athletes compared with men, and Fresno State spent $193,000 less. In much larger universities in the most competitive sports conferences, disparities can be larger. Regardless of whether this is legal under current Title IX regulations, it isn't fair.

Those figures come from data that the law compels colleges and universities to provide under the Equity in Athletics Disclosure Act. There still is no law requiring high schools to do the same, making it harder to track athletics discrimination there. And that's the point.

Schools backslide on their Title IX obligations unless watchdogs stand guard. Shoreline Community College near Seattle considered cutting men's and women's soccer in January 2020 until Herb Dempsey of the Old Guys for Title IX wrote to them, pointing out (which they surely knew) that even before the proposed cuts, women were 51 percent of the college's students but received only 40 percent of athletic opportunities. The college changed its mind and kept women's soccer, knowing Dempsey was watching.

Thanks to Title IX, athletics scholarships helped many more low-income and minority women afford a college education. But that's not enough by itself to be called athletics equity in an intersectional world. Even simply splitting sports budgets equally between men and women is not enough when the women athletes being recruited increasingly are those who can afford to pay sports club fees, or whose high schools have the resources to offer sports teams.

If society deems athletics to be an important part of education, we need to find innovative ways to make the full gamut of education accessible to those who least can afford it. Recent calls by some politicians to make college free might help.

Conflict and crises also create opportunities for major change. Budget stresses from the coronavirus pandemic coincided with surveys by the Knight Commission on Intercollegiate Athletics showing widespread support for "big solutions" rather than incremental changes to fix the out-of-whack commercialization of college sports in order to reprioritize athletes' education, health, and safety.[9]

An equitable "big solution" under Title IX must tackle problems that won't be solved even if we achieve the dream of equal division of athletics resources to men and women. What about the lack of athletics for students of any gender with disabilities? The men/women divide also doesn't accommodate intersex athletes or those with nonbinary gender identities. If athletics are an important part of education, they should be available to everyone.

Conservatives and right-wing religious groups in recent years co-opted feminist terminology to build a hysteria around transgender girls and women competing in school sports. Instead of harping on the old myth that Title IX is destroying men's athletics by shunting resources to women—a myth that took a good three and a half decades to wither—conservatives now claim that Title IX is destroying women's athletics by letting transgender women "steal" playing opportunities from cisgender women. Both arguments distract from the bigger issue: there's ongoing neglect of athletics for women of any kind, so why not direct attention to expanding equity for all women? They'd rather attack transgender girls than acknowledge that boys' sports still hog the resources, or reorganize the system to include everyone.

Staunch Title IX defenders like the National Women's Law Center (NWLC), the American Civil Liberties Union (ACLU), and Know Your IX (KYIX) support transgender rights and don't see them as a threat. Many student athletes don't either. Nearly 550 athletes from at least eighty-five colleges and universities demanded in a March 2021 letter that the NCAA stop holding championships and events in states that consider or pass laws effectively banning transgender athletes from competing.

In fact, a *USA Today* investigation found only thirty transgender athletes in high schools and only two complaints about them competing. Hardly any of the state legislators advocating anti-transgender bills could point to a single case in their states that the bills would address. Stories about trans-gender girls dominating sports were lies or exaggerations being flogged in a national fear-mongering campaign by the conservative group Alliance Defending Freedom, which drafted many of the bills.[10] Compare that with the thousands of playing opportunities that go to high school boys instead of girls in violation of Title IX, documented year after year, and one has to question the motives of conservatives who ignore this yet say they are defending girls.

Still, the more than 110 anti-trans bills proposed in state legislatures in the first half of 2021 most commonly focused on banning transgender girls from competing on girls' teams.

Conservatives' arguments resonated with a small but surprisingly siz-able number of feminists in knee-jerk reactions to the claim that "men" were once again taking resources from women. They'd seen most athlet-ics opportunities and resources go to boys and men throughout Title IX's history and they were tired of it. They also weren't ready to recognize transgender girls as girls. At its heart, though, feminism tries to find ways to include everyone on the playing field.

What *is* the fairest way to include postpubertal transgender girls, who may or may not have hormones that could provide a competitive advan-tage compared with the "average" cisgender girl? Or to include intersex or gender-neutral athletes who may not fit neatly into binary gender cat-egories? The issue revives the question of whether sex or gender should be the guiding principle at all in school athletics structures. The debate harkens back to discussions during the formulation of Title IX's original regulations about whether there may be a better way, such as organizing competitions based on weight, age, or height, or using different methods of scoring. Perhaps those ideas were ahead of their time. Are we ready for them now?

While these questions eventually may alter athletics significantly, anoth-er issue is changing a different part of athletics. The movement against sexual violence has challenged the protected status of abuser athletes.

When the criminal justice system failed victims of sexual assault and harassment on campus, Title IX offered a lifeline. Activists like Pamela Price, Alexandra Brodsky, and Andrea Pino woke up schools about their

responsibilities under Title IX to not let sexual misconduct interrupt victims' education. Momentum on campus in the past decade helped spark
a worldwide movement that has given more women than ever the courage to demand an end to sexual violence and better support for survivors. Yet academic programs recently still ranked second among industries
in their rate of sexual harassment—affecting 58 percent of students and
faculty—behind only the military.[11]

Despite decades of efforts, the growing prominence of the movement
against sexual violence, and OCR's increased attention to sexual misconduct under Title IX, rates of campus sexual misconduct hadn't decreased
significantly by 2019. In the Association of American Universities' climate
survey of 181,752 students, nearly 33 percent of undergraduates reported
that during their time in college they experienced nonconsensual sexual
contact by force or inability to give consent or stop what was happening.
Survivors included 26 percent of undergraduate women and 7 percent of
undergraduate men in the survey. Extrapolated to the 16.6 million undergraduates enrolled in 2018, that means more than 5 million students were
affected.[12]

Sexual misconduct led the reasons for Title IX complaints to OCR in
the past half-decade and accounted for 29 percent of Title IX violations
reported in fiscal year 2019.[13] But OCR's enforcement depends on the
willingness of the political party in charge of the executive branch and on
the federal resources allocated to the agency. After the idea that government must be shrunk took hold in the Reagan era, Office for Civil Rights
(OCR) full-time staff levels decreased drastically between 1980 and 2014
under both Republican and Democratic administrations, from 1,148
employees to 544. At the same time, the number of complaints received
annually climbed from 3,497 to 9,989.[14]

Only a reinvigorated OCR could begin to do these numbers justice.
OCR never has been funded well enough to do its job completely. Besides
the question of funding, OCR never has been willing to enforce Title IX
using the strongest tool at its disposal: cutting off all federal funding to
a school or district, which undoubtedly would produce swift changes at
other laggard schools.

And what of school administrators? Within each institution, some try to change the conditions that foster sex discrimination while others do the minimum necessary to avoid legal liability. The high-pressure jobs of today's Title IX coordinators operating with inadequate resources, some of whom encounter obstruction from higher administrators, leave many feeling overwhelmed, emotionally drained, or burned out, *Chronicle of Higher Education* interviews with three dozen of them found.[15]

Still, 97 percent of administrators in January 2020 felt very or somewhat confident that they had improved their efforts to prevent and respond to sexual misconduct since the 2011 Dear Colleague letter, another *Chronicle* survey of 567 colleges and universities reported. Eighty-six percent of the institutions had hired or appointed a Title IX coordinator and 91 percent revised their sexual-misconduct policies since 2011. The most effective steps, they felt, were using the "preponderance of evidence" standard, introducing anonymous online reporting, and increasing advocacy for survivors or victims.[16]

Only a minority measured success in a way that could tell whether prevention efforts were succeeding, though: 40 percent looked for a decreased incidence of sexual misconduct as reported in anonymous campus climate surveys. More commonly, 85 percent gauged improvement by the numbers of students, faculty, or staff participating in prevention efforts like mandatory online training.

Those online trainings required by the Clery Act don't necessarily inform campus members about their Title IX rights, but they do allow schools to say they've complied with the law.

In her first month at Fresno State in September 2020, Jacqueline Gonzalez sped through the online training about sexual assault, dating violence, and stalking that new and returning students were required to complete.[17] She took notes too, knowing she had to score at least 80 percent correct on a post-training test to finish the training.

Gonzalez liked the video messages by a diverse cast of students—young people of color, white students, queer people, people in wheelchairs—and especially the true-life testimonials by survivors of sexual violence or stalking. She learned more than she knew about alcohol potency through pictures of different levels of hard liquor in clear plastic beer cups.

Students at around seven hundred colleges and universities that semester took the same "Not Anymore" training, designed to foster empathy, dispel myths about sexual assault, and teach bystander interventions to help prevent sexual misconduct.

A slide at the very beginning listed Fresno State's Title IX office and nondiscrimination policy but went by so fast it hardly was noticed. It seemed disconnected from the rest anyway, its paragraph about discrimination disjointed from the individualistic and situational vignettes stressing personal thoughts, actions, and morals and the physical and psychological effects of assault.

A few slides gave Fresno State space to modify the training for its students. Each time, a screen popped up showing California State Universities Executive Order 1097, which provided details of the university system's policies in a long scroll of tiny, dense type virtually guaranteed to be unread by students. Gonzalez read a portion for ten to fifteen seconds before moving on. She checked the box saying she'd read it, so Fresno State could check its own virtual box proving that it complied with some Title IX and Clery Act requirements.

Topics that might have been useful particularly to Fresno State students went unmentioned. Can a student report sexual assault anonymously? If the student has a police record, or they have a relative at home with undocumented immigration status, is it safe to seek help for sexual assault? What if they witness sexual harassment of a student off campus, where most Fresno State students live?

Gonzalez liked what she saw and learned from the program; she rated it "excellent" overall. Students couldn't rate what they didn't see, didn't learn. They didn't learn how sexual harassment and assault can be sex discrimination, or about the school's responsibility to provide a fair education to all. The discussions about the psychological consequences of sexual misconduct didn't mention how such impacts can interrupt education or lead to long-standing financial deficits. They didn't describe the school's duty to provide services or accommodations to survivors. You can't access a right that you don't know exists.

The only discussion in the training of consequences for perpetrators alluded to the possibility of jail time if a student sexually assaults someone while drunk or high, just as they might go to jail if they drove a car while

drunk or high and hit someone. The training didn't mention possible sus-
pension or expulsion for sexual harassment or assault. In the real world,
perpetrators of sexual assault rarely go to jail. Sexual assault survivors who
don't necessarily want the assaulter incarcerated might avoid reporting the
assault, potentially missing out on services that could help the survivor stay
in school.

An optional tab for "Resources" at the end of the computer-based training listed three on-campus resources including the victim advocate's office
and student health center, but not the Title IX office. At the top of the
list: the Fresno State Police Department, prioritizing a criminal justice
approach that many students shy away from and that nearly ignores the
civil protections provided by Title IX.

The "Not Anymore" training didn't teach students their Title IX rights.
In fact, it didn't mention Title IX at all except for the fleeting slide at the
start. That one sparse slide was the only information Gonzalez remembers
receiving about Title IX her entire first semester.[18] Teaching students from
a young age, and their parents, about their civil rights could empower
them to demand change when needed.

And schools that train teachers, education administrators, and coaches
need to do a better job of teaching them about Title IX too, Sandler once
said, because these groups generally show little knowledge of the law.

Lasting change requires modifying cultures—institutions, cultural privileges of power, notions of masculinity, and more.

In 2013 Dana Bolger noted that Amherst College's fifty-five-page
committee report about sexual misconduct on campus lacked the words
"sexism," "masculinity," and "patriarchy." There's little point to discussing rape prevention and response "without understanding the underlying
causes of sexual violence in the first place," she wrote. The report repeatedly characterized rape as a bizarre event out of the blue. Yet seven of the
nine rapists she knew of at college were repeat offenders, a pattern that
researchers say is motivated by rapists' desire to exert power or control over
bodies to which they feel entitled.[19]

In the past decade many educational institutions started the systemic data
collection needed to assess the problem of campus sexual misconduct and
to evaluate potential solutions, Professor Jennifer Freyd of the University

of Oregon said in a February 2019 symposium at Stanford University. Some have done more than that, trying to do better than past institutional betrayal of sexual assault survivors. In Corvallis, Oregon, for example, Oregon State University local police for six years ignored Brenda Tracy's 1998 report of gang rape by four men (including two university football players) until she and a journalist turned up the public heat in 2014. Then university officials apologized, admitted failures, changed their policies, and hired Tracy as a consultant for two years. Part of Tracy's job: talking to football teams to prevent sexual violence.[20]

Freyd named this second kind of response "institutional courage"—the opposite of institutional betrayal—and founded the Center for Institutional Courage in May 2020 to help schools and companies "seek the truth and engage in moral action" and "protect and care for those who depend on the institution."[21]

That's one way forward that can expand on Title IX's success. Another is an old idea: finally passing the Equal Rights Amendment. Or reaching beyond education rights to add "sex" to Title VI of the Civil Rights Act of 1964 so that sex discrimination is banned in many more sectors of society. When Rep. Edith Green's staff first drafted the bill that evolved into Title IX, most feminists advocated for cohesion in civil rights, arguing to add "sex" to "race, color, or national origin" as protected categories in Title VI. Instead, politicians split the different groups, sometimes out of political necessity and sometimes as a divide-and-conquer strategy. They borrowed words from Title VI to make Title IX, banning sex discrimination in education, then used essentially the same words for separate laws banning discrimination based on disability or age, all with different sets of regulations.

One consequence is that campus procedures for handling discrimination often vary by the type of discrimination, a conundrum for someone facing intersectional discrimination. College administrators report that even when students know where to go with a Title IX complaint, they seldom know who to talk to about harassment or discrimination related to race, disability, or religion.[22] What's a woman of color to do, for example? Merging sexual-misconduct prevention with anti-racism efforts and campus programs targeting other kinds of discrimination and harassment might help.

But even adding "sex" to Title VI wouldn't be enough today. The "simple" three-letter word is a more complicated concept than people conceived of fifty years ago. LGBTQ advocates are championing a bill called the Equality Act, which would add "sex (including sexual orientation and gender identity)" to Title VI and some other parts of the Civil Rights Act of 1964. The bill passed the U.S. House of Representatives in early 2021 (H.R. 5) but faced stiffer obstacles in the Senate.

Meanwhile, a "Survivors' Agenda" could lead the way in modeling an approach to dealing with sexual assault that's based on understandings of intersectional discrimination and social justice feminism.

Four women of color—Mónica Ramírez, Tarana Burke, Ai-jen Poo, and the NWLC's Fatima Goss Graves, all of them among the founders of the legal network Time's Up—in 2020 organized an effort to channel #metoo momentum into laws and policies. They surveyed more than eleven hundred survivors and formed a steering committee of twenty-one groups including the NWLC, Equal Rights Advocates, and the National Organization of Sisters of Color Ending Sexual Assault. More than sixty organizations signed on as partners, including the ACLU, End Rape on Campus (EROC), and KYIX. Forty-plus representatives met weekly for months, developing an agenda and then presenting it to a virtual summit for survivors in September 2020.[23]

The Survivors' Agenda doesn't include abolishing police or prisons but also doesn't emphasize punitive measures, instead advocating actions that could make life better for survivors. It proposes actions like ending the criminalization of survivors who defend themselves, repealing the Trump administration's changes to the Title IX regulations, universal health care, consent education starting in preschool, sex education (including the concept of consent) starting no later than middle school, and much, much more. The agenda recommends funding for culturally rooted community programs, non-police "crisis teams," and restorative justice programs. It calls for investments addressing factors that increase the risk of sexual violence such as poverty, substance abuse, lack of housing or transportation, and societal norms that prop up patriarchal violence and white supremacy.[24]

Title IX so far has helped many millions of people—women, men, and in between—access education and jobs in education, play school sports, and change policies to better help survivors of sexual harassment and assault. It also has kept some pregnant students in school, created a few protections for queer and transgender students, opened a crack for students to pursue Career and Technical Education regardless of stereotypes about who should be welders or beauticians, and so much more. By many measures, Title IX's first fifty years were a success.

But every single one of these Title IX battles still is being fought, and we have far to go. Those who've benefited disproportionately are white, financially comfortable, able-bodied, cisgender, heterosexual, native-born. If we don't address the reasons why that privilege exists—the racism, economic barriers, and other factors that intersect with sexism—Title IX never will be fully a success.

Fortunately, many are embracing the concepts of social justice feminism, and youth are not waiting for older adults to figure it all out. In the past decade they've surged in activist and political leadership to an extent not seen for half a century. They've turbocharged multiple movements to stop sexual violence, economic oppression, the deep racism that permeates every aspect of U.S. society, climate change, gun violence, police brutality, and other evils.

They will face backlashes and setbacks, same as it ever was. But there's hope in the future.

16

The Next Fifty Years

SHORTLY AFTER THE 2016 ELECTION OF PRESIDENT TRUMP, ONE OF BERNICE Sandler's daughters called her, distraught and worried about how Sandler might be taking the news. "The road goes up and down. You've got to take the long view and the high road," Sandler consoled her. "Women in the suffrage movement didn't give up because of bumps in the road. They didn't stop because of the obstacles and the unsupportive world they lived in. They knew they wouldn't see the results of their work in their lifetimes. But they kept going."[1]

Sandler kept going as Title IX's longest advocate despite twenty-eight years of attacks on Title IX or neglect under Republican presidents and better but inadequate efforts under Democratic administrations. Beyond her lifetime, younger activists carry the movements for equity and justice forward.

"Somehow we've weathered and witnessed a nation that isn't broken but simply unfinished," Amanda Gorman recited at President Joe Biden's inauguration, brightening the dais in a vivid yellow coat and crowned by a scarlet satin headband. A young Black woman chosen as the first National Youth Poet Laureate in 2017, Gorman inspired not just the politicians present that day in January 2021, but any listeners committed to civil rights and the creation of a fair and healthy world. She ended with a call to action:

> For there is always light,
> if only we're brave enough to see it
> If only we're brave enough to be it.[2]

Five days earlier Pamela Price announced her next political candidacy, running again for district attorney of Alameda County, California, in 2022. Events of 2020 such as police killings and the Black Lives Matter protests "pulled back the curtain on the broken system of criminal justice, clearly exposing the racial, socioeconomic and gender disparities within our criminal justice system," Price wrote to supporters in an email blast on January 28, 2021. She promised a corporate-free, grassroots, people-powered campaign, daring once more to be a light leading toward fairness under the slogan "Justice with Compassion."

A *Fresno Bee* analysis of police department data described one of those persistent disparities affecting all of California: being stopped by police for "driving while black," as Fresno State coach Britt King had been twenty years earlier. Police in the first half of 2020 stopped Black drivers in Fresno at twice the rate they stopped white and Hispanic drivers. They searched, arrested, and handcuffed Black drivers at disproportionate rates, though police were more likely to find contraband on white drivers.[3]

While Price continued to battle racial and gender disparities through law and politics, in Fresno Diane Milutinovich carried on as a watchdog for equity in athletics. Still a Bulldogs fan, she regularly attended softball games in Fresno State's beautiful stadium before the pandemic canceled competition. Milutinovich enjoyed season tickets to softball, men's basketball, and football as part of the settlement to her lawsuit.

She attended every meeting—in person or virtual—of Fresno State's Athletic Corporation, the only attendee specifically concerned about gender equity other than an occasional *Fresno Bee* reporter. "If somebody's not looking over their shoulder, some things squeak by" that may violate Title IX, she said.

Milutinovich traveled to annual galas benefiting the National Women's Law Center (NWLC) and the Women's Sports Foundation along with meetings related to Title IX or women in athletics, squeezing in side trips to see Broadway shows in New York City any time she ventured east of the Mississippi River. In the pandemic those connections became virtual, but her cell phone rang often. Coaches, administrators, and attorneys around the country asked for advice or strategy on Title IX issues—including athletes suing their colleges for cutting women's teams during the pandemic.

"Information is power," she'd tell them. Are they studying their college's Equity in Athletics Disclosure Act reports? Do they know their school's policy for adding or dropping sports? Do they know how to tap resources and build relationships on campus so they can speak up without getting fired?

Milutinovich calculated she'd be seventy-four on Title IX's fiftieth birthday in 2022. She had no watchdog-in-waiting coming up behind her, no protégé to promote Title IX whenever her time is done. Individual athletics professionals she spoke with feared being seen as the "other," not as a team player, feared they wouldn't be promoted, feared losing their job if they demanded equity. Those legitimate fears make the work of less vulnerable groups like the NWLC, the Women's Sports Foundation, and Champion Women all the more important.

Champion Women, founded in 2014 by lawyer and three-time Olympic gold medalist Nancy Hogshead-Makar, calculated that in college athletics alone men still get nearly $1 billion more in scholarships and recruitment dollars, and 200,000 more chances to play than do women athletes. Ninety percent of colleges and universities are violating Title IX by discriminating against women athletes, the group estimated. It teamed up with the Equality League to try and recruit college women in all fifty states to take legal action by the law's fiftieth anniversary on June 23, 2022.[4] The rippling effects of Title IX getting more women into law schools and athletics continue to rock the boat.

Milutinovich may not yet have a replacement for herself on the local level, but she and the wider Title IX revolution in athletics have left a legacy. Thirty-three years after graduating from Park Ridge High School in New Jersey, Liza Heller Eto accompanied her father to the school's 2018 athletics awards ceremony, where he received a booster award. The sheer numbers of girls on teams amazed her. That night the girls received the same tributes as boys—season highlights recited, recognitions for toughness or teamwork. Afterward, she made her way to the athletics director. "When I started as a student here, there were no girls' teams. I joined the first-ever girls' track team," she told him, adding how pleased she was by the program now. The younger man had trouble believing that things had been so lopsided. He had no idea.

Younger Title IX activists are just starting to level out a lopsidedness in the epidemic of sexual violence on campus, but they've found their voices and won't be quieted. Alexandra Brodsky became a civil rights attorney in the nonprofit legal advocacy group Public Justice. She dissected the polarized debates about "due process" under Title IX in her first book, *Sexual Justice: Supporting Victims, Ensuring Due Process, and Resisting the Conservative Backlash* (Metropolitan, 2021). For Brodsky and others of her generation, their Title IX activism didn't define them, but always would be a part of them.

Andrea Pino woke up on March 10, 2020, and just knew. She didn't need to look at a calendar; she could feel that this was the day she'd been raped eight years earlier. "But I didn't wake up sad," she tweeted to followers. "I woke up hopeful, because I feel loved, by others and by myself. To all who can't feel joy right now: there will always be a Spring at the end of each Winter."

Still in their twenties, Brodsky and Pino and their peers had aged out of student leadership. The organizations they helped build supported their replacements.

At the 2018 Women's March Convention in Detroit, Jess Davidson, the interim executive director of End Rape on Campus, staffed a literature table. A girl and her friend stopped by. They looked to be around thirteen or fourteen years old.

"I have an anti-rape club on my campus," one girl said.

The day before, some slightly older teens stopped by the table and one told Davidson, "I work on sexual assault in my high school." Their words lifted an invisible weight off her shoulders.

At age twenty-two Davidson was a veteran of the anti-sexual violence movement. After being raped her junior year at the University of Denver, she'd been advocating almost nonstop for better sexual assault policies on campuses. It was hard work, emotionally taxing. She noticed at one point that she was developing symptoms of post-traumatic stress disorder. The exhilaration of progress on specific campuses ebbed when she considered the exhausting amount of work still needed.

Then younger people would show up and remind her that they were ready to carry the torch. Davidson hadn't even heard of affirmative consent until sometime in college. Here were kids in middle school and high school familiar with feminist concepts and goals for stopping sexual violence— kids who were doing something about it.

The change is *definitely* coming, she thought.

Chaos theory tells us that the flap of a butterfly's wings can trigger a tornado thousands of miles away. Small actions can have large effects under the right conditions. The movements for sexual and gender equity are like legions of butterflies, Catharine MacKinnon said in 2017. Some go splat on the windshield, but still they come. Their strength lies in the "collaborative effects of collective repetition," a phrase she borrowed from feminist author Kate Millett.[5]

Title IX's history is a kaleidoscope of butterflies, a tale of ongoing movements and new beginnings, a chronicle of progress and setbacks and forging ahead even if you're unaware of the previous progress and setbacks. The ending to this book is simply that there's no end to this story. Culture change may lag legal change, or vice versa, but trends toward recognizing the fundamental fairness of civil rights aren't easily undone. Once problems get named they can be changed. People who have lost their blinders won't unsee what they've seen.

One excited scream of discovery can turn into millions. Then there's no going back.

Acknowledgments

I'VE BEEN THE STUDENT OF MANY TEACHERS IN THIS PROJECT ON TITLE IX.

Many high-profile, longtime champions of Title IX do not get the credit they deserve from this book, alas. Title IX lives through each of those not represented here, too. The major characters in this telling—Bernice Sandler, Pamela Price, and Diane Milutinovich—intersected with Title IX and struggles against discrimination for decades. I could have followed other decades-long Title IX advocates mentioned herein or those omitted due to limited space, and I hope other writers will.

Wonderful staff at research libraries and archives opened the past to me, especially at: the Schlesinger Library on the History of Women in America, Cambridge, Massachusetts; the Library of Congress, Washington, DC; the Oregon Historical Society, Portland; Indiana University Libraries, Bloomington; Yale University's Sterling Memorial Library, New Haven, Connecticut; California State University, Fresno's Henry Madden Library; and Smith College's Sophia Smith Collection, Northampton, Massachusetts.

The generosity of at least seventy-two people who granted more than a hundred interviews made this book come alive. Some also shared their personal archives and photos or offered feedback on manuscript drafts, for which I can never thank them enough. Bernice Sandler, Pamela Price, Diane Milutinovich, and Margaret Dunkle especially were generous in telling Title IX's story.

I'm also grateful to the sources listed below, listed alphabetically within groups (though some belong in more than one group), and to others who asked to remain anonymous.

Former Office for Civil Rights directors: Cynthia Brown, Martin Gerry, and Catherine Lhamon.

Washington government sources from Title IX's early days: Deborah Ashford, Jason Berman, Alexandra Buek, Barbara Dixon, Arvonne Fraser, Ellen Hoffman, and Vincent Macaluso.

People currently or formerly with the National Women's Law Center: Neena Chaudhry, Marcia Greenberger, and Margaret (Margy) Kohn. *Former PSEW staff:* Julie Ehrhart, Jean Hughes, Francelia Gleaves McKindra, and Kay Meckes. *Other "foremothers" familiar with the NCWGE:* Holly Knox, Mary Ann Millsap, Julia (Judy) Norrell, and Margot Polivy.

Relatives of some key characters in this book: Rora Brodwin, Richard Green, JJ Hersh, Gwendolyn Mink, and Deborah Sandler.

People connected to Yale or Pamela Price: Phyllis L. Crocker, Ann Olivarius, Chase Olivarius, Kathryn Olivarius, P. Bobby Shukla, and Anne E. Simon. *Activists and academics in the campus movement against sexual assault:* Dana Bolger, Alexandra Brodsky, Sage Carson, Annie E. Clark, Jess Davidson, Jennifer Freyd, Mahroh Jahangiri, Carly Mee, Wendy Murphy, Andrea Pino-Silva, Betsy Salkind, Carly Smith, and Wagatwe Wanjuki.

Sources with insights about Fresno State University: Jessica Adams, Deborah Adishian-Astone, Stephanie Canales, Rayma Church, Kathryn Forbes, Karen Humphrey, Britt King, Meg Newman, Leilani Overstreet, Donna Pickel, Lindy Vivas, and Margie Wright. *Other athletics activists:* Herb Dempsey and Rollin Haffer. *And in various categories:* Kirby Dick, Noreen Farrell, Tyler Kingkade, Marty Langelan, Lenora Lapidus, Judith L. Lichtman, Terry Saario, Daniel Swinton, and others who wished to remain anonymous.

Organizations that facilitated interviews with some sources or provided other information include the American Civil Liberties Union, the Center for Institutional Courage, Equal Rights Advocates, End Rape on Campus, Know Your IX, the National Center for Lesbian Rights, National Women's Law Center, and SurvJustice.

Liza Heller Eto, attorney and friend extraordinaire, saved me from legal blunders; any remaining in this book belong to me alone. I'm grateful to readers-of-drafts Naakai Addy, Richard Morse, and Eliana Salazar, and to S. Daniel Carter for taking and sharing his photographs. Thanks go to Elliot and Phyllis Prager of Santa Barbara, California, and Cambridge, Massachusetts, and to Pam Jacklin of Portland, Oregon, for their hospitality in providing housing during research trips.

Writing residencies at the Djerassi Resident Artists Program, Mesa Refuge, and Hypatia-in-the-Woods gave me precious time and space to think and write uninterrupted.

I'm grateful to Gail Ross and Dara Kaye at the Ross Yoon Agency for believing in this book and to Julie R. Enszer at The New Press for her skillful editing.

Even though I was among the first women students to coeducate a formerly all-men college in the 1970s, I knew nothing about Title IX—never heard of it—until the mid-1980s. My wife and greatest teacher, Meg Newman, introduced me and made this book possible in incalculable ways.

To all the youth and allies demanding a fair and livable world, I send my biggest thanks.

Text of Title IX of the Education Amendments of 1972

Congress passed the original text on June 23, 1972: Title IX of Public Law 92-318—Prohibition of Sex Discrimination. Congress amended it in 1974 to add paragraph (6) to the first section and again in 1976 to add paragraphs (7) through (9) to that section. The 1988 Civil Rights Restoration Act added two more sections at the end, listed here as 1687 and 1688. For a complete version minus the original part below on "Amendments to Other Laws," see 20 U.S. Code Sections 1681–1688 on the U.S. Department of Justice site at https://www.justice.gov/crt /title-ix-education-amendments-1972.

20 U.S.C. Sections 1681–1688, Title 20 – Education
Chapter 38 – Discrimination Based on Sex or Blindness
  Sec. 1681. Sex.

(a) **Prohibition against discrimination; exceptions**

No person in the United States shall, on the basis of sex, be excluded from participation in, be denied the benefits of, or be subjected to discrimination under any education program or activity receiving Federal financial assistance, except that:

(1) **Classes of educational institutions subject to prohibition**

in regard to admissions to educational institutions, this section shall apply only to institutions of vocational education, professional education, and graduate higher education, and to public institutions of undergraduate higher education;

(2) Educational institutions commencing planned change in admissions

in regard to admissions to educational institutions, this section shall not apply

(A) for one year from the date of enactment, June 23, 1972, nor for six years after such date in the case of an educational institution which has begun the process of changing from being an institution which admits only students of one sex to being an institution which admits students of both sexes, but only if it is carrying out a plan for such a change which is approved by the Secretary of Education or

(B) for seven years from the date an educational institution begins the process of changing from being an institution which admits only students of only one sex to being an institution which admits students of both sexes, but only if it is carrying out a plan for such a change which is approved by the Secretary of Education, whichever is the later;

(3) Educational institutions of religious organizations with contrary religious tenets

this section shall not apply to an educational institution which is controlled by a religious organization if the application of this subsection would not be consistent with the religious tenets of such organization;

(4) Educational institutions training individuals for military services or merchant marine

this section shall not apply to an educational institution whose primary purpose is the training of individuals for the military services of the United States, or the merchant marine;

(5) Public educational institutions with traditional and continuing admissions policy in regard to admissions

this section shall not apply to any public institution of under-graduate higher education which is an institution that tradi-tionally and continually from its establishment has had a policy of admitting only students of one sex;

(6) Social fraternities or sororities; voluntary youth service organizations

this section shall not apply to membership practices—

(A) of a social fraternity or social sorority which is exempt from taxation under section 501(a) of title 26, the active member-ship of which consists primarily of students in attendance at an institution of higher education; or

(B) of the Young Men's Christian Association, Young Women's Christian Association, Girl Scouts, Boy Scouts, Camp Fire Girls, and voluntary youth service organizations which are so exempt, the membership of which has traditionally been limited to persons of one sex and principally to persons of less than nineteen years of age;

(7) Boy or Girl conferences

this section shall not apply to—

(A) any program or activity of the American Legion undertaken in connection with the organization or operation of any Boys State conference, Boys Nation conference, Girls State conference, or Girls Nation conference, or

(B) any program or activity of any secondary school or educa-tional institution specifically for—

   (i) the promotion of any Boys State conference, Boys Na-tion conference, Girls State conference, or Girls Nation conference; or

   (ii) the selection of students to attend any such conference;

(8) Father–son or mother–daughter activities at educational institutions

this section shall not preclude father–son or mother–daughter activities at an educational institution, but if such activities are provided for students of one sex, opportunities for reasonably comparable activities shall be provided for students of the other sex; and

(9) Institution of higher education scholarship awards in "beauty" pageants

this section shall not apply with respect to any scholarship or other financial assistance awarded by an institution of higher education to any individual because such individual has received such award in any pageant in which the attainment of such award is based upon a combination of factors related to the personal appearance, poise, and talent of such individual and in which participation is limited to individuals of one sex only, so long as such pageant is in compliance with other nondiscrimination provisions of Federal law.

(b) Preferential or disparate treatment because of imbalance in participation or receipt of Federal benefits; statistical evidence of imbalance

Nothing contained in subsection (a) of this section shall be interpreted to require any educational institution to grant preferential or disparate treatment to the members of one sex on account of an imbalance which may exist with respect to the total number or percentage of persons of that sex participating in or receiving the benefits of any federally supported program or activity, in comparison with the total number or percentage of persons of that sex in any community, State, section, or other area: *Provided,* That this subsection shall not be construed to prevent the consideration in any hearing or proceeding under this title of statistical evidence tending to show that such an imbalance exists with respect to the participation in, or receipt of the benefits of, any such program or activity by the members of one sex.

(c) "Educational institution" defined

For the purposes of this chapter an educational institution means any public or private preschool, elementary, or secondary school, or any institution of vocational, professional or higher education, except that in the case of an educational institution composed of more than one school, college, or department which are administratively separate units, such term means each such school, college, or department.

Sec. 1682. Federal administrative enforcement; report to Congressional committees

Each Federal department and agency which is empowered to extend Federal financial assistance to any education program or activity, by way of grant, loan, or contract other than a contract of insurance or guaranty, is authorized and directed to effectuate the provisions of section 1681 with respect to such program or activity by issuing rules, regulations, or orders of general applicability which shall be consistent with achievement of the objectives of the statute authorizing the financial assistance in connection with which the action is taken. No such rule, regulation, or order shall become effective unless and until approved by the President. Compliance with any requirement adopted pursuant to this section may be effected (1) by the termination of or refusal to grant or to continue assistance under such program or activity to any recipient as to whom there has been an express finding on the record, after opportunity for hearing, of a failure to comply with such requirement, but such termination or refusal shall be limited to the particular political entity, or part thereof, or other recipient as to whom such a finding has been made, and shall be limited in its effect to the particular program, or part thereof, in which such noncompliance has been found, or (2) by any other means authorized by law: *Provided, however,* That no such action shall be taken until the department or agency concerned has advised the appropriate person or persons of the failure to comply with the requirement and has determined that compliance cannot be secured by voluntary means. In the case of any action terminating, or refusing to grant or continue, assistance because of failure to comply with a requirement imposed pursuant to this section, the head of the Federal department or agency shall file with the committees of the House and Senate having legislative jurisdiction over the program or activity involved a full written report of the circumstances and the grounds for such action. No such action shall become effective until thirty days have elapsed after the filing of such report.

Sec. 1683. Judicial review

Any department or agency action taken pursuant to section 1682 of this title shall be subject to such judicial review as may otherwise be provided by law for similar action taken by such department or agency on other grounds. In the case of action, not otherwise subject to judicial review, terminating or refusing to grant or to continue financial assistance upon a finding of failure to comply with any requirement imposed pursuant to section 1682 of this title, any person aggrieved (including any State or political subdivision thereof and any agency of either) may obtain judicial review of such action in accordance with chapter 7 of title 5, United States Code, and such action shall not be deemed committed to unreviewable agency discretion within the meaning of section 701 of that title.

Sec. 1684. Blindness or visual impairment; prohibition against discrimination

No person in the United States shall, on the ground of blindness or severely impaired vision, be denied admission in any course of study by a recipient of Federal financial assistance for any education program or activity, but nothing herein shall be construed to require any such institution to provide any special services to such person because of his blindness or visual impairment.

Sec. 1685. Authority under other laws unaffected

Nothing in this chapter shall add to or detract from any existing authority with respect to any program or activity under which Federal financial assistance is extended by way of a contract of insurance or guaranty.

(Author's note: The next part appeared in the original bill as Section 906 but does not appear in online text for Title IX in the U.S. Code.)

Amendments to Other Laws.

Sec. 906.

(a) Sections 401(b), 407(a)(2), 410, and 902 of the Civil Rights Act of 1964 (42 U.S.C. 2000c(b), 2000c-6(a)(2), 2000c-9, and 2000h-2) are each amended by inserting the word "sex" after the word "religion".

(b) (1) Section 13(a) of the Fair Labor Standards Act of 1938 (29 U.S.C. 213(a)) is amended by inserting after the words "the provisions of section 6" the following: "(except section 6(d) in the case of paragraph (1) of this subsection)".

(2) Paragraph (1) of subsection 3(r) of such Act (29 U.S.C. 203(r)(1)) is amended by deleting "an elementary or secondary school" and inserting in lieu thereof "a preschool, elementary or secondary school".

(3) Section 3(s)(4) of such Act (29 U.S.C. 203(s)(4)) is amended by deleting "an elementary or secondary school" and inserting in lieu thereof "a preschool, elementary or secondary school".

Sec. 1686. Interpretation with respect to living facilities

Notwithstanding anything to the contrary contained in this chapter, nothing contained herein shall be construed to prohibit any educational institution receiving funds under this Act, from maintaining separate living facilities for the different sexes.

Sec. 1687. Interpretation of "program or activity"

For the purposes of this subchapter, the term "program or activity" and the term "program" mean all of the operations of—

(1)(A) a department, agency, special purpose district, or other instrumentality of a State or of a local government; or

(B) the entity of such State or local government that distributes such assistance and each such department or agency (and each other State or local government entity) to which the assistance is extended, in the case of assistance to a State or local government;

(2)(A) a college, university, or other postsecondary institution, or a public system of higher education; or

(B) a local educational agency (as defined in section 198(a)(10) of the Elementary and Secondary Education Act of 1965), system of vocational education, or other school system;

(3)(A) an entire corporation, partnership, or other private organization, or an entire sole proprietorship—

(i) if assistance is extended to such corporation, partnership, private organization, or sole proprietorship as a whole; or

(ii) which is principally engaged in the business of providing education, health care, housing, social services, or parks and recreation; or

(B) the entire plant or other comparable, geographically separate facility to which Federal financial assistance is extended, in the case of any other corporation, partnership, private organization, or sole proprietorship; or

(4) any other entity which is established by two or more of the entities described in paragraph (1), (2), or (3);

any part of which is extended Federal financial assistance, except that such term does not include any operation of an entity which is controlled by a religious organization if the application of section 1681 of this title to such operation would not be consistent with the religious tenets of such organization.

Sec. 1688. Neutrality with respect to abortion

Nothing in this chapter shall be construed to require or prohibit any person, or public or private entity, to provide or pay for any benefit or service, including the use of facilities, related to an abortion. Nothing in this section shall be construed to permit a penalty to be imposed on any person or individual because such person or individual is seeking or has received any benefit or service related to a legal abortion.

List of Characters and Acronyms

Main recurring characters (in order of appearance)

Bernice Resnick Sandler, the godmother of Title IX
Pamela Y. Price, plaintiff in *Alexander v. Yale* and a civil rights attorney
Diane Milutinovich, athletics administrator, California State University, Fresno

Other key characters (alphabetically)

Sen. Birch Bayh
Marvella Bayh, Birch's first wife
Dana Bolger, KYIX co-founder
Alexandra Brodsky, KYIX co-founder
Rep. Shirley Chisholm
Annie E. Clark, EROC co-founder
Margaret Dunkle, PSEW and NCWGE
Francelia Gleaves (later McKindra), PSEW
Rep. Edith Green
Marcia Greenberger, NWLC co-founder
Holly Knox, PEER founder
Rep. Patsy Takemoto Mink
Ann Olivarius, plaintiff in *Alexander v. Yale*
Andrea Pino-Silva, EROC co-founder

Margot Polivy, AIAW counsel

Lindy Vivas, volleyball coach, California State University, Fresno

Wagatwe Wanjuki, anti-rape activist, writer, and educator

Margie Wright, softball coach, California State University, Fresno

Acronyms

AAC—Association of American Colleges ("and Universities" added later)

AIAW—Association for Intercollegiate Athletics for Women

EADA—Equity in Athletics Disclosure Act

EEOC—Equal Employment Opportunity Commission

ERA—Equal Rights Amendment

EROC—End Rape on Campus

HEW—U.S. Department of Health, Education, and Welfare (until the Department of Education split off in 1980)

KYIX—Know Your IX

LCCR—Leadership Conference on Civil Rights (later: "Civil and Human Rights")

LGBTQ—Lesbian, gay, bisexual, transgender, queer

NCAA—National Collegiate Athletic Association

NCWGE—National Coalition for Women and Girls in Education

NOW—National Organization for Women

NWLC—National Women's Law Center

OCR—Office for Civil Rights, in HEW until 1980 and then the U.S. Department of Education

OFCC—Office of Federal Contract Compliance ("Programs" added in 1975), U.S. Department of Labor

PE—Physical education

PEER—Project on Equal Education Rights of the NOW Legal Defense Fund

PSEW—Project on the Status and Education of Women, Association of American Colleges

UNC—University of North Carolina, Chapel Hill

WEAL—Women's Equity Action League

Notes

Citations from research archives list the name of the archive, box number, folder number or folder name, and the source item. After the first reference for Bernice Sandler's papers, for example, "Sandler papers, 51.10" indicates box 51, folder 10 in Sandler's papers at that archive. Other items cited below were retrieved online unless otherwise specified.

1. Strong—1969

1. U.S. Census data, 1952. Few Black women, on the other hand, had the option of *not* working even if married; they knew they'd have to work to survive. They and other women of color had even less access to education and were more likely than white women, or men of any race, to do low-paying work such as household help.

2. A Women's Equity Action League complaint to the U.S. Department of Health, Education, and Welfare (HEW) dated November 29, 1971, noted that only 4 percent of full professors and 9 percent of associate professors at Indiana University were women. Women's Equity Action League (WEAL) Records, 1967–1990, MC 500, Schlesinger Library on the History of Women in America, Radcliffe Institute, Harvard University (hereafter cited as WEAL MC 500).

3. Friedan interview in *She's Beautiful When She's Angry*, directed by Mary Dore and Nancy Kennedy (Music Box Films, 2014).

4. Papers of Bernice Resnick Sandler, 1963–2008, MC 558 Schlesinger Library, box 34, folder 3 (hereafter cited as Sandler papers).

5. Katherine Turk, *Equality on Trial: Gender and Rights in the Modern American Workplace* (Philadelphia: University of Pennsylvania Press, 2016), 14.

6. National Organization for Women, "NOW Bill of Rights," 1968 (adopted at its 1967 national conference), https://350fem.blogs.brynmawr.edu/about/1968-bill-of -rights/.

7. Ruth Rosen, *The World Split Open: How the Modern Women's Movement Changed America* (New York: Penguin Books, 2000); Molly Vorwerck, "Groundbreaking 1968 Pageant Proved Black Is Beautiful," *USA Today,* February 15, 2018.

8. Author interviews with Bernice Sandler on July 25, September 17, and November 4 and 5, 2014; January 20, April 10, July 13, October 21, and December 6, 2015, and April 6, November 28, and December 6, 2016. Other interviewers sometimes give a different version of this epiphany taking place in a classroom, as in Katherine Hanson, Vivian Guilfoy, and Sarita Pillai, *More Than Title IX: How Equity in Education Has Shaped the Nation* (Lanham, MD: Rowman & Littlefield, 2009), 13.

9. Bernice Resnick Sandler, "Title IX: How We Got It and What a Difference It Made," *Cleveland State Law Review* 55, no. 4 (2007): 473.

10. Excerpt from transcript of oral history interview with Glaser, Penn State University Libraries, https://libraries.psu.edu/about/collections/few-good-women/vera-glaser.

11. Bernice said Jerry earlier also played a key role in lobbying Congress about public broadcasting, specifically to get radio included along with public television, so he had a better sense of politics than she. Bernice also learned on-the-job politics from him, such as how to ask for a raise. Women's Equity Action League (WEAL) Records, 1967–1990, MC 311, box 152 (hereafter cited as WEAL MC 311).

12. Title VI (U.S.C., vol. 42, sec. 2000d) states that "no person in the United States shall, on the ground of race, color, or national origin, be excluded from, be denied the benefits of, or be subjected to discrimination under any program or activity receiving Federal financial assistance."

13. U.S.C., vol. 42, sec. 2000e. "Titles" are sections of a statute and run consecutively within that legislation, unrelated to title numbers in other legislation. Title IX refers to Title IX of the Education Amendments of 1972; it is not part of the Civil Rights Act of 1964, as are the Titles VI and VII described here.

14. For a brief history of executive orders related to 8802, see https://www.dol.gov/agencies/ofccp/about/executive-order-11246-history, though it's interesting that at this writing, in the year 2021, the page does not mention Executive Order 11375.

15. Verbal communication from Esther Peterson to Bernice Sandler.

16. EO 11375 of October 13, 1967, 32 FR 14303, 3 CFR, 1966–1970 Comp., p. 684.

2. Complaints—1970

1. He'd been working on executive order guidelines (though not specifically for education) before Sandler found him. Rep. Martha Griffiths wrote to the acting director of the OFCC on February 5, 1969, sending comments on "the proposed Guidelines on Sex Discrimination, published as 41 C.J.R. Part 60.20, in the Federal Register of Jan. 17, 1969 (34 J.R. 758)." Patsy T. Mink Papers, 1883–2005, MSS 84957, Library of Congress, box 393.2 (hereafter cited as Mink papers LOC to differentiate the collection from Mink papers at Smith College). The OFCC, created in 1965, became the Office of Federal Contract Compliance Programs (OFCCP) in 1975.

2. Correspondence from Sandler to Nancy Dowding of WEAL, Sandler papers, 148.

3. "'Second-Wave' Feminism on Campus," University of Chicago Library, https://www.lib.uchicago.edu/collex/exhibits/exoet/second-wave-feminism/.

4. Amelia Thomson-DeVeaux, "When Women Came to Princeton," *Princeton Alumni Weekly*, October 5, 2016.

5. *WEAL National Newsletter* 1, no. 2 (June 1975); Mink papers LOC, 184.11.

6. But APGA delayed follow-through, so Sandler filed complaints with the EEOC in April 1970 against the APGA and the American Psychological Association for violating Title VII in job placement services, and with the Department of Labor for violating the executive orders. Sandler papers, 44.7 and 49.7.

7. Sandler papers, 51.1.

8. Correspondence from Sandler to Dr. Dolan, cc'd to WEAL's Boyer, October 2, 1969, WEAL MC 311, 147.

9. Bernice Sandler, "Sex Discrimination at the University of Maryland," Sandler papers, 51.1.

10. Correspondence from Sandler to Boyer, November 10, 1969, WEAL MC 311, 53.

11. Correspondence from Sandler to WEAL's Nancy Dowding, December 10, 1969, WEAL MC 311, 148, folder "FCCE—Nov–Dec '69."

12. Correspondence from Sandler to Dowding, January 2, 1970, WEAL MC 311, 149.

13. Correspondence from Sandler cc'd to Boyer, October 2, 1969, WEAL MC 311, 147.

14. Correspondence from Betty Boyer to Jo Freeman, January 15, 1969, asking Freeman (who did the study "Women on the Social Science Faculty Since 1892") to send Sandler data on Chicago; WEAL MC 311, 149.

15. Nicholas von Hoffman, "Women Scholars: Stymied by System," *Washington Post*, February 24, 1969, Sandler papers, 51.1.

16. Judith Anderson, "Academic Equality," *San Francisco Chronicle*, September 28, 1971, 21, in Edith Green Papers, 1955–1975, Mss 1424, Oregon Historical Society, box 196, folder "Education: Sex Discrimination" (hereafter cited as Green papers).

17. Linda Greenhouse, "Columbia Accused of Bias on Women," *New York Times*, January 11, 1970, Sandler papers, 51.1.

18. For example, see the January 6, 1970, reply from Lawrence A. Simpson, director of placement at the University of Virginia, Charlottesville, to Sandler's request for his 1968 dissertation at Penn State University. Sandler papers, 51.2.

19. In the University of Maryland's School of Education (widely considered to be a "nurturing" field more accepting of women), a woman headed only one department: Special Education. Overall, only 8 percent of the university's 120 full professors were women, and 12 percent of all 436 faculty members were women. Sandler papers, 51.1.

20. Correspondence from Sandler to Dowding, December 22, 1969, Sandler papers, 148, folder "FCCE—Nov–Dec '69"; and February 12–28, 1970, Sandler papers, 150, folder "FCCE Feb. 12–28, 1970."

21. Sandler papers, 10 and 149.

22. From the WEAL complaint: women's share of college faculties decreased from

more than a third in 1879 to 28 percent in 1940 and 22 percent in 1960 (but only 10 percent [of faculty] at prestigious private universities). Cited in Edwin C. Lewis, *Developing Women's Potential* (Ames: Iowa State University Press, 1968).

23. "Report of the Virginia Commission for the Study of Educational Facilities in the State of Virginia, 1964," cited in the February 6–8, 1964, debate in the U.S. House of Representatives on Title VII of the Civil Rights Act, and subsequently cited in WEAL's complaint.

24. Correspondence from Sandler to Dowding, February 6, 1970, WEAL MC 311, 149, folder "FCCE Jan.–Feb. 11, 1970."

25. Correspondence from Sandler to Vincent Macaluso, February 6, 1970, WEAL MC 311, 149.

26. Correspondence from Sandler to Dowding, February 6, 1970, refers to the *Washington Post*'s story that day, "Women Charge Sex Bias," WEAL MC 311, 149, folder "FCCE Jan.–Feb. 11, 1970."

27. Sandler papers, 51.1.

28. The reference sections of some major libraries have copies of the 1971 two-volume publication compiled by Sandler for Rep. Edith Green, *Discrimination Against Women: Hearings Before the Special Subcommittee on Education of the Committee on Education and Labor, House of Representatives, Ninety-First Congress, Second Session, on Section 805 of H.R. 16098* (Washington, DC: Congressional Printing Office, 1970). R.R. Bowker Company published an abridged version in 1973, *Discrimination Against Women: Congressional Hearings on Equal Rights in Education and Employment*, copies of which may be more accessible. These endnotes cite the former as *Hearings* Part I or II, with the relevant page number followed by the Bowker page number in parentheses if available. So, for this citation, "Statement of Bernice Sandler, Chairman, Action Committee for Federal Contract Compliance in Education, WEAL," *Hearings* Part I, 307 (Bowker 422).

29. From *She's Beautiful When She's Angry*.

30. Jessica Bennett and Jesse Ellison, "Young Women, Newsweek, and Sexism," *Newsweek*, March 18, 2010.

31. Georgiana Vines, "The Day Women Broke the Rules and Wore Pants in the News Sentinel Newsroom," *News Sentinel*, August 26, 2019.

32. Mary Ann Millsap, "Advocates for Sex Equity in Federal Education Law: The National Coalition for Women and Girls in Education" (dissertation, Harvard University, 1988), courtesy of Millsap.

33. Correspondence from Sandler to Joan Joesting, Sandler papers, 51.2.

34. Arvonne Fraser, *She's No Lady: Politics, Family, and International Feminism* (Minneapolis: Nodin Press, 2007).

35. Thomas D. Snyder, ed., *120 Years of American Education: A Statistical Portrait*, U.S. Department of Education, National Center for Education Statistics, Office of Educational Research and Improvement, January 1993.

36. Sandler papers, 47.15.

37. Sandler papers, 49.15.

38. Sandler, "Title IX: How We Got It."

39. Sandler papers, 7.

40. Sandler had read Millett's *Sexual Politics* and passed it on to Rep. Green, who "thinks it is brilliant," Sandler wrote in correspondence to Kate Millett, August 23, 1970, WEAL MC 311, 156, folder "FCCE Aug '70."

41. Correspondence from Sandler to Ann Scott, April 14, 1970, WEAL MC 311, 152, folder "FCCE Apr '70."

42. See various correspondence by Sandler and Scott, WEAL MC 311, 151.

43. Sandler papers, 55.6.

44. Sandler papers, 49.14.

45. Sandler papers, 51.7, 51.9, and 55.6. Letter from Arthur A. Fletcher, assistant secretary of labor, to Bernice Sandler, June 2, 1970, Sandler papers, 51.9.

46. "Michigan U. to Lose Aid Contracts for Bias," *Washington Post*, November 6, 1970, and other news articles about Michigan's case in Mink papers LOC, 195.1 and 195.2. For a detailed account of the University of Michigan activism, see Sara Fitzgerald, *Conquering Heroines: How Women Fought Sex Bias at Michigan and Paved the Way for Title IX* (Ann Arbor: University of Michigan Press, 2020).

47. Sandler papers, 47.15.

48. *Higher Education and National Affairs* 19, no. 13 (April 10, 1970), Mink papers LOC, 195.1. U.S. Census Bureau data at https://www.census.gov/content/dam /Census/library/working-papers/2002/demo/POP-twps0056.pdf.

49. "Facts About Women's Absenteeism and Labor Turnover," U.S. Department of Labor, August 1969.

50. "Fact Sheet on the Earning Gap," *Higher Education and National Affairs* 19, no. 13 (April 10, 1970), Mink papers LOC, 195.1.

51. Correspondence from Ann Scott to Sandler, March 30, 1970, WEAL MC 311, 151.

52. Correspondence from Sandler to George Shultz, May 27, 1980, Sandler papers, 51.11.

53. Ann Scott, "A Plan for Affirmative Action to End Discrimination Against Women," Mink papers LOC, 195.1.

54. See *Women's Liberation* (Marlene Sanders, ABC News, ABC Media Concepts, 1970), listed at worldcat.org.

3. Congress—1970–1972

1. See author's note on citations for the *Hearings* at endnote 28 in the previous chapter. Rep. Edith Green held hearings on her sex-discrimination provision on June 17, 19, 26, 29, and 30 and July 1 and 31, 1970. See a description in Karen Blumenthal, *Let Me Play: The Story of Title IX* (New York: Atheneum Books for Young Readers, 2005), 30.

2. Later in her career, Mink described how she and Green—both members of the House Education and Labor Committee—often commiserated in the late 1960s and early 1970s about the need for legislation to address sex discrimination in education. Mink was much more of a natural feminist than Green, but Green had more legislative success: she authored the Equal Pay Act and led a multi-year campaign culminating in its passage in 1963. Sources say Green had long wanted to sponsor a bill like Title

IX but wasn't convinced there were enough data or a large enough constituency to fight for it until Sandler filed her complaints. Undoubtedly, Green conferred with the few other women in Congress about it, including Mink (who was leading the push to pass a bill for national day care at the time), Rep. Martha Griffiths (who was leading efforts to pass the ERA in the House), and others. Green eventually got the bill through her hostile subcommittee (all men except her) in 1971 and approved by the full Committee on Education and Labor; thus, all thirty-seven of the committee members were listed as co-sponsors, including Mink. Many people misconstrue this to mean that Mink wrote Title IX; she is widely credited on the internet as Title IX's author. Neither Green's nor Mink's papers nor interviews with their contemporaries support this claim.

3. "Statement of Bernice Sandler," *Hearings*, 297–328 (Bowker 60–67).

4. Sandler submitted a written statement to be appended to her testimony, updating the story of her first "win." The APGA's Placement Bulletin in March 1970 still listed ads by sex as a job qualification: "Assistant or Associate Professor, male preferred (Northeastern Illinois State College, Chicago)"; "Counselor . . . man (Mercer County Community College, Trenton, NJ)." This, despite the multiple correspondence between Sandler (on behalf of WEAL) and APGA executive director Willis Dugan in which he promised that the offending policy would be eliminated. In Sandler's rough tabulation of some 343 college and university departments of counselor education, the data suggested that 85 percent of departments had one or no women on their faculty even though women accounted for 21 percent of doctorates in the counseling and guidance field (Sandler papers, 10). She based her estimate on data from the *Directory of Counselor Educators, 1967–68* (OE-25036-N).

5. Jack Anderson, "On Washington Merry-Go-Round," *El Paso Times*, September 7, 1969, and other articles, Green papers, 375, folder "Edith Green Scrapbook—1969 Personal."

6. Interview with Green's son Richard Green.

7. Roy Wilkins, director of the NAACP, told Portland, Oregon, citizens in May 1972 that Green was "no friend of yours. . . . The only way to get your kids a good education is by bus," he said. And: "We never heard a word about busing while they were busing to segregate; now it's a terrible thing to bus to integrate." Green papers, 375, folders "Scrapbook 1972 Education" and "Edith Green Scrapbook—1969 Personal."

8. Correspondence from Sandler to Ann Scott, October 31, 1970, WEAL MC 311, 54, folder "Corr. 1970."

9. Indritz became such a valuable and beloved fixture on Capitol Hill that even after he retired in the early 1970s, Congress kept a special desk and phone for him in House office buildings until 1994. Bart Barnes, "Phineas Indritz Dies at 81," *Washington Post*, October 18, 1997.

10. Correspondence from Green to Sandler, February 6, 1970, Green papers, 191, folder "Control Files, 1970."

11. Sandler started work at HEW on February 9, 1970. Sandler papers, 8.6, and WEAL MC 311, 149. Martha Griffiths speaking on sex discrimination, 91st Cong., 2nd sess., *Congressional Record* 116, pt. 5 (March 9, 1970): 6398-6400.

12. Correspondence from Sandler to Betty Boyer, March 8, 1970, WEAL MC 311, 150, folder "FCCE Feb. 12–28, 1970."

13. Simchak's fix for the Equal Pay Act in Section 906(b) of Title IX on June 23, 1972, read: (b)(1) Section 13(a) of the Fair Labor Standards Act of 1938 (29 U.S.C. 213(a)) is amended by inserting after the words "the provisions of section 6" the following: "(except section 6(d) in the case of paragraph (1) of this subsection)."

14. "Morag Simchak, 64, Ex-Adviser on Women's Activities for AID," obituary in *Washington Post*, September 17, 1978; "Daughters of the Stars: Lives of Local Women," Shenandoah County Library. Also, interviews with Bernice Sandler.

15. *A Matter of Simple Justice*, Presidential Task Force on Women's Rights and Responsibilities, December 15, 1969. Also in *Hearings* Part I, 37–75.

16. Sandler papers, 49.14.

17. Women made up only 18 percent of the freshman class of 1969 and 30 percent of all undergraduates at the University of North Carolina, Chapel Hill, according to a report from its Office of Undergraduate Admissions. The report stated that the university could not accept all qualified applicants and "admission of women on the freshman level will be restricted to those who are especially well qualified." In other words, average or below-average men could be admitted, but only exceptional women. As a result, the 1970 freshman class admitted nearly 1,900 men and only 426 women. Sandler papers, 51.1. At the City University of New York's Borough of Manhattan Community College, women made up 41 percent of the 227 faculty, mostly clustered in the lower-ranking positions. Only 7 of 25 professors (28 percent) were women. Sandler papers, 52.14.

18. Correspondence from Sandler to Jane Pollock, April 6, 1970, WEAL MC 311, 152.

19. First submitted in 1923 and many times thereafter, the ERA seemed like it might finally have a chance of passing as the second-wave women's movement surged. In case it didn't, women's advocates also pursued bills targeting specific sectors of sex discrimination such as education, banking, and more. See Patsy Mink's remarks to the House Judiciary Subcommittee Number Four in support of H.R. 916, Patsy T. Mink Papers, 1965–1982, Sophia Smith Collection, Smith College, Northampton, MA, box 4, folder 10.

20. Harry Hogan, who took the call from the ACE lobbyist, told Sandler this story.

21. "Statement of Dr. Pauli Murray, Professor of American Studies, Brandeis University," *Hearings* Part I, 328–82 (Bowker 67–86).

22. Murray co-founded NOW in 1966 but soon left its board because she felt it didn't adequately address the needs of minority women. Her testimony at Green's hearings emphasized the need to address multiple kinds of discrimination. "In neglecting to appreciate fully the indivisibility of human rights . . . we have often reacted with the squeaky-wheel-gets-the-grease approach and not given sufficient attention to the legitimate claims of other disadvantaged groups—poor whites, women, American Indians, Americans of Puerto Rican, Mexican, and Oriental origin, and the like. In so doing we have often set in motion conditions which have created a backlash." "Statement of Pauli Murray," in *Hearings* Part I.

23. See Rosalind Rosenberg, *Jane Crow: The Life of Pauli Murray* (New York: Oxford University Press, 2017).

24. "Statement of Hon. Shirley Chisholm, a Representative in Congress from the State of New York," *Hearings* Part II, 617–22 (Bowker, 189–94). Note: Rep. Patsy

Mink did not testify at the hearings but submitted a written statement supporting Green's legislation. *Hearings* Part I, 433–34.

25. The descriptions of Chisholm draw from: Barbara Winslow, *Shirley Chisholm: Catalyst for Change* (Boulder, CO: Westview Press, 2014); "Dear Representative Shirley Chisholm: An Avoice Issue Forum Honoring Her Historic Leadership," African American Voices in Congress, September 25, 2009.

26. "Statement of Hon. Frankie M. Freeman, Commissioner, U.S. Commission on Civil Rights; Accompanied by Howard H. Glickstein, Staff Director; Judith Lichtman, Staff Member, and John H. Powell, Jr., Counsel," *Hearings* Part II, 661–76 (Bowker 222–33). Civil Rights Commission staff director Howard H. Glickstein shared Freeman's priorities. In a memo from Hogan to Green on June 30, 1970, he noted a recent speech in which Glickstein said that within civil rights the problems facing Blacks were primary and the rights of women secondary. Green papers, 191, folder "Control Files—1970." For a list of commissioners in 1970, see *Stranger in One's Land*, U.S. Commission on Civil Rights Clearinghouse Publication No. 19, May 1970.

27. "Statement of Mrs. Elizabeth Duncan Koontz, Director, Women's Bureau; Accompanied by Carol Cox, Solicitor's Office; and Mrs. Pearl Spindler, Women's Bureau," *Hearings* Part II, 691–704 (Bowker 249–61).

28. See testimonies of Peter Muirhead, assistant secretary, HEW (*Hearings* Part II, 642–61; Bowker, 208–22), Frankie M. Freeman (endnote 93), and Jerris Leonard, assistant attorney general, Department of Justice (*Hearings* Part II, 677–91; Bowker 235–49), who each argued that Section 805's amending of Title VI would restrict the ability to have single-sex gyms or recreational and physical education activities. The topic of sports came up twice in Senate debates on the iterations of Title IX. In 1971 Bayh said the bill would not require the desegregation of football. See 92nd Cong., 1st sess., *Congressional Record* 117, pt. 23 (August 6, 1971): 30407. In 1972 he said Title IX's provisions would maintain personal privacy in sports facilities. See 92nd Cong., 2nd sess., *Congressional Record* 118, pt. 5 (February 28, 1972): 5807.

29. "Statement of Dr. Pauli Murray," *Hearings* Part I.

30. Later, Sandler and others vaguely recalled that leaders of racial minority groups opposed amending Title VI out of fear that this would open the door to hostile amendments that could weaken Title VI. Perhaps they were thinking of Freeman's testimony. I found no evidence of other communications about this in the papers of Green, Sandler, Bayh, Mink, and others, but it's the kind of thing that may not have been documented. In another line of thought, National Women's Law Center co-founder Marcia Greenberger remembers that opposition to amending Title VI had an economic element similar to opposition to the ERA: people with entrenched financial interests did not want to rethink business models based on sex discrimination, such as charging women more for insurance. "It became clear that under no circumstances was that going anywhere," so legislators' focus shrank to education. Dunkle notes that a broader bill, such as amending Title VI, would have crossed into the jurisdictions of multiple congressional committees (Ways and Means, Health, Finance), so fears that joint referrals to committees might doom the bill could have played a role in narrowing it. See discussions in "Video History from Women Behind Title IX," Woman's National Democratic Club, Washington, DC, January 26, 2015, posted at sherryboschert.com, February 21, 2015. Also, Green papers, 195, folder "Memos to Mrs. Green," and correspondence from Glickstein to Rep. Carl D. Perkins, May 11, 1971, Green papers, 214, "Women Folder 4 of 4."

31. Murray and Sandler frequently wrote each other throughout the early 1970s. Sandler papers, 7.

32. "Title IX: A Brief History," WEEA Equity Resource Center, August 1997, Mink papers LOC, 2041.5.

33. Sandler papers, 7.

34. Correspondence from Ruth B. Ginsburg to Sandler, June 29, 1970, Sandler papers, 51.10.

35. The first letter from Ginsburg came June 29, 1969; they consulted each other by mail on and off for nearly a decade. WEAL MC 311, 154.

36. Correspondence from Ginsburg to Sandler, September 8, 1970, Sandler papers, 51.10.

37. Green papers, 184, "Education and Labor: Sex Discrimination Folder 1."

38. Catharine R. Stimpson, "Introduction," *Hearings* (only in Bowker, xiv).

39. Correspondence from Sandler to Murray, October 15, 1970, Sandler papers, 7.9.

40. Sandler papers, 7.

41. Sandler papers, 10.

42. "Pocketbook Politics," *Women's Wear Daily*, October 5, 1970, in Green papers, 775, folder "Scrapbook—1970 Equal Rights (Women)."

43. "List of Universities and Colleges Charged with Sex Discrimination," up to around April 1972, WEAL MC 311, 160, folder "FCCE May 71–1973, n.d."

44. Sandler papers, 58.2. Also, Additional Records of the National Organization for Women, 1970–2011, MC 666, Schlesinger Library (hereafter NOW MC 666), 209.25.

45. Bernice R. Sandler, "Too Strong for a Woman—the Five Words that Created Title IX," *Journal of Equity & Excellence in Education* 33, no. 1 (2000): 9–13. Amy Erdman Farrell, *Yours in Sisterhood: Ms. Magazine and the Promise of Popular Feminism* (Chapel Hill: University of North Carolina Press, 1998), quoted in Susan Ware, *Game, Set, Match: Billie Jean King and the Revolution in Women's Sports* (Chapel Hill: University of North Carolina Press, 2011), 48.

46. Green papers, 214, "Folder 4 of 4 Women."

47. Correspondence from Ginsburg to Rep. Edith Green, June 22, 1971, and other dates, Green papers, 214, "Folder 2 of 4 Women."

48. Marvella's story comes from her autobiography, published six months after her death from breast cancer in 1979: *Marvella: A Personal Journey* (New York and London: Harcourt Brace Jovanovich, 1979).

49. Senators Bayh and Dominick speaking on S. 659, 91st Cong., 1st sess., *Congressional Record* 117, pt. 23 (August 6, 1971): 30407.

50. Bayh's amendment lost 50–32. "Sex Bias Ban for Colleges Urged on Hill," *Washington Post*, August 31, 1971, A2, Green papers, 375, folder "Edith Green Scrapbook 1981 Equal Rights (Women)."

51. Marvella became a volunteer spokesperson and then a paid consultant for the American Cancer Society. She also was a roving reporter for an NBC affiliate doing feature interviews leading up to the 1976 U.S. Bicentennial. After Marvella died in April 1979, Birch remarried.

52. That bill, H.R. 18728, died in the Committee on the Judiciary. Its 1971 version, "The Women's Equality Act," was H.R. 916. Like Green's bill but broader, it aimed to amend the Fair Labor Standards Act / Equal Pay Act to remove exemptions for professional women. It also would increase the enforcement powers of the EEOC, Justice Department, and Civil Rights Commission to bar sex discrimination in employment, education, and housing, change Social Security laws so husbands and widowers could get benefits for disabled or deceased wives, and let working women deduct payments for day care or housekeeping as business expenses. These examples are from the 1971 version of the bill. Lynn Langway, "Women's Equality Act Pushed," *New York Times* (exclusive from the *Washington Post*), undated but the context suggests 1971.

53. In 1969 Creighton University and Vanderbilt University accepted no women into their medical schools. "Statement of Frances S. Norris, M.D., Washington, DC," *Hearings* Part I, 510–84 (Bowker 162–77).

54. Richard Nixon, "Statement on Signing the Health Manpower and Nurse Training Bills," November 18, 1971, online at Gerhard Peters and John T. Woolley, *The American Presidency Project*, http://www.presidency.ucsb.edu/ws/?pid-3223.

55. See the Comprehensive Health Manpower Training Act of 1971 and the Nurse Training Amendments Act of 1971 legislative history at *Congressional Record* 117, pt. 23: 222–64, 25: 119–22, 25, and 25: 181–86 (1971).

56. Here Sandler is referring to committee members Rep. John Brademas (D-IN) and Rep. Albert Quie (R-MN). Correspondence from Sandler to Sen. Edmund Muskie, NOW MC 666, 209.82.

57. Green papers, 214, folder "2 of 4 Women."

58. She was later known as Francelia Gleaves McKindra.

59. Author interviews with Francelia Gleaves McKindra, January 26 and 28, 2015.

60. Correspondence from Sandler to Murray, September 12, 1971, Sandler papers, 7.9.

61. Judith Anderson, "Academic Equality," *San Francisco Chronicle*, September 28, 1971, 21, Green papers, 196, folder "Education: Sex Discrimination."

62. Correspondence from Green to Mr. and Mrs. Richard Feeney, September 24, 1971, Green papers, 328, folder "EG/Personal, 2 of 6."

63. See a list of House Education and Labor Committee members in the Ninety-Second Congress at https://www.c-span.org/congress/committee/?2109&congress =92.

64. "Sex Bias Bill Gains in House," *Wall Street Journal*, September 30, 1971, Green papers, 375, folder "Edith Green Scrapbook 1971 Education."

65. "Sex Balance by Edict," *New York Times*, August 15, 1971, sec. 4, 14. "Women's Rights and the Colleges," *Washington Post*, September 16, 1971, A18, cited in Blumenthal, *Let Me Play*, 35.

66. Correspondence from Green to Avery Russell, Carnegie Corporation, December 17, 1971, Green papers, 196, folder "Education: Sex Discrimination."

67. See letters from these and other college presidents entered into the record by Erlenborn: Extensions of Remarks, "Opposition to Title X of the Higher Education Bill," Hon. John N. Erlenborn, 92nd Cong. 1st sess., *Congressional Record* 117: pt. 29 (November 1, 1971): 38639–42.

68. Higher Education Act of 1971, HR 7248, 92nd Cong., 1st sess., *Congressional Record* 117, pt. 30 (November 4, 1971): 39248–365.

69. "Higher Education Conference Report," Democratic Study Group Fact Sheet 92-26, June 2, 1972, Mink papers LOC, 182:12.

70. *Higher Education Act of 1971*, H.R. 7248, 92nd Cong., 1st sess., *Congressional Record* 117, pt. 30 (November 4, 1971): 39353-54.

71. Extensions of Remarks, "Day of Catastrophe," Patsy T. Mink, 92nd Cong., 1st sess., *Congressional Record* 117, pt. 30 (November 5, 1971): 39672-73.

72. U.S. Association of Former Members of Congress, Edith Green Oral History Interview, 103, Manuscript Room, Library of Congress, Washington, DC.

73. Green papers, 196, folder "Education: Sex Discrimination."

74. Correspondence from Green to NOW's Academic Task Force chairwoman Suzanne Gwiazda, December 8, 1971, Green papers, 214, folder "2 of 4 Women."

75. Memo from Paul Vanture to Green, November 10, 1971, 195, folder "Memos: To Mrs. Green."

76. Green papers, 218, folder "Ad Hoc Subcommittee on Discrimination: Folder 1 of 2." Of those, more than one hundred complaints charged 273 colleges and universities, according to "List of Universities and Colleges Charged with Sex Discrimination," up to around April 1972, WEAL MC 311, 160, folder "FCCE May 71–1973, n.d."

77. That grew to fifty-two meetings and conferences in 1973–74. "Meetings 1971–72," Records of the Project on the Status and Education of Women (Association of American Colleges), 1969–1991 (inclusive), 1971–1985 (bulk), MC 577, Schlesinger Library (hereafter PSEW records), 53.3.

78. Interview with former Ford Foundation staffer Terry Saario, June 14, 2016.

79. A daughter of Armenian immigrants, Chamberlain earned a PhD in economics from Harvard University, a rare achievement for a woman in that era. She became director of the Ford Foundation's higher education program in 1967 and a program director from 1971 to 1981. She arranged about $5 million in grants that made an incalculable impact on education by and about women, earning her a reputation as "the fairy godmother of women's studies." "Mariam Chamberlain, Women's Champion, Dies at 94," *New York Times*, April 7, 2013. When the foundation fired her in the early 1980s, Chamberlain alleged age discrimination and negotiated a healthy settlement, according to Terry Saario. See also Susan M. Hartmann, *The Other Feminists: Activists in the Liberal Establishment* (New Haven, CT: Yale University Press, 1998).

80. NOW MC 666, 23.60.

81. Rep. Mink's name also was on the presidential ballot in Oregon, running on an anti-war platform.

82. Amendment 874 to S. 659.

83. Sen. Bayh, speaking on Amendment 874 to S. 659, 92nd Cong., 2nd sess., *Congressional Record* 118, pt. 5 (February 28, 1972): 5802–16.

84. Bernice Sandler, "The Status of Women: Employment and Admissions," 92nd Cong., 2nd sess., *Congressional Record* 118, pt. 5 (February 28, 1972): 5809–12.

85. "On Campus with Women," PSEW newsletter, no. 3 (April 1972), PSEW records.

86. The ERA passed Congress on March 22, 1972, but needed ratification by the states and only would affect actions of the state, not private actions. It would apply to public schools and universities but not private ones, so women still needed a Title IX. On the differences between House and Senate bills, see memo from Green to Sally, March 2, 1972, Green papers, 195, folder "Memos to Mrs. Green," and Green letter to Ricki Ninomiya, March 10, 1972, 324, folder "4 of 4."

87. Green correspondence to NOW leader, March 14, 1972, Green papers, 218, folder "Women—Miscellaneous."

88. "Higher Education Conference Report."

89. Blumenthal, *Let Me Play*, 46–48.

90. The Senate approved the conference bill on May 24, 1972, by a vote of 63 to 15. "Higher Education Conference Report."

91. At some point before passage of Title IX in June 1972, a few representatives of women's groups met with Green and offered to lobby for the bill or do whatever she wanted them to do, Sandler recalled. Green was adamant that they not lobby, fearing it would increase awareness and thus opposition, Sandler said. "I thought Rep. Green was crazy, but we had to follow her," Sandler said in multiple interviews. In her memory, Green's strategy was meant to protect Title IX. But it's unclear exactly when that meeting happened, so it's possible that Green already was aiming to defeat the entire omnibus education bill even if it meant sacrificing Title IX, and thus did not want women's advocates lobbying *for* the bill. Up until then, she had urged nearly everyone who contacted her office (and there were many) to lobby their elected representatives in favor of the anti-discrimination amendment, her papers show. For example, the National Congress of Parents and Teachers declared its support for Section 805 after the first day of Green's hearings in June 1970, reasoning that equal pay for teachers would enhance the quality of teacher preparation. Green papers, 289, folder "H.R. 16098 – Section 805 (Discrimination Against Women)," and Sandler, "Title IX: How We Got It."

92. Green papers, 215, folder "1 of 2: H.R. 7248 Education & Labor Committee."

93. Green letter and Sanford memo, Mink papers LOC, 183.1.

94. Correspondence from La Raza National Lawyers Association president Mario G. Obledo to Mink, June 7, 1972, Mink papers LOC, 183.1.

95. Rep. Martha Griffiths did not vote. See the vote of 218 to 180 to approve the conference report at 92nd Cong., 2nd sess., *Congressional Record* 118, pt. 16 (June 8, 1972): 5446–47.

96. Public Law 92-318. 20 U.S.C. Section 1681 and what follows.

97. Robert B. Semple Jr., "President Signs School Aid Bill; Scores Congress," *New York Times*, June 24, 1972, A1.

98. Following Title IX's omission of an amendment to Title VI, later laws written to prohibit discrimination based on age or disability followed the same format of passing separate legislation rather than amending Title VI.

99. Staff summary comparing House and Senate versions, March 3, 1972, Green papers, 209, folder "1972 Controls A-L." Also, correspondence from Bayh to Arvonne Fraser, February 24, 1972, WEAL MC 311, 160, folder "FCCE May '71–1973, n.d."

100. Correspondence from Green to Sandler, August 12, 1972, Green papers, 215,

folder "Ad Hoc Subcommittee (to investigate discrimination against women)."

101. Interviews with Sandler and Margaret Dunkle.

4. Implementation—1972–1977

1. "Revolution in Women's Sports," special section of *womenSports* magazine, September 1974. For a summary of Title IX in the courts, see Linda Jean Carpenter and R. Vivian Acosta, *Title IX* (Champaign, IL: Human Kinetics, 2005), chapters 6 and 7, 115–64.

2. Adele Simmons et al., *Exploitation from 9 to 5: Report of the Twentieth Century Fund Task Force on Women and Employment* (Lexington, MA: Lexington Books, 1975), 151; *Brenden v. Independent School District* 742, 342 F. Supp. 1224 (D. Minn. 1972); *Reed v. Nebraska School Activities Association*, 341 F. Supp. 258 (D. Neb. 1972); *Haas v. South Bend Community School Corporation, et al.*, No. 10715309 (Indiana Supreme Court, 1972).

3. Newman is the author's wife.

4. Author interview with Meg Newman on April 20, 2018.

5. The proportion of girls among high school athletes grew from 1 in 13 in 1971 to 1 in 5 by 1973 and 1 in 4 by 1974, before the federal government finished writing regulations for applying Title IX to athletics in 1975. By the end of the decade, girls made up one in three high school athletes. Blumenthal, *Let Me Play*, 41 and 52, and Ware, *Game, Set, Match*, 129–30.

6. Despite the rising numbers of female students, a 1970 survey found that women composed only 22 percent of faculties and 9 percent of full professors. A mean of three women headed departments at each school, though 90 percent of schools claimed they applied the same promotion policies to men and women. One in four boards of trustees were 100 percent men. Ruth M. Oltman, "Campus 1970: Where Do Women Stand?," American Association of University Women, Mink papers LOC 183.4.

7. Welch Suggs, *A Place on the Team: The Triumph and Tragedy of Title IX* (Princeton, NJ: Princeton University Press, 2005), 50.

8. Mary Jo Festle, *Playing Nice: Politics and Apologies in Women's Sports* (New York: Columbia University Press, 1996), 122.

9. Author interview with Margot Polivy, January 27, 2015.

10. James S. Murphy, "The Office for Civil Rights's Volatile Power," *The Atlantic*, March 13, 2017.

11. Correspondence from Margaret Dunkle to OCR's Bertrand Taylor, August 9, 1972, thanked him for their conversation the day before about athletics and sent him resources from the *Women's Rights Law Reporter* and more. PSEW records, 9.12.

12. Correspondence from Sandler to Ginsburg, December 20, 1972, saying she'd heard that Ginsburg had written some materials on coed sports versus "separate but equal" athletics and letting her know HEW was wrestling with how Title IX should apply to sports. Ginsburg and Dunkle corresponded on the topic too. PSEW records, 30.13.

13. Ware, *Game, Set, Match*, 50–51, cites October 4 and October 20, 1972, memos from OCR attorney Gwen Gregory to OCR Director J. Stanley Pottinger on "Sex

Discrimination in Athletics," in the Papers of Margaret Dunkle, 1957–1993, MC 530, Schlesinger Library (hereafter Dunkle papers).

14. The two legislators to be honored as racial civil rights stalwarts but who fought the ERA were Rep. Emanuel Celler and Rep. William McCulloch. See correspondence and memos in Records of the National Organization for Women, 1959–2002 (inclusive), 1966–1988 (bulk), MC 496, M 152, Schlesinger Library (hereafter NOW MC 496), 55.1, folder "Leadership Conference on Civil Rights, 1972–1976."

15. Simmons et al., *Exploitation from 9 to 5*, 146–47, 160.

16. Bill Gilbert and Nancy Williamson, "Sport Is Unfair to Women (Part 1)," *Sports Illustrated*, May 28, 1973, 88–98, cited in Nancy Hogshead-Makar and Andrew Zimbalist, eds., *Equal Play: Title IX and Social Change* (Philadelphia: Temple University Press, 2007), 35–48.

17. Ware, *Game, Set, Match*, 63.

18. Two years after Greenberger's LSAT, draft deferments for graduate students had ended, but a man taking the LSAT at Harvard University confronted a young Hillary Rodham (later Clinton) in the same way. "What do you think you're doing?" he scolded her. "If you get into law school, you're going to take my position. You've got no right to do this. Why don't you go home and get married?" Clinton recounted the memory in a "Humans of New York" interview on Facebook, September 8, 2015. See also "Fact Checker: Hillary Clinton's Story of a Vietnam Era Confrontation over Law School Admissions," *Washington Post*, September 14, 2016.

19. Once the draft deferment ended, many of the men in her cohort dropped out, reducing its size.

20. Greenberger eventually found work initially at the Washington firm of Caplin & Drysdale. Author interview with Marcia Greenberger, January 26, 2015.

21. Simmons et al., *Exploitation from 9 to 5*, 148–51.

22. These included Shirley McCune (who was working on sex equity through the National Education Association), Olya Margolin (longtime lobbyist for the National Congress of Jewish Women), Joy Simonson (president of the Interstate Association of Commissions for Women), and longtime federal lawyer and women's activist Marguerite Rawalt. See Millsap, "Advocates for Sex Equity in Federal Education Law."

23. That's the equivalent of $192 million in 2020 dollars.

24. Author interviews with Wendy Mink, September 17, 2014, and January 20, 2015. Supporting the 40 percent figure, see "Academic Equality," *San Francisco Chronicle*, September 25, 1971, p. 21.

25. Hearings Before the Subcommittee on Education of the Senate Committee on Labor and Public Welfare, on S. 2518, October 17 and November 9, 1973. Subcommittee Chair Sen. Claiborne Pell (D-RI) let Mondale chair the hearings.

26. Ware, *Game, Set, Match*, 1–14.

27. Blumenthal, *Let Me Play*, 62–63, and Festle, *Playing Nice*, 159.

28. Mink introduced a revised WEEA (H.R. 11149) on October 19, 1973, that would authorize up to $15 million for fiscal year 1975, $25 million for 1976, and $40 million for 1977. It also would create a National Advisory Council on Women's Educational Programs to advise the education secretary. NOW MC 666, 50.50.

29. Ware, *Game, Set, Match*, 54.

30. Correspondence from Mink to Morgan, July 5, 1974, NOW MC 666, 50.50.

31. The Women's Educational Equity Act of 1974, 20 USC 1866, in Public Law 93-380, the Education Amendments of 1974. See https://www.congress.gov/93 /statute/STATUTE-88/STATUTE-88-Pg484.pdf.

32. WEAL Fund paper on WEEA history, July 1977, WEAL MC 500, 77.58.

33. Of the forty-one pending bills, ten were authored by Bella Abzug and seven by Martha Griffiths. WEAL "Washington Reporter" newsletter, September 20, 1973, Green papers, 224, folder "Women."

34. Ware, *Game, Set, Match*, 56.

35. "What Constitutes Equality for Women in Sport?," Project on the Status and Education of Women, April 1974. Accessed online at https://files.eric.ed.gov/fulltext /ED089640.pdf.

36. Deborah L. Brake, *Getting in the Game: Title IX and the Women's Sports Revolution* (New York: New York University Press, 2010), 8–13, succinctly describes the eclectic strands of feminism and how they manifested in Title IX debates. Sandler, Ginsburg, WEAL, and others were liberal feminists emphasizing formal equality—equal treatment on the same terms for men and women without questioning the male-dominated structure of sports. Some of NOW's proposals reflected anti-subordination feminism (which questions whether a practice or law operates to disadvantage or oppress women) or cultural feminism (also called "different voice" feminism or "relational" feminism, in reference to the way that women's "culture" values relationships and connections with others). The latter forms of feminism aim for more substantive equality, calling for law and policies to recognize and value women's distinctive interests, needs, and experiences as much as those of men. The final Title IX athletics regulations in 1975 incorporated aspects of all these. Another strand, critical race feminism (also called "social justice" feminism), makes the case that feminist approaches that don't also address intersectional discriminations (racism, homophobia, and so on) end up implicitly privileging white straight women and can never succeed because they leave other women behind—the fate of Title IX up to today.

37. Sandler, "Title IX: How We Got It."

38. Another suit by the NAACP in 1975 focused on elementary and secondary education discrimination in thirty-three Northern and Western states.

39. Plaintiffs included WEAL, NOW, the National Education Association, the Federation of Organizations for Professional Women, and American Women in Science. WEAL press release, November 28, 1974, WEAL MC 500, 42.28.

40. *PEER Perspective* 1, no. 1 (January 1975), Records of the Project on Equal Education Rights, 1966–1991, MC 607, Schlesinger Library (hereafter PEER records). Section 504 was inserted near the end of the Rehabilitation Act of 1973; when President Nixon signed the act on September 26, 1973, Section 504 became perhaps the strongest legal tool for people with disabilities until the passage of the Americans with Disabilities Act in 1990. See Lennard J. Davis, *Enabling Acts: The Hidden Story of How the Americans with Disabilities Act Gave the Largest US Minority Its Rights* (Boston: Beacon Press, 2015).

41. The *Adams/WEAL* cases established that the government has a lot of discretion about how it enforces the law but it can't *not* enforce the law. They also established the expectation that OCR would investigate and resolve complaints it receives of

discrimination. With other kinds of complaints—such as to the EEOC under Title VII of the Civil Rights Act—the individual had to follow up and file suit themselves.

42. Among Senate staff, Ellen Hoffman in Mondale's office, Barbara Dixon on Bayh's staff, and Arvonne Fraser in Rep. Don Fraser's office probably were the main allies to the network of advocates for women's education.

43. Millsap "Advocates for Sex Equity in Federal Education Law."

44. Passed on May 20, 1974, the Javits amendment read in full: "Provision Relating to Sex Discrimination. Sec. 844 of the Education Amendments of 1974. The secretary shall prepare and publish, not later than 30 days after the date of enactment of this act, //20 USC 1681 Note.// proposed regulations implementing the provision of Title IX of the Education Amendments of 1972 //86 Stat. 373, 10 USC 1681.// relating to the prohibition of sex discrimination in federally assisted education programs which shall include with respect to intercollegiate athletic activities reasonable provisions considering the nature of particular sports." Hogshead-Makar and Zimbalist, *Equal Play*, 64.

45. Festle, *Playing Nice*, 178.

46. Carpenter and Acosta, *Title IX*, 6, and Millsap, "Advocates for Sex Equity."

47. *PEER Perspective* newsletter 1, no. 1 (January 1975), 1, in PEER records.

48. Author interviews with Holly Knox, January 2015, and Millsap, "Advocates for Sex Equity."

49. "A Look at Women in Education: Issues and Answers for HEW," 1972, cited in *PEER Perspective* 1, no. 1 (January 1975), PEER records.

50. Terry Saario at Ford actively recruited Knox and other promising feminists to bring their ideas to her for funding. By 1978 Saario and Ford's Mariam Chamberlain had sent $676,000 to PEER ($2.8 million in 2020 dollars), $181,00 to PSEW ($750,000), $200,000 each ($829,000 each) to Greenberger at the Center for Law and Social Policy and to the ACLU's Women's Rights Project, and $150,000 to WEAL ($622,000)—$1.4 million of the nearly $8 million ($33 million) Ford gave to women's education projects in those six years. Saario shared with me the internal Ford report, "The Education and Research Division's Program on Sex Discrimination and Equality of Opportunity for Women: Information Paper for the Education Committee," March 1978.

51. Others in the early group that evolved into the National Coalition for Women and Girls in Education included Mary Ellen Verheyden-Hillyard from NOW; WEAL's Lois Schiffer; Donna Shavlik of the American Council on Education; the National Education Association's Shirley McCune and Marty Matthews; Olya Margolin of the National Conference of Jewish Women; Judith Lichtman of the Women's Legal Defense Fund; Julia Lear of the Federation of Organizations for Professional Women; and the League of Women Voters' Marlene Provisor.

52. Millsap, "Advocates for Sex Equity." See also a luncheon discussion at the Woman's National Democratic Club in Washington, DC, on January 26, 2015, among eleven women's advocates who were involved in Title IX's early years, which the author video recorded: http://www.sherryboschert.com/women-behind-title-ix -video.

53. Title IX would no longer govern the membership practices of the Boy Scouts, Girl Scouts, Camp Fire Girls, the Young Men's or Young Women's Christian Associations (YMCA/YWCA), or other single-sex "voluntary youth service organizations"

whose members are chiefly under age nineteen (though recreational youth groups like Little League were still covered if they received federal funds or "significant assistance" from institutions that got federal funds). Title IX also would no longer apply to the membership practices of social fraternities or sororities (but honorary or professional fraternities or sororities still were covered). See Section 3 of P.L. 93-568. Margaret Dunkle and Cecile Richards, *Sex Discrimination in Education: A Policy Handbook*, August 1977, National Coalition for Women and Girls in Education. Also, Margaret Dunkle and Bernice Sandler, "Sex Discrimination Against Students: Implications of Title IX of the Education Amendments of 1972," *Inequality in Education* (October 1974), 12; Bernice Sandler, "Title IX: Antisexism's Big Legal Stick," *American Education* 13, no. 4 (May 1977).

54. Sandler papers, box 7.8.

55. In Sandler's telling, she could not remember the exact year in the 1970s this took place, or who in the executive branch they met with, or exactly what they talked about. Negotiations around the regulations went on for years. But she vividly remembered her angst about her clothes.

56. Neither Sandler nor Polivy could remember whom they met with at the White House.

57. Among them: Complainants must exhaust their school's grievance procedures before asking OCR for help—something not required by other civil rights laws. No time limits meant schools could bury complaints forever. Gone were sections encouraging affirmative steps to overcome past discrimination and requiring yearly assessments of sports interest. "Tougher Sex Bias Laws Eyed," *Washington Post*, April 27, 1975, Mink papers LOC 186.3.

58. Release from Bayh plus letter to Ford and memorandum with suggested changes, April 20, 1975, PEER records, 20.5.

59. The conference was held at Clark College in Georgia in April 1975. *On Campus with Women*, no. 12 (November 1975).

60. Published in 40 Fed. Reg. 24, 128 (June 4, 1975). I heard two theories from former OCR directors about why President Ford didn't exempt football from Title IX, as the coaches asked. Peter Holmes (OCR director 1973–1975) said government lawyers had advised Ford that no sports could be exempt; he met with coaches as a courtesy so they could tell backers they'd tried everything. Football coaches that trekked to Washington included Bo Schembechler of the University of Michigan, Darrell Royal of the University of Texas, and Barry Switzer of the University of Oklahoma. Interview with Holmes by Eileen H. Tamura, March 15 and 22, 2016, courtesy of Prof. Tamura. The second theory came from Martin Gerry (1975–77), who believed that Ford thought exempting football would be unfair, in part because he had a daughter. In fact, Gerry said, all the men in the top chain of command to produce the Title IX regulation had daughters, including himself, Ford, HEW secretary Weinberger, and the secretary after him, Dave Mathews. "Whenever I would be arguing or trying to persuade somebody, I'd try to get them to think about a daughter," Gerry said. OCR in these years did get the regulations out but did little to enforce them.

61. Nationwide, college budgets for women's sports amounted to 2 percent of men's budgets. Margaret Dunkle, "Title IX: New Rules for an Old Game," *Capitol Hill Forum*, 1, no. 8 (July 1975).

62. Jocelyn Samuels and Kristen Galles, "In Defense of Title IX: Why Current

Policies Are Required to Ensure Equality of Opportunity," *Marquette Sports Law Review* 14, no. 1 (2003). The law that allowed review of regulations was Section 431(d)(1) of the General Education Provisions Act, Pub. L. 93-380, 88 Stat. 567, as amended, 20 U.S.C. Section 1232(d)(1) (2000). A similar requirement for congressional approval was later invalidated by the Supreme Court.

63. In 1973, three years after the ACE lobbyist ignored Rep. Green's Section 805 and her hearings on sex discrimination, ACE created its Office on Women in Higher Education.

64. See a thoughtful, detailed analysis of this in Ware, *Game, Set, Match*, chapter 5: "The Feminist Moment That Wasn't," especially pp. 171–78.

65. Millsap, "Advocates for Sex Equity," and conversation between Dunkle and Donna Shavlik.

66. Millsap, "Advocates for Sex Equity," and luncheon discussion on January 26, 2015, among eleven women's advocates, recorded by the author.

67. Sandler interview, November 4, 2014. Author interview with Julia (Judy) Norrell, January 25, 2015, Washington, DC, who was the lobbyist for the League of Women Voters at that time. Olya Margolin of the National Council of Jewish Women also educated NCWGE members on lobbying skills, Dunkle said.

68. Mink papers LOC 184.7.

69. Samuels and Galles, "In Defense of Title IX." And in Dunkle's "Title IX: New Rules for An Old Game," she lists anti–Title IX resolutions by Sen. James Martin (R-NC), Sen. Jesse Helms (R-NC), Rep. James O'Hara (D-MI), and Rep. Bob Casey (D-TX).

70. Interview with Julia (Judy) Norrell, January 25, 2015.

71. Mink papers LOC 184.11, 184.12.

72. Rep. James O'Hara and Sen. Tower each introduced bills to stop Title IX in athletics. WEAL sent out a national alert in August 1975: "Title IX is in trouble. We need your help, now." WEAL MC 311, box 139, folder "Educ. Comm. 1969–78"; Letter from Arvonne Fraser, August 27, 1975. Pressure from Bayh, AIAW, and other women's advocates stopped both bills.

73. "Ban on Sex Integration Is Rejected," *Washington Post*, July 19, 1974, p. 1, PEER records, 55.9.

74. WEAL MC 500, box 5.18.

75. "Rep. Mink Wins a Vote Even While in Ithica," *Ithica Journal*, July 19, 1975, Mink 184.7. Also, 94th Cong., 1st sess., *Congressional Record* 121, pt. 18 (July 18, 1975): 23504-09.

76. Dunkle 4.7 and 4.8.

77. C.F.R. Section 106 (2003). Donna Shavlik of the American Council on Education (ACE) took the lead on getting the self-evaluations included in the regulations, then published a document to help colleges and universities implement the self-evaluation. "We also took this opportunity to work with the Office of Minorities in Higher Education to address Title VI to produce a similar document on assessing institutional progress serving minorities in higher education, even though there was not such a requirement with regard to Title VI." Email from Shavlik to Dunkle for the January 25, 2015, luncheon, "Video History from Women Behind Title IX,"

sherryboschert.com. Shavlik and Sherry Penney of the State University of New York traveled to many campuses in that system to guide them in implementing the self-evaluation and other parts of Title IX. That work led to other programs in ACE to boost women in education.

78. Sandler said she originated the Title IX coordinator idea.

79. The Consolidated Procedural Rules for Administration and Enforcement of Certain Civil Rights Laws, June 4, 1975. This would apply not just to complaints of sex discrimination under Title IX but discrimination based on race, ethnicity, or national origin under Title VI and against people with disabilities (referred to as "handicaps" in that era) under Section 504. Later that year, in November 1975, Congress enacted the Age Discrimination Act; the proposed Consolidated Procedural Rules would have applied to it too. Like Title IX, the Age Discrimination Act adapted the wording from Title VI: "No person in the United States shall, on the basis of age, be excluded from participation in, be denied the benefits of, or be subjected to discrimination under, any program or activity receiving Federal financial assistance."

80. Memo from Susan Kakesako to Mink, June 9, 1975, Mink papers LOC 185.1.

81. This section draws mainly from three sources: Millsap's description of the response to the consolidated procedural regulations in "Advocates for Sex Equity"; Dunkle and Richards, *Sex Discrimination in Education*; and "Speech of Sen. Birch Bayh to the New York Women's Political Caucus," November 23, 1975, in Hogshead-Makar and Zimbalist, *Equal Play*, 56–58. Also, "Rights Groups Assail E.D. To Reduce Investigations of Bias," *New York Times*, July 16, 1975, PEER records, 55.9.

82. What started as the *Adams v. Richardson* case against HEW secretary Elliot Richardson and OCR to demand enforcement of civil rights laws changed names over time as plaintiffs pursued the case under successive administrations. By this point, it was *Adams v. Weinberger* because Caspar Weinberger headed HEW.

83. "HEW Yields to Protests on Rules," *Washington Star*, March 16, 1976, WEAL MC 500, 42.28.

84. NACWEP's first meeting was June 18–20, 1975; attendees included Sandler and Knox. Sandler papers, 40.7.

85. Sandler nominated Dunkle to chair the NCWGE. It wasn't what Sandler wanted to do and, besides, her plate was full. In 1976–77 alone she served on eighteen boards and advisory committees, spoke to dozens of groups, and testified before Congress twice.

86. PSEW records, 10.4.

87. Memo from OCR director Peter E. Holmes in September 1975 on "Elimination of Sex Discrimination in Athletic Programs," accessed on Department of Education website.

88. Margaret Dunkle, "Competitive Athletics: In Search of Equal Opportunity," HEW Office of Education. Dunkle contracted with OCR and the Resource Center on Sex Roles in Education.

89. The court's decision came January 9, 1978. *NCAA v. Califano*, 444 F. Supp. 425 (D. Kan. 1978). An appeals court later ruled that while the NCAA did not have standing to sue on its own, it could file suits on behalf of its members. 622 F.2d 1382 (10th Cir. 1980). But the threat of this lawsuit to Title IX had passed. Hogshead-Makar and Zimbalist, *Equal Play*, 52–54 and 84.

90. "Students Free 14 Trustees Held at a College for Black Women," Associated Press, April 23, 1976, published in *New York Times*, April 24, 1976, 20. Spelman College's website says that in 1976 Dr. Donald Stewart replaced a Black man as president, who was preceded by four white women presidents.

91. Correspondence from Margaret Dunkle for the NCWGE to HEW secretary F. David Mathews, September 30, 1976, in Dunkle and Richards, *Sex Discrimination in Education*.

92. Thanks to Millsap, "Advocates for Sex Equity," for this insight.

93. Bayh led defeat of one bill that tried to redefine "education program or activity" as only those that are curriculum or graduation requirements, which could allow discrimination in other areas such as scholarships, employment, or extracurricular activities. Another bill would have exempted schools that receive only indirect federal financial assistance such as student financial aid even though the aid benefits both the university and the student. 92nd Cong., 2nd sess., *Congressional Record* 122, pt. 22 (1976): 28136–48. Three bills wanted to exempt certain youth groups. Another would exempt scholarships for beauty pageant winners in such broad terms that it could allow most athletic scholarships to go to men. One tried to exempt professional and honorary societies. One bill would lengthen the process to resolve complaints; another tried to outlaw admissions "quotas, goals" and so on and would block statistics from being collected. The pageants bill was H.R. 10418 by Rep. Jack Edwards (R-AL). Youth-group bills included H.R. 11428, H.R. 11630, and S.2881. Rep. Dawson Mathis (D-GA) sponsored the societies exemption. Sandler's notes list at least two other bills in play. PSEW records, 5.7. Memos from Susan Kakesako to Mink, June 22, 1976, describe plans by Rep. Ralph Regula (R-OH) to amend an appropriations bill so the government could not require coed PE; opposition convinced him to back off. Mink papers LOC, 185.5.

94. "Ford Reinstates 'Father-Son' Activities," *Washington Star*, July 7, 1976, A10; "Ford Acts to Permit Schools to Hold Father-Son Events," *Washington Post*, July 8, 1976, A1; "Civil Rights Madness," *Washington Post*, July 8, 1976, A18; Correspondence to Mink from U.S. Civil Rights Commission staff director John A. Buggs, with text of letter to President Ford, September 17, 1976. All from Mink papers LOC, 183.8.

95. The NCWGE submitted eighteen pages of comments on the proposed regulations in January 1977 and another eleven pages in May. Millsap, "Advocates for Sex Equity," and correspondence from the NCWGE, May 2 and 9, 1977, in Dunkle and Richards, *Sex Discrimination in Education*.

96. Correspondence from the NCWGE to the director of the Office of Education's Women's Program Staff, December 6, 1976, in Dunkle and Richards, *Sex Discrimination in Education*.

5. Sexual Harassment—1977–1980

1. "The Black Panther Raid and the Death of Fred Hampton," *Chicago Tribune*, December 19, 2007.

2. Price's foster caretakers were Alice Aaron, Amy Jenkins, and Lorena O'Donnell.

3. The Umoja Community program "promotes student success and improved life outcomes for all students through a curriculum that is responsive to the legacy of the

African and African American Diasporas." See umojacommunity.org.

4. Based on interviews with Price and her accounts in legal records.

5. Judge Ellen Bree Burns's July 2, 1978, Memorandum of Decision in the resulting lawsuit varies slightly in recounting this timeline. It says Price and another student reported the incident to Balogh that night, then Price told Lum seventeen days later and, at his request, typed up her account, which he then sent to administrators. Price says Burns erred, and that she reported it to Balogh immediately and left New Haven within days of this incident. Author's interviews with Price. Yale Women's Center Records, RU 1130, Yale Sterling Memorial Library (hereafter Yale Women's Center records), 3, folder "Alexander v. Yale 1977–1980"; Ellen Lesser, "Sexus et Veritas: Yale Sued for Sexual Harassment," *Seven Days*, February 23, 1979, 25–26, Records of Women Organized Against Sexual Harassment, 1978–1980, Schlesinger Library (hereafter WOASH records), 1.2.

6. "Yale Women Strip to Protest a Lack of Crew's Showers," *New York Times*, March 4, 1976, 47; *A Hero for Daisy*, directed by Mary Mazzio (50 Eggs, 1999). This may have been the second time Yale woman athletes stripped in protest. Ann Olivarius says she organized a similar strip by women swimmers seeking suits a few years earlier, but I found no news coverage of the event.

7. Other co-founders included Katherine Tyson (Yale 75), "Women's Caucus Fights Oppression," *Yale Daily News*, November 11, 1974.

8. "Rough Draft . . . Statement on the Corporation Report in Regard to Third World Women," Yale Women's Center records, 4, folder "Third World Women 1979–80." Also in the box is a three-page letter to the Yale Corporation, November 3, 1979, detailing policies and actions of Yale that "consciously neglect and in fact aggravate the conditions facing Third World people" (unsigned copy), and an eight-page critique of Yale's decision not to disinvest in companies doing business with the apartheid regime of South Africa, signed by seven campus organizations including the Yale Undergraduate Women's Caucus.

9. Author interview with Ann Olivarius, February 14, 2017; "A Report to the Yale Corporation from the Yale Undergraduate Women's Caucus," March 1977, accessed online, and a March 1977 draft in Yale Secretary's Office Records, 1938–2007, RU 52, Yale Sterling Memorial Library, 16.337.

10. "Female Protesters Disrupt Rape Lecture," *Springfield Union*, April 17, 1975, NOW MC 666, 31.6; "Rape! Storaska Rebuked," *the uwm post*, University of Wisconsin-Milwaukee student publication, November 6, 1975, 1, accessed online; *Do it NOW* 8, no. 4 (July/Aug 1975), in NOW records.

11. For more, see Danielle L. McGuire, *At the Dark End of the Street: Black Women, Rape, and Resistance—a New History of the Civil Rights Movement from Rosa Parks to the Rise of Black Power* (New York: Penguin Random House, 2011).

12. Much of the historical account beyond Yale in this chapter relies on Carri N. Baker, *The Women's Movement Against Sexual Harassment* (New York: Cambridge University Press, 2008), 14.

13. *On Campus with Women*, no. 6 (May 1973), PSEW records; "Coeds Air Problems of Rape," *Washington Star*, April 10, 1972, and other articles, Sandler papers, 69.6. See also Takebackthenight.org history online and Rape Counseling Services of Fresno, rcsfresno.org.

14. Mary Ann Largen, Rape Task Force Report, February 28, 1974, NOW MCC 666, 49.5.

15. *WEAL National Newsletter* 1, no. 2 (June 1975), Mink papers LOC, 184.11.

16. National Crime Victimization Survey, 2010–2016 (2017), Department of Justice, Office of Justice Programs, Bureau of Justice Statistics, Rape, Abuse, and Incest National Network (RAINN) website.

17. NOW Rape Task Force report on "The Case of Joan Little," Yale Women's Center records, 4, folder "Rape 1976–1985." Also, "Aug. 15: 1975: Joan Little Acquitted," Zinn Education Project, online.

18. The group later moved to New York, renaming itself the Working Women United Institute and then simply Working Women Institute.

19. Paulette Barnes, *Barnes v. Train*; Diane Williams, *Williams v. Saxbe*; Margaret Miller, *Miller v. Bank of America*; Adrienne Tomkins, *Tomkins v. Public Service Electric and Gas*; Jane Corne and Geneva DeVane, *Corne v. Bausch and Lomb*; Darla Jeanne Garber, *Garber v. Saxon Business Products*.

20. Claire Safran, "What Men Do to Women on the Job," *Redbook* 148 (1976): 149, cited in Phyllis L. Crocker and Anne E. Simon, "Sexual Harassment in Education," *Capital University Law Review* 10 (1980–81): 541.

21. Sources for Olivarius's story include: author interview, February 14, 2017; "In Court and On Campus: How Sex Education Fights Sexual Harassment," Yale Sex Week keynote speech by Olivarius, February 4, 2012; Nicole Allan, "To Break the Silence" (senior thesis, Yale University, 2009); and Ann Olivarius, "Title IX: Taking Yale to Court," *New Journal* 42, no. 55 (April 2020), online.

22. Lesser, "Sexus et Veritas," WOASH records, 1.2.

23. Anne E. Simon, "Alexander v. Yale University: An Informal History," in *Directions in Sexual Harassment Law*, ed. Catharine A. MacKinnon and Reva B. Siegel (New Haven, CT: Yale University Press, 2004), 51–59.

24. Supreme Court opinions affirming that sexual harassment at work is sex discrimination under Title VII did not start appearing until the summer of 1977, after *Alexander v. Yale* was filed. For Title IX, too, key issues took years to wend through the legal system. The Supreme Court affirmed a private right to sue under Title IX in *Cannon v. University of Chicago*, 441 U.S. 677 (1979). The Court declared that Title IX covers employment discrimination in *North Haven Board of Education v. Bell*, 456 U.S. 512 (1982).

25. Jack Winkler, on Yale's faculty 1974–79, helped found the women's studies program. In 1977, the year he joined *Alexander v. Yale*, he was the only faculty member to help organize Yale's first Gay Rights Week, the first event of its kind on a U.S. university campus. As a member of the Gay Alliance at Yale, Winkler argued to convince members that there could be no gay rights without women's rights and civil rights for racial minorities. He often joined picket lines for causes like abortion rights or protesting a gay bar that denied entry to African Americans or supporting the Yale service workers' strike. Winkler co-produced a weekly LGBT radio show featuring men from the Gay Alliance and women from Yalesbians at a time when queers of different sexes hardly worked together. He moved to Stanford University's faculty in 1979. Winkler went on sabbatical in 1987 after being diagnosed with AIDS and died in 1990 in Palo Alto, California. See the Yale AIDS Memorial Project at yamp.org/profiles/jackwinkler.

26. "Alexander v. Yale 1977–1980," Yale Women's Center records, 3.

27. Diane Henry, "Yale Faculty Members Charged with Sexual Harassment in Suit," *New York Times*, August 22, 1977, 30, WOASH records, 2.6.

28. The original five plaintiffs in July 1977 were Alexander, Olivarius, Stone, Winkler, and student Eugenia Leftwich. In the amended complaint in November 1977, Leftwich decided to drop out and Price and Reifler joined the suit. Diane Henry, "Yale Faculty Members Charged."

29. "Sexual Harassment: A Hidden Issue," Project on the Status and Education of Women, June 1978, Sandler papers, 41.8.

30. WEAL records, 38.34.

31. Simon, "Alexander v. Yale University: An Informal History."

32. Allan, "To Break the Silence."

33. Author interview with Anne E. Simon, January 19, 2017.

34. F. Supp. 1 (D. Conn. 1977).

35. F.2d 178 (2d Cir. 1980).

36. Baker, *The Women's Movement Against Sexual Harassment*, 98, cites *Alexander v. Yale: Collected Documents from the Yale Undergraduate Women's Caucus and Grievance Committee*, Yale University, 1978.

37. Pamela Price statement, December 21, 1977, Yale Women's Center records, 3, folder "Alexander v. Yale 1977–1980." Also, WEAL records, 38.34.

38. Baker, *The Women's Movement Against Sexual Harassment*, 181.

39. Yale Women's Center records, 3, folder "Alexander v. Yale 1977–1980."

40. *Van Arsdel v. Texas A&M*, 628 F2d 344 (5th Cir. 1980).

41. Correspondence from Sandler to Martha C. Dean, January 27, 1995, Sandler papers, 32.3.

42. A court ruling about workplace harassment moved Sandler to write the sexual harassment paper (J.Y. Smith, "Court Supports Job Rights of Women Rejecting Boss," *Washington Post*, July 23, 1977). Her paper followed the era's focus on harassment of employees or students by managers or faculty (not peer harassment). It's interesting that the paper offers some wiggle room in its recommendations. A grievance procedure "need not be identical to other grievance mechanisms if not appropriate," and "institutions might also develop different procedures for students and for employees." Those common kinds of thinking contributed to different standards that made it harder for complainants and easier for respondents in sexual harassment cases than in other kinds of misconduct. *Sexual Harassment: A Hidden Issue* and *The Problem of Rape on Campus*, PSEW records, 83.9, and WEAL MC 500, 77.61.

43. Alexandra Buek, *Sexual Harassment: A Fact of Life or Violation of Law? University Liability Under Title IX*, July 1, 1978, Sandler papers, 42.4.

44. Marcy Kates, "Sex Harassment: 'Bad Odds,'" *Independent and Gazette*, August 14, 1979, WOASH records, 2.6.

45. WEAL records, 38.34.

46. Lesser, "Sexus et Veritas," WOASH records, 1.2.

47. Memorandum of Decision, July 2, 1978, *Pamela Price v. Yale University*, Civil No.

N-77-277, Yale Women's Center records, 3, folder "Alexander v. Yale 1977–1980."

48. Undated statement, Yale Women's Center records, 3, folder "Alexander v. Yale 1977–1980."

49. These included the legal defense and education funds for NOW and WEAL, Greenberger's team at the Center for Law and Social Policy, Equal Rights Advocates in San Francisco, the ACLU, the National Conference of Black Lawyers, Black Women Organized for Political Action, WOASH, the Working Women's Institute, and others.

50. Baker, *The Women's Movement Against Sexual Harassment*, 92–93.

51. *On Campus with Women*, Summer/Fall 1979, PSEW records.

52. Baker, *The Women's Movement Against Sexual Harassment*, 82–89.

53. Donna J. Benson and Gregg E. Thomson, "Sexual Harassment on a University Campus: The Confluence of Authority Relations, Sexual Interest, and Gender Stratification," *Social Problems* 29, no. 3 (1982): 236–51, cited in Linda M. Blum and Ethel L. Mickey, "Women Organized Against Sexual Harassment: A Grassroots Struggle for Title IX Enforcement, 1978–1980," *Feminist Formations* 30, no. 2 (Summer 2018): 175–201.

54. "Feminists Push Case Against UC," *San Francisco Examiner*, March 2, 1979, 4, WOASH records, 1.1.

55. Kates, "Sex Harassment."

56. For a fascinating account of WOASH history interpreted by a WOASH member and a millennial academic, see Linda M. Blum and Ethel L. Mickey, "Women Organized Against Sexual Harassment: A Grassroots Struggle for Title IX Enforcement, 1978–1980," *Feminist Formations* 30, no. 2 (Summer 2018): 175–201.

57. Sally Lehrman, "Senate Wants Disclosure of UC Sexual Harassment Report," November 30, 1979, WOASH records, 1.1.

58. Author interview with Phyllis L. Crocker, June 10, 2019.

59. "None of the written procedures that have come to the authors' attention provide substantial assurance that they will produce adequate responses." Crocker and Simon, "Sexual Harassment in Education."

60. A review of grievance procedures at ten large universities found the worst ones at MIT and Michigan State University, neither of which had a grievance board for sexual harassment and encouraged students to confront the offending faculty member directly. The University of Minnesota had the best: it proposed specific sanctions and was the only one requiring a written response from the accused, not just a written complaint from the accuser, but even it did not commit to collecting and publishing statistics about complaints and their resolutions. Yale neither required a written response nor specified sanctions, leaving decisions to the dean of Yale College. The University of Wisconsin and Brown and Stanford Universities had a separate Sexual Harassment Grievance Board but did not define its powers, procedures, or structure, presumably making it impotent. "Where Does Yale Stand on Sexual Harassment?," *Aurora*, Fall 1981–Winter 1982, 15, Yale Women's Center records, 1.

61. Blum and Mickey, "Women Organized Against Sexual Harassment."

62. Simon, in MacKinnon and Siegel, *Directions in Sexual Harassment Law*, cites Louise F. Fitzgerald, "Institutional Policies and Procedures," in *Combatting Sexual Harass-*

ment in Higher Education, ed. Bernice Lott and Mary Ellen Reilly (1996), 130, which cites Claire Robertson, Constance E. Dyer, and D'Ann Campbell, "Campus Harassment: Sexual Harassment Policies and Procedures at Institutions of Higher Learning," *Signs: Journal of Women in Culture and Society* 13, no. 4 (1988): 792. Among the students pushing for grievance policies was Patsy Mink's daughter Gwendolyn (Wendy), while a graduate student at Cornell University. Author interviews with Wendy Mink, September 14, 2014, and January 20, 2015.

6. Enforcement—1975–1979

1. Not uncommonly, non-faculty women affiliated with a school started these courses. At Yale University, for example, most courses on women in the early 1970s were taught by graduate students, faculty wives, or visiting faculty who had separate financial support from foundations. Simmons et al., *Exploitation from 9 to 5*, 156.

2. There's no indication in Green's papers that she went to Fresno. Record of phone call from Bonne Newman, February 18, 1971, Green papers, 207, folder "Telephone Sheets Jan. Thru March 1971."

3. Margot Polivy confirmed that many of the coaches and administrators she represented in the AIAW were conservative, discreet lesbians; others faced repercussions for being perceived as lesbians.

4. Descriptions of the 1977 National Women's Conference and the competing "Pro-Life, Pro-Family" rally draw from: Marjorie J. Spruill, *Divided We Stand: The Battle over Women's Rights and Family Values That Polarized American Politics* (New York: Bloomsbury, 2017), 205–61; Gloria Steinem, *My Life on the Road* (New York: Random House, 2016); "Equal Rights Plan and Abortion Are Opposed by 15,000 at Rally," *New York Times*, November 20, 1977, 32; and "Women's Conference Approves Planks on Abortion and Rights for Homosexuals," *New York Times*, November 21, 1977, 44.

5. Spruill, *Divided We Stand*, 227.

6. "Phyllis Schlafly, 'Mrs. America,' Was a Secret Member of the John Birch Society," *Daily Beast*, April 22, 2020.

7. Paraphrased from Sandler's memory.

8. The same issue cleaved the annual WEAL convention the year before. When much of WEAL's new board backed a resolution opposing discrimination based on "lifestyle and sexual orientation," WEAL founder Betty Boyer wrote to Sandler in a panic: "The North Carolina women sitting behind me were aghast, upset, WORRIED— said if this sort of thing started they would be simply cooked in North Carolina—to say nothing of the ERA effort, and I BELIEVE THEM." Correspondence from Betty Boyer to WEAL president, "Eileen," June 2, 1976, WEAL MC 311, 81, folder "Corr., May 18–Aug. 76." See also correspondence from Boyer to WEAL board and officers, June 9, 1976, WEAL MC 311, 205, folder "Bert Hartry, WEAL, 1976, WEAL Fund, 1978," with snarky notes by Hartry, WEAL's first executive director. Though Boyer for years shared her Cleveland home with a woman, Maida E. Taylor, she never spoke publicly of her sexual orientation, as far as I know. When Sandler stayed with them on a WEAL trip, she noticed a framed photo of Taylor on Boyer's nightstand. Whether Boyer was straight or lesbian, she clearly feared that supporting gay rights would splinter WEAL.

9. Correspondence from Sandler to Lila, June 13, 1999, Sandler papers, 34.6.

10. Correspondence from Sandler to Jing Lyman, May 9, 1979, PSEW records, 16.5.

11. Correspondence from Sandler to Margaret Hardy, July 10, 1978, PSEW records, 16.4.

12. The number of Title IX complaints increased from 129 in 1973, to 208 in 1974, and to 424 in the first ten months of 1976. *Stalled at the Start: Government Action on Sex Bias in the Schools*, Project on Equal Education Rights, 1977, 1978. Thanks go to Holly Knox for sharing her copy.

13. California State University, Fresno papers on Title IX, Henry Madden Library, California State University, Fresno, CA (hereafter Fresno Title IX papers), and *Stalled at the Start* data forms for Fresno, CA, 1975–1976, PEER records, 34.27.

14. Correspondence from Meg Newman to Joanne Schroll, Pat Thomson, Gene Bourdet, Gaylord O. Graham, and Norman Baxter, March 1977, provided by Newman.

15. Kathy Freeman, "Discrimination: Women Athletes Want Equitable Funding; Possible Suit," and "Athlete Claims CSUF Sex Discrimination," *Collegian* (Fresno State student newspaper), approximately spring 1977, Diane Milutinovich papers, shared with the author.

16. Abbe Smith, undated report, Yale Women's Center records, 3, folder "Athletics 1976–1985."

17. "Testimony on Extension of the Women's Educational Equity Act Before the Subcommittee on Elementary, Secondary and Vocational Education, House Education and Labor Committee," July 14, 1977, in Dunkle and Richards, *Sex Discrimination in Education*. Speaking were Holly Knox of PEER, Dunkle as chair of the NCWGE, Carol Parr of WEAL, and Donna Shavlik of the Federation of Organizations for Professional Women. WEEA was set to expire in September 1978; the hearings were on a bill to reauthorize WEEA.

18. The four states were Georgia, Indiana, South Dakota, and Vermont. *Title IX and the State: A Report on State Agency Compliance, 1976*, PEER records, 54.9.

19. *Stalled at the Start*, PEER records.

20. U.S. Commission on Civil Rights, *More Hurdles to Clear: Women and Girls in Competitive Athletics*, 33, cited in Suggs, *A Place on the Team*, 83.

21. "A Policy Interpretation: Title IX and Intercollegiate Athletics," *Federal Register* 44, no. 239 (December 1979), at 71413.

22. See items in *Title IX News*, August 24, 1978, PSEW records, 134.1.

23. Designed for intercollegiate athletics, the Policy Interpretation's general principles also applied to club, intramural, and interscholastic athletic programs, OCR said.

24. Correspondence from Terry Sanford to college leaders, July 5, 1979, Dunkle papers, 85.6, and correspondence from Edith Green to HEW secretary Harris, November 17, 1979.

25. Her entire life, it irked Brown that the U.S. has no civil rights laws to protect against discrimination based on poverty.

26. Author interviews with Cynthia Brown, January 23 and 26, 2015. Also, Cynthia G. Brown, "40 Years After Title IX, Men Still Get Better Sports Opportunities," *U.S. News and World Report*, June 27, 2012.

27. *Cannon v. University of Chicago*, 441 U.S. 677 (1979); "High Court Strengthens Sex Bias Law," article in unidentified newspaper, May 15, 1979, B6, in WOASH records, 1.2.

28. "Coaches May Sue CSUF for Title IX Violation," *Insight*, February 28, 1979, 1, copy provided by Leilani Overstreet.

29. "'Hold the Line': Women Athletes Campaign for Anti-Bias Law," *Washington Post*, April 23, 1979, plus articles in the *Chicago Tribune* and *Philadelphia Inquirer*, April 24, 1979, Dunkle papers, 22.3.

30. Festle, *Playing Nice*, 189–90.

31. PSEW records, 16.5.

32. WEAL MC 500, 5.37. Ware, *Game, Set, Match*, 95.

33. The total included a backlog of 1,003 complaints and 368 opened in 1977 but not finished. Some were employment discrimination cases that OCR delayed addressing, pending court decisions. OCR set aside athletics cases while working on the Policy Interpretation. Per author interview with Cynthia Brown, January 23, 2015. Memo from Joan Z. Bernstein in the General Counsel's office to the Secretary of HEW, November 19, 1979, Dunkle papers, 85.6.

34. "Title IX of the Education Amendments of 1972; A Policy Interpretation: Title IX and Intercollegiate Athletics," *Federal Register* 44, no. 239 (December 1979), accessed on the Department of Education website. WEAL records, 43.11. The 1979 Policy Interpretation has been upheld by every one of the eight federal appeals courts that has considered its legality. Hogshead-Makar and Zimbalist, *Equal Play*, 52–54.

35. The thirteen areas of compliance: athletic opportunities accommodating interests and abilities; equipment and supplies; game and practice scheduling; travel and per diem allowances; opportunities for coaching and academic tutoring; assignment and compensation of coaches and tutors; locker rooms and facilities for practice and competition; medical and training facilities and services; housing and dining facilities and services; publicity; recruitment; support services; and financial assistance (scholarships).

36. Sandler, "Title IX: How We Got It." Polivy and others also told me that men's advocates, not women's groups, pushed for the compromise.

37. The clarification was clear and had teeth, Greenberger said at the January 16, 2015, "Video History from Women Behind Title IX," so "there wasn't a lot of legal room" for institutions to get away with doing nothing about sex discrimination in athletics. Dunkle said in an email to the author, November 2, 2015, that the 1975 regulations already had been clear and the 1979 clarification conveyed that OCR was ready to enforce it: "The political message was at least as important as the content."

38. National Center for Education Statistics, Digest of Education Statistics, at https://nces.ed.gov/programs/digest/d13/tables/dt13_303.10.asp.

39. Author interview with Sandler, July 25, 2014.

40. Dunkle later published a detailed side-by-side comparison of the 1975 Title IX regulation and the 1979 Policy Interpretation in the *Chronicle of Higher Education*, June 21, 1989; PSEW records, 11.4.

41. Statement by Knox for PEER, December 4, 1979, NOW MC 496, 87.42.

42. Author interview with Leilani Overstreet, July 12, 2018. Enrollment data are from Institutional Research Office records, box 1, Henry Madden Library, California State University, Fresno.

43. Blumenthal, *Let Me Play*, 52 and 97.

44. Festle, *Playing Nice*, 190–191.

45. "Women & Sports: A Summary of Major Court Cases," WEAL report, WEAL MC 500, 27.10.

46. *Enforcing Title IX: A Report of the United States Commission on Civil Rights*, October 1980.

47. Ware, *Game, Set, Match*, 69.

7. Backlash—1980–1990

1. Terrel H. Bell, *The Thirteenth Man: A Reagan Cabinet Memoir* (New York: Free Press, 1988), 2, cited in Suggs, *A Place on the Team*, 87.

2. Ronald Reagan Presidential Library and Museum, "The Reagan Presidency," https://www.reaganlibrary.gov/reagans/reagan-administration/reagan-presidency.

3. James S. Murphy, "The Office for Civil Rights's Volatile Power," *The Atlantic*, March 13, 2017.

4. Millsap, "Advocates for Sex Equity."

5. Millsap, "Advocates for Sex Equity"; and U.S. General Accounting Office, *Women's Educational Equity Act: A Review of Program Goals and Strategies Needed*, December 1994.

6. Dunkle papers, 22.2.

7. College students participated in the campaign to pressure Congress members. For example, students at the University of Indiana sent postcards and twelve hundred petition signatures, those at the University of Nebraska sent a thousand postcards, and at the University of California, Davis, students sent 150 letters and three hundred petition signatures. Dunkle papers, 22.2. Phyllis Cheng, executive director of the Los Angeles School District's Commission on Women and a WEEA grantee, organized a campaign that sent fifteen hundred letters to Congress. Millsap, "Advocates for Sex Equity."

8. Sen. Orrin Hatch (R-UT), for example, introduced S. 1361 to limit Title IX coverage to students, not employees, and only to programs paid for directly by federal funds. A separate "Family Protection Act" would have eliminated the potential penalty of withholding federal funds from discriminatory institutions and programs. *WEAL Washington Report*, October–November 1981, WEAL records.

9. PSEW records, 66.23.

10. Millsap, "Advocates for Sex Equity," and PEER *Equal Education Alert* 2, no. 7 (1982), PEER records.

11. Virginia Allan, who chaired Nixon's Presidential Task Force on Women's Rights and Responsibilities, chaired the shadow council. Members included former Rep. Mink, who said, "The women of this country have been betrayed. [Reagan's NACWEP is] abdicating its responsibility." Congress eliminated NACWEP entirely in 1988 while reauthorizing WEEA in the Hawkins-Stafford Amendments of 1988. Millsap, "Advocates for Sex Equity," and PSEW records, 6.10.

12. In 1981 82, 11,902 women enrolled in law schools. Blumenthal, *Let Me Play*, 97.

13. The North Haven School District in Connecticut refused to rehire tenured special education teacher Eileen Dove after a one-year maternity leave and wouldn't cooperate with OCR's investigation, arguing that Title IX covers only students, not employees. When OCR moved to rescind the district's federal funding, school officials sued HEW. Conflicting rulings in similar cases pushed the matter to the Supreme Court. Greenberger's team weighed in with an amicus brief explaining that part of the confusion came from Title IX being modeled on Title VI. While Title VI made an exception for employment, Title IX did not. The Supreme Court agreed. The wording of Title IX and its regulations covered employment, and Congress had accepted the regulations. The Education Department then found cause to withhold federal funds because the North Haven school board retaliated against Dove for asserting her civil rights. Though Dove sought job reinstatement plus $124,000 in back pay and legal fees, a settlement in June 1985 provided $50,000. "News Update," *Education Week*, August 22, 1985. Author interviews with Marcia Greenberger, January 26, 2015, August 24, 2016, and January 4, 2021.

14. *Haffer et al. v. Temple U. of the Commonwealth System of Higher Education et al.*, 524 Supp. 531 (E.D. Pa. 1981), affirmed, 688 F. 2d 14 (3d Cir. 1982).

15. Other significant suits included *U. of Richmond v. Bell*, 543 F. Supp. 321 (E.D. Va. 1982), a suit by Hillsdale College, and one at West Texas State University.

16. *Grove City College v. Bell*, 687 F. 2d 691 (3d Cir. 1982), affirmed, 465 U.S. 555 (1984). The majority opinion was written by Justice Byron White, who'd been a star football player for the University of Colorado.

17. "Questions and Answers About Grove City College v. Bell," NCWGE, March 19, 1984, Dunkle papers, 84.11.

18. The example came from PEER's "Injustice Under the Law: The Impact of the Grove City College Decision on Civil Rights in America," in PSEW *Update*, April 11, 1985, PSEW records, 83.16.

19. Carpenter and Acosta, *Title IX*, 119–121.

20. Marcia Greenberger and C.A. Beier, "Federal Funding of Discrimination: The Impact of Grove City v. Bell," pamphlet, PSEW records, cited in *On Campus with Women* 17, no. 2 (Fall 1987).

21. "Civil Rights Stalemate," *Washington Post*, March 12, 1986, PSEW records, 99.11. OCR's closed cases included complaints from handicapped students who couldn't get into dorms and a Black high school student at the top of her class who was denied an invitation to the National Honor Society. Blumenthal, *Let Me Play*, 95–96. Locations of closed cases included the Universities of Maryland and Washington, both of which had been found to discriminate against women athletes, Penn State University, the University of Alabama, Duke University, Idaho State University, Mississippi College, Auburn University in Alabama, and elsewhere, as reported in "23 Cases on Civil Rights Closed After Court Rules," *New York Times*, June 3, 1984, NOW MC 496, 89.18. "As Debate Continues on Grove City Ruling, U.S. Delays Action on Complaints of Bias," *Chronicle of Higher Education*, April 3, 1984, PSEW records, 99.10. National Women's Law Center, "Federal Funding of Discrimination: The Impact of *Grove City v Bell*," in Greenberger's testimony before the U.S. Senate, *Hearings Before the Committee on Labor and Human Resources on S. 557*, 100th Cong., 1st sess., March 19 and April 1, 1997, cited in Festle, *Playing Nice*, 348n102.

22. PSEW *On Campus with Women* 14, no. 4 (Spring 1984), PSEW records.

23. Between fiscal years 1976 and 1982, OCR received the most complaints (5,935) about discrimination under Title VI; it also received 5,820 complaints under Section 504, 3,782 under Title IX, 240 involving more than one, and twenty-eight others. WEAL MC 500, 42.27.

24. Millsap, "Advocates for Sex Equity."

25. Millsap, "Advocates for Sex Equity."

26. "Education Secretary Backs Civil Rights Proposal," *Washington Post,* May 24, 1984, PSEW records, 99.11. As it had for years, the NCWGE pushed OCR in a September 10, 1984, press release to "examine the special problems of girls and women who experience double or triple discrimination" during its investigations and compliance reviews to identify any patterns. "For example, what is the experience of the Hispanic female students in contrast to Hispanic male students and also in contrast to white female students? Are Black disabled female students treated differently from non-minority disabled female students and also from Black disabled male students?" Dunkle and Richards, *Sex Discrimination in Education.*

27. Sen. John Danforth (R-MO) proposed exempting abortion so that it would not be required in equitable health services under Title IX, as did Reps. Thomas J. Tauke (R-IA) and F. James Sensenbrenner Jr. (R-WI) in the House. Hundreds of women descended on Capitol Hill in March 1986 to lobby against this and an amendment that would broaden religious exemptions. "Women Lobby Congress on Abortion Rules," *New York Times,* March 19, 1986, PSEW records, 99.11. The amendment that passed neither required nor prohibited abortion coverage; Hogshead-Makar and Zimbalist, *Equal Play,* 116.

28. The author's interviews with Greenberger and an interview with Judith L. Lichtman, February 23, 2021, describe this scenario. Also, see transcript of an oral history interview with Lichtman (April 10, 2006; April 17, 2006; May 5, 2006; March 18, 2010), https://abawtp.law.stanford.edu/exhibits/show/judith-lichtman. Interestingly, Catherine East, the Labor Department employee whose networking in the 1960s and 1970s earned her the nickname "midwife to the women's movement," sent a ten-page plea to allies to accept the abortion amendment if they had to. "What would women gain if the bill doesn't pass? Some few women would retain the right to health insurance coverage for abortion in those cases where the Office for Civil Rights had jurisdiction in spite of the *Grove City* decision. They would not regain the full coverage of Title IX that existed prior to the *Grove City* decision," she wrote. Dunkle papers, 5.3.

29. *National NOW Times* 20, no. 5 (December 1977/January 1988), NOW records.

30. U.S.C. section 1687 (1988), Public Law 100-259. Carpenter and Acosta, *Title IX,* 32, and https://www.govtrack.us/congress/bills/100/s557.

31. *Haffer* also provided a format for comparing the benefits received by the men's and women's athletic programs. Suggs, *A Place on the Team,* 93–94.

32. "Hats Off to Fresno State's New Sports Administrator," *Fresno Bee,* July 31, 1981, D2.

33. The NCAA started offering Division II and III women's championships in 1981–82 and Division 1 in 1982–83. The NCAA offered to pay membership expenses for schools that attended its women's championships and not the AIAW's. The

NCAA's TV and radio contracts required broadcasters to air its women's championships and not the AIAW's. An antitrust suit by the AIAW against the NCAA failed in 1983. Author interviews with Margot Polivy, January 25, 2014, January 20, 2015, and November 4, 2019; Carpenter and Acosta, *Title IX*, 114.

34. Office for Civil Rights, "Interim Title IX Intercollegiate Athletics Manual," July 28, 1980, and "Guidance for Writing Title IX Intercollegiate Athletics Letters of Finding," 1982.

35. All the women on the U.S. Olympic basketball and volleyball teams plus some of its swimmers had athletic scholarships in college thanks to Title IX. *The Eleanor Smeal Report*, August 31, 1984, NOW records, 89.18.

36. The California Sex Equity in Education Act (SEEA), AB 3133, Chapter 1117, enacted in 1982, barred sex discrimination in educational institutions receiving or benefiting from state financial assistance or that enroll students receiving state financial aid. Also, AB 1559, Chapter 789, enacted in 1975, required equality in participation and funding for high school athletic programs. California SB 2252, Chapter 1371, enacted in 1984, clarified that the SEEA covers sexual harassment. Per "Women and Equality: A California Review of Women's Equity Issues in Civil Rights, Education and the Workplace," California Senate Office of Research, February 1999. The California law was more comprehensive than Title IX, explicitly covering athletics, employment, pregnancy, and more. Other states followed with specific prohibitions against sex discrimination in athletics, such as Alaska, Florida, Georgia, Hawaii, Illinois, Iowa, Maine, Minnesota, Nebraska, New Jersey, New York, Rhode Island, South Dakota, and Washington. Hogshead-Makar and Zimbalist, *Equal Play*, 104.

37. The PEER report *Toward Educational Equity: An Overview of the Law* (circa 1985) identified Title IX–like laws in Alaska, California, Colorado, Connecticut, Florida, Hawaii, Illinois, Iowa, Massachusetts, Minnesota, Montana, Nebraska, New Jersey, Oregon, Pennsylvania, and Washington, and with bills in progress in Michigan, Ohio, and New York. PEER records, 54.10.

38. Ware calls this strategy the "essence of liberal feminism." *Game, Set, Match*, 97.

39. "Where Does Yale Stand on Sexual Harassment?," *Aurora*, 15, Yale Women's Center records, 1, folder "*Aurora*: Fall 1981–Winter 1982." Cherríe Moraga and Gloria Anzaldúa, eds., *This Bridge Called My Back: Writings by Radical Women of Color* (New York: Kitchen Table; Women of Color Press, 1981).

40. Caroline Kitchener, "When Helping Rape Victims Hurts a College's Reputation," *The Atlantic*, December 17, 2014, in PEER records, 54.17.

41. OCR Policy Memorandum from Antonio J. Califa to Regional Civil Rights Directors, August 31, 1981, as quoted in *Sexual Harassment: It's Not Academic*, pamphlet published by OCR in September 1988. The memo from Califa, OCR's director for Litigation, Enforcement, and Policy Service, broadly defined sexual harassment based on EEOC guidelines and court rulings on lawsuits under Title VII. Baker, *The Women's Movement Against Sexual Harassment*, 126.

42. PSEW shared news of sexual harassment at Harvard, Princeton, MIT, Penn State, the Universities of Michigan and Minnesota, St. Louis University, Minnesota Law School, Hillsborough Community College, Ramapo College (New Jersey), and others. See *On Campus with Women* issues in the PSEW records.

43. Yale Women's Center records, 1.17.

44. Baker, *The Women's Movement Against Sexual Harassment*, 158–59.

45. Complaints increased from 3,661 in 1981 to 5,557 in 1990. Baker, *The Women's Movement*, 170.

46. For example, male professors accused of harassing male students at Ball State University, Muncie, Indiana, and female students at the University of Texas, El Paso, sued their universities in 1984 and 1985, claiming violation of their constitutional rights to due process or equal protection. A sociology professor at Clark University sued two students, two professors, and a secretary, claiming they damaged his name and reputation. Usually, these cases settled out of court or were dismissed for lack of evidence. Baker, *The Women's Movement*, 140–43.

47. Baker, *The Women's Movement*, 135–61, 170.

48. Sandler had quit for up to a year or two (and once for six years) before it stuck. Sandler made a list of more than thirty reasons to quit smoking; whenever she wanted a cigarette, she made herself recite from memory at least twenty-five reasons not to have one. If she still wanted one after that, she could have one, but she rarely did. Sandler papers, 1.4–1.5.

49. Sandler speech, "The Classroom Climate—a Chilly One for Women," PSEW records, 20.2.

50. By Roberta M. Hall with assistance from Bernice R. Sandler, PSEW records, 83.13.

51. Mentioned in PSEW's report to the Ford Foundation, January 15, 1987, PSEW records, 6.11.

52. The phrase "gang bang" later became racialized to evoke images of African American men doing the raping rather than mostly white fraternity brothers.

53. PSEW records, 98.3.

54. Authored by Julie K. Ehrhart and Bernice R. Sandler.

55. The study drew coverage by *Time* and *Newsweek* magazines, NPR, CBC, and many other media outlets.

56. The paper quotes Andrew Merton of the University of New Hampshire.

57. The Campus Sexual Assault Study reported in October 2007, for instance, that 6 percent of 1,375 undergraduate men said they had experienced a completed or attempted sexual assault: https://www.ojp.gov/pdffiles1/nij/grants/221153.pdf.

58. Helen Zia, "The University of Michigan's Silent Crime," *Metropolitan Detroit*, January 1985, PSEW records, 98.2.

59. PSEW records, 98.1, 98.2, and 98.3.

60. Mary P. Koss, Christine A. Gidycz, and Nadine Wisniewski, "The Scope of Rape: Incidence and Prevalence of Sexual Aggression and Victimization in a National Sample of Higher Education Students," *Journal of Consulting and Clinical Psychology* 55, no. 2 (1987): 162–70.

61. *Women's Education Equity Act: A Review of Program Goals and Strategies Needed*, General Accounting Office, December 1994.

62. The conservative "education reform" movement that emphasized going "back to basics" in the 1980s failed to address issues facing minorities, girls and women, and

financially underprivileged students. Among PEER's recommendations: train teachers to overcome sexism, racism, and classism; make sure curricular and standardized texts are not biased; create school programs to curb racial and sexual harassment; and offer on-site day care so pregnant and parenting teens don't drop out. *The PEER Report Card: Update on Women and Girls in America's Schools—a State-by-State Survey*, Autumn 1985, PEER records, 55.4; *The Heart of Excellence: Equal Opportunities and Educational Reform*, September 1987 (which was inspired in part by comments at PEER's 1986 speak-out), PEER records, 54.17.

63. By Drs. Akasha (Gloria T.) Hull, Patricia Bell Scott, and Barbara Smith, cited in Nancy Chi Cantalupo, "And Even More of Us Are Brave: Intersectionality & Sexual Harassment of Women Students of Color," *Harvard Journal of Law and Gender* 42, no. 1 (2018): 3.

64. Kimberlé Crenshaw, "Demarginalizing the Intersection of Race and Sex: A Black Feminist Critique of Antidiscrimination Doctrine, Feminist Theory and Anti-racist Politics," *University of Chicago Legal Forum*, no. 1 (1989): 139–67; and "Mapping the Margins: Intersectionality, Identity Politics, and Violence Against Women of Color," *Stanford Law Review* 43, no. 6 (1991): 1241–99.

65. Email from Sandler to daughters Deborah and Emily, October 30, 2005, Sandler papers, 8.3.

66. Both papers were authored by Jean O'Gorman Hughes and Bernice Sandler.

67. Correspondence from Sandler to Martha Church, cc'd to President Chandler, Board Chair Bette E. Landman, and AAC's incoming president, Paula Brownlee, August 2, 1990, Sandler papers, 27.4, 27.8.

68. *On Campus with Women*, 19, no. 1 (Summer 1989), PSEW records.

69. Yale Women's Center records, 3, folder "Crime 1989 & Unrelated." See "Rifleman Slays 15 'Feminists' at University," Associated Press, in *New Haven Register*, December 7, 1989, 1.

70. The descriptions of Sandler's accomplishments and reactions to being fired come from interviews with her, PSEW's annual reports, and correspondence in the Sandler papers, 27.

71. A decade earlier, PSEW's champion at the Ford Foundation, Mariam Chamberlain, and three others had filed an EEOC complaint for age discrimination after the foundation's new president fired dozens of program officers in 1981. (PEER's champion, Terry Saario, had left shortly before what Ford Foundation employees called the "Monday massacre.") Chamberlain reached a financial settlement that helped her found a nonprofit organization to continue some of the work she'd been doing at Ford. "Cracks in the Foundation?" *Newsweek*, September 7, 1981, 87, PSEW records, 6.3. Also, author interview with Terry Saario, June 14, 2016; "Mariam Chamberlain, Women's Champion, Dies at 94," *New York Times*, April 7, 2013.

72. "Head of College Association's Project on Women Dismissed After 20 Years in Advocacy Role," *Chronicle of Higher Education*, December 5, 1990, Sandler papers, 1.9. My review of PSEW's *On Campus with Women* found that it rarely mentioned discrimination, harassment, or sexual assault after Sandler was gone, even though these issues led to some of the most significant developments in Title IX history in the 1990s.

8. Christine, Jackie, Rebecca, Nicole, Alida, LaShonda—1991–1999

1. Jim Staats, "Former Marin City Administrator Returns to Help Community," *Marin Independent Journal*, July 31, 2008.

2. The account of the case comes from court filings. Also, Suggs, *A Place on the Team*, 105–6; Mark Walsh, "Issue of Sexual Harassment in Schools Moves to Supreme Court," *Education Week*, December 11, 1991; and Dan H. Wishnietsky, *Establishing School Policies on Sexual Harassment*, Phi Delta Kappa Educational Foundation, 1994.

3. For the effects of *Franklin*, see Suggs, *A Place on the Team*, 105–6; Carpenter and Acosta, *Title IX*, 124–25 and 131–33; Hogshead-Makar and Zimbalist, *Equal Play*, 133; and Brake, *Getting in the Game*, 73 and 147.

4. Groups that signed NWLC's amicus brief to the Supreme Court include the National Education Association, the American Association of University Women, the ACLU, NOW, and groups advocating for Mexican Americans, people with disabilities, and others. WEAL records, 33.37.

5. Linda P. Campbell, "Court Weighs Allowing Students to Collect Damages in Sex Bias Cases," *Chicago Tribune*, December 12, 1991.

6. *Franklin v. Gwinnett County Public Schools*, 911 F. 2d 617 (11th Cir. 1990), reversed by Supreme Court 503 U.S. 60 (1992).

7. Paul M. Anderson, "Title IX at Forty: An Introduction and Historical Review of Forty Legal Developments That Shaped Gender Equity Law," *Marquette Sports Law Review* 22, no. 2 (2012): 325.

8. The three others were Angela Wright, Rose Jourdain, and Sukari Hardnett. Annys Shin and Libby Casey, "Anita Hill and Her 1991 Congressional Defenders to Joe Biden: You Were Part of the Problem," *Washington Post*, November 22, 2017.

9. Baker, *The Women's Movement Against Sexual Harassment*, 144, 152.

10. Thomas's reaction typified responses to accusations of sexual harassment, a strategy that Professor Jennifer Freyd of the University of Oregon later named DARVO (deny, attack, and reverse the victim and offender).

11. Turk, *Equality on Trial*, 199.

12. Chris Mills Rodrigo, "Timeline: A History of the Joe Biden–Anita Hill Controversy," *The Hill*, May 4, 2019.

13. One of the older men in the House approached Rep. Patricia Schroeder (D-CO) when the new Congress convened, still around 90 percent men. "Well, I hope you're happy," he said to her. "What do you mean?" Schroeder asked. He said, "This place looks like a shopping mall." Schroeder looked at him. "Where do you shop?" Shin and Casey, "Anita Hill and Her 1991 Congressional Defenders."

14. The account of the *Patricia H.* case comes from the judge's preliminary hearing decision in *Patricia H. v. Berkeley Unified Sch. Dist.*, 830 F. Supp. 1288 (N.D.CA 1993), from author interviews with Pamela Price on January 13, 2017, and January 21 and February 5, 2020, and from posts on Price's website.

15. According to the National Sexual Violence Resource Center, rape is the most underreported crime: only 37 percent is reported to police, and only 12 percent of

child sexual abuse is reported to authorities. "Statistics About Sexual Violence," 2015, NSVRC.org.

16. This account is based on Price's recollection, not the deposition transcription.

17. In 1994 Congress amended the Federal Rules of Evidence to make evidence of a plaintiff's "sexual predisposition" or "other sexual behavior" inadmissible in sexual harassment lawsuits. California Evidence Code section 1106 and Baker, *The Women's Movement Against Sexual Harassment*, 174.

18. Signers to the amicus included NWLC, NOW, Equal Rights Advocates, the American Association of University Women, California Women's Law Center, and the Women's Legal Defense Fund.

19. For example, see *Doe by and Through Doe v. Petaluma City School Dist.*, 949 F. Supp. 1415 (N.D. Cal. 1996).

20. "Berkeley District to Pay $800,000 to Settle Sexual-Abuse Suit," *Education Week*, September 7, 1994. According to the article, the total value of the structured settlement was $1.8 million.

21. "With Campus Crimes Capturing Public Attention, Colleges Re-evaluate Security Measures and Stiffen Some Penalties," *Chronicle of Higher Education*, February 6, 1991, Sandler papers, 68.3.

22. The conference was in October 1991. Sandler papers, 12.20.

23. Duke University appointed her in the fall of 1992. Sandler papers, 28.3.

24. Congress originally passed the law as Title II of the Student Right-to-Know and Campus Security Act of 1990 (P.L. 101-542), which was an amendment to the Higher Education Act of 1965, then renamed it the Jeanne Clery Disclosure of Campus Security Policy and Campus Crime Statistics Act (Clery Act, 20 U.S.C. 1092) in the Higher Education Amendments of 1998. The Clerys sued Lehigh, saying their daughter would not have enrolled if the crime rate there was public. They settled for $2 million and founded a nonprofit organization, Security on Campus. The murderer received a life sentence. Gail McCallion, "History of the Clery Act: Fact Sheet," Congressional Research Service, October 20, 2014; "Ex-Lehigh Student Sentenced to Electric Chair for Murder," *New York Times*, April 30, 1987, B9; Valerie J. Nelson, "Crusader for Increased Campus Security After Daughter's Murder," *Los Angeles Times*, January 12, 2008.

25. Center for Public Integrity, *Sexual Assault on Campus: A Frustrating Search for Justice*, 2010, https://publicintegrity.org/topics/education/sexual-assault-on-campus.

26. William Celis 3d, "Date Rape and a List at Brown," *New York Times*, November 18, 1990, section 1, p. 26.

27. "Campus Life: Stanford; Task Force Seeks Revised Handling of Rape Charges," *New York Times*, February 10, 1991.

28. "Women's Group Proposes Curfew for Men," *National NOW Times*, December 1991, 6.

29. Sandler records, 68.3.

30. Correspondence from Kathryn Allot to Sandler, December 13, 1993, Sandler records, 28.4.

31. Memo from NOW legal intern Jill Weissman to Ginny Montes and Nancy Buermeyer, July 6, 1992, NOW MC 666, 97.16.

32. Baker, *The Women's Movement Against Sexual Harassment*, 173–75; Bernice R. Sandler and Robert J. Shoop, eds., *Sexual Harassment on Campus: A Guide for Administrators, Faculty, and Students*, to be marketed by the National Middle School Association, Sandler records, 10.4.

33. From Sandler's talk in October 1996 to the Grand Valley State University Women's Commission, Allendale, MI, Sandler papers, 10.1.

34. Demand for these materials increased in 1992–93. WEEA Program biennial evaluation report for fiscal year 1993–94, DFDA No. 84.083.

35. *Women's Educational Equity Act: A Review of Program Goals and Strategies Needed*, General Accounting Office, December 1994.

36. Memo from Verna Williams to Sandler, August 21, 1996, Sandler papers, 33.2.

37. Correspondence from OCR Region X director Gary D. Jackson to Jane Jervis, president of Evergreen State College, April 4, 1995. See www.ncherm.org/documents /193-EvergreenStateCollege10922064.pdf.

38. NOW's executive vice president, Kim Gandy, a former prosecutor, argued in the *NOW National Times* Fall 1999 issue that "college disciplinary boards have no business adjudicating rape cases. They should be turned over to the criminal justice system." Ironically, in the same issue a lengthy article described the case of an exotic dancer who sought police help—and how that backfired against her—after Delta Chi fraternity men allegedly gang-raped her on February 27, 1999, at the University of Florida, Gainesville. Lisa Gier King ran naked from the party and called her mother, who called university police. An ambulance drove King to a hospital on a stretcher in a neck brace. On a video shot and edited by the fraternity men, some chant "rape" several times during the alleged assault. One can be heard telling King he will "break her neck" if she resists. He seems to choke her and asks, "What do you want? Your circulation back?" The men titled their tape "The Raping of a White-Trash, Crackhead Bitch." A male judge said he found no evidence of sexual assault and made the videotape public; someone offered it for sale on the internet as a "live frat rape tape." University police arrested King, not the alleged rapists, on March 1 for "falsifying a police report." Florida state attorney Rod Smith never interviewed King and reportedly did nothing about the rape charges despite four other women complaining to NOW about Smith's mishandling of their rape cases. NOW held weekly pickets and gathered three thousand signatures on a petition to support King, who accepted a plea deal in July of six months of probation for operating an escort service without a license in exchange for police dropping charges of prostitution and lewdness. The university suspended the fraternity from campus for three years.

39. For the first time, OCR addressed sexual orientation under Title IX, saying that the law does not prohibit discrimination based on sexual orientation, but it does prohibit harassing *conduct* of a sexual nature regardless of the orientation of the harasser or the harassed. The Supreme Court ruled the next year that Title VII covers on-the-job same-sex harassment because usually such harassment is based on stereotypes about masculinity and femininity. *Oncale v. Sundowner Offshore Services*, 523 U.S. 75.

40. *Sexual Harassment Guidance: Harassment of Students by School Employees, Other Students, or Third Parties*, 62 Federal Register (March 13, 1997), 12034 and what follows.

41. Sandler papers, 28.1, 28.2.

42. Sandler papers, 32.5.

43. Sandler papers, 35.1.

44. Sandler papers, 33.2, 33.3, 33.7.

45. Email from Ali P. Crown, director of the Women's Center at Emory, to Sandler, September 22, 1997, Sandler papers, 33.7.

46. Blumenthal, *Let Me Play*, 107.

47. "Title IX: A Brief History," WEEA Equity Resource Center, August 1997, Mink papers LOC, 2041.5.

48. NCWGE, *Title IX at 25: Report Card on Gender Equity* (Washington, DC: National Women's Law Center, 1997), cited in Susan J. Smith, "Title IX and Sexual Harassment," *WEEA Digest*, October 1998; and a 1993 Louis Harris and Associates survey of 1,600 public school students commissioned by the American Association of University Women. See http://www2.edc.org/WomensEquity/pubs/digests/digest -title9-harass.html.

49. "Celebrate the 25th Anniversary of Title IX," Mink's "Dear Colleague" letter of June 23, 1997, asked the committee members to sign on to the concurrent resolution. Mink papers LOC, 2041.2, 2041.3.

50. MacKinnon and Siegel, *Directions in Sexual Harassment Law*, 61 (emphasis in original).

51. *Nicole M. v. Martinez Unified School Dist.*, 964 F. Supp. 1369 (N.D. Cal. 1997).

52. Emily Gurnon, "Women Object to Sex Suit Costs," *San Francisco Examiner*, July 15, 1997.

53. U.S. 274 (1998).

54. *Catherine M. v. San Francisco Community College District*, Nos. A078308 and A079443 (Cal. Ct. App. August 27, 1998). The appeals court affirmed the grant of summary judgment on totally unrelated grounds by the lower court.

55. U.S. 629 (1999).

56. For a fuller discussion, see Cantalupo, "And Even More of Us Are Brave."

57. Blumenthal, *Let Me Play*, 113.

58. Michele Goodwin, "Sex, Theory, & Practice: Reconciling Davis v. Monroe & the Harms Caused by Children," *DePaul Law Review* 51, no. 3 (2002): 805, 821.

59. Correspondence in August 1998 and January 1999 from the secretary of education to school superintendents and college and university presidents, respectively. Also, Office for Civil Rights, *Revised Sexual Harassment Guidance: Harassment of Students by School Employees, Other Students, or Third Parties*, January 2001.

60. Pamela Y. Price, "Eradicating Sexual Harassment in Education," in MacKinnon and Siegel, *Directions in Sexual Harassment Law*, 64.

61. Price's client, Claude Reissner, was a Jewish nurse working at Pelican Bay State Prison, where guards and officers subjected him to racial slurs and anti-Semitism because he treated the African American inmates humanely, forcing him to leave his job. After a three-week trial, a federal jury awarded him more than $501,000 as compensation for discrimination. Pamela Y. Price, in MacKinnon and Siegel, *Directions in Sexual Harassment Law*, 66.

62. Price won three awards by judges and juries against the California Department of Corrections, two for $1.3 million and one for $629,000. She also won $825,000

for a City of Oakland employee sexually assaulted by her boss, and $905,000 for racial discrimination against an oil refinery mechanic.

9. Athletics—1992–1999

1. *Favia v. Indiana University of Pennsylvania*, 812 F. Supp. 578 (W.D. Pa. 1993).

2. "National Collegiate Athletic Association: Final Report of the NCAA Gender-Equity Task Force, July 26, 1993," in Susan Ware, *Title IX: A Brief History with Documents* (Boston: Bedford/St. Martin's, 2007), 86.

3. Debra E. Blum, "A Different 'Equity,'" *Chronicle of Higher Education*, May 18, 1994, A35, and "Forum Examines Discrimination Against Black Women in College Sports," *Chronicle of Higher Education*, April 21, 1993, A39, cited in Festle, *Playing Nice*, 273.

4. Kenneth Tolo, "Gender Equity in Athletics: The Inadequacy of Title IX Enforcement by the U.S. Office for Civil Rights," Lyndon B. Johnson School of Public Affairs, University of Texas, Austin, 1993, cited in both Hogshead-Makar and Zimbalist, *Equal Play*, 136–37, and Suggs, *A Place on the Team*, 128–29. See also "Equal Opportunity in Intercollegiate Athletics," OCR, 1991.

5. *Gender Equity: Men's and Women's Participation in Higher Education*, U.S. General Accounting Office Report to the Ranking Minority Member, Subcommittee on Criminal Justice, Drug Policy and Human Resources, Committee on Government Reform, House of Representatives, December 2000.

6. "Intercollegiate Athletics: Status of Efforts to Promote Gender Equity," General Accounting Office, HEHS-97-10, October 25, 1996; Suggs, *A Place on the Team*, 129; Hogshead-Makar and Zimbalist, *Equal Play*, 137.

7. Author's analysis of data requested from OCR.

8. *National NOW Times*, June 1993, NOW records.

9. Memo from Linda Joplin, California NOW Athletic Equity Committee Chair, to Women Athletic Administrators, September 17, 1993, Milutinovich papers.

10. Carpenter and Acosta, *Title IX*, 131.

11. Brake, *Getting in the Game*, 74–77. See *Cohen v. Brown University*, 809 F. Supp. 978 (D.R.I. 1992), affirmed, 991 F.2d 888 (1st Cir. 1993), remanded to, 879 F. Supp. 185 (D.R.I. 1995), affirmed in part and reversed in part, 101 F.3d 155 (1st Cir. 1996), cert. denied, 520 U.S. 1186 (1997). Also, Suggs, *A Place on the Team*, 109–23.

12. Carpenter and Acosta, *Title IX*, 133–24; Hogshead-Makar and Zimbalist, *Equal Play*, 135; Festle, *Playing Nice*, 173–279. Deborah Brake and Elizabeth Catlin, "The Path of Most Resistance: The Long Road Toward Gender Equity in Intercollegiate Athletics," *Duke Journal of Gender Law & Policy* 3, no. 51 (1996): 51–92.

13. Scenes involving Milutinovich in this and other chapters draw from the author's interviews with her on April 23, 2018, February 1 and 13, 2019, and December 18–20, 2019, as well as news accounts.

14. George Hostetter, "Spencer Out as FSU Women's Basketball Coach," *Fresno Bee*, March 30, 1993, C1.

15. Scenes in this chapter and others involving Lindy Vivas or Margie Wright draw on the author's interviews with Vivas on February 19, 2019, with Wright on February 16, 2019, and with Milutinovich on six days in 2018 and 2019.

16. The vast majority of dropped teams were in NCAA Division I, especially in wrestling and men's gymnastics. The number of football and men's basketball players grew or stayed the same in all NCAA divisions. Suggs, *A Place on the Team*, 139.

17. NCAA, *1982–2001 Sports Sponsorship and Participation Statistics Report*, cited in Hogshead-Makar and Zimbalist, *Equal Play*, 105–6.

18. Samantha Schmidt, "Judge Bars Disgraced Former House Speaker Dennis Hastert from Being Alone with Children," *Washington Post*, December 13, 2017.

19. Eric Lipton and Monica Davey, "Wrestling Propelled Hastert's Career, and Provided Opportunity for Abuse," *New York Times*, April 22, 2016.

20. Statements by NCAA executive director Richard D. Schultz and NWLC's Ellen J. Vargyas before the House Subcommittee on Commerce, Consumer Protection, and Competitiveness, April 9, 1992, Mink papers LOC, 2041.7.

21. See *Miami U. Wrestling Club v. Miami U.*, 302 F. 3d 608 (6th Cir. 2002), *Gonyo v. Drake University*, 879 F. Supp. 1000 (S.D. Iowa 1995), and *Kelley v. Board of Trustees*, 35 F. 3d 265 (7th Cir. 1994), cited in Brake and Catlin, "The Path of Most Resistance," 68. Also see Deborah E. Blum, "Slow Progress on Equity," *Chronicle of Higher Education*, October 26, 1994, A47.

22. Mike Digiovanna, "Cal State System's Plan to Bring Women's Opportunities in Line with Men's Could Have Nationwide Ramifications," *Los Angeles Times*, October 22, 1993.

23. Jim Wasserman, "No Excuse for Ignoring FSU Sports for Women," *Fresno Bee*, August 29, 1993, Milutinovich papers.

24. Correspondence and report from John E. Palomino, OCR regional civil rights director, to Dr. John Welty, April 6, 1994, Milutinovich papers.

25. Carol Herwig, "Federal Office Gets Tougher with Title IX," *USA Today*, July 21, 1994, Milutinovich papers.

26. Former Fresno mayor Karen Humphrey (the city's first woman mayor) and attorney Mary Louise Frampton co-founded the coalition.

27. Bill McEwen, "Women Aren't Sinking Bulldogs," *Fresno Bee*, November 9, 1995, D1. Christopher Livingston, "The 'Wright' Honor: 'Dogs Dedicate Softball Diamond to Applaud Winningest Coach," *Collegian*, May 4, 2014. Author interview with Margie Wright, February 16, 2019.

28. Equity in Athletics Disclosure Act, 20 USC 1092 [g].

29. Corrective Action Plan Correspondence and Corrective Action Plan from OCR regional director John Palomino to John D. Welty, June 20, 1994, Milutinovich papers.

30. *Data Books, Students, 1997*, Institutional Research Office records, box 1 of 2, Madden Library, California State University, Fresno.

31. "Excerpts from *Hearing on Title IX of the Education Amendments Act of 1972: Hearing Before the Subcommittee on Postsecondary Education, Training, and Life-Long Learning of the Committee on Economic and Educational Opportunities*, House of Representatives, 104th Cong., 1st sess., May 9, 1995," in Ware, *Title IX: A Brief History*, 96–114.

32. Aaron Sorkin, *The American President* screenplay, on dailyscript.com.

33. "Dear Colleague" letter and "Clarification of Intercollegiate Athletics Policy Guidance: The Three-Part Test," January 16, 1996, Office for Civil Rights.

NOTES

34. "Dear Colleague" letter from Norma Cantú to Bowling Green State University, July 23, 1998, and made available to other institutions.

35. Questioned as a witness during Lindy Vivas's 2007 trial, Raymond denied having said that.

36. Vandals burned down the LGBT students' booth at Fresno State in the late 1980s. The Ku Klux Klan planned to disrupt a gay, lesbian, and bisexual students' conference and attack its keynote speaker there in February 1989, but campus police kept them off campus. Milutinovich papers; Dan Waterhouse, "Sexual Orientation an Issue in CSU Fresno Athletic Department," *Community Alliance*, December 2007, 9, Milutinovich papers.

37. Robert Lipsyte, "Penn State Coach Will Abide by Lesbian Policy, but Won't Discuss It," *New York Times*, December 20, 1991, B14, cited in Festle, *Playing Nice*, 267–68.

38. Excerpts from Lucy Jane Bledsoe, "Team Sports Brought Us Together," *Harvard Gay & Lesbian Review* 4, no. 3 (1997), 18–20, as "Lucy Jane Bledsoe: Homophobia in Women's Sports, 1997," in Ware, *Title IX: A Brief History*, 147.

39. Unofficial transcript of the Appleton broadcast on October 26, 1995, Milutinovich papers.

40. KMJ press release, June 16, 1997, Milutinovich papers.

41. Suggs, *A Place on the Team*, 132–34; Brake, *Getting in the Game*, 159; "Advocacy Group Charges 25 Colleges with Violating Title IX, *Chronicle of Higher Education*, June 13, 1997.

42. OCR also did five compliance reviews focused on sexual harassment, five focused on admissions, and one other one. *Gender Equity: Men's and Women's Participation in Higher Education*, U.S. General Accounting Office Report to the Ranking Minority Member, Subcommittee on Criminal Justice, Drug Policy and Human Resources, Committee on Government Reform, House of Representatives, December 2000.

43. At the event the NCWGE also issued *Title IX at 25: Report Card on Gender Equity*.

44. "Nondiscrimination on the Basis of Sex in Education Programs or Activities Receiving Federal Financial Assistance; Final Common Rule," *Federal Register* 65, no. 169 (August 30, 2000): 52857.

45. *Title IX: 25 Years of Progress*, Department of Education, 1997, Mink papers LOC, 2041.5. Also, OCR's January 1999 fact sheet.

46. *Women and Equality: A California Review of Women's Equity Issues in Civil Rights, Education and the Workplace*, California Senate Office of Research, February 1999.

47. Milutinovich papers.

48. Blumenthal, *Let Me Play*, 110.

49. Not all the facilities improvements were for women. They included: a $4.1 million softball stadium and press box; a $1.2 million women's locker room; the addition of chair-back seating and air conditioning for $688,000 in the North Gym where women's basketball and volleyball played; and the renovation of the women's soccer office, soccer fields, swimming locker room, and more.

50. Fresno State's 1993 football squad had 110 players. Michele Kort, "Full Court Press," *Ms.*, Spring 2008, 46–51.

51. Correspondence from OCR's Robert E. Scott to John D. Welty, September 27,

2001, Milutinovich papers; Jill Lieber Steeg, "Disputes Reflect Continuing Tension over Title IX," *USA Today*, May 13, 2008, A1.

10. Retaliation—2000–2010

1. "2000 Republican Party Platform," July 31, 2000, online at The American Presidency Project, University of California, Santa Barbara.

2. By 1997 women made up 56 percent of undergraduate students and were as likely as men to receive financial aid. Between 1972 and 1997, the share of law degrees going to women increased from 7 percent to 44 percent, and the share of medical degrees increased from 9 percent to 41 percent. *Gender Equity: Men's and Women's Participation in Higher Education*, U.S. General Accounting Office Report to the Ranking Minority Member, Subcommittee on Criminal Justice, Drug Policy and Human Resources, Committee on Government Reform, House of Representatives, December 2000.

3. Krista Kafer, "Gender Equity Program in the Chairman's Mark," The Heritage Foundation, May 9, 2001, Mink papers LOC 2041.9.

4. "Women's Educational Equity, Funding Status: Archived Information," U.S. Department of Education website.

5. Mary Jo Sylvester, "Hispanic Girls in Sport Held Back by Tradition," *USA Today*, March 29, 2005; Brake, *Getting in the Game*, 116.

6. Excerpts from Welch Suggs, "Left Behind: Title IX Has Done Little for Minority Female Athletes—Because of Socioeconomic and Cultural Factors, and Indifference," *Chronicle of Higher Education*, November 30, 2001, p. 35, in Ware, *Title IX: A Brief History*, 140–47.

7. Ware, *Title IX*, 35.

8. *Title IX and Race in Intercollegiate Sport*, Women's Sports Foundation, June 2003.

9. Correspondence from Milutinovich to NCAA assistant director for health and safety Randall W. Dick, November 26, 2001, Milutinovich papers. See Guideline 3b in the NCAA's *Sports Medicine Handbook 1999–2000*.

10. Amy Rainey, "What Athletes Can Expect When They're Expecting," *Chronicle of Higher Education*, May 26, 2006.

11. See Brake, *Getting in the Game*, 171, 186–87.

12. Press packet for Milutinovich's October 9, 2002, press conference, Piccadilly Inn Hotel, Fresno, Milutinovich papers.

13. Hogshead-Makar and Zimbalist, *Equal Play*, 2; Carpenter and Acosta, *Title IX*, 84.

14. *Title IX at 30 Report Card on Gender Equity*, National Coalition for Women and Girls in Education, June 2002, Mink papers LOC, 2041.2.

15. Bernice Sandler, "Wrestling with Title IX," letter to the editor of the *Chronicle of Higher Education*, March 8, 2002, Mink papers LOC 2041.1.

16. Bill Pennington, "More Men's Teams Benched as Colleges Level the Field," *New York Times*, May 9, 2002, Mink papers LOC 2041.1.

17. *National Wrestling Coaches Association v. Department of Education*, 366 F.3d 930 (D.C. Cir. 2004), cert. denied 545 U.S. 1004.

18. Memo from "RLV" to Mink, June 27, 2002, with notes from the Senate Committee on Health, Education, Labor, and Pensions hearing on "Title IX: Building on 30 Years of Progress," Mink papers LOC, 2041.1. Also, Suggs, *A Place on the Team*, 157–58.

19. Welch Suggs, "Federal Commission Considers Reinterpreting Title IX," *Chronicle of Higher Education*, September 6, 2002.

20. "More Men's Teams Benched"; excerpt from Nancy Hogshead-Makar, "A Critique of *Tilting the Playing Field: Schools, Sports, Sex and Title IX* by Jessica Gavora," *UCLA Women's Law Journal*, Fall/Winter 2003; *Intercollegiate Athletics: Four-Year Colleges' Experiences Adding and Discontinuing Teams*, U.S. General Accounting Office, March 2001, cited in Hogshead-Makar and Zimbalist, *Equal Play*, 197–217.

21. College football mushroomed from an average of eighty-two players on 497 teams in 1981 to ninety-four players on 603 teams in 2000, the NCAA reported. "NCAA Report on Sports Participation Reveals Upswing for Women and a Drop for Men," *Chronicle of Higher Education*, April 19, 2002, Mink papers LOC, 2041.1.

22. Andrew Zimbalist, "What to Do About Title IX," based on his testimony before the U.S. Department of Education's Commission on Title IX, San Diego, November 20, 2002, in Hogshead-Makar and Zimbalist, *Equal Play*, 239–42.

23. *Patsy Mink: Ahead of the Majority*, directed by Kimberlee Bassford (Making Wave Films, 2008, including outtakes).

24. Correspondence from Secretary Paige to Mink, April 10, 2002, Mink papers LOC, 2041.1.

25. Mink papers LOC, 2041.1.

26. *National NOW Times*, Fall/Winter 2002, NOW records.

27. "Statement by Congresswoman Patsy T. Mink in the House of Representatives Celebrating the 30th Anniversary of Title IX of the Education Act Amendments of 1972," June 19, 2002, Mink papers LOC, 2041.1.

28. H.J.R. 113 and S.J.R. 49, which President Bush signed October 21, 2002. House members gave their tributes on September 30 and October 2 and 7, 2002.

29. *Patsy T. Mink, Late a Representative from Hawaii: Memorial Addresses and Other Tributes* (Washington, DC: U.S. Government Printing Office, 2003).

30. Welch Suggs, "Smoke Obscures Fire in Title IX Debate as Federal Panel Adjourns," *Chronicle of Higher Education*, February 7, 2003, A31.

31. Donna de Varona and Julie Foudy, "Minority Views on the Report of the Commission on Opportunity in Athletics," in Hogshead-Makar and Zimbalist, *Equal Play*, 256–75.

32. "Further Clarification of Intercollegiate Athletics Policy Guidance Regarding Title IX Compliance," Dear Colleague letter, Office for Civil Rights, July 11, 2003.

33. Press packet from Milutinovich's October 9, 2002, press conference, Milutinovich papers.

34. Andy Boogaard, "Milutinovich: Switch Was Payback," *Fresno Bee*, October 20, 2007, D1.

35. Kort, "Full Court Press," 46–51; Bryant-Jon Anteola, "Local Law Firm Will Not Represent Vivas," *Fresno Bee*, December 23, 2004, Milutinovich papers.

36. E.J. Schultz, "Panel on Title IX Bias Targets Fresno State in Heated Hearing," *Sacramento Bee*, July 25, 2007, A3.

37. Correspondence from Milutinovich to OCR's Pat Shelton, February 3, 2004, Milutinovich papers.

38. Correspondence from Charles R. Love of OCR's San Francisco office to Rayma Church, April 26, 2004, Milutinovich papers. The women's swim team refused to get in the pool in fall 2004 after a month of increasing rashes, hair loss, and breathing difficulties. University doctors blamed it on stress. Staff claims that the water quality was fine were based on faulty chemical testing. The county health department finally determined an untrained staff person had been adding eight times more chlorine to the pool than is considered healthy. Team members sued for personal injury and eventually reached a settlement. Robert Rodriguez and Robert Kuwada, "Female Swimmers Sue Fresno State over Pool Chlorine," *Fresno Bee*, October 21, 2003, A1.

39. Kort, "Full Court Press," 46–51; Dan Waterhouse, "Sexual Orientation an Issue in CSU Fresno Athletic Department," *Community Alliance*, December 2007, 9.

40. In court testimony later, Johnson denied making the alleged remarks, and two witnesses vouched for his and Welty's fairness toward lesbians. Bryant-Jon Anteola, "Defense Contests Anti-gay Portrait," *Fresno Bee*, June 26, 2007, Milutinovich papers; Waterhouse, "Sexual Orientation an Issue."

41. Melanie Warner, "Think You Know Stacy? Think Again! 52 Things You Didn't Know About Stacy Johnson-Klein," *Fresno Magazine*, February 2005, 34–40.

42. From Donna Pickel's notes at the Johnson-Klein trial. Fred Farrar, "The Scandal Zone," *Fresno Magazine*, April 2005, 51–54; Jeff Davis, "Bulldogs Women's Basketball Coach Put on Leave," *Fresno Bee*, February 9, 2005.

43. Pickel's notes at Johnson-Klein trial.

44. Waterhouse, "Sexual Orientation an Issue," 9.

45. Dear Colleague letter from James F. Manning, "Additional Clarification of Intercollegiate Athletics Policy: Three-Part Test—Part Three," and "User's Guide to Developing Student Interest Surveys Under Title IX," March 17, 2005.

46. Hogshead-Makar and Zimbalist, *Equal Play*, 285.

47. *Jackson v. Birmingham Board of Education*, 544 U.S. 167.

48. Christine Lagorio, "From Grimy Gym to Supreme Court," Associated Press, November 26, 2004, online on CBS News site.

49. *Equity in Athletics, Inc. v. Dept. of Educ.*, March 8, 2011, 639 F3d 91 (4th Cir. 2011).

50. "Building on the Success of 35 Years of Title IX," Hearing Before the Subcommittee on Higher Education, Lifelong Learning, and Competitiveness, Committee on Education and Labor, U.S. House of Representatives, June 19, 2007, Serial No. 110-48. The materials released by NWLC included the survey results, the *Barriers to Fair Play* report on OCR's enforcement, the *Who's Playing College Sports* analysis, the *Breaking Down Barriers* manual, and the FairPlayNow.org website.

51. *Vivas v. Bd. of Trs. of the Cal. St. Univ.*, No. 06CECG00440 (Cal. Super. Ct. Fresno County, February 9, 2006).

52. Legal awards were to be paid by the California State University Risk Management Authority, a quasi-public entity that pooled insurance services to the state

universities. George Hostetter, "Fresno State Suit Is Settled for $3.5m," *Fresno Bee*, October 12, 2007, A1.

53. Hostetter, "Fresno State Suit Is Settled for $3.5m."

54. Associated Press, "Upheaval at Fresno State," *Deseret News*, March 29, 2005.

55. Jill Lieber Steeg, "Record Awards Follow Ruling Allowing Suits by Title IX Whistleblowers," *USA Today*, May 13, 2008, 2A, Milutinovich papers.

56. Schools that paid through verdicts or settlements included Florida Gulf Coast, Howard, and Oregon State Universities. As of 2008, other suits were filed against the University of California, Davis, Montana State University, the University of Hawaii, California State Universities at Sonoma, San Diego, and Northridge, the University of Southern California, and four junior colleges in California. Milutinovich papers and Lieber Steeg, "Record Awards."

57. Kort, "Full Court Press," 46–51.

58. According to Milutinovich and the California State Universities Committee of the Whole report dated March 11–12, 2008, Athletics Department Secretary Iris Levesque complained of discrimination and policy violations by Men's Basketball Coach Ray Lopes. The school laid off Levesque in 2005, claiming a budget crisis, and refused to hire her for other positions. Fresno State agreed to pay $125,000 to settle her retaliation complaint. The throws coach for track, Ramona Pagel, said Fresno State forced her out after she applied for the track head coach position against the wishes of men in the athletics department; the school settled her lawsuit for $300,000 in 2009. And there were others.

59. "Margie Wright Diamond," Fresno State website, gobulldogs.com.

60. Author interviews with Herb Dempsey November 28, 2018, and February 12, 2020; Alexander Wolff, "Father Figures: A Girl's Best Friend in the Fight for Playing Time Was Often Her Dad," *Sports Illustrated*, May 7, 2012, 65.

61. Tom Goldman, "40 Years On, Title IX Still Shapes Female Athletes," *All Things Considered*, National Public Radio, June 22, 2012.

62. Correspondence from Linda E. Mangel, Seattle office director, to Dr. Joseph I. Castro, February 9, 2016.

63. Jill Lieber Steeg, "Disputes Reflect Continuing Tension over Title IX," *USA Today*, 1A, quotes Title IX consultant Valerie Bonnette of San Diego, whose clients included Fresno State.

64. Criteria for a sport include a team's structure and administration, team preparation, and competition. Dear Colleague letter from Stephanie Monroe, assistant secretary for civil rights, September 17, 2008.

65. The "High School Sports Information Collection Act" died in 2009.

66. Dear Colleague letter from Russlynn Ali, April 20, 2010: "Intercollegiate Athletics Policy Clarification: The Three-Part Test—Part Three," with accompanying "User's Guide to Student Interest Surveys Under Title IX" and a related technical report.

67. "Division I FBS Athletics: Revenues and Expenses," NCAA flyer, 2011, Milutinovich papers.

68. Katie Thomas, "Colleges Cut Men's Programs to Satisfy Title IX," *New York Times*, May 1, 2011; Erin Buzuvis and Kristine Newhall, "Coaches' Title IX Literacy Called into Question," *Title IX Blog*, July 2, 2010.

69. *Go Out and Play: Youth Sports in America*, Women's Sports Foundation, October 2008.

70. Katie Thomas, "A City Team's Struggle Shows Disparity in Girls' Sports," *New York Times*, June 13, 2009, cited in Brake, *Getting in the Game*, 117-18.

11. Sexual Assault—2000–2010

1. Office for Civil Rights, "Revised Sexual Harassment Guidance: Harassment of Students by School Employees, Other Students, or Third Parties," *Federal Register*, January 19, 2001.

2. David Lisak and Paul M. Miller, "Repeat Rape and Multiple Offending Among Undetected Rapists," *Violence and Victims* 17, no. 1 (2002): 73, 80.

3. It also stopped distributing information about workplace rights for women. U.S. Commission on Civil Rights, *Redefining Rights in America: The Civil Rights Record of the George W. Bush Administration, 2001–2004*, September 2004 draft report, accessed online.

4. Per former OCR official C. Todd Jones, in Center for Public Integrity, *Sexual Assault on Campus*.

5. Center for Public Integrity, *Sexual Assault on Campus*, 25–26.

6. Correspondence from OCR's District of Columbia office team leader Sheralyn Goldbecker to Georgetown University president John J. DeGioia, May 5, 2004, regarding a complaint about the school's handling of an April 2002 sexual assault. In response to OCR's investigation, Georgetown revised its student code of conduct guidelines in 2003–4 to use the preponderance of evidence standard. Also, correspondence from Howard Kallem, chief attorney, OCR's DC Enforcement Office, to Jane E. Genster of Georgetown University, October 16, 2003.

7. Deborah L. Brake, "Fighting the Rape Culture Wars Through the Preponderance of the Evidence Standard," *Montana Law Review* 78, no. 1 (2017): 109, 128; Nancy Chi Cantalupo, "Title IX's Civil Rights Approach and the Criminal Justice System," in *The Crisis of Campus Sexual Violence: Critical Perspectives on Prevention and Response*, ed. Sara Carrigan Wooten and Roland W. Mitchell (New York: Routledge, 2015), 134.

8. Heather M. Karjane, Bonnie S. Fisher, and Francis T. Cullen, *Campus Sexual Assault: How America's Institutions of Higher Education Respond*, final report to the National Institute of Justice, No. 196676.

9. Center for Public Integrity, *Sexual Assault on Campus*, 49–50, 51–54.

10. Sources for Wanjuki's story include the following: Author's interview, June 4, 2018; the films *It Was Rape*, directed by Jennifer Baumgardner (Soapbox Productions, 2013), and *The Hunting Ground*, directed by Kirby Dick and Amy Ziering (Chain Camera Pictures, 2016); Wanjukie's blog, rapedattufts.tumblr.com; Wagatwe Wanjuki, "The Conversation That Needs to Happen About Sexual Violence on Campus," Cosmopolitan.com, October 29, 2014; Tyler Kingkade, "The Woman Behind #SurvivorPrivilege Was Kicked Out of School After Being Raped," *HuffPost*, June 12, 2014; Wagatwe Wanjuki, "Dear Tufts Administrators Who Expelled Me After My Sexual Assaults," theestablishment.co, April 21, 2016; Dana Bolger, "Gender-Based Violence Costs: Schools' Financial Obligations Under Title IX," *Yale Law Journal* 125, no. 7 (2016): 2106–30.

11. Wendy J. Murphy, "Using Title IX's 'Prompt and Equitable' Hearing

Requirements to Force Schools to Provide Fair Judicial Proceedings to Redress Sexual Assault on Campus," *New England Law Review* 40, no. 40 (2006): 1007–22; Center for Public Integrity, *Sexual Assault on Campus*, 79–80.

12. Kristina M. Kamis and Susan V. Iverson, "Powerful or Playful? A Case Study of 'Walk a Mile in Her Shoes,'" in *Preventing Sexual Violence on Campus: Challenging Traditional Approaches Through Program Innovation*, ed. Sara Carrigan Wooten and Roland W. Mitchell (New York: Routledge, 2016).

13. See https://www.nsvrc.org/organizations/3521.

14. Sandra E. Garcia, "The Woman Who Created #MeToo Long Before Hashtags," *New York Times*, October 20, 2017.

15. Clarissa Brooks, "How HBCUs Can Make It Hard for Sexual Assault Survivors to Speak Up," *Teen Vogue*, December 21, 2017.

16. Center for Public Integrity, *Sexual Assault on Campus*, 24–25.

17. Gail McCallion, "History of the Clery Act: Fact Sheet," Congressional Research Service, October 20, 2014.

18. Center for Public Integrity, *Sexual Assault on Campus*, 75–77.

19. Among the schools reprimanded were Metropolitan College of New York, Oklahoma State University, and Temple University. Center for Public Integrity, *Sexual Assault on Campus*, 31–45, 65, 77.

20. J. Campbell et al., "Intimate Partner Violence and Physical Health Consequences," *Archives of Internal Medicine* 162, no. 10 (2002): 1157–63. Rebecca C. Thurston et al., "Association of Sexual Harassment and Sexual Assault with Midlife Women's Mental and Physical Health," *JAMA Internal Medicine* 179, no. 1 (2019): 48–53, 10.1001/jamainternmed.2018.4886.

21. U.S. Commission on Civil Rights, *Sexual Assault in the Military*, 2013. Reports of sexual assaults in the military drew national attention in 1991, 1996, and 2003. See https://www.usccr.gov/pubs/docs/09242013_Statutory_Enforcement_Report_Sexual_Assault_in_the_Military.pdf. The *Boston Globe* published a Pulitzer Prize–winning series in 2002 on the Catholic Church's cover-up of pedophile priests (which was depicted in a 2015 film, *Spotlight*, winner of an Academy Award for best picture). See https://www3.bostonglobe.com/arts/movies/spotlight-movie/?arc404=true.

22. The two plaintiffs were Debbie Keller and Melissa Jennings, cited in Brake, *Getting in the Game*, 215. *Jennings v. University of North Carolina*, 481 F.3d 686 (4th Cir. 2007). "North Carolina and Coach Dorrance Settle 1998 Harassment Suit for $385,000," *Women in Higher Education*, February 1, 2007, 3.

23. Correspondence from Ayesha Z. DeMond of *The Jane Pauley Show* to Sandler, November 20, 2004, Sandler papers, 36.5.

24. Bernice Resnick Sandler and Harriett M. Stonehill, *Student-to-Student Sexual Harassment, K-12: Strategies and Solutions for Educators to Use in the Classroom, School, and Community* (Lanham, MD: R&L Education, August 11, 2005).

25. Center for Public Integrity, *Sexual Assault on Campus*, 21–22; *Simpson v. Univ. of Colo. Boulder*, 500 F.3d 1170 (10th Cir. 2007).

26. Allison C. Aosved and Patricia J. Long, "Co-occurrence of Rape Myth Acceptance, Sexism, Racism, Homophobia, Ageism, Classism, and Religious Intolerance," *Sex Roles* 55, no. 7 (2006): 481–92.

27. Sarah K. Murnen & Marla H. Kohlman, "Athletic Participation, Fraternity Membership, and Sexual Aggression Among College Men: A Meta-analytic Review," *Sex Roles* 57, nos. 1–2 (2007): 145, 147, cited in Deborah L. Brake, "Back to Basics: Excavating the Sex Discrimination Roots of Campus Sexual Assault," *Tennessee Journal of Race, Gender, & Social Justice* 6, no. 1 (2017): 7–39.

28. Sumi K. Cho, "Converging Stereotypes in Racialized Sexual Harassment: Where the Model Minority Meets Suzie Wong," in *Critical Race Feminism: A Reader,* ed. Adrien Katherine Wing (New York: New York University Press, 2003).

29. William D. Cohan, "Remembering (And Misremembering) the Duke Lacrosse Case," *Vanity Fair,* March 10, 2016; Reeves Wiedeman, "The Duke Lacrosse Scandal and the Birth of the Alt-Right," *The Intelligencer,* April 14, 2017.

30. Kristin Kalsem and Verna L. Williams, "Social Justice Feminism," *UCLA Women's Law Journal* 18, no. 1 (2010), 131–93.

31. Kalsem and Williams, "Social Justice Feminism."

32. Boy Scouts of America Equal Access Act (Boy Scouts Act), 20 U.S.C. 7905, 34 C.F.R. Part 108.

33. James Barron, "Nearly 8,000 Boy Scout Leaders Have Been Accused of Sexual Abuse Since 1944, Researcher Found," *New York Times,* April 23, 2019; Timothy Bella and Gina Harkins, "Boy Scouts of America Settles for $850 Million with More Than 84,000 Sexual Abuse Victims," *Washington Post,* July 2, 2021.

34. *Issues Involving Single-Gender Schools and Programs,* U.S. Government Accountability Office, 1996.

35. Sandler, "Title IX: How We Got It."

36. "Building on the Success of 35 Years of Title IX," Hearing Before the Subcommittee on Higher Education, Lifelong Learning, and Competitiveness, Committee on Education and Labor, U.S. House of Representatives, June 19, 2007, Serial No. 110-48.

37. Jodi Pilson, ed., *Hostile Hallways: Bullying, Teasing, and Sexual Harassment in Schools,* American Association of University Women Educational Foundation (AAUWEF), 2001; Catherine Hill and Elena Silva, *Drawing the Line: Sexual Harassment on Campus,* AAUWEF, 2006.

38. U.S. 246 (2009); *Fitzgerald v. Barnstable School Committee,* 504 F.3d 165, 170 (1st Cir. 2007).

39. Center for Public Integrity, *Sexual Assault on Campus,* 38, 74, 81.

40. Sources for Brodsky's story include the author's interview with Brodsky, March 1, 2018; correspondence with Brodsky via Twitter; and *The Hunting Ground* film.

41. Alumna Naomi Wolf described in a 2004 *New York Magazine* story how Yale officials ignored her nine months of calls and emails about "sexual encroachment" by an English professor. Hailey Fuchs and Adelaide Feibel, "Students Revive Sexual Misconduct Allegations Against Three Yale Professors," *Yale Daily News,* December 16, 2017.

42. Center for Public Integrity, *Sexual Assault on Campus,* 49. Also, *Burhans v. Yale,* 23, at https://cdn.atixa.org/website-media/atixa.org/wp-content/uploads/2013/01/12194339/Burhans-v-Yale-Title-IX-Retaliation-Complaint.pdf.

43. Tess Korobkin, "Silencing Rape Victims Sanctions the Crime," *Yale Daily News,* April 15, 2015; Presca Ahn, "Why We Filed the Title IX Complaint," *Yale Daily News,* April 1, 2011.

44. Christine Hung and Annette Wong, "Racially Based Humor Reflects Badly on School," *Yale Daily News*, April 17, 2006; "AASA Accuses Publications of Racism," *Yale Daily News*, April 17, 2006.

45. Accounts involving the Olivarius sisters or Yale in general draw from the author's interviews with Chase Olivarius on March 10, 2017, Kathryn Olivarius on March 20, 2017, and Ann Olivarius on February 14, 2017, as well as news accounts and records in Yale's archives.

46. Divya Subrahmanyam, "Med. School to Revise Anti-sexual-harassment Policies," *Yale Daily News*, March 6, 2008.

47. Alexandra Schwartz, "Days Later, Officials Still Ignoring 'Sluts' Incident," *Yale Daily News*, January 30, 2008.

48. Ahn, "Why We Filed."

49. Lauren Rosenthal and Vivian Yee, "Vulgar E-mail Targets Freshmen," *Yale Daily News*, September 3, 2009.

50. Sam Greenberg, "DKE Chants on Old Campus Spark Controversy," *Yale Daily News*, October 14, 2010; Nora Caplan-Bricker, "Thinking Aloud," *Yale Daily News*, April 27, 2012; Ahn, "Why We Filed."

51. Christina Huffington, "Yale Students File Title IX Complaint Against University," *Yale Herald*, March 31, 2011.

52. Christine Chen, Suraiya Jetha, Chris Lapinig, Peter Lu, Altaf Saadi, and Annette Wong, "Title IX's Resonances for Race," *Yale Daily News*, April 18, 2011.

53. Center for Public Integrity, *Sexual Assault on Campus*; Kristine Villanueva, "Q&A: Kristen Lombardi on the Legacy of Her Sexual Assault on Campus Series," Center for Public Integrity, December 6, 2019.

54. "Vice President Biden Announces New Administration Effort to Help Nation's Schools Address Sexual Violence," Department of Education press release, April 4, 2011; "At Yale, Some Say Misogyny Goes Unheeded," *New York Times*, April 7, 2011.

12. Acceleration—2011–2014

1. Ruth Milkman, "A New Political Generation: Millennials and the Post-2008 Wave of Protest," *American Sociological Review* 82, no. 1 (2017): 1–31.

2. Milkman, "A New Political Generation."

3. OCR Voluntary Resolution Agreement with Yale, Complaint No. 01-11-2027.

4. Celene Reynolds, "The Mobilization of Title IX Across U.S. Colleges and Universities, 1994–2014," *Social Problems* 66, no. 2 (2019): 245–73.

5. Angela F. Amar et al., "Administrators' Perceptions of College Campus Protocols, Response, and Student Prevention Efforts for Campus Sexual Assault," *Violence and Victims* 29, no. 4 (2014): 579, 584, cited in Brake, "Fighting the Rape Culture Wars."

6. Amar et al., "Administrators' Perceptions of College Campus Protocols."

7. *The Invisible War*, directed by Kirby Dick (Chain Camera Pictures, 2012).

8. Anne McClintock, "Who's Afraid of Title IX?," *Jacobin*, October 24, 2017.

9. "Lead a Good Life, Everyone: Trey Malone's Suicide Note," The Good Men Project, November 5, 2012.

10. Angie Epifano, "An Account of Sexual Assault at Amherst College," *Amherst Student*, October 17, 2012; Dana Bolger and Jisoo Lee, "Surviving, at Amherst College," *It Happens Here*, October 23, 2012; Richard Pérez-Peña, "Student's Account Has Rape in Spotlight," *New York Times*, October 26, 2012.

11. Rebecca Johnson, "Campus Sexual Assault: Annie E. Clark and Andrea Pino Are Fighting Back—and Shaping the National Debate," *Vogue*, October 9, 2014.

12. Cecilia Mengo and Beverly M. Black, "Violence Victimization on a College Campus: Impact on GPA and School Dropout," *Journal of College Student Retention: Research, Theory & Practice* 18, no. 2 (2015).

13. Michele Kort, "Interview: The Activist Survivors of 'The Hunting Ground,'" *Ms.*, February 28, 2015.

14. Forty-six percent of students reporting rape or attempted rape were betrayed by their schools. Carly Parnitzke Smith and Jennifer J. Freyd, "Institutional Betrayal," *American Psychologist* 69, no. 6 (2014): 575, 578–83, and other studies by Freyd and associates.

15. *The Hunting Ground* film.

16. Tyler Kingkade, "University of North Carolina Routinely Violates Sexual Assault Survivor Rights, Students Claim," *Huffington Post*, January 16, 2013.

17. *The Hunting Ground* film shows a screenshot of that tweet from April 14, 2013.

18. *Freitag v. Department of Corrections*. See Price's website, pypesq.com.

19. Erin Whiteside and Amber Roessner, "Forgotten and Left Behind: Political Apathy and Privilege at Title IX's 40th Anniversary," *Communications and Sport* 6, no. 1 (2018): 3–24. Statistics on athletics participation are from Pamela Bass, "Second Generation Gender Bias in College Coaching: Can the Law Reach That Far?," *Marquette Sports Law Review* 26, no. 2 (2016), 671.

20. William C. Rhoden, "Black and White Women Far from Equal Under Title IX," *New York Times*, June 10, 2012.

21. Rhoden, "Black and White Women Far from Equal." The Aspen Institute Sports and Society Program hosted the latter panel, "Title IX and Beyond: How Do We Get the Rest of Our Girls in the Game?"

22. From part 2 of the 2009–10 Civil Rights Data Collection, cited in the NCWGE 2017 report for Title IX's forty-fifth anniversary, *Title IX: Advancing Opportunity Through Equity in Education*.

23. Matthew J. Breiding et al., "Prevalence and Characteristics of Sexual Violence, Stalking, and Intimate Partner Violence Victimization—National Intimate Partner and Sexual Violence Survey, United States, 2011," *Morbidity and Mortality Weekly Report* 63, no. 8 (2014).

24. *The Hunting Ground* footage of the protest.

25. Author interviews with Alexandra Brodsky March 1, 2018, and Dana Bolger May 27, 2018. Allie Grasgreen, "Enforcement for the Enforcers," *Inside Higher Ed*, July 16, 2013.

26. Laura L. Dunn, "Afterword: The Anti-campus Sexual Assault Activism Movement Under Title IX," in *Preventing Sexual Violence on Campus: Challenging Traditional Approaches Through Program Innovation*, ed. Sara Carrigan Wooten and Roland W. Mitchell (New York: Routledge, 2016).

27. Richard Pérez-Peña, "College Groups Connect to Fight Sexual Assault," *New York Times*, March 19, 2013.

28. In 2014, Pino reported taxable income of around $2,000 from one speaking engagement, she said.

29. The Campus SaVE Act was H.R. 2016 and S. 834. Gail McCallion, "History of the Clery Act: Fact Sheet," Congressional Research Service, October 20, 2014.

30. Dear Colleague letter from Seth Galanter and accompanying pamphlet, "Supporting the Academic Success of Pregnant and Parenting Students Under Title IX of the Education Amendments of 1972," June 25, 2013.

31. ACLU of California, *Breaking Down Educational Barriers for California's Pregnant & Parenting Students,* January 2015.

32. National Women's Law Center and the NAACP Legal Defense Fund, *Unlocking Opportunity for African American Girls: A Call to Action for Educational Equity*, 2014.

33. Dear Colleague letter from Catherine E. Lhamon, May 14, 2014.

34. Ruth Tam, "Activists Applaud White House Effort to Fight Campus Rape," *Washington Post*, January 25, 2014.

35. Rebecca Solnit, "Listen Up: Women Are Telling Their Story Now," *The Guardian*, December 30, 2014.

36. T. Rees Shapiro, "Columbia University Settles Title IX Lawsuit with Former Student Involving 'Mattress Girl' Case," *Washington Post*, July 13, 2017; Jia Tolentino, "Safe Spaces: Could Small Changes in Campus Life Reduce the Risk of Sexual Assault?," *New Yorker*, February 12 and 19, 2018.

37. Nicole Ng and Vivian Want, "Despite Progress, Sexual Misconduct Policies Still Draw Ire," *Yale Daily News*, November 21, 2014.

38. Tweet by Alexandra Brodsky (@azbrodsky), January 22, 2021.

39. Author interview with Brodsky March 1, 2018, and text messages through Twitter.

40. See a video of Sandler's meeting at Fresno State, at http://www.sherryboschert .com/fresno-tied-title-ix-decades.

41. Brigid Schulte, "D.C. Schools Agree to Give Girls Opportunity to Play Sports to Settle Civil Rights Complaints," *Washington Post*, October 1, 2013.

42. "Failure to Enforce Title IX?," *Inside Higher Ed*, April 22, 2014; Christina Jedra, "Title IX Complaint Alleges Gender Discrimination in Emerson Athletics," *Berkeley Beacon*, September 10, 2014.

43. *Sexual Violence on Campus: How Too Many Institutions of Higher Education Are Failing to Protect Students*, U.S. Senate Subcommittee on Financial and Contracting Oversight, July 9, 2014.

44. *Audrie & Daisy*, directed by Bonni Cohen and Jon Shenk (AfterImage Public Media, Actual Films, 2016); *It Happened Here*, directed by Lisa F. Jackson (Neponsit Pictures, 2014).

45. "Writing Rape: How U.S. Media Cover Campus Rape and Sexual Assault," Women's Media Center, 2015.

46. Katherine Mangan, "Feuding over Sex-Assault Scandal Intensifies Spotlight on Baylor," *Chronicle of Higher Education*, November 11, 2016, A26; Brad Wolverton, "An

Icon Falls, and a President with Him," *Chronicle of Higher Education*, November 18, 2011, A1; "In the News," *Chronicle of Higher Education*, November 11, 2016, A3, and November 18, 2016, A3.

13. Critical Mass—2015–2016

1. Sandler papers, 32.3.

2. Susan Stryker, *Transgender History: The Roots of Today's Revolution* (New York: Hachette, 2008; repr. 2017).

3. Stryker, *Transgender History*, 202.

4. Amy Graff, "New Guidelines Aim to Protect Transgender Students," *San Francisco Chronicle*, August 6, 2015.

5. Erin Buzuvis, "Best Gender Equality Quote from a High School Student . . . ," *Title IX Blog*, April 22, 2007; Kevin Fagan, "Obama's Restroom Policy Is Reversed," *San Francisco Chronicle*, February 23, 2017.

6. Laura Onstot, "Shoulder Pads, Pom-Poms, and the Angry Inch," *Seattle Weekly*, October 16, 2007.

7. Josh Fischel, "Beyond the Bathroom," *Amherst Magazine*, Summer 2017, 28–35.

8. Author interviews with Sandler; "Interview with Martin Gerry, 1985," Dunkle papers, 88.10.

9. "Questions and Answers on Title IX and Single-Sex Elementary and Secondary Classes and Extracurricular Activities," Office for Civil Rights, December 1, 2014.

10. Sue Klein, "Reinvigorating the Role of the Title IX Coordinator: A Requirement and Resource," Feminist Majority Foundation, September 2016. The American Association of University Women anecdote is from NCWGE, "Title IX: Advancing Opportunity Through Equity in Education," 2017.

11. Dear Colleague letter from Catherine Lhamon and Vanita Gupta, May 13, 2016, including "Examples of Policies and Emerging Practices for Supporting Transgender Students."

12. Mackenzie Mays, "Becoming Mr. Love: Fresno State ID Means Better Life for Trans Student," *Fresno Bee*, October 21, 2016.

13. Association of American Universities, *AAU Climate Survey on Sexual Assault and Sexual Misconduct*, 2015.

14. Chris Loschiavo and Jennifer L. Waller, "The Preponderance of Evidence Standard: Use in Higher Education Campus Conduct Processes," Association for Student Conduct Administration.

15. Sarah Brown, "Education Dept. Cites Title IX Rights of Student Accused of Sex Assault," *Chronicle of Higher Education*, October 21, 2016, A18.

16. Jeremy Bauer-Wolf, "Title IX Lawsuits Have Skyrocketed in Recent Years, Analysis Shows," *Education Dive*, January 5, 2020.

17. Sage Carson and Sarah Nesbitt, "Balancing the Scales: Student Survivors' Interests and the Mathews Analysis," *Harvard Journal of Law & Gender* 43, no. 2 (Summer 2020): 319–74, which drew the Michigan data from "Student Sexual Misconduct Annual Report," Office for Institutional Equity, University of Michigan, 14. Anemona Hartocollis and Christina Capecchi, "'Willing to Do Everything':

Mothers Defend Sons Accused of Campus Sexual Assaults," *New York Times*, October 22, 2017.

18. Cantalupo, "Title IX's Civil Rights Approach," 125–46; Alexandra Brodsky, "Against Taking Rape 'Seriously': The Case Against Mandatory Referral Laws for Campus Gender Violence," *Harvard Civil Rights–Civil Liberties Law Review* 53, no. 1 (2018): 131–66.

19. Dana Bolger, "Where Rape Gets a Pass," *New York Daily News*, July 6, 2014; "Testimony of Dana Bolger Before the Senate Committee on Health, Education, Labor and Pensions, Hearing on Reauthorizing the Higher Education Act: Combating Campus Sexual Assault," July 29, 2015.

20. John Eligon, "Black Lives Matter Grows as Movement While Facing New Challenges," *New York Times*, August 28, 2020.

21. Tyler Kingkade, "Stop Attacking the Education Department for Enforcing Title IX, 80 Advocacy Groups Say," *Huffington Post*, July 13, 2016.

22. *Republican Party Platform*, July 18, 2016, posted online by The American Presidency Project, University of California, Santa Barbara.

23. Dorian Lynskey, "How Dangerous Is Jordan B. Peterson, the Rightwing Professor Who 'Hit a Hornets' Nest'?," *The Guardian*, February 7, 2018.

24. Nellie Bowles, "Jordan Peterson, Custodian of the Patriarchy," *New York Times*, May 18, 2018.

25. Brodsky, "Against Taking Rape 'Seriously.'"

26. Briana Burroughs, "Just Say It," *Yale Daily News*, November 3, 2015.

27. Beth McMurtrie, "A 'Devastating Account' of Yale's Efforts to Diversify Its Faculty," *Chronicle of Higher Education*, June 10, 2016, A10.

28. Sarah Brown, "Activist Athletes," *Chronicle of Higher Education: The Trends Report*, March 3, 2017, B10, B13.

29. Fatima Goss Graves et al., *Finishing Last: Girls of Color and School Sports Opportunities*, National Women's Law Center, 2015.

30. National Women's Law Center, *Let Her Learn: A Toolkit to Stop School Push Out for Girls of Color*, November 2016; Monique W. Morris, *Pushout: The Criminalization of Black Girls in Schools* (New York: The New Press, 2016).

31. NWLC, *Let Her Learn*. Also, three reports by the NWLC: *Dress Coded: Black Girls, Bodies, and Bias in D.C. Schools*, April 2018; *Dress Coded II: Protest, Progress and Power in D.C. Schools*, September 2019; and *We Are Not Invisible: Latina Girls, Mental Health, and Philadelphia Schools*.

32. Author interview with Andrea Pino, June 14, 2019, Washington, DC.

33. Author interview with Daniel Swinton, ATIXA senior associate executive director, October 26, 2016.

34. Cantalupo, "And Even More of Us Are Brave."

35. *It Was Rape* film.

36. Alex Flanagan, John Kelly, Phoenix Tso, and Ruby Vail, "She's Earned It," *Tufts Daily*, September 17, 2014.

37. Tyler Kingkade, "The Woman Behind #SurvivorPrivilege Was Kicked Out of School After Being Raped," *Huffington Post*, June 12, 2014.

38. Allison Pohle, "Seeking an Apology, Local College Alumni Burn Belongings to Protest Sexual Assault Policies," *Boston Globe*, August 24, 2016.

39. Kirby Dick and Amy Ziering, *The Hunting Ground: The Inside Story of Sexual Assault on American College Campuses* (New York: Hot Books, 2016), companion book to film, 40–41.

40. Anna Voremberg, "Anna's This-Isn't-Goodbye Goodbye Blog," EROC website, June 30, 2017.

41. *The Hunting Ground* film.

42. Chloe Allred, "An Artist and Survivor Joins Lady Gaga on Stage at the Oscars," *Huffington Post*, March 4, 2016.

43. Andrea L. Pino, "Our Hermanitas' Heroes," in *Colonize This! Young Women of Color on Today's Feminism*, ed. Daisy Hernández and Bushra Rehman (New York: Seal Press, 2019), 239–44.

44. From MacKinnon's talk and post-talk discussion at the University of California, Berkeley, Center for Law and Social Policy, September 11, 2017. For more on affirmative consent laws passed or considered, see http://affirmativeconsent.com/affirmative-consent-laws-state-by-state/.

45. Constance Matthiessen, "Introduction," in Kirby Dick and Amy Ziering, *The Hunting Ground* (New York: Hot Books, 2016), v.

46. Tyler Kingkade, "124 Colleges, 40 School Districts Under Investigation for Handling of Sexual Assault," *Huffington Post*, July 24, 2015.

47. Tyler Kingkade, "There Are Far More Title IX Investigations of Colleges Than Most People Know," *Huffington Post*, June 16, 2016.

48. Sarah Brown, "An Uncertain Future for Title IX Consultants," *Chronicle of Higher Education*, February 10, 2017; Alexandra Brodsky and Elizabeth Deutsch, "The Promise of Title IX: Sexual Violence and the Law," *Dissent Magazine*, Fall 2015.

49. Jack Stripling, "Behind Ugly Locker-Room Talk, Divisions of Class and Race," *Chronicle of Higher Education*, February 24, 2017, A13–A17.

50. Nicole Chavez, "Ex-Frat Leader's Plea Deal Is the Latest in a Series of Baylor Sex Assault Scandals," CNN, December 12, 2018.

51. "Accountability," *Chronicle of Higher Education*, July 8, 2016; Kelly McLaughlin, "A Stunning New Report Details How Michigan State University's 'Dream Team' Recruiting Class Crumbled After 4 Football Players Were Accused of Sexual Assault," *Business Insider*, January 15, 2020.

14. Backlash—2017–2020

1. "IX-CAN Newsletter: What You Should Know," Know Your IX, December 2, 2016.

2. Cantalupo, "And Even More of Us Are Brave."

3. Marty Langelan, "The Godmother of Title IX," *Ms.*, Spring 2019, 40–41; De Elizabeth, "40 Signs from the Women's March on Washington," *Teen Vogue*, January 21, 2017.

4. Emmarie Huetteman and Yamiche Alcindor, "Betsy DeVos Confirmed as Education Secretary; Pence Breaks Tie," *New York Times*, February 7, 2017.

5. Linda Jacobson, "DeVos on the Docket: With 455 Lawsuits Against Her Department and Counting, Education Secretary Is Left to Defend Much of Her Agenda in Court," *The 74*, October 26, 2020.

6. Author interview with Catherine Lhamon, March 6, 2018, Washington, DC.

7. Dear Colleague letter from Sandra Battle and T.E. Wheeler II, February 22, 2017. OCR then sent "Instructions to the Field re Complaints Involving Transgender Students" to staff on June 6, 2017, and an updated Case Processing Manual on November 19, 2018.

8. "Supreme Court Allows School District Restroom Policies Supporting Transgender Students to Stand," ACLU press release, May 28, 2019; Erin Buzuvis, "Supreme Court Cancels Hearing in Transgender Bathroom Case," *Title IX Blog*, March 6, 2017; Moriah Balingit, "Court Sides with Transgender Student in His Fight to Use the Boys' Bathroom," *Washington Post*, May 22, 2018. In addition to *Grimm*, see *Doe v. Boyertown Area Sch. Dist.*, 2018 WL 3581456 (3d Cir. July 26, 2018), and *Parents for Privacy v. Dallas Sch. Dist. No. 2*, 2018 WL 3550267 (D. Or. July 24, 2018).

9. "Fourth Circuit Court of Appeals Again Rules in Favor of Gavin Grimm," ACLU press release, August 26, 2020; 13News Now Staff, "ACLU: Circuit Court Denies Appeal in Gavin Grimm Case," WVEC-TV, September 22, 2020.

10. Susan Miller, "Onslaught of Anti-LGBT Bills in 2017 Has Activists 'Playing Defense,'" *USA Today*, June 1, 2017.

11. Associated Press, Sadie Gurman and David Crary, "Feds End Job Protections," *San Francisco Chronicle*, October 6, 2017.

12. Nico Lang, "Hawaii Governor Signs Bill Banning Discrimination Against LGBTQ Students," *Into*, July 16, 2018. For a full list of the sixteen states, see National Center for Transgender Equality, "School Action Center."

13. Clarissa Brooks, "How HBCUs Can Make It Hard for Sexual Assault Survivors to Speak Up," *Teen Vogue*, December 21, 2017.

14. Vanessa Romo, "9-Day Student Protest at Howard University Ends with a Deal," National Public Radio, April 6, 2018.

15. Nina Petrovic, "DU Campaign Against Sexual Assault and Gender Violence Goes National," *Westword*, March 23, 2020; Kaitlin Quigley, "Sexual Violence Allegations Linked to Loyola Surface on Instagram," *Greyhound*, June 27, 2020; Caitlynn Peetz, "MCPS, Police Investigating Dozens of Sexual Assault and Harassment Claims," *Bethesda Magazine*, June 26, 2020.

16. Leily Rezvani, "Students Hang Banner with Sexual Misconduct Statistic in Big Game Demonstration," *Stanford Daily*, November 23, 2019.

17. *Karasek v. Regents of the Univ. of Cal.*, 948 F.3d 1150 (9th Cir. Jan. 30, 2020); Greta Anderson, "Increased Legal Scrutiny for Sexual Assault Policies," *Inside Higher Ed*, January 31, 2020.

18. Nanette Asimov, "UC Settles in Former Student's Rape Case," *San Francisco Chronicle*, February 1, 2017; Nanette Asimov and Jill Tucker, "How UC Handled Sexual Offenses," *San Francisco Chronicle*, March 3, 2017; Nanette Asimov, "UC Settles Sex Harassment Lawsuit for $1.7 million," *San Francisco Chronicle*, April 19, 2017; Nanette Asimov and Cynthia Dizikes, "UC Pays $80,000 in Harassment Settlement," *San Francisco Chronicle*, December 20, 2017; Catherine Ho, "UCSF Professor Faces Sex Harassment Lawsuit," *San Francisco Chronicle*, December 10, 2017, A16.

19. Marjorie Lundstrom, "From Hidden Cameras to Crotch-Watching: California Pays Out Millions for Sexual Harassment," *Sacramento Bee*, January 26, 2018.

20. Kim Kozlowski, "UM's Cost from Anderson Allegations: $10.7M and Rising," *Detroit News*, October 21, 2020; Erica L. Green, "Record Federal Fine Levied on University in Abuse Case," *San Francisco Chronicle*, September 7, 2019, A6; Susan Svrluga, "Former Michigan State President Arraigned on Charges of Lying to Police About Nassar Sex-Abuse Scandal," *Washington Post*, November 26, 2018; David Eggert and Mike Householder, "Sports Doctor Gets 40 to 175 Years in Prison," Associated Press, *San Francisco Chronicle*, January 25, 2018, A7.

21. Nick Anderson, "Dartmouth Plans $14 Million Settlement of Suit Accusing College of 'Animal House' Climate on Sexual Misconduct," *Washington Post*, August 8, 2019; Michael Casey, "Alumni Pressure Dartmouth over Sex-Abuse Claims," Associated Press, *San Francisco Chronicle*, November 30, 2018, A12.

22. Kantele Franko and Julie Carr Smyth, "University Was Aware of Abuse, Report Says," Association Press, *San Francisco Chronicle*, May 18, 2019; Anna Clark, "Robert Anderson's Survivors Are Seeking Justice from the University That Ignored Them for Decades," Michigan Radio, August 25, 2020; Associated Press, "Ohio State Tallies Hundreds More Instances of Abuse by Doctor," *Sports Illustrated*, December 18, 2020; Associated Press, "More Men Were Abused by Former Ohio State Doctor, New Lawsuit Says," *Sports Illustrated*, June 29, 2021.

23. Shawn Hubler, Tim Arango, and Anemona Hartocollis, "U.S.C. Agrees to Pay $1.1 Billion to Patients of Gynecologist Accused of Abuse," *New York Times*, March 25, 2021; Eli Meixler, "93 More Women Accuse Former USC Gynecologist George Tyndall of Sexual Misconduct," *Time*, October 19, 2018; Erin Richards, "'Extraordinarily Egregious': USC Slammed for Not Stopping Predatory Doctor George Tyndall," *USA Today*, February 27, 2020; James Queally, "Six More Counts of Sex Assault, Battery Filed Against Former USC Gynecologist George Tyndall," *Los Angeles Times*, July 9, 2020.

24. National Coalition for Women and Girls in Education, *Title IX: Advancing Opportunity Through Equity in Education*, June 2017.

25. "Title IX—Play Fair," Women's Sports Foundation flyer, 2017, Milutinovich papers.

26. "Fatima Goss Graves Appointed Next CEO and President of the National Women's Law Center; Co-Presidents Greenberger and Campbell Stepping Down in July," NWLC press release, February 23, 2017.

27. Erica L. Green and Sheryl Gay Stolberg, "Campus Rape Policies Get a New Look as the Accused Get DeVos's Ear," *New York Times*, July 12, 2017; Editorial Board, "Myths About Sexual Assault on Campus from the Department of Education," *Washington Post*, July 14, 2017.

28. Hélène Barthelemy, "How Men's Rights Groups Helped Rewrite Regulations on Campus Rape," *The Nation*, August 14, 2020.

29. Dear Colleague letter from Candice Jackson, September 22, 2017, and "Q&A on Campus Sexual Misconduct"; Nanette Asimov, "Sexual Assault Rules Set to Change," *San Francisco Chronicle*, September 8, 2017, A1.

30. Britton O'Daly, "Alumni Urge Yale to Stand By Title IX," *Yale Daily News*, September 27, 2017.

31. Annie Waldman, "DeVos Has Scuttled More Than 1,200 Civil Rights Probes Inherited from Obama," ProPublica, June 21, 2018.

32. National Women's Law Center, *Dress Coded II: Protest, Progress and Power in D.C. Schools*, September 2019.

33. Author interview with Sage Carson, KYIX manager, March 4, 2018; "Student Phone Call with Organization Leaders to Discuss Title IX and the Campus Sexual Assault Movement," EROC announcement, n.d.

34. Kathryn Joyce, "The Takedown of Title IX: Inside the Fight over Federal Rules on Campus Sexual Assault," *New York Times Magazine*, December 5, 2017.

35. Sandra E. Garcia, "The Woman Who Created #MeToo Long Before Hashtags," *New York Times*, October 20, 2017; Monica Anderson, "How Social Media Users Have Discussed Sexual Harassment Since #MeToo Went Viral," Pew Research Center, October 11, 2018.

36. *Time* staff, "700,000 Female Farmworkers Say They Stand with Hollywood Actors Against Sexual Assault," *Time*, November 10, 2017; "'I Guess This Is My Life. I Have No Options.' Why #MeToo Matters More Than Ever Now," *Just Matters* blog, Ford Foundation, May 11, 2020; Jake Coyle, "United Front in a Sea of Black," *San Francisco Chronicle*, January 8, 2018.

37. German Lopez, "A Year After the First Women's March, Millions Are Still Actively Protesting Trump," *Vox*, January 23, 2018.

38. Email from EROC interim executive director Jess Davidson to the author, July 28, 2018; EROC hiring announcement, late August 2018.

39. Email from EROC chief of staff (later executive director) Kenyora Parham, October 30, 2019.

40. Charlie McGee, "UNC Found in Violation of Crime and Safety Reporting by U.S. Department of Education," *Daily Tar Heel*, November 18, 2019.

41. Robin McDowell, Reese Dunklin, Emily Schmall, and Justin Pritchard, "Hidden Horror of School Sex Assaults Revealed by AP," Associated Press, May 1, 2017.

42. Correspondence from OCR director Kenneth L. Marcus to Sen. Ron Wyden, October 8, 2019.

43. David Jackson, Jennifer Smith Richards, Juan Perez Jr., and Gary Marx, "Federal Officials Withhold Grant Money from Chicago Public Schools, Citing Failure to Protect Students from Sexual Abuse," *Chicago Tribune*, September 28, 2018; Emily Zantow, "Chicago Schools Sue Feds for Pulling $4M Grant," *Courthouse News Service*, December 3, 2018; Nicole Gaudiano, "Education Department Reaches Agreement with Chicago Schools After Sexual Misconduct Investigation," *Politico*, September 13, 2019.

44. Paula A. Johnson et al., *Sexual Harassment of Women: Climate, Culture, and Consequences in Academic Sciences, Engineering, and Medicine, A Consensus Study Report of the National Academies of Sciences, Engineering, and Medicine* (Washington, DC: National Academies Press, 2018).

45. "Report of Complaints of Sexual Misconduct," Yale University, January 1, 2019, through June 30, 2019, and July 1, 2019, through December 31, 2019; "2019–2020 Title IX Annual Report," California State University, Fresno.

46. Dino-Ray Ramos, "Disneyland's Pirates of the Caribbean Ride Makes Some Changes to Controversial Bride Auction Scene," *Deadline*, March 21, 2018.

47. Emily Peck and Paul Blumenthal, "Brett Kavanaugh Controversy Rocks Yale Law School," *Huffington Post*, September 21, 2018; Susan Svrluga, "'This Is an Extraordinary Moment': Yale Law Faculty Call on Senate Committee to Treat Allegations Seriously in Kavanaugh Nomination," and "Yale Law Students Sit Out Class, Travel to Supreme Court to Protest Kavanaugh," *Washington Post*, September 21 and 24, 2018, respectively. Tweet by Dana Bolger (@DanaBolger), September 24, 2018: "Yale Law Students are lining the halls of the Senate. We. Will. Not. Go. Back. #metoo #IBelieveChristine." Tweet by Jesse Tripathi (@jessetripathi), September 24, 2018: "Outside Sen Flake's office. Remember: A majority of YLS professors signed a letter calling for a full investigation, 100+ YLS students are protesting in DC today, and the school itself has been effectively shut down by a sit-in. YLS does not support Kavanaugh #CancelKavanaugh." Also, Advocates for Youth 2018 annual report.

48. Rachel Swan, "East Bay D.A. Race Draws Interest and Money," *San Francisco Chronicle*, May 12, 2018. Also, e-newsletter from Pamela Price, September 27, 2019; "Voters Choose Nancy O'Malley over Pamela Price for Alameda County District Attorney," KTVU Fox 2, June 6, 2018.

49. "Oakland Mayor Libby Schaaf Wins Re-election," ABC7 News, November 7, 2018.

50. Dana Bolger, "Betsy DeVos's New Harassment Rules Protect Schools, Not Students," *New York Times*, November 27, 2018.

51. "Nondiscrimination on the Basis of Sex in Education Programs or Activities Receiving Federal Financial Assistance: A Proposed Rule by the Education Department," 85 FR 30026, pages 30026–578, Docket ID ED-2018-OCR-0064, RIN 1870-AA14.

52. American College of Trial Lawyers, "White Paper on Campus Sexual Assault Investigations," March 2017; "ACLU Comment on Department of Education's Final Title IX Rule on Sexual Harassment," ACLU press release, May 6, 2020.

53. Remarks by Emily Sanders at Sandler's memorial, June 26, 2019.

54. "United States COVID-19 Cases and Deaths by State," U.S. Centers for Disease Control and Prevention, updated November 23, 2020; "COVID-19 Situation Update Worldwide, as of 24 November 2020," European Centre for Disease Prevention and Control.

55. "Coronavirus Live Updates," *San Francisco Chronicle*, November 21, 2020; "Tracking the Coronavirus at U.S. Colleges and Universities," *New York Times*, updated November 19, 2020.

56. Robert Kuwada, "As Revenue Declines, Fresno State Drops 3 Sports Including One It Just Brought Back," *Fresno Bee*, October 16, 2020; "Women's Lacrosse Players File Sex Discrimination Class Action Against Fresno State for Eliminating Team and Violating Title IX," press release by Bailey Glasser LLP, attorneys for Fresno State women's lacrosse players, February 12, 2021; Kristine Newhall, "COVID and the Cuts," *Title IX Blog*, January 15, 2021; Kayla Gaskins, "The Battle to Save the Tribe: What It Took to Keep Three Collegiate Women's Teams on Campus," WAVY News 10, October 22, 2020.

57. Juan Perez Jr., "NCAA Delays New Sexual Violence Policy, Months After Approval," *Politico*, November 18, 2020.

58. Kenny Jacoby, *USA Today* "Predator Pipeline" series: "NCAA Looks the Other

Way as College Athletes Punished for Sex Offenses Play On," "A Football Star Was Expelled for Rape Twice. A Secret Deal Scrubbed It from His Transcript," and "College Athletes More Likely to Be Disciplined for Sex Assault," published December 12, 2019; "NCAA Defends Sexual Assault Policy," *USA Today*, December 20, 2019; Scott M. Reid, "NCAA Argues in Former Texas Track Coach Alleged Sex Abuse Case It Has No Legal Duty to Protect Athletes," *Orange County Register*, June 3, 2020; "NCAA Adjusts Sexual Violence Policy, Requires Disclosure," Associated Press, May 1, 2020.

59. Jillian Kramer, "The Virus Moved Female Faculty to the Brink. Will Universities Help?," *New York Times*, October 6, 2020.

60. Larry Buchanan, Bui, and Patel, "Black Lives Matter May Be the Largest Movement in U.S. History," *New York Times*, July 3, 2020.

61. Buchanan, Bui, and Patel, "Black Lives Matter May Be the Largest Movement in U.S. History."

62. "Moment of Truth: Statement of Commitment to Black Lives," Washington State Coalition Against Domestic Violence website, June 30, 2020.

63. Talya Minsberg, "'Boys Are Boys and Girls Are Girls': Idaho Is First State to Bar Some Transgender Athletes," *New York Times*, April 1, 2020.

64. Mark Walsh, "Education Dept.: High Court Ruling Does Not Support Transgender Athletes," *Education Week*, September 14, 2020.

65. Bob Egelko, "U.S. Supreme Court Rules Discrimination Based on Sexual Orientation or Gender Identity Is Illegal," *San Francisco Chronicle*, June 15, 2020.

66. Michael Stratford, "Court Rules 'Resoundingly Yes' for Transgender Rights in Gavin Grimm Bathroom Access Battle," *Politico,* August 26, 2020.

67. Laura Meckler, "Betsy DeVos Announces New Rules on Campus Sexual Assault, Offering More Rights to the Accused," *Washington Post*, May 6, 2020.

68. Fatima Goss Graves and Derrick Johnson, "NAACP and National Women's Law Center: Attack on Title IX Is Attack on All Civil Rights," *Atlanta Journal-Constitution*, May 6, 2020.

69. Erica L. Green, "DeVos's Rules Bolster Rights of Students Accused of Sexual Misconduct," *New York Times*, May 6, 2020.

70. Collin Binkley and Aamer Madhani, "Biden Order Could Change How Colleges Handle Sex Misconduct," Associated Press, *San Francisco Chronicle* March 8, 2021.

71. Jacobson, "DeVos on the Docket." Greta Anderson, "Lawsuit Against DeVos, Title IX Rules Is Dismissed," *Inside Higher Ed*, October 22, 2020; Bob Egelko, "S.F. Court Dismisses Challenge to Harassment Changes," *San Francisco Chronicle*, October 2, 2018; Greta Anderson, "Attorneys General Sue DeVos, Education Department Over Title IX Rule," *Inside Higher Ed*, June 5, 2020; Barthelemy, "How Men's Rights Groups Helped Rewrite Regulations."

72. "Women in the U.S. Congress 2021," Rutgers Center for American Women and Politics, https://cawp.rutgers.edu/women-us-congress-2021.

73. Valerie Strauss, "Title IX Protects Transgender Students, Biden's Education Department Says," *Washington Post*, June 16, 2021.

74. Alison Durkee, "Supreme Court Declines to Hear Landmark Transgender Bathroom Case, Leaving Gavin Grimm Victory in Place," *Forbes*, June 28, 2021.

75. Gavin Grimm, "Opinion: I Fought for Years in Court for My Basic Rights as a Trans Kid. It Shouldn't Have Been This Hard," *Washington Post*, June 30, 2021.

76. Sam Levin and Rashida Kamal, "Mapping the Anti-trans Laws Sweeping America: 'A War on 100 Fronts,'" *The Guardian*, June 14, 2021.

15. Fifty Years

1. "More Women Than Men Enrolled in U.S. Medical Schools in 2017," Association of American Medical Colleges press release, December 18, 2017.

2. "Fast Facts: Race/Ethnicity of College Faculty," U.S. Department of Education, National Center for Education Statistics, 2020, https://nces.ed.gov/fastfacts/display.asp?id=61.

3. Sarah Brown, "Race on Campus: How One Campus Nearly Doubled Its Black Faculty," *Chronicle of Higher Education*, March 2, 2021.

4. Colleen Flaherty, "Even More White Lies," *Inside Higher Ed*, October 29, 2020.

5. Emily Shugerman, "'Don't Forget the White Women!': Members Say Racism Ran Rampant at NOW," *Daily Beast*, June 6, 2020.

6. "Diversity Research: NCAA Race and Gender Demographics Database," NCAA, http://www.ncaa.org/about/resources/research/diversity-research; U.S. Census Bureau, "More Than 76 Million Students Enrolled in U.S. Schools, Census Bureau Reports," December 11, 2018.

7. Erica L. Ayala, "The NBA's Walkout Is Historic. But the WNBA Paved the Way," *Washington Post*, August 29, 2020.

8. Lauren Hubbard, "12 Powerful Quotes from Ruth Bader Ginsburg," *Town & Country Magazine*, September 19, 2020.

9. "Knight Commission Examining Major Restructuring of College Sports," December 16, 2019, and "Groundbreaking Knight Commission Survey Finds Division I Leaders Overwhelmingly Support Major Reform," October 13, 2020, Knight Commission on Intercollegiate Athletics; Ross Dellenger, "NCAA Reform, Congress and the Most Consequential Election in U.S. College Sports History," *Sports Illustrated*, November 2, 2020.

10. Rachel Axon and Brent Schrotenboer, "Conservatives Want to Ban Transgender Athletes from Girls Sports. Their Evidence Is Shaky," *USA Today*, June 30, 2021.

11. U.S. Census Bureau, Table A-6. Age Distribution of College Students 14 Years Old and Over, by Sex: October 1947 to 2017; "Ending the Pushout of Women in Scientific Research," Equal Rights Advocates press release, September 4, 2019.

12. Association of American Universities, *Report on the AAU Campus Climate Survey on Sexual Assault and Misconduct*, January 17, 2020. "Undergraduate Enrollment," National Center for Education Statistics, updated May 2020.

13. "Annual Report to the Secretary, the President, and the Congress, Fiscal Year 2019," U.S. Department of Education Office for Civil Rights, July 2020. Sexual or gender harassment or violence accounted for 29 percent of the 2,418 violations of Title IX alleged in 1,802 complaints in fiscal year 2019 (7 percent for sexual violence and 22 percent for sexual/gender harassment). These were followed by allegations of discriminatory treatment or denial of benefits (23 percent), retaliation (18 percent), violations in athletics (6 percent) or employment (5 percent), and more.

14. Andy Thomason, "The Strain on the Education Dept.'s Office for Civil Rights, in 2 Charts," *Chronicle of Higher Education*, April 30, 2015.

15. Sarah Brown, "Life Inside the Title IX Pressure Cooker," *Chronicle of Higher Education*, September 5, 2019.

16. "Where Colleges Stand on Sexual Misconduct and Title IX," *Chronicle of Higher Education*, October 15, 2020.

17. Gonzalez (not her real name) let the author watch as she took the training. Because she is a current student as this book is being published, her name has been changed to avoid any potential repercussions for giving the author access.

18. In the fall of 2020 students at Fresno State attended classes remotely via technology to avoid the risk of coronavirus infection. Had Gonzalez been on campus, perhaps she would have learned about Title IX some other way, but the failure of this online training to teach about Title IX was a lost opportunity.

19. Dana Bolger, "New Amherst College Report on Sexual Violence: 'Something [Went] Wrong,'" *It Happens Here*, February 5, 2013.

20. Scott Jaschik, "What Oregon State Knew on 1998 Gang Rape Allegation," *Inside Higher Ed*, January 2, 2015.

21. See jjfreyd.com and institutionalcourage.org. Her comments are from a February 12, 2019, panel at the Center for Advanced Study in the Behavioral Sciences, Stanford University.

22. "Where Colleges Stand on Sexual Misconduct and Title IX."

23. Madison Pauly, "A Radical New Plan for MeToo Turns Away from 'Law and Order' Feminism," *Mother Jones*, October 26, 2020.

24. See survivorsagenda.org.

16. The Next Fifty Years

1. Emily Sanders's remarks at Sandler's memorial, June 26, 2019, Washington, DC.

2. "READ: Youth Poet Laureate Amanda Gorman's Inaugural Poem," CNN, January 20, 2021.

3. Manuela Tobias, "Fresno Police Stop Black Drivers More Often. Chief Says It's Not Racist, Others Disagree," *Fresno Bee*, February 25, 2021.

4. Equality League and Champion Women webinar to launch the "Title IX 50 By 50" campaign, June 22, 2021; video of the event posted online June 23, 2021 at https://www.youtube.com/watch?v=hpI-17-In2A.

5. From MacKinnon's talk, September 11, 2017, at the University of California, Berkeley Center for Law and Social Policy. Also, Catharine A. MacKinnon, *Butterfly Politics* (Cambridge, MA: Belknap Press of Harvard University Press, 2017).

Index

```\

`段段?

段段段段

段
```

Price, Pamela Y., 72–76, 83–89, *107*, 141–147; arrest and trial, 119–120; and civil rights movement, 72–74; early life, 72–74; electoral politics and campaigns, 235, 257, 280; first marriage, 130; honors and awards, 209–210, 235, 257; and intersectional discrimination, 84–85, 87–88; law practice and sexual harassment cases, 120, 130, 132–135, 141–147, 209–210, 235, 335n62; as single mother, 119–120; Yale sexual harassment incident, 74–76, 84–85, 319n5; and Yale women's lawsuit (*Alexander v. Yale*), 80–89, 119, 134, 319n5, 321n28
Price v. Yale, 86. See also *Alexander v. Yale*
Princeton University, 13, 118, 242
prisons, 121, 214, 234–235, 236–237
The Problem of Rape on Campus (1978 PSEW paper), 85–86
Professional Women's Caucus, 24
professors, women, 3, 15, 16–17, 90, 140, 249, 266–267, 299n2, 301n19, 311n6
Project on Equal Education Rights of the NOW Legal Defense Fund (PEER): dissolution, 129; Knox and creation of, 62–63; *Stalled at the Start* (1977 report), 97–98; state "report cards" on progress in equitable education, 125–126, 330–331n60; and Title IX implementation and enforcement, 69, 97–98
Project on the Status and Education of Women (PSEW): "chilly climate" papers, 121–123; Dunkle's 1974 paper on sex discrimination in athletics, 58; newsletter *On Campus with Women*, 118, 125; OCR's 1979 clarification and new guidelines on compliance, 102–103; papers on sexual harassment, 85–86, 126–128, 321n42; papers on sexual violence and rape, 85–86, 121–124, 126–128; Sandler as director of, 40, 43, 90, 95, 121; and Sandler's firing from the AAC, 128–129; sharing news about

sexual harassment on campus, 118, 125, 329n42; staff photo, *106*; and Title IX implementing regulations, 51, 61, 68–69; and Yale students' Title IX complaint about sexual harassment, 83
Provisor, Marlene, 314n51
Public Health Service Act, 39, 67
Public Justice (nonprofit legal advocacy group), 264, 282
Purdue University, 264

"queer" identity, 226, 240. *See also* transgender people
Quie, Albert, 39–40, 41

racial discrimination, 232–238; Black Lives Matter movement, 203, 214, 235, 237, 261, 267; and Black women coaches at Fresno State, 167–168; Chisholm on sexism and, 33–34; and the criminal justice system, 121, 232–233, 234–235, 261; Freeman on sexism and, 34; Jim Crow, 33; KYIX's criminal justice campaign, 234–235; Murray on, 32–33, 34–35, 305n22; myth that Title IX gender equity is racist toward athletes of color, 158–159, 168–169; at NOW, 267; OCR's 2014 Dear Colleague letter, 214; and police violence, 202–203, 232–233, 261, 280; and school punishment/discipline, 214, 236–237; University of Missouri-Columbia, 236; white academics impersonating people of color, 267; Yale University, 235–236. *See also* intersectional discrimination
Raffel, Dorothy, 59
Rahman, Laura Holman, 189
Ramírez, Mónica, 252–253, 277
@RapedAtSpelman (Twitter account), 246
@RapedAtTufts (Twitter account and blog), 188, 211
Raymond, Jeannine, 160
Reagan, Ronald: conservative attacks on civil rights laws and Title IX, 108–115, 118–121; and OCR budget cuts, 109, 112

About the Author

Sherry Boschert is an award-winning journalist and the author of *Plug-in Hybrids: The Cars That Will Recharge America*. Among her many honors, she received a Distinguished Service Award from the Society of Professional Journalists for her efforts to promote equity within the news industry. She lives in New Hampshire.